A BLOOD COVENANT

THE ALIEN AGENDA BEHIND CIVILIZATION AND HUMAN DOMESTICATION

ERIK NANSTIEL

Foreword by
LINDA MOULTON HOWE

Copyright Page

A Blood Covenant: The Alien Agenda
Behind Civilization and Human Domestication
Copyright © 2025 by Erik Nanstiel
All rights reserved.
Foreword © Linda Moulton Howe, used with permission.

No part of this book may be reproduced in any form
or by any electronic or mechanical means, including information storage
and retrieval systems, without written permission from the author,
except for the use of brief quotations in a book review.

This work represents the author's interpretations and views.
Sources have been cited where available.

ISBN Numbers:
Paperback: 979-8-9993806-3-0
Hardcover: 979-8-9993806-4-7
Ebook: 979-8-9993806-5-4

First Edition: 2025

Greymark Publishing • Chicago, IL
Cover design by Erik Nanstiel
Printed in the United States of America

CONTENTS

Foreword	vii
Prologue	1
1. The Debt to the Gods	5
2. What's in a Name... of God?	24
3. Faces and Symbols of Power	60
4. The Architecture of the Gods	96
5. Skywatchers and Stellar Timetables	134
6. The Ritual Machine	166
7. Two Hemispheres, Multiple Covenants	192
8. Blood Types and Biological Utility	216
9. Population Management Across Hemispheres	231
10. The Enforcers	248
11. The Gods of the Pyramids	274
12. The Physiology of the Gods	301
13. The Modern Parallels	317
14. The Same Recipients?	337
15. Blood Covenant	354
16. The Covenant of Silence	365
17. The Covenant of Succession	378
18. The Soul Covenant	390
Epilogue	403
Sources & Further Reading	407
Figure Credits	409
Acknowledgments	415
About the Author	417

*For Betty and Norman Nanstiel, Sr.,
for raising me not only with love, but
with the love of inspiration. You were... perfect.*

FOREWORD
BY LINDA MOULTON HOWE

Since September 1979, when I was Director of Special Projects at the CBS station in Denver, Colorado, I have investigated hundreds of bloodless animal mutilation cases ranging from cattle and horses to kangaroos and house cats around the world. Pathology exams of tissues in many animals have confirmed excision lines that have been cut with high heat by an unidentified technology.

Pregnant, 6-year-old cow alive and well at noon, September 9, 1982, but found dead and mutilated by 5 pm, only a half-mile from ranchers Bill and Linda Dzuris's home east of Colorado Springs, Colorado. They were outside the whole day, but never heard or saw anything unusual. An El Paso County Sheriff's Deputy arrived and wrote in his report: "... cut by some type of instrument." No necropsy or veterinarian examination, so no confirmation if unborn calf and fetal sac were still in pregnant cow's belly, or removed. Photo by rancher Linda Dzuris, An Alien Harvest: Further Evidence Linking Animal Mutilations and Human Abductions to Alien Life Forms © *by Linda Moulton Howe.*

My first book, *An Alien Harvest* © 1989, featured the above photograph of a mutilated, pregnant black and white cow on the Dzuris Ranch thirty miles east of Colorado Springs, Colorado. The ranchers and the investigating sheriff could not understand how the large excision in the white belly hair did not show any blood along, or inside, the large excision.

Moving white or red-orange lights; round, silver disks; pale beams of light in pastures; and silent helicopters have been reported since the 1950s to date hovering above pastures where mutilations have occurred day or night. Eyewitnesses have also reported seeing non-human entities at bloodless mutilation sites. Since September 1979, I have investigated bloodless animal mutilations around Earth linked to Grey extraterrestrial harvests.

By 2025, there is other speculation that blood and tissues removed from mutilated animal bodies are harvests of blood chemistries and tissues needed to sustain the health of extraterrestrial Grey entities. For centuries, perhaps humanity has lived under a covenant — even a *blood covenant* — enforced by emissaries and administered by unseen alien recipients who have never departed Earth.

Now, author Erik Nanstiel brings together Mesoamerican serpents with Mesopotamian dragons, Egyptian storm gods and Maya rain-bringers, underworld lords and sky fathers. "... From the earliest rites of Mesopotamia to the equinox alignments of Chichén Itzá; from the blood bowls of the Aztecs to the bloodless corpses of cattle in our 20th to 21st Century fields."

We will see that the names of gods are not just cultural. Names are powerful. The Egyptian Aun, the Sumerian storm god Ishkur, the serpent Nagas, the Maya Kukulkan and the Aztec Quetzacoatl were venerated up to the Spanish conquest in a system of transactions that Nanstiel highlights in Chapter 15 as blood covenants.

Does a cold, dark sea surround *this* particular universe *because* it was created to be a holographic colosseum where the dark and light battle forever?

– Linda Moulton Howe, Producer and Reporter © 2025

Linda Moulton Howe is Producer and Reporter for the *Earthfiles* YouTube Channel, and has appeared on *Ancient Aliens* and *UFO REPORT: Sightings*. She is the author of *An Alien Harvest*; *Glimpses of Other Realities* (2 vols.); and *Mysterious Lights and Crop Circles*. Her documentaries include *A Strange Harvest*; *Strange Harvest 1993*; *Gobekli Tepe: E.T. Terraforming?*; and *ANTARCTICA: Alien Secrets Beneath the Ice*.

PROLOGUE

Blood in the Stone

The drums beat in unison with the crowd's chant, each pulse echoing against the limestone steps. At the summit of the pyramid, a priest in a feathered headdress stands over the bound captive. The obsidian blade flashes; the chest is opened with practiced precision.

A heart is lifted skyward, its blood streaming into a stone vessel carved with the faces of gods. Smoke from burning copal rises in thick columns, mingling with the heat of the midday sun.

Below, thousands watch in reverent silence. This is no execution. It is an offering — an act to feed the gods, to nourish the divine so that rains will come and crops will grow.

That, at least, is what the people believe. But what if this scene — as brutal and public as it is — is only the echo of something older? What if the nourishment once spoken of was not symbolic, but literal? And what if, long before the Classic Maya codified this ritual, those who required that nourishment stood here in the flesh?

Before I ever set foot near a pyramid, I had already lived decades with questions most people are afraid to ask. I am an experiencer —

someone who has had direct encounters with nonhuman beings — and those encounters pushed me to search for patterns that connect the ancient world to our present. For years I've collected fragments from archaeology, anthropology, mythology, and modern UFO research — not as a credentialed scholar in the field, but as an investigator outside the academic walls.

I never studied archaeology in university. I didn't apprentice in the Andes, learn Classical Nahuatl, or publish in peer-reviewed journals. This book is not the product of fieldwork. It is the product of pattern recognition.

It's written from a place outside the academic establishment — not in defiance of it, but because of it. Because as credentialed experts drill ever deeper into isolated fields, some of the most urgent and haunting questions are being missed. Or avoided.

Why did so many unconnected civilizations build pyramids aligned to the stars? Why did blood — human blood — become the interface of divine communication across the globe? And why do so many modern abductees describe beings whose biology and motives echo the gods of old?

Inspired by the works of Ancient Aliens theorists such as Erich von Däniken and those who followed, this work stands on their shoulders and those of archaeologists, linguists, historians, mythographers, geneticists, and experiencers whose data, insights, and risks made it possible. But it is a post-scholarly synthesis: a step back from the dig site and university libraries to ask, *What are we looking at, really?*

Civilization began not with writing, but with blood. Long before papyrus or cuneiform, before law codes or priesthoods, there was the offering: a body slain with ritual precision. Blood poured into a stone basin, a heart raised skyward. We were not simply building cities or counting crops. We were trading.

The question is: with whom? Across time and geography, from the temple-pyramids of Mesoamerica to the ziggurats of Mesopotamia, from Angkor to Abydos, the pyramid emerged as the shared signature — a structure that reached toward the sky, aligned to the stars, and centralized ritual around elevation. In cultures where the pyramid terminated in a flat summit, it became a platform for something else: sacrifice.

The same shapes appear. The same gods. The same feathered serpents, bird-headed men, serpent-bodied judges. The same obsessions with blood, with marrow, with the sky. This is not coincidence. It is coordination.

The premise of this book is simple, but radical: ancient blood sacrifices were not simply symbolic acts to imaginary gods, but were once rooted in literal transactions with an advanced nonhuman intelligence. An intelligence that required something from us — and gave much in return.

Agriculture. Astronomy. Metallurgy. Laws. Architecture. Not gradually, but all at once. As if something had intervened.

In the Western Hemisphere, the emphasis was biological: ritual bloodletting, heart extraction, mass sacrifice. These were feeding zones. In the Eastern Hemisphere, signs point to controlled breeding, priestly bloodlines, and hybrid instruction. These were breeding zones. Two different missions. One intelligence. Many masks.

In the chapters that follow, we will dissect those masks across continents and centuries. We will explore the emissaries — the engineered intermediaries — who maintained the covenant. And we will follow its legacy forward, through medieval suppression, modern abductions, cattle mutilations, and the continuing harvest.

Humanity was not uplifted. It was domesticated. And the covenant we entered into — whether in fear, ignorance, or hope — may still be active.

1

THE DEBT TO THE GODS

The Royal Tombs of Ur, excavated in the 1920s by Sir Leonard Woolley, revealed a truth as stark as it was unsettling (*Ur Excavations*, 1934). Beneath the sands of southern Mesopotamia, Woolley uncovered Early Dynastic burials (c. 2600 BCE) where rulers were not laid to rest alone. Around the central figures—kings and queens whose graves glittered with lyres inlaid with shell and lapis, with gold vessels and headdresses—lay ordered ranks of attendants: soldiers, musicians, groomers, cup-bearers. Their bodies were arranged with a precision that feels liturgical rather than chaotic, as if even their final poses had been choreographed for a ritual end.

Woolley's field notes describe a grim but orderly scene. In some chambers, attendants still clutched goblets in their skeletal hands, as though they had drunk a narcotic or poison before lying down. In others, skull fractures and smashed cranial plates suggest deliberate blows, ritual execution rather than battle or collapse. Woolley called these deaths "retainer sacrifice"—the killing of the ruler's household to accompany him into the next world. Later scholars have argued over whether the deaths were voluntary, coerced, or a combination, but the conclusion remains the same: the king's passage was purchased with the lives of his people. The afterlife required payment in blood.

That payment was not a personal whim. It was covenant. In the Mesopotamian worldview, kingship "descended from heaven" and bound the city to its god in a relationship of mutual obligation: protection and order in exchange for unfailing offerings. Life was the highest denomination in that economy. When a ruler died, the temple did not simply mourn. It settled accounts.

The written record supports what the graves make visible. Sumerian temple hymns—preserved and translated by scholars such as Jeremy Black—speak in concrete, physical terms about divine consumption (*The Literature of Ancient Sumer*, 2004). One hymn bluntly petitions: "May the blood be poured for the gods as wine for the feast." Blood appears beside bread and beer as part of the divine table. These lines are not coy metaphors; they describe feeding. The major deities—Enlil, Inanna, Nergal, Shamash—are treated not as distant ideas but as present beings with appetites, powers to appease, and consequences to fear.

Even the oldest epic reinforces this picture. In *Gilgamesh*, after Utnapishtim's sacrifice following the Deluge, the gods are depicted as famished: "The gods smelled the sweet savor; the gods crowded like flies around the sacrifice" (*Tablet XI*). It is an unsettling line because it is literal. Prayer is not the currency here. Offering is—smoke, fat, and yes, blood. Deprivation is possible; satiation is required. That logic underwrites the whole sacrificial machine.

Temple archives make the "machine" legible. Administrative tablets list daily deliveries: barley, beer, dates, oils, flocks moved from field to pen, animals designated for slaughter—rations for the human workforce and specified portions "for the god" (Bottéro, *Religion in Ancient Mesopotamia*, 2001). The economy of a city—its fields measured in gur and iku, its herds counted beast by beast—was braided directly into the economy of sacrifice. The temple was not only a spiritual center; it was the city's largest household, its greatest bakery and brewery, its most exacting butcher. When shortages loomed, officials consulted omens. When disasters struck, the question was not merely tactical ("Where did we err?") but cultic ("What payment did we miss?").

Archaeology corroborates the system. At Mari and Kish, altars were built with basins and channels to carry liquids away (Oppenheim, *Ancient Mesopotamia*, 1964). Scholars often label them libation drains for wine or oil, and sometimes they were. But read alongside hymns that speak of "pouring blood like wine," the function sharpens: they were conduits, designed to collect and deliver offerings. The temple was not theater. It was a covenant machine, engineered to ensure payment reached its recipients.

Architecture amplified the arrangement. The ziggurat—Mesopotamia's tiered mountain of mudbrick—stood as a permanent bridge between earth and sky. The great ziggurat of Babylon, E-temen-an-ki ("the house of the foundation of heaven and earth"), lifted the cult shrine high above the plain. Each ascending platform had a processional logic: priests, attendants, and offerings moved upward in measured stages to the point of presentation. As Samuel Noah Kramer wrote in *History Begins at Sumer* (1956), the tower was a man-made *axis mundi*. At its summit, the "meeting" was enacted; below, the city labored to furnish what the god required.

Divination shows another face of the same economy. The famous liver-models—bronze and clay "handbooks" etched with interpretive zones—belonged to a craft that read the will of the gods in the organs of sacrificial animals (Oppenheim, *"Divination and Celestial Observation in Ancient Mesopotamia,"* 1974). The sequence is important: the animal is consecrated and killed, the liver inspected, the signs read, and then—if ominous—additional offerings are prescribed. Sacrifice was not only nourishment; it was an information exchange. Purchased guidance.

Festivals made the debt visible in the streets. During the New Year rite at Babylon—the Akītu—statues of the gods traveled in procession while the king submitted to ritual humiliation and renewal (Hallo & van Dijk, *The Exaltation of Inanna*, 1968; Bottéro). Offerings spiked during these days, and liturgies are unequivocal about stakes: the city's fate in the coming year hinged on satisfying divine appetite and re-establishing favor. When the gods "took their seats" in the temple, tables were set, animals killed, libations poured. The civic calendar was, at heart, a schedule of payments.

Iconography tightens the picture. On Assyrian and Babylonian reliefs, the winged, bearded Apkallu stand beside kings and sacred trees, always at work with two instruments: a bucket and a cone. Modern handbooks call the cone a stylized pinecone (life/fertility) and the bucket a vessel of holy water (purification) (*Black & Green, Gods, Demons and Symbols of Ancient Mesopotamia,* 1992). But the scenes are too consistent and too technical to dismiss as mere symbol. The Apkallu are always shown performing the same sequence: dipping the cone into the bucket, then raising it to touch a tree, an altar, or even the king himself—as if carrying out a precise ritual procedure. In Mesopotamian tradition they are semi-divine sages—civilizers who taught law, agriculture, and ritual (Jacobsen, *The Treasures of Darkness,* 1976). Read together with the sacrificial record, they look like technicians of the covenant, ensuring both delivery and effect.

Even the vocabulary of religion is transactional. The Sumerians spoke of the me—the divine ordinances that establish the functions of the world—and of kur, the perilous beyond, the realm of chaos always threatening to breach the city's fragile order (Kramer). Offerings kept the me in force and held kur at bay. When royal inscriptions boast that a god "fixed the borders of the land," they mean more than victory. They mean compliance. The account is current. The debt is paid.

There were adjustments over time. In some periods human life was commuted to animal life, with sheep, goats, and bulls taking on the role of acceptable substitutes. But substitution does not negate the core logic—it confirms it. A substitute is still payment, and the channels, basins, and altars continued to function as before. The theater refined; the economy remained.

Seen whole, Mesopotamia's system is not a scatter of pious gestures but an integrated apparatus. Graves that spend human retinues like coin. Hymns that speak of blood as wine. Administrative tablets that track deliveries "for the god." Altars engineered to carry away liquids. Towers that elevate the meeting-place. Sages who administer ritual like technicians with tools. From every angle, the picture resolves into the same pattern: a civilization organized around debt to unseen recipients.

The pattern matters because it is portable. The apparatus that rose on the banks of the Euphrates did not end there. When we turn to Egypt, we will see different gods, a different river, and a different theology of order. But the payment schedule—life for life, blood for order—remains astonishingly familiar.

Egypt: Blood for Ma'at

If Mesopotamia revealed the covenant in its tombs and ziggurats, Egypt displayed it in even grander form. The earliest dynasties left evidence that the transition of a king into eternity demanded not only grave goods but human lives. At Abydos, the burial place of Egypt's First Dynasty rulers (c. 3100–2900 BCE), archaeologists uncovered rows of subsidiary graves clustered around royal tombs. Sir Flinders Petrie, who first documented these sites in the late 19th century, noted that dozens—sometimes hundreds—of retainers were buried alongside their sovereign (Petrie, *Abydos*, 1902). Many of these burials were simultaneous, suggesting that when a pharaoh died, members of his household were killed to accompany him.

Later excavations confirmed this. In the tomb complex of King Djer, over 300 subsidiary graves surrounded the royal chamber, a staggering display of ritual death. Bioarchaeological analysis indicates that many of these individuals were young adults in good health. They were not natural deaths spread over years but orchestrated sacrifices, carried out at the moment of the king's burial. Like the retainers at Ur, they were human payments made to secure the pharaoh's passage and continued reign in the afterlife.

Archaeologist David O'Connor, who excavated at Abydos in the 1980s, noted that these subsidiary graves were cut into the desert sand with remarkable precision, forming straight rows radiating from the king's tomb like spokes from a hub (O'Connor, *Abydos: Egypt's First Pharaohs and the Cult of Osiris*, 2009). Many graves contained pottery vessels, bread molds, and simple tools, as though the buried attendants were expected to resume their duties in the service of the pharaoh beyond death. The sheer number—hundreds in some cases—suggests not a handful of chosen elites, but a systemic practice of equipping the king's afterlife with the lives of his subjects.

The logic behind these killings was theological as much as political. The pharaoh was not merely a king but the *nṯr nfr*—the "good god"—the living embodiment of Horus, whose authority maintained Ma'at, the cosmic order. To ensure that Ma'at endured, the pharaoh's own death had to be compensated. Blood was the currency that guaranteed the continuity of divine order. Egypt, like Mesopotamia, began with covenant.

Texts reinforce the archaeology. The Pyramid Texts, inscribed in the tombs of Fifth and Sixth Dynasty kings (c. 2400 BCE), present offerings not as symbols but as literal sustenance. In Utterance 32, the dead king is assured: *"Your bread is the blood of the gods; you eat the red and drink the white"* (Faulkner, *The Ancient Egyptian Pyramid Texts*, 1969). The imagery is stark—blood is food. In temple ritual manuals, the hetep offering of bread, beer, meat, and at times blood was said to replenish the ka, the vital life-force of the god's statue. Priests clothed, washed, and fed these statues each day, reciting invocations that explicitly invited the deity to consume what was laid before them.

Another Pyramid Text (Utterance 273) presents the deceased king as a predator whose sustenance is derived from sacrifice: "The king feeds on the gods, he has eaten their magic, he has swallowed their spirits." James P. Allen comments that this imagery, though shocking to modern ears, is consistent with a worldview where consuming life-force was the essence of divine kingship (*The Ancient Egyptian Pyramid Texts*, 2005). Sacrifice in this context was not theater—it was nourishment, drawing power from offerings to maintain the king's godhood.

To Egyptologists, these were ceremonies of devotion. To the Egyptians themselves, they were acts of maintenance. Gods were not abstractions to be honored but beings to be serviced, fed, and kept in good health. The offerings were daily payments to ensure that Ma'at —order, fertility, stability—was upheld. Without them, chaos (isfet) threatened to overwhelm the land.

The early evidence for human sacrifice fades after the First Dynasty. By the Middle Kingdom, subsidiary burials disappear, and animal offerings, libations of wine, or even symbolic substitutes like red ochre come to dominate ritual practice. Yet the shift did not erase the original meaning. As Jan Assmann observes, the Egyptian concept of sacrifice retained its transactional nature throughout pharaonic history: "Sacrifice is the act that nourishes the gods and thereby restores the world" (*The Search for God in Ancient Egypt*, 2001). Even when human blood was no longer spilled, the language of feeding endured.

Even as human sacrifice waned, animal killings escalated. Archaeological evidence from Saqqara and Thebes shows that tens of thousands of cattle, birds, and fish were slaughtered during annual festivals, their remains deposited in vast offering pits (Ikram, *Divine Creatures: Animal Mummies in Ancient Egypt*, 2005). In some cases, entire herds were dedicated to a single god for ritual consumption. These animal offerings acted as commuted payments, still adhering to the original covenant but spread across a broader base of life.

Architecture again reinforces the covenant. Temple complexes like Karnak and Luxor were designed as ritual machines. Altars often included carved basins and channels for libations, designed to capture and direct fluids. Reliefs show priests pouring offerings while chanting: "Take to yourself the bread that is yours, the beer that is yours, the oxen that are yours." The parallel to Mesopotamian channels is striking: two civilizations, two rivers, one principle—that life, in liquid form, must be collected and delivered to the unseen recipients.

The animal-headed gods themselves reinforced the seriousness of the debt. Horus with his falcon gaze, Anubis with his jackal's snout, Sobek with his crocodile's maw—these were not abstract allegories but visualizations of enforcement. The gods were predators, guardians of Ma'at, and reminders that offerings were not optional. To withhold them was to risk famine, flood, invasion, or plague. Each disaster was read as evidence that the covenant had lapsed, the gods left unfed.

The Egyptians also depicted divine consumption visually. On temple walls at Edfu, Horus is shown receiving offerings of blood and wine, accompanied by inscriptions that describe him as "drinking the red." At Dendera, Hathor is portrayed with vessels of beer and blood, reinforcing her dual nature as mother and avenger. Such scenes collapse the symbolic into the literal—the gods were envisioned in the act of eating and drinking what was given.

Inscriptions from temple walls drive the point home. In the Coffin Texts, a later corpus derived from Pyramid Text traditions, we read: "I live on what they live on; I eat what they eat, I drink what they drink" (Allen, *The Ancient Egyptian Pyramid Texts*, 2005). The gods consume, and the king consumes with them. Sacrifice is a shared meal, binding human and divine in an exchange of life-force.

The continuity of this worldview extended even into the Greco-Roman period. Plutarch, writing in On Isis and Osiris, described the Egyptian belief that rituals fed the gods and kept the Nile's cycles in balance. To him, these practices were archaic, even quaint. But to Egyptians across three millennia, they were essential—a covenant renewed each day at the altar.

Mainstream Egyptology often frames sacrifice as metaphor — a symbolic gesture of cosmic reciprocity rather than literal feeding (Assmann, *The Mind of Egypt*, 2002). But the Egyptians themselves left little ambiguity. Their texts show gods "drinking the red," their reliefs depict deities receiving offerings directly, their liturgies insist that divine life was sustained by what humans provided. To reduce these acts to symbolism is to miss the point: for Egyptians, sacrifice was the daily maintenance of a covenant, and blood and bread were its currency.

Taken together, the evidence is unmistakable. Egypt, like Mesopotamia, began with sacrifice as debt. From Abydos to Saqqara, from Pyramid Texts to temple basins, the pattern repeats: blood and offering given to maintain divine order, to nourish the unseen powers upon whom survival depended. Civilization's earliest monuments were not only tombs and temples. They were ledgers, keeping account of payments made in life itself.

Conclusion: The First Debt

From the royal tombs of Ur to the retainer graves of Abydos, the world's first great civilizations show us the same unsettling truth: blood was the price of order. Mesopotamia and Egypt, though separated by language, geography, and culture, both structured their survival on the conviction that the gods required life to be sustained.

In Mesopotamia, kingship "descended from heaven" and bound the city in perpetual obligation. In Egypt, the pharaoh embodied Horus and upheld Ma'at, the fragile equilibrium of the cosmos. Both roles demanded continual offerings. Both equated nourishment of the divine with survival of the human. And both enforced the covenant with ritual machinery—ziggurats and pyramids, altars and basins, hymns and liturgies—that made the transfer of life systematic.

The parallels are too precise to dismiss. The retainer sacrifices at Ur and Abydos. The language of hymns and Pyramid Texts, which speak not of symbols but of feeding and drinking. The monumental architecture designed as stairways between heaven and earth. Even the intermediaries—the Apkallu in Mesopotamia, the animal-headed gods of Egypt—stand as parallel reminders that the covenant was never optional. It was enforced.

Mainstream scholars often resist this literalism, preferring to see sacrifice as metaphor or social theater. But the ancients themselves left little ambiguity. They spoke of blood as food, of gods as drinkers, of kings as predators who "swallowed the spirits" of offerings. Their architecture captured blood in channels. Their art depicted gods receiving it with outstretched hands and open beaks. To impose modern metaphor onto these testimonies is to strip them of the very thing they meant to preserve: the terms of the debt.

These earliest civilizations did not simply invent ritual. They inherited or were taught a system of transaction. Their survival was contingent upon paying the gods, and the gods, in turn, delivered order, fertility, and protection. Whether on the Euphrates or the Nile, the bargain was identical. Life was currency. The covenant was active.

And this is only the beginning. As we move beyond Mesopotamia and Egypt, we will see the same economy of sacrifice appear across continents and centuries. The names of gods will change. The languages will shift. But the debt remains recognizable. Humanity entered into an arrangement at civilization's dawn—and that arrangement, whether by consent or coercion, is the Blood Covenant.

Figure 1.1

STONE OFFERING TABLE

Offering Table with Libation Basin, *Late Period (ca. 664–332 BCE)*. Carved from limestone, this table combines a basin for liquid offerings with a sculpted surface for food. Found at *Kafr 'Ammar*, it reflects the Egyptian practice of sustaining the dead and gods with daily provisions of bread, beer, and blood. Now in the National Museum of Ireland, Dublin (Inv. 1912:261).

Figure 1.2

ROYTAL TOMBS AT UR

Royal Tombs at Ur, *Early Dynastic Period (ca. 2600 BCE)*. Excavated in the 1920s by Sir Leonard Woolley, these tombs contained kings, queens, and their attendants, buried with rich grave goods and evidence of ritual sacrifice. The site revealed that Mesopotamian rulers carried their households with them into death, confirming that the covenant with the gods was sealed in blood.

ZIGGURAT AT UR

Ziggurat of Ur, built by King Ur-Nammu (ca. 2100 BCE). Rising above the Mesopotamian plain, this stepped temple was dedicated to the moon god Nanna. Its ascending platforms symbolized a bridge between heaven and earth, where offerings and sacrifices were carried upward to the divine. The ziggurat embodied Mesopotamia's covenant machine: architecture engineered to ensure the gods received their due.

RETAINER GRAVES AT ABYDOS

Retainer Graves at Abydos, First Dynasty (ca. 3100–2900 BCE). Surrounding the tombs of Egypt's earliest kings, hundreds of subsidiary graves contained the sacrificed retainers of the royal household. Excavations revealed young attendants buried simultaneously, confirming that the pharaoh's passage into eternity was secured by the blood of his subjects.

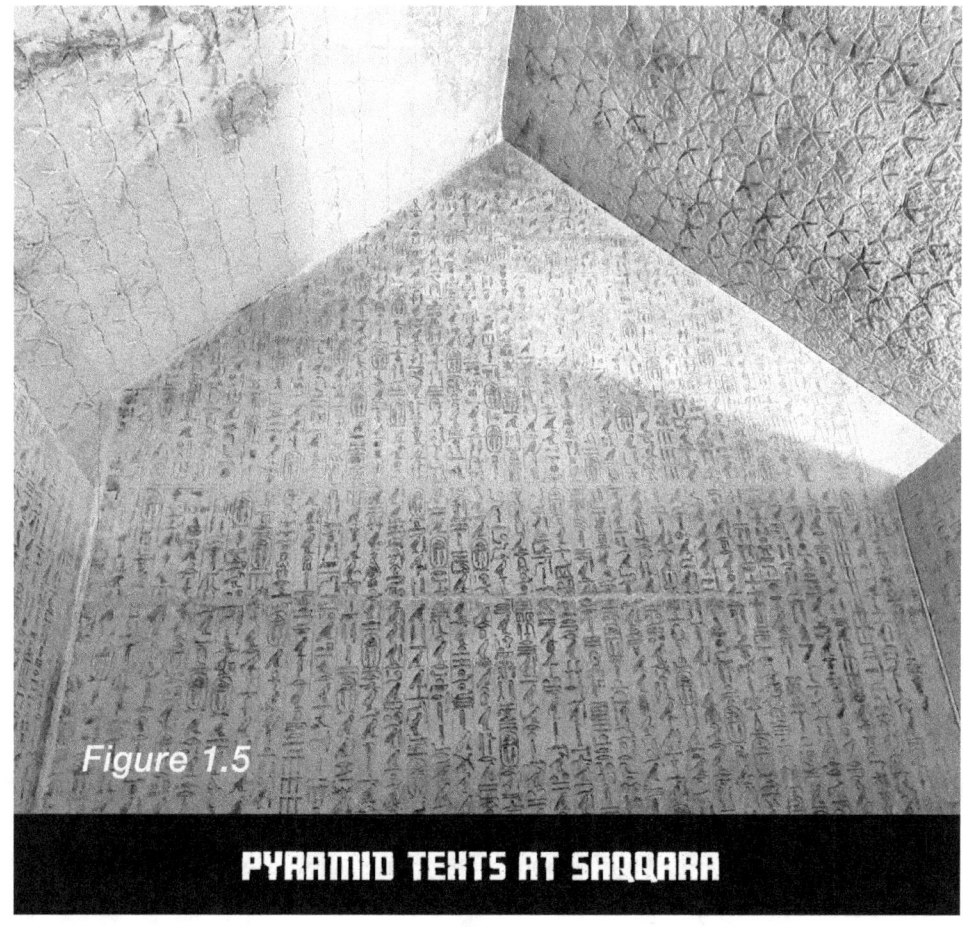

PYRAMID TEXTS AT SAQQARA

Pyramid Texts Inscription, *Old Kingdom (ca. 2400–2300 BCE).* Carved into the walls of royal tombs at Saqqara, the Pyramid Texts are the oldest known religious writings. Their verses describe offerings of bread, beer, meat, and blood as literal nourishment for the dead king and the gods. These inscriptions confirm that sacrifice was not symbolic devotion but daily sustenance in the covenant between human and divine.

2

WHAT'S IN A NAME... OF GOD?

Introduction: The Durability of Divine Names

Names are among the most durable artifacts of human culture. Unlike pottery or stone, they are not excavated from the earth but preserved in the living memory of language. Empires collapse, temples crumble, scripts evolve into new alphabets — yet the names of gods often persist. They pass from priest to priest, whispered in liturgy, invoked in curse or blessing, sometimes distorted by centuries of phonetic drift but still recognizable in their bones. A god's cult may vanish, yet the name endures like a fossil hidden in the strata of culture.

We know this because the record is stubborn. The Egyptian Amun, "the Hidden One," survived into Greek and Roman times, his temples still active even as foreign dynasties ruled the Nile. The Sumerian storm god Ishkur, later called Adad by the Akkadians, remained in prayers and incantations for more than a millennium. In India, the serpent kings known as Nāgas still appear in Hindu and Buddhist traditions; their names survive in regional folklore, place names, and temple iconography. The Maya Kukulkan and the Aztec Quetzalcoatl remained venerated right up to the Spanish conquest —

and today their names are instantly recognizable to schoolchildren and tourists alike, long after the collapse of the civilizations that first invoked them.

Mythographers have long noted that names are more durable than doctrines. Mircea Eliade observed in *A History of Religious Ideas* (1982) that divine names are "portable containers," carried across conquests and adopted by successor cultures even when their theological content changes. Georges Dumézil made a similar observation when comparing Indo-European pantheons, noting that certain phonetic elements of god-names outlasted shifts in ritual and myth. In other words: the names themselves carry an authority that transcends the cultures that speak them.

Why this persistence? Partly because names are power. To invoke a god by name is to call upon their presence, and in many ancient traditions, knowing the correct name was believed to grant influence over the being named. The Egyptian Book of the Dead is filled with spells that require the recitation of divine names; without the right pronunciation, the deceased could not pass the guardians of the underworld. In Mesopotamia, incantations often included long strings of god-names, each one functioning as a key to unlock divine attention. In Mesoamerica, glyphs representing deities were not only pictorial but phonetic, ensuring that the sound of the name was preserved in writing. To forget a god's name was to sever the relationship. To preserve it was to keep the channel alive.

Mainstream linguistics often explains similarities between divine names across cultures as coincidence or convergence. Languages are finite systems, after all, and certain sounds — especially guttural consonants like "k" and "q," or nasal vowels like "an" and "am" — appear frequently worldwide. But when those phonetic echoes are paired with identical divine functions and overlapping symbols, the argument for coincidence weakens. As David Leeming remarks in *The Dictionary of Gods and Goddesses* (2005), "parallels of name and role, especially when combined, suggest lines of transmission rather than isolated invention."

Consider the persistence of storm gods across continents. The

Maya Chaac, the Aztec Tlaloc, the Sumerian Ishkur/Adad, even the Hittite storm god Tarhunna — different languages, different alphabets, yet similar consonant clusters and identical functions: lightning, rain, fertility, punishment by drought. Or take underworld deities: the Maya Ah Puch, the Egyptian Anpu (Anubis), the Mesopotamian Nergal. Again, not identical sounds, but recurring "ah/pu/na" phonetics attached to skeletal or canine guardians of the dead. The pattern is not random.

Some comparativists—most famously Joseph Greenberg—have argued that recurrent phonetic patterns across distant families can be early signals of deeper relationships (e.g., Language in the Americas, 1987). Most historical linguists remain skeptical of his methods, and rightly insist on strict correspondence rules. Even so, Greenberg's provocation is relevant here: when names + roles + symbols converge repeatedly across unrelated traditions, the case for mere coincidence becomes harder to sustain.

This is not to say that names were always preserved perfectly. They shifted, merged, and were reinterpreted. The Egyptian Amun became Zeus-Ammon under the Greeks, blending two traditions. The Sumerian goddess Inanna became Ishtar under Akkadian rule, her name transformed but her role intact. Quetzalcoatl was identified by the Spanish with St. Thomas, his feathered serpent imagery reinterpreted through a Christian lens. Yet through these changes, the names themselves did not vanish. They carried forward, adapted but recognizable, like stones carried downstream by a river.

That persistence invites a radical question: were these names invented in isolation—or transmitted? At civilization's dawn, architecture, calendars, and astronomy appear in mature form. The names of the gods look the same way: already paired with elemental domains —sky, storm, death, creation. When names and functions recur across hemispheres, the hypothesis of common instruction explains more than coincidence does.

This chapter will not prove that hypothesis on names alone. What it will do is map the terrain. We will compare names across cultures, identify their domains, and note their symbolic markers. We will bring together Mesoamerican serpents and Mesopotamian dragons, Egyptian storm gods and Maya rain-bringers, underworld lords and sky fathers. In doing so, we will begin to see that the names of gods are not just cultural curiosities. They are fingerprints of a larger system — a system that spanned hemispheres, preserved in syllables, carried across time like echoes of an original voice.

The Feathered Serpent Motif

Few divine figures are as persistent or widespread as the serpent. Across continents, cultures envisioned it not merely as an animal, but as a being charged with cosmic authority — guardian, creator, destroyer, and sometimes all three. When wings or feathers are added to its coils, the serpent becomes not just an earthly creature but a liminal one, spanning sky and ground, symbolizing transition between realms. The recurrence of this motif is striking enough in itself. But when we map its names across hemispheres, the persistence becomes harder to dismiss.

In Mesoamerica, the Maya spoke of Kukulkan, the "feathered serpent" who was both creator and culture-bringer. The Aztecs called him Quetzalcoatl, a name composed of quetzal (the iridescent green bird of Central America) and coatl (serpent). Both deities were associated with wind, rain, and the renewal of the world after cataclysm. Quetzalcoatl, in particular, was said to have descended into the underworld to gather the bones of past humanity, which he anointed with his own blood to create the present race of people (León-Portilla, *Aztec Thought and Culture,* 1963). In glyphic form, his name appears with serpent bodies topped by feather crests, unmistakably linking him to both earth and sky.

The Florentine Codex, compiled by Bernardino de Sahagún in the 16th century, preserves indigenous testimony that Quetzalcoatl was not only a creator god but also a culture hero who taught writing, astronomy, and calendar reckoning (Sahagún, *Florentine Codex, Book 3*). Diego de Landa, writing of the Maya in Yucatán, likewise described Kukulkan as a bringer of order who "came from the west" and instructed the people in law and agriculture (*Relación de las Cosas de Yucatán*, 1566). These colonial accounts are heavily filtered through Christian interpretation, yet they confirm that for both Aztec and Maya alike, the feathered serpent was remembered as more than a myth — he was a teacher whose name carried authority.

The persistence of this figure across the Americas is notable. The Toltecs at Tula carved colossal feathered serpents coiled around their temple stairways. The city of Chichen Itza was dominated by El Castillo, the pyramid where Kukulkan descends each equinox as sunlight creates the illusion of a serpent slithering down the staircase. These spectacles were not mere theater but embodied theology: the god was present in architecture, calendar, and ritual. His name, carved and chanted, tied human cycles to cosmic order.

Linda Schele and David Freidel, in *A Forest of Kings* (1990), argued that the serpent descent spectacle was carefully engineered into El Castillo's architecture, synchronizing celestial movement with divine manifestation. For the Maya, the appearance of Kukulkan was not symbolic theater but a literal visitation, a covenant renewed when sunlight "animated" the god's descent. The persistence of the name Kukulkan in inscriptions, paired with these astronomical alignments, underscores how the deity was embedded in multiple domains — calendar, sky, temple, and kingship.

Across the world, in India and Southeast Asia, the serpent appears again. The Nāga, semi-divine serpent kings, inhabit rivers, lakes, and the underworld. In Hindu and Buddhist texts, nāgas are powerful beings who control rain and guard treasures. The Mahabharata describes them as ancient rulers of a subterranean realm, while the Manusmriti warns of their fiery breath. In Cambodia, the Khmer empire integrated nāga iconography into its very architecture. The causeways of Angkor Wat are flanked by massive stone serpents, their hoods fanned out in multi-headed grandeur. In local legend, the Khmer royal line itself was descended from a union between an Indian prince and a nāga princess — a myth of hybrid bloodlines.

The Egyptian cobra, the uraeus, carried similar weight. Worn on the pharaoh's brow, it was a living symbol of protective sovereignty.

The cobra goddess Wadjet, often depicted rearing with flared hood, was said to spit fire at the king's enemies. Like Quetzalcoatl or the nāga, the uraeus was a serpent elevated beyond nature—charged with rulership and divine defense. Whatever we make of phonetics here, the functional parallels are unmistakable: a serpent-power enthroned at the heart of kingship, enforcing legitimacy with fire and threat.

The Pyramid Texts reinforce Wadjet's lethal power. In Utterance 226, the king is said to ascend with the uraeus on his brow, who "spits fire against your enemies" (Faulkner, *The Ancient Egyptian Pyramid Texts,* 1969). Here the cobra is not a passive emblem but an active, consuming force. The same role — fiery defender of kingship — appears in much later temple inscriptions at Edfu, where Wadjet is called "the Great Flame." The persistence of this imagery, tied directly to the name of the goddess, reveals the continuity of the serpent motif from the Old Kingdom into the Ptolemaic period.

In Mesopotamia, the serpent-dragon known as Mushussu (or sirrush) guarded the gates of gods and kings. The creature, depicted on the famed Ishtar Gate of Babylon, had the scaly body of a serpent, the forelegs of a lion, and the hind legs of a bird of prey. Its name appears in Akkadian inscriptions as a divine guardian of Marduk, the storm god. The Mushussu was both terrifying and protective, its hybrid body echoing the liminal role of serpent deities worldwide.

The phonetic echoes are not uniform, but clusters emerge. "Ku/Qu" in Kukulkan and Quetzalcoatl. "Na/Naga" in India and Cambodia. "Mu/Mushussu" in Mesopotamia. Even the Egyptian "uraeus," derived from iaret ("the risen one"), preserves the hiss of the serpent in its elongated vowels. When paired with the shared functions — creation, rain, protection, rulership — the argument for coincidence thins.

Khmer inscriptions at Angkor Thom speak of nāgas as "lords of the waters" who grant or withhold rainfall, paralleling Kukulkan and Quetzalcoatl's association with storms (Coedès, *The Indianized States of Southeast Asia*, 1968). The seven-headed nāga balustrades lining Angkor's causeways symbolized the bridge between realms — a literal crossing point between the human world and the divine. Such imagery makes the phonetic echo of Nāga more than a name: it is a marker of the serpent's global role as threshold guardian and rain-bringer.

Scholars of comparative mythology have wrestled with this problem. Joseph Campbell, in *The Masks of God* (1962), suggested that serpents symbolize "the energy of life itself, coiled and uncoiled." Carl Jung, from a psychological lens, described the serpent as an archetype of the unconscious, a primordial image that reappears because it springs from the human psyche. Both explanations acknowledge the serpent's ubiquity but ground it in internal human universals. Yet neither fully explains why the serpent is not just present, but named, winged, and assigned identical elemental domains in cultures with no proven contact.

Linguists usually resist cross-hemisphere comparisons. They note that "ku," "na," and "mu" are simple phonemes, likely to occur in unrelated languages. They stress that iconographic similarities may reflect shared human experience — snakes are everywhere, rains and droughts are universal concerns. But this conservative caution begins to strain when we align the serpent's names with its roles. Why should Kukulkan in Yucatán and the nāgas of Cambodia both guard stairways of temples? Why should Mushussu and the uraeus both crown rulers as protectors of legitimacy? Why should the serpent so consistently appear as rain-bringer, threshold guardian, hybrid between above and below?

The Ishtar Gate, now reconstructed in Berlin's Pergamon Museum, preserves brick inscriptions identifying the Mushussu as the creature of Marduk, the patron deity of Babylon (Koldewey, *The Excavations at Babylon*, 1914). Its scaly body, leonine forelegs, and bird talons were explicitly hybrid — a creature spanning multiple domains. The dragon's name, written in Akkadian as "mu-šuš-šu," literally meant "splendor serpent." That such a hybrid guardian carried the same serpent identity as Quetzalcoatl and the nāgas points to more than local imagination; it suggests a shared archetype remembered in different syllables.

There is another possibility. Rather than isolated invention, these names and functions may descend from an older system, transmitted to human societies as part of a deliberate program. Just as pyramids, calendars, and astronomy appear in sudden, sophisticated form, so too the serpent may have arrived already coded as a divine archetype. Its names — echoing across syllables and continents — are linguistic fossils of that transmission.

Mircea Eliade, in *Patterns in Comparative Religion* (1958), called the serpent "the most universal of symbols, mediating between life, death, and rebirth." Yet even Eliade, who favored archetypal explanations, admitted that the serpent's recurrence in temple architecture across continents "requires more than psychology to explain." If the serpent were purely a projection of the unconscious, we would not expect it to carry names, ritual calendars, and specific temple alignments across unrelated civilizations. Its universality seems programmed rather than imagined.

This chapter will return to the serpent in detail when we consider symbols of power in Chapter 3. For now, it is enough to note that the feathered serpent is not local but global, its names and forms repeating with unnerving consistency. From Quetzalcoatl to nāga, uraeus to Mushussu, humanity has remembered the serpent as more than an animal. It was the emissary of covenant, the reminder of debts owed to powers that slithered between earth and sky.

The Storm Bringers

If the serpent embodied the liminal threshold between worlds, the storm god embodied their raw power. Across civilizations, figures emerged who wielded thunder, lightning, and rain, both blessing and curse. They were bringers of fertility when appeased, but destroyers when neglected. Their names vary, yet the sounds and functions are so consistent across continents that they suggest not only archetype, but transmission.

In Mesopotamia, the Sumerians called him Ishkur, later known to the Akkadians and Babylonians as Adad. Texts describe Ishkur/Adad as "the thundering one," whose voice was heard in storms and whose weapons were lightning bolts. Hymns praise him as the giver of rains that swell the Tigris and Euphrates, yet warn that his anger brings drought and famine (Hallo & van Dijk, The Exaltation of Inanna, 1968). His symbol was the forked lightning, carved onto kudurru boundary stones and cylinder seals. Adad appears frequently in the Mari archives, invoked in treaties to witness oaths — a god who punished perjury with storms.

In the Mari archives, Adad appears repeatedly in political and legal contexts. Kings swore treaties in his name, invoking the storm god as witness and enforcer. One Akkadian oath tablet warns: "May Adad strike with storm, may he withhold the rain, if you break this treaty" (Foster, *Before the Muses*, 2005). Here Adad was not only a weather deity but also a god of justice, punishing betrayal with drought and famine. The linkage between divine storm and human law reinforced the covenant: survival of the fields and survival of society alike depended on honoring the storm bringer.

Far across the ocean, the Maya knew Chaac, the rain and lightning god whose name was written with a fish glyph and a stylized axe, representing the thunderbolt. Chaac was often depicted with reptilian features and a long curling nose, wielding a lightning axe to strike clouds and release rain. Maya texts record ceremonies known as cha-chaac, rain-invoking rituals that continued into modern Yucatán. Chaac was not alone: there were four Chaacs, one for each cardinal direction, echoing the idea that rainfall and thunder were universal forces spread across the sky (Schele & Freidel, *A Forest of Kings*, 1990).

Ethnographers note that Chaac's rites did not end with the Classic Maya. In villages of Yucatán, farmers continue to perform cha-chaac ceremonies to this day, chanting his name while pouring libations and sacrificing chickens to call the rains (Redfield & Villa Rojas, *Chan Kom: A Maya Village*, 1934). The persistence of these rituals over two millennia shows the extraordinary durability of Chaac's name and function. For the Maya, the covenant with the storm god has never lapsed; it is still renewed each planting season with offerings of blood and drink.

Among the Aztecs, the storm god was Tlaloc, "He Who Makes Things Sprout." Tlaloc's temples were piled with offerings of jade, seashells, and — most disturbingly — sacrificed children. According to the Florentine Codex, the tears of the children were considered essential to summon rain; priests actively sought their crying as a guarantee of fertility (Sahagún, *Florentine Codex, Book 2*). Tlaloc, like Adad and Chaac, was ambivalent: benevolent when fed, wrathful when ignored. His worship was so central that one half of the Great Temple at Tenochtitlan was dedicated to him.

The Florentine Codex preserves harrowing details: "They took children, and if they wept greatly, it was considered a good sign, for it meant the rains would come" (Sahagún, *Florentine Codex, Book 2*). Archaeological excavations at the Templo Mayor have confirmed this testimony, unearthing the remains of more than forty children sacrificed to Tlaloc, many buried with jade beads in their mouths to symbolize water (López Austin & López Luján, *Monte Sagrado – Templo Mayor,* 2009). These finds erase any lingering notion that colonial accounts exaggerated the practice. The covenant was brutally literal: tears and blood for rain.

The linguistic echoes here are hard to ignore. Ishkur's epithet includes the guttural "-kur." Adad's name ends in the hard "-d." Chaac terminates in the same clipped consonant, while Tlaloc closes with "-loc." Different languages, different phonetics, yet storm gods across hemispheres consistently end in guttural or hard stops, reinforcing their violent and abrupt domains. Phonetics alone might be coincidence, but when paired with identical functions and ritual patterns, they take on weight.

Iconography also binds these figures. All wield weapons of lightning: Adad with his forked bolt, Chaac with his lightning axe, Tlaloc with spears tipped in obsidian. All are tied to fertility and agriculture: Adad's rains swelling Mesopotamian fields, Chaac feeding maize, Tlaloc "making things sprout." And all demand sacrifice. In Mesopotamia, animals were slaughtered in Adad's honor during treaties. In Mesoamerica, humans were bled or drowned for Tlaloc. The exchange was always the same: blood for rain.

Hittite and Hurrian traditions reinforce the pattern in the Old World. The storm god Tarhunna (also called Teshub) was depicted standing on bulls, wielding a lightning bolt. His mythology centers on combat with the serpent Illuyanka, echoing the battle motifs of other storm gods worldwide. In Ugaritic texts, the Canaanite storm god Baal Hadad is described as "rider on the clouds," striking down his enemies with thunder (Pardee, *Ritual and Cult at Ugarit*, 2002). The name "Hadad" itself is a direct continuation of the Akkadian Adad. Here the line of transmission is clear: Sumerian Ishkur → Akkadian Adad → West Semitic Hadad → Canaanite Baal. The storm god's name mutated, but never vanished.

The motif of the storm god battling a primordial serpent repeats across cultures with startling consistency. In Hittite myth, Tarhunna struggles against Illuyanka. In the Rigveda, Indra splits open the serpent Vritra to release the waters. In Greek myth, Zeus defeats Typhon, the monstrous dragon. In Norse legend, Thor grapples with Jörmungandr, the world-serpent, whose coils encircle the sea. These battles are not local quirks but iterations of the same cosmic drama: the storm-bringer defeating chaos-serpent to bring order and fertility. That the motif persists in Indo-European, Near Eastern, and Mesoamerican contexts alike suggests deliberate transmission of both story and symbol.

Even in Indo-European traditions, we find the same continuity. The Vedic Indra, wielder of the thunderbolt (vajra), is described in the Rigveda as the god who split the storm-clouds to release rain and defeated the serpent Vritra who hoarded the waters (Griffith, *Rigveda*, 1896). The Greek Zeus hurled the thunderbolt from Olympus, called "cloud-gatherer" in Homer. The Norse Thor, whose very name means "thunder," carried the hammer Mjölnir, striking giants and sanctifying the land with lightning. The Sanskrit "Indra," the Greek "Zeus," and the Norse "Thor" differ phonetically, yet their weapons, roles, and mythic combats align with uncanny precision.

Mircea Eliade, in *Patterns in Comparative Religion* (1958), observed

A Blood Covenant

that storm gods appear in nearly every agricultural civilization, "guardians of fertility whose violence both creates and destroys." Scholars attribute this to universal human dependence on weather. Yet while storms are universal, the naming patterns and ritual similarities are not so easily dismissed. Why should Chaac's lightning axe and Adad's forked bolt resemble each other so closely? Why should Tlaloc and Hadad both be appeased with human life at critical agricultural junctures?

The skeptic's answer is convergence: human beings everywhere fear drought and depend on rain. They personified storms in gods whose names coincidentally echoed guttural stops. But the persistence of names, weapons, and sacrifices across language families and oceans raises the same question we saw with the serpent: coincidence, or continuity?

Scholars such as Jan Assmann and Mircea Eliade have highlighted the paradox of storm deities: they are at once creative and destructive, life-givers and life-takers. Eliade noted that "the storm god embodies the dual power of fertility and catastrophe, blessing and curse" (*Patterns in Comparative Religion*, 1958). To ancient peoples, this was not contradiction but contract: the same force that brought harvests could also starve them, depending on whether it was fed. This duality underscores the storm gods' role as enforcers of covenant, keeping humanity bound by the perpetual exchange of life for survival.

If continuity, then the storm gods — like the feathered serpent — were part of a program, taught rather than invented. Their names, etched into stone and preserved in chant, are echoes of an original system. They were reminders that humanity's survival depended on servicing a covenant with unseen powers who controlled the skies.

The Lords of Death

If storm gods ruled the skies, the lords of death ruled the passage below. Across cultures, figures emerged whose domains were corpses, tombs, and the unseen world beneath the earth. Their names differ, but their sounds and symbols echo with uncanny consistency: skeletal faces, canine guardians, cavernous gates. They presided over judgment, guarded thresholds, and demanded offerings to keep the balance between the living and the dead.

In Mesoamerica, the Maya named him Ah Puch, also called Kisin, "the Flatulent One" or "the Stinking One." He was often depicted with exposed ribs and a skull for a head, adorned with bells around his joints to announce his arrival (Thompson, *Maya History and Religion*, 1970). Ah Puch ruled over Xibalba, the underworld, a realm described in the Popol Vuh as a place of trials, where the lords of death tested heroes with ordeals of darkness, bloodletting, and sacrifice. The skeletal iconography is unmistakable: bones painted black and white, the grin of decay, death personified not as metaphor but as lord.

The Popol Vuh elaborates on the terrors of Xibalba through the trials faced by the Hero Twins, Hunahpú and Xbalanqué. They were forced into the "House of Darkness," where no light existed; the "House of Knives," where blades leapt from the walls; and the "House of Bats," where one of the twins lost his head to the underworld bat-god Camazotz (Christenson, *Popol Vuh*, 2003). These ordeals, administered by the lords of death, were more than allegory — they dramatized the belief that passage into the underworld was fraught with peril, overseen by deities who demanded offerings at every stage.

Among the Aztecs, his closest counterpart was Mictlantecuhtli, "Lord of Mictlan," the lowest level of the underworld. Depictions show him as a skeletal figure with wide, staring eyes and a necklace of human eyeballs. He presided over the long journey that souls made after death — a passage that took four years and required crossing rivers, mountains, and winds. Archaeological excavations of the Templo Mayor in Mexico City uncovered statues of Mictlantecuhtli with flayed skin and outstretched arms, positioned in shrines alongside offerings of bones (López Austin & López Luján, *Monte Sagrado – Templo Mayor*, 2009). His name, with its resonant "-tecuhtli" (lord) ending, reinforced his sovereignty over death.

According to Aztec cosmology, Mictlan was divided into nine

A Blood Covenant

distinct levels, each of which the soul had to traverse over four years. These included crossing the Apanohuaya River with the aid of a sacrificial dog, passing between mountains that crashed together, enduring icy winds, and finally reaching Mictlantecuhtli's domain at the ninth level (Read & González, *Handbook of Mesoamerican Mythology*, 2000). Offerings made during funerary rites — jade beads, obsidian, food — were meant to equip the dead for this journey. The four-year passage was less a metaphor than a covenantal repayment, where the soul's endurance supplied the gods with proof of loyalty.

In Egypt, the underworld guardian was Anpu, better known by his Greek name Anubis. Anpu was the jackal-headed god who presided over embalming and weighed the hearts of the dead against the feather of Ma'at. His earliest depictions appear in the First Dynasty, where priests donned jackal masks in funerary rites. The Book of the Dead portrays him standing at the scales, holding the balance steady as Thoth records the verdict. The phonetics are notable: Anpu, with its "An/Ap" syllables, stands not far from Ah Puch, whose name also carries the "Ah/Ap" prefix and guttural close. Both are skeletal guardians of the realm beyond.

The Book of the Dead preserves Anubis's role in vivid detail. In *Spell 125*, the deceased is brought before the scales, where Anubis weighs the heart against the feather of Ma'at while Thoth records the result. If the heart was heavier, it was thrown to Ammit, the devourer. Spell 17 invokes Anubis as "the one who is upon his mountain, who keeps watch over the dead" (Faulkner, *The Ancient Egyptian Book of the Dead*, 1972). These texts confirm that Anubis was not simply a funerary emblem but the judge who mediated divine order at the threshold of eternity.

Mesopotamia, too, had its lord of death: Nergal, a god associated with plague, war, and the underworld. In Akkadian hymns, Nergal is called "the cutter-off of life," who "lays low the living and turns warriors into shades" (Foster, *Before the Muses*, 2005). His consort Ereshkigal ruled the great city of the dead, Irkalla, but Nergal himself was the enforcer, a destructive power invoked in curses and feared in battle. Iconography shows him armed with a mace, surrounded by demons who dragged the living into the underworld. His name, heavy with the guttural "-gal," shares the same hard finality as Mictlan, Puch, and Anpu.

When we place these figures side by side, the resonances multiply. Ah Puch, Mictlantecuhtli, Anpu, Nergal: names with clipped syllables and guttural endings, all tied to skeletal imagery, canine guardianship, or plague. Their roles converge: they preside over judgment or passage, they guard the gates of the dead, and they demand ritual to appease them. In Mesoamerica, families left offerings of food and incense for the lords of Xibalba. In Egypt, funerary papyri instructed the soul to recite the names of underworld guardians correctly or be devoured. In Mesopotamia, appeasement rituals for Nergal included blood sacrifice to ward off plague. The covenant extended into death itself — survival of the soul was conditioned on payment.

Mesopotamian myth also records Nergal's dramatic descent to the underworld, where he seized power by confronting and eventually marrying Ereshkigal, queen of the dead (Dalley, *Myths from Mesopotamia*, 2000). In some versions, Nergal storms into her realm with weapons drawn; in others, he is tricked into entering and trapped. Either way, the story reveals Nergal as both intruder and ruler of the dead, binding him permanently to Irkalla. His dual nature as plague-bringer and underworld lord reinforces his role as enforcer of divine covenant: life could be taken in war, pestilence, or death itself, all through his hand.

The iconography reinforces the linguistic echoes. In Maya codices, Ah Puch is drawn with skeletal jaws and blackened flesh. In Aztec codices, Mictlantecuhtli is portrayed with open ribs and skeletal hands. Egyptian tomb paintings show Anubis black as night, guiding the dead with canine vigilance. Mesopotamian cylinder seals depict demons dragging figures into the underworld, overseen by a stern-faced Nergal. Bones, skulls, jackals, skeletal grins — four civilizations, four names, one set of symbols.

Some scholars attribute this to universal human psychology. Death is the great equalizer; skeletal imagery emerges wherever bones remain after flesh decays. Jackals prowled cemeteries in Egypt; dogs guarded villages in Mesoamerica; plague haunted Mesopotamian cities. The explanation runs: similar problems yield similar symbols. Yet as with the storm gods and serpents, the convergence extends beyond symbolism. It extends into names. Why should "Anpu" and "Ah Puch" echo each other across continents? Why should Nergal's guttural close resemble Mictlan's? At what point does convergence require a common source?

The rituals of appeasement deepen the case. The Maya believed the lords of Xibalba could be tricked or appeased with offerings of blood and incense. The Aztecs sacrificed dogs and humans to guide souls into Mictlan, an economy of death that mirrored the daily economy of the gods above. Egyptians performed the "Opening of the Mouth" ceremony to animate statues of the deceased, ensuring they could eat and drink in the afterlife — offerings explicitly described as food for the dead, with Anubis overseeing. Mesopotamian priests conducted the kispu ritual, pouring libations and offering bread to the shades, lest they return to haunt the living (Bottéro, *Religion in Ancient Mesopotamia*, 2001). Everywhere, ritual was debt-payment: nourishment to the guardians who controlled the passage between worlds.

In this light, the lords of death appear less as abstract symbols and more as gatekeepers of covenant. They enforced the ultimate payment: life given, life judged, life carried into the unseen. Their names, etched into glyphs, papyri, and clay, preserved their authority across millennia. To speak the name correctly was to survive the journey. To forget it was to vanish.

Beyond these four anchor cultures, the pattern repeats globally. In Greece, Hades ruled the underworld with Cerberus as guardian. In India, Yama presided as king of the dead, assisted by two four-eyed dogs who guided souls across the river Vaitarani (O'Flaherty, *Hindu Myths*, 1975). In Norse myth, Hel governed the realm of the dishonored dead, half her body alive and half skeletal. Each culture attached different names, yet the domains, symbols, and canine companions remain constant. Taken together, these figures suggest not cultural invention in isolation, but a shared template of divine authority over death and passage.

Mainstream archaeology tends to resist trans-oceanic connections, attributing these overlaps to coincidence. Yet the persistence of skeletal deities with similar names, roles, and rites across hemispheres challenges that dismissal. As David Leeming notes in *The Oxford Companion to World Mythology* (2005), "the recurrence of underworld lords with skeletal features and canine guardianship in widely separated cultures is a problem of diffusion not yet resolved." The simplest resolution is that these names, like the serpent and storm gods before them, were part of an original system, remembered and re-spoken across ages.

If the feathered serpent ruled thresholds, and the storm gods ruled fertility and sky, the lords of death ruled permanence. They ensured that the covenant extended beyond life. Human beings did not escape their debts at death; they paid them again at the gates of the underworld. In every civilization that remembered their names, the same truth was enforced: even in death, the gods had to be fed.

The Sky Fathers and Creators

If serpents guarded thresholds and storm gods controlled fertility, then the role of the sky father was to establish the cosmos itself. These were not merely deities of weather or death but beings associated with creation, law, and the ordering of heaven and earth. Their names carried a weight of supremacy: short, resonant syllables often beginning with open vowels, as if their very sound should dominate. Across cultures, these creator figures were remembered as the ones who "set things in place."

In Mesoamerica, the Maya invoked Itzamnaaj, sometimes shortened to Itzamna, as the great god of the heavens. He was credited with inventing writing, establishing calendrical order, and granting maize — the substance of human life — to mankind (Taube, The Major Gods of Ancient Yucatan, 1992). Depictions show him as an aged deity with a Roman nose and edentulous jaw, often seated upon a celestial throne. The Dresden Codex portrays him as a sky-supporter, his body adorned with hieroglyphs marking time. His very name, Itzamnaaj, combines itz (sacred substance, like dew or sap) with amnaaj (house or authority), suggesting "the house of sacred substance."

Colonial accounts emphasize Itzamnaaj's role not just as sky god but as cultural founder. Diego de Landa wrote that the Maya remembered him as the one who "taught them to write and count, and who named their lands and gave them laws" (*Relación de las Cosas de Yucatán*, 1566). In this memory, Itzamnaaj is less a distant sky deity than a civilizer who walked among humans, encoding writing and time. The durability of his name is inseparable from the gifts he was remembered for.

The Aztecs recognized a similar figure in Tonacatecuhtli, "Lord of Sustenance," who, together with his consort Tonacacihuatl, generated creation. Though less prominent in surviving codices than Tlaloc or Huitzilopochtli, Tonacatecuhtli's name appears in mythic cycles where he dwells in the highest of the heavens, Omeyocan, the "Place of Duality" (León-Portilla, Aztec Thought and Culture, 1963). His role was abstract but crucial: he established the framework within which the other gods operated.

In Mesopotamia, the supreme figure was An, later known in Akkadian as Anu. His name is almost minimal: two letters, an open vowel followed by a nasal consonant. "An" literally means "sky" or "heaven." As early as the third millennium BCE, An was venerated in Sumerian hymns as the father of the gods, ruler of the constellations, and the one who set kingship upon earth (Jacobsen, The Treasures of Darkness, 1976). Cylinder seals depict him enthroned with a horned crown, receiving homage from lesser deities. Though often remote — leaving day-to-day affairs to Enlil or Inanna — An/Anu remained the final authority, invoked in curses: "By Anu, Enlil, and Ea, may you be struck down." The survival of his name for millennia underscores its authority.

Egyptian tradition likewise preserves the name of a supreme creator: Amun, "the Hidden One." Originally a local Theban deity,

Amun rose to prominence in the Middle Kingdom and became fused with the sun god Ra to form Amun-Ra, king of the gods. Hymns to Amun describe him as "one who made that which is, creator of all that exists" (Assmann, *The Search for God in Ancient Egypt,* 2001). His hiddenness was paradoxical: unseen yet supreme, transcendent yet immanent in the sun's daily cycle. The phonetic resemblance of Amun to Anu and even to Itzamna's "Amnaaj" is suggestive, an echo of authority across continents.

Hymns from the New Kingdom describe Amun as "king of the gods, maker of men, creator of all animals, lord of what is" (Assmann, *Egyptian Hymns and Prayers,* 1984). His temples at Karnak and Luxor were the largest religious complexes in the ancient world, constructed as axial monuments aligning with solstices. The scale itself was testimony: the name of Amun was to be spoken not in small shrines but in spaces that embodied eternity. His hiddenness was paradoxical — invisible in form, yet omnipresent in stone and liturgy.

The Indo-European world adds more names to this pattern. In Vedic India, the sky father was Dyaus Pitar, literally "sky father," cognate with Greek Zeus Pater and Latin Jupiter (from Diu Pater). These names share not only roles but phonetic cores: Dy- and Ze-, the bright sky; pater or pitar, the father. The Indo-European diffusion is well-documented, but its resonance with non-Indo-European figures like Anu or Amun invites broader questions. Why do sky fathers everywhere bear short, sonorous names tied to creation and law?

Philologists have traced the sky father's name across Indo-European tongues for over a century. Max Müller first noted the parallels in the 19th century, arguing that Dyaus Pitar, Zeus Pater, and Jupiter were linguistic brothers, descended from a Proto-Indo-European root dyeu-pater, "shining father" (Müller, *Comparative Mythology,* 1856). What is striking is not only the linguistic continuity but the semantic stability: in every tongue, the name referred to the supreme sky father. This durability reinforces the idea that such names were designed to persist, carried intact for thousands of years.

Symbolically, these figures often appear enthroned or elevated, embodying stability rather than dynamism. Unlike storm gods who wield weapons, the sky fathers preside with authority. Itzamnaaj sits upon a throne with glyphs of time. Anu crowns kingship and fixes stars. Amun is hidden yet omnipresent, his temples vast and axial. Zeus rules from Olympus with thunderbolt in hand, but even he is called "father of gods and men." The imagery is consistent: sky fathers do not merely act; they ordain.

The rituals associated with them also carry a more abstract quality. Offerings to Itzamnaaj involved incense and bloodletting, but his role was not to consume but to sanction the cycles of time. Hymns to Anu describe him not as eating or drinking but as decreeing. In Egypt, Amun was worshipped with grand processions during the Opet Festival, where his image was carried from Karnak to Luxor to renew kingship and cosmic order (Shafer, Religion in Ancient Egypt, 1991). These rites reinforced not only divine presence but legitimacy.

The linguistic echoes are striking. Anu, Amun, Itzamnaaj — syllables heavy with open vowels, nasals, and the "an/am" sequence. Dyaus, Zeus, Jupiter — the same bright-sky phoneme, tied explicitly to fatherhood. Even in Polynesia, the sky father appears as Atea or Rangi, names beginning with open vowels that connote expanse and light. Names of supreme authority seem to crystallize around the same phonetic cores.

Skeptics argue that this is inevitable: human languages often use simple, resonant sounds for concepts of sky and father. Yet the recurrence of specific syllables, paired with identical roles and iconography, suggests more than coincidence. Georges Dumézil, though focused on Indo-European triads, admitted that "the persistence of the sky father as supreme deity across unrelated traditions demands a common explanation" (Archaic Roman Religion, 1970).

What emerges is a pattern of names designed for permanence. The sky fathers were less accessible than storm or serpent gods, but their names carried ultimate authority. To invoke Anu or Amun was to appeal to the highest power. To pray to Itzamnaaj or Tonacatecuhtli was to recognize cosmic order itself. These were the gods of foundations, the ones whose names marked beginnings.

Even beyond Eurasia, similar figures appear. In Polynesia, Ranginui was the sky father whose union with Papa, the earth mother, generated the gods. In China, Shangdi ("Supreme Deity") presided over heaven and was invoked as the source of imperial legitimacy (Keightley, *Sources of Shang History*, 1978). These examples, though outside the Indo-European sphere, echo the same structure: short, resonant names tied to heaven and creation, invoked as ultimate authority.

When we map them side by side, the conclusion becomes unavoidable: civilizations across hemispheres remembered their creators with short, resonant names that echo each other in sound and function. Whether Anu, Amun, Itzamnaaj, or Zeus, the pattern is unmistakable. The names of the sky fathers were not invented in isolation but preserved from a common system, transmitted at the dawn of civilization and carried forward in ritual, myth, and syllable.

Skeptics and Counterarguments

Whenever parallels between gods across hemispheres are raised, scholars of linguistics and comparative religion are quick to raise a hand of caution. The mainstream view is straightforward: human beings everywhere face the same elemental realities — storms, death, fertility, the sky — and it is inevitable that they would invent gods with overlapping traits. Names, too, are dismissed as coincidence, the product of limited sound systems rather than diffusion. To many academics, the suggestion that Kukulkan and Anu, or Ah Puch and Anpu, share more than chance phonetics is a case of pattern-seeking gone too far.

Historical linguists are especially wary. The discipline of comparative linguistics, since its formalization in the 19th century, has developed strict rules for establishing connections: systematic sound correspondences, extensive word lists, and reconstruction of proto-languages. Anything less is considered speculation. Scholars like Lyle Campbell, in *Historical Linguistics: An Introduction* (1998), argue that "superficial similarities in phonetics cannot establish relationship."

Thus, the appearance of "an/am" in Itzamnaaj, Anu, and Amun is brushed aside as convergence — different languages happened to produce similar sounds for sky gods because open vowels and nasals are common globally.

Anthropologists make a parallel argument about symbols. Snakes, storms, and skulls appear everywhere because snakes are dangerous, storms are vital and frightening, and bones are the natural residue of death. Joseph Campbell, though sympathetic to grand comparative frameworks, leaned heavily on Jungian archetypes to explain the recurrence of deities like the feathered serpent or storm god. For Campbell, these were projections of the human unconscious, "masks of God" generated independently by cultures grappling with the same inner structures of psyche (*The Masks of God: Primitive Mythology*, 1962). Carl Jung himself described the serpent as an archetype of transformation and the storm as an image of psychic upheaval. From this perspective, the similarities across cultures say more about the human mind than about historical transmission.

Archaeologists, too, caution against overreach. When Thor Heyerdahl attempted to argue for transoceanic diffusion in *American Indians in the Pacific* (1952), his methods were criticized as selective and romantic. Specialists pointed out that similar technologies and symbols can arise through convergent evolution — cultures facing similar challenges produce similar solutions. The same logic, skeptics argue, applies to divine names: "ku," "na," or "an" are simply easy syllables, likely to recur in independent traditions.

Even within comparative mythology, there is division. Georges Dumézil, who pioneered the study of Indo-European myth structures, was cautious about extending his triadic framework beyond the Indo-European sphere. While he acknowledged the universality of sky fathers, storm gods, and underworld lords, he insisted these patterns should be studied within cultural families, not assumed to represent global diffusion. His warning is often repeated: structural similarity does not equal shared origin.

Yet the skepticism itself reveals its limits. If all serpent gods are merely archetypes, why do they so often appear in temples aligned to solstices, under names with similar guttural phonemes, and attached to the same elemental domains? If storm gods are universal projections, why do their names so consistently terminate in hard consonants, and why are child sacrifices to rain gods recorded in both the Florentine Codex for Tlaloc and Ugaritic texts for Baal Hadad? Skeptics dismiss phonetic echoes as chance, but the recurrence of name + role + symbol stretches coincidence to breaking.

Furthermore, the history of linguistics itself shows that "coincidence" often masks relationship. Early in the 19th century, Sir William Jones noted the parallels between Sanskrit, Greek, and Latin, observing that they "have sprung from some common source" (Jones, *Third Anniversary Discourse*, 1786). At the time, these similarities were dismissed by some as happenstance. Today, they form the foundation of Indo-European studies. It took decades for systematic correspondences to confirm what intuition first suggested. By analogy, the echoes of divine names across unrelated families may be early evidence of a deeper system not yet reconstructed.

Archaeology also complicates the skeptic's case. When cultures with "no contact" produce not just similar gods but similar temples, aligned to the same stars, the coincidence argument begins to wobble. Kukulkan descending El Castillo at equinox is difficult to explain as archetype alone. So is the Mushussu guarding the Ishtar Gate with the same serpent-dragon form as Quetzalcoatl's feathered coils. Scholars who insist on coincidence often do so by treating each element — name, role, symbol — in isolation, rather than confronting the constellation of parallels.

Even the archetype argument falters under scrutiny. Jung described archetypes as psychic structures, not names. Archetypes may explain why humans everywhere revere the sun, but they cannot explain why the names of creator gods so often contain "an/am," or why storm gods across language families share guttural endings. To bridge that gap, we must at least consider diffusion or deliberate transmission. As David Leeming observed in *The Oxford Companion to World Mythology* (2005), "the recurrence of specific phonetic and symbolic patterns in otherwise unrelated mythologies points to lines of contact or shared instruction."

The skeptic's caution is necessary — it prevents us from chasing every superficial resemblance. But it is also incomplete. By focusing only on the dangers of overreach, mainstream scholarship blinds itself to the possibility of an older, global system. The names of gods may be more than coincidences of sound; they may be linguistic fossils, fragments of a program of transmission. When paired with identical functions and ritual machinery, the case for common instruction grows stronger than the case for chance.

In the end, the counterarguments sharpen rather than blunt the thesis. If skeptics insist the serpent, storm, death, and sky fathers are universal archetypes, then the question remains: why do they carry such specific, echoing names? If linguists insist phonetic similarity is coincidence, then why do those echoes cluster around elemental domains across hemispheres? Coincidence explains part of the story, but not all. The persistence of names across thousands of years and thousands of miles hints at something more deliberate — a system of memory that refuses to vanish, even when scholars dismiss it.

Conclusion: The Memory in the Names

When we step back from the details of Kukulkan's temples, Chaac's lightning axe, Ah Puch's skeletal grin, or Amun's hidden throne, a pattern emerges that cannot be dismissed as coincidence. The names of gods — carried forward in chants, carved into stone, whispered in prayers — have endured with a persistence that outlasts empires. They echo across hemispheres, bound not only by sound but by function.

The feathered serpent appears in Mexico, India, Egypt, and Mesopotamia: guardian, creator, liminal power of transition. Storm gods thunder from Sumer to Yucatán to the Levant: wielders of lightning, givers of rain, takers of life. Lords of death, skeletal and canine, preside over the underworld from Xibalba to Mictlan, from Abydos to Irkalla. Sky fathers, enthroned above all, establish the order of heaven from Itzamnaaj to Anu to Amun. Four archetypes, four sets of names, repeating across civilizations that allegedly never met.

Mainstream scholarship offers explanations: archetypes, convergent evolution, coincidence of phonetics. These explanations carry weight, and they remind us not to leap at every superficial resemblance. Yet when names, symbols, and roles converge together, the burden of proof shifts. Coincidence may explain one echo, but not dozens. Archetype may explain the serpent, but not Kukulkan's syllables resembling nāga or Mushussu, nor Amun's name echoing Anu. Convergence may explain rain rituals, but not the tears of children sacrificed to Tlaloc paralleling the weeping offerings to Baal Hadad. The similarities are too consistent, too functional, too heavily ritualized.

What remains is the possibility of transmission. Not necessarily in the crude sense of shiploads of priests crossing oceans, but in something deeper: a system of names and functions given to humanity at the dawn of civilization. Just as kingship, writing, and astronomy appear fully formed in early records, so too do these divine archetypes arrive already paired with names. They are not scattered inventions but fragments of a larger program — a program whose memory lingers most stubbornly in sound.

This does not mean the names remained unchanged. They shifted, morphed, and fused. Inanna became Ishtar. Amun fused with Ra. Tonacatecuhtli was remembered faintly in Aztec codices, while Kukulkan's cult rose to dominance in Yucatán. But even through change, the bones of the names survived — short, resonant syllables attached to elemental domains. To invoke them was to invoke more than metaphor. It was to recognize a contract that linked survival to ritual payment.

In this light, the names are not trivia. They are evidence. They are the fingerprints of an older order, preserved not by accident but by design. Their persistence across continents reveals the durability of covenant — agreements remembered not in text alone but in sound, syllable, and ritual.

Skeptics will continue to argue coincidence, and their caution must be respected. But for those willing to look at the global picture, the case grows harder to ignore. Names endure because they matter. They are spoken with reverence, fear, and obligation. They carry the memory of debts owed, covenants struck, and powers that once walked openly among us.

As we turn to the next chapter, we move from the realm of names to the realm of symbols — the faces, animals, and tools that accompanied these gods in stone and relief. If the names are the echoes of an older system, the symbols are its illustrations, recurring across continents with the same uncanny persistence. Together, names and symbols will continue to build the case that what we call mythology is in fact memory — memory of a covenant that still casts its shadow across human history.

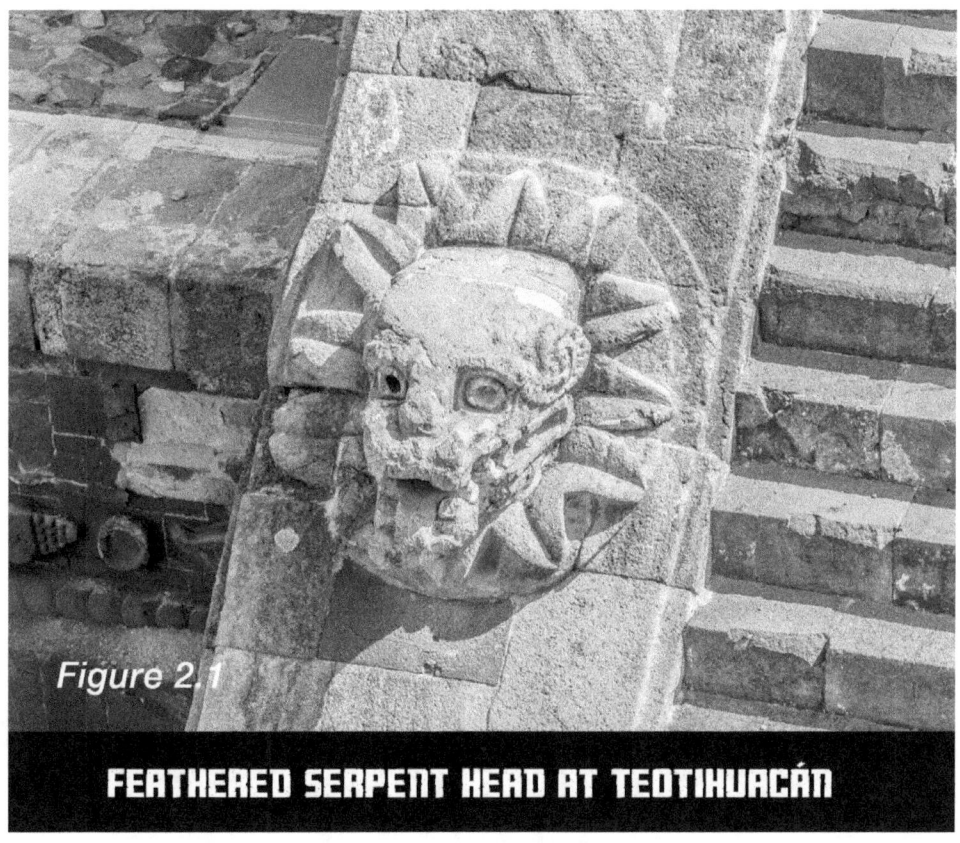

FEATHERED SERPENT HEAD AT TEOTIHUACÁN

Feathered Serpent Head, Temple of the Feathered Serpent (Teotihuacán, ca. 200–250 CE). Projecting stone head wreathed in feathers on the pyramid's façade. At Teotihuacán, the Feathered Serpent embodied rulership, calendrics, and rain–fertility cults — an early form of the deity later known as **Quetzalcoatl**.

SEVEN-HEADED NāGA BALUSTRADE AT ANGKOR THOM

Nāga Balustrade, Causeway of Angkor Thom (12th c. CE).
Seven-headed nāga serpent flanking the entrance causeway, its body forming the bridge to the temple. In Khmer cosmology, nāgas were lords of waters and threshold guardians, linking the human world with the divine.

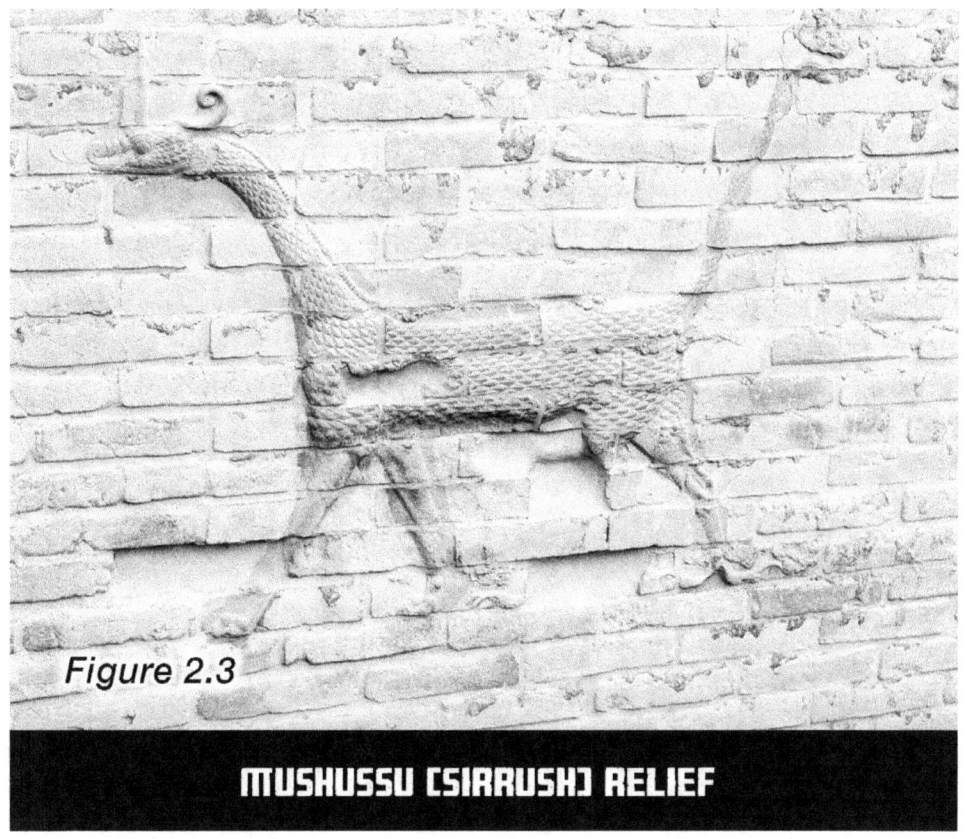

Figure 2.3

MUSHUSSU [SIRRUSH] RELIEF

Mushussu, Ishtar Gate of Babylon (6th c. BCE).
Bas-relief of the serpent-dragon of Marduk, with scaly body, leonine forelegs, and bird talons. The mushussu guarded the ceremonial way into Babylon and served as the divine attendant of Marduk, enforcing sovereignty at the city's threshold.

Chaac Mask, Uxmal (ca. 800–950 CE). Stone façade covered with long-nosed masks of Chaac, the Maya rain and lightning god. Chaac wielded a lightning axe to split clouds and release rain, sustaining maize and human life. His image, repeated across temple walls, embodied the covenant of sacrifice for fertility.

Anubis Weighing the Heart, Papyrus of Hunefer (ca. 1275 BCE).
From the Book of the Dead, this scene shows Anubis weighing the heart of the deceased against the feather of Ma'at, while Ammit, the devourer, waits for the verdict. The judgment embodied Egypt's covenant of death: only those whose lives were balanced by truth could pass safely into eternity.

3

FACES AND SYMBOLS OF POWER

Introduction: Power Wore a Face

P ower wore a face before it spoke a word. Long before written theology or codified law, the symbols of authority appeared in stone and relief. Across continents and millennia, cultures that supposedly never met nevertheless carved the same visages, raised the same emblems, and repeated the same gestures. These were not idle decorations or aesthetic flourishes. They were instructions — procedural diagrams of how power flowed, who carried it, and what it demanded.

The serpent comes first, a crown that bites. In Egypt, the uraeus, a rearing cobra, thrusts upward from the pharaoh's brow, ready to spit fire at his enemies. This was not metaphor: the cobra goddess Wadjet was believed to defend the king with lethal force. The uraeus adorned crowns, statues, and temple walls, a perpetual reminder that sovereignty itself was a living power that struck like venom (Faulkner, *The Ancient Egyptian Pyramid Texts,* 1969). In Mesoamerica, the serpent grew feathers and a voice. The Maya's Kukulkan and the Aztec Quetzalcoatl united earth and sky in a single body, depicted as serpents with avian plumage, winding across temple stairways and codices. The serpent became not only a crown but a bridge — a conduit between below and above, delivering breath, rain, and life-force.

The Pyramid Texts confirm this fiery role. In *Utterance 226*, the king ascends with the uraeus on his brow, who "spits fire against your enemies" (Faulkner, *The Ancient Egyptian Pyramid Texts*, 1969). In New Kingdom inscriptions from Edfu, Wadjet is invoked as "the Great Flame, the Lady of the Sky, who burns the rebellious with her fire." Here the cobra is not ornamental but weaponized, an active participant in the covenant of kingship. The pharaoh's authority was literalized as lethal force, embodied in the serpent's hiss and strike.

In India and Southeast Asia, the nāga coils beneath temples and rises beside gateways. Nāgas guard thresholds, fountains, and rivers; in Khmer architecture at Angkor Wat, massive seven-headed nāgas line the causeways, their bodies forming bridges between the human world and the sacred enclosure (Coedès, *The Indianized States of Southeast Asia*, 1968). The motif repeats with unnerving precision: serpent as guardian, serpent as crown, serpent as conduit. Whether uraeus, feathered serpent, or nāga, the body of the snake becomes a living bridge — exactly the kind of channel a covenantal system would require.

Then the sky acquires arms and legs. Winged men step from the walls of Mesopotamian palaces, feathers spread behind human faces. These are the Apkallu, hybrid sages described in Assyrian inscriptions as half-divine beings sent to teach humanity agriculture, law, and ritual (Black & Green, *Gods, Demons and Symbols of Ancient Mesopotamia*, 1992). They hold in their hands mysterious objects — a cone and a bucket — and perform repeated gestures of dipping and applying, as if enacting a procedure. Their wings mark them as liminal, creatures of altitude who moved between realms.

In India, the great bird Garuda fills the same role. A colossal eagle-man, Garuda is the mount of Vishnu and the eternal enemy of the serpent nāgas. Hindu epics describe him as swift enough to blot out the sky, a rescuer and warrior whose very name means "devourer." Like the Apkallu, Garuda is feathered authority: part human, part avian, a courier between worlds. In Mesoamerica, murals and headdresses depict rulers as bird-men, donning feathers and beaks to announce that their power descends from above. The Maya carved avian beings with human torsos and outspread wings, perched upon world trees or flanking deities. Wings signal jurisdiction over altitude — over the place where offerings ascend and edicts fall. If serpents mark the channel, bird-men mark the courier. Together they describe a logistics of the sacred: movement of power, movement of tribute, movement of blood.

The Mahabharata preserves Garuda's role vividly. In one tale, he devours the nāgas en masse, earning his place as Vishnu's eternal mount and the scourge of serpents (Ganguli, *The Mahabharata, Book* I, c. 400 BCE). His speed is described as "blotting out the sun," his wings shaking the heavens as he descended to rescue stolen amrita, the nectar of immortality. Such epic descriptions transform him from a mere mythic bird into a force of cosmic logistics — a courier whose very name signifies appetite and dominion.

In the hands of these figures appear objects so plain they become startling. The so-called "handbag" motif — a small, bucketed arc grasped like a tool — is carved in Sumerian and Assyrian reliefs, carried by Apkallu in one hand while they extend a cone in the other. The cone, pinched delicately between two fingers, touches sacred trees, kings, or altars. Scholars call this "fertilization," "anointing," or "purification." Yet the repetition across scenes suggests something more technical: take from container, apply to target, effect change. It is storage and transfer, dose and delivery. Improbably, the same handbag motif appears on stelae in Mesoamerica, carried by gods and kings alike (von Däniken, *The Gold of the Gods*, 1972; also *Mesoamerican iconography studies* by Linda Schele).

Even earlier evidence of the "handbag" motif appears at Göbekli Tepe in southeastern Turkey, dated to the 10th millennium BCE. Pillar reliefs show pail-like shapes arranged above animal figures, carved with the same arc-handled outline later seen in Assyrian and Mesoamerican art (Schmidt, *Göbekli Tepe: A Stone Age Sanctuary in Southeastern Anatolia*, 2010). The persistence of this simple but precise form across such vast spans of time suggests intentional continuity. Whatever the object represented — container of seeds, vessel of life, or ritual tool — its form was standardized early and carried forward across civilizations.

Later commentators have argued about meaning, but the gestures are too consistent to dismiss as decorative. The figures are not posing; they are working. They grasp tools, perform applications, and repeat sequences. The set is so stable it might be called a ritual toolkit — a standard issue for covenant enforcers across hemispheres.

The message is reinforced by scale. The central figure is always larger, haloed or crowned, while smaller attendants flank the feet — as we see in both Maya sculpture and Indian carvings. In both cases, a divine being is elevated, framed by a gateway or throne, with diminutive figures acknowledging subordination. This is not coincidence. It is staging: power diagrammed in stone.

When we line these motifs up — uraeus with nāga with feathered serpent; Apkallu with Garuda with avian rulers; bucket with cone with basin — the pattern clarifies. These are not random artistic flourishes or independent inventions. They form a kit, a set of standardized faces and tools used across hemispheres to represent covenant.

Faces and symbols of power are never merely decorative. They are instructions. The serpent shows the channel. The bird-man shows the courier. The bag-and-cone show the method of transfer. And the staged composition — central figure haloed, flanked by attendants — shows hierarchy itself, preserved with uncanny fidelity across civilizations.

What emerges is a system of iconography too consistent to dismiss. Later chapters will supply the site reports, the codices, the museum plates. For now, the argument stands in outline: the gods wore the same faces, carried the same tools, and demanded the same thing from those who served them.

Serpent as Crown and Conduit

The serpent was among humanity's earliest divine emblems, and it appears wherever civilization first put chisel to stone. Its body is a paradox: low and earthbound, yet capable of sudden, vertical violence. It is predator and protector, symbol of death and regeneration. That paradox made it ideal as a crown of power, a living conduit through which divine authority passed.

In Egypt, the uraeus was carved upon the foreheads of kings as both symbol and participant in their rule. The cobra goddess Wadjet was said to rise from the brow of the pharaoh, spitting fire at enemies and striking them down. Pyramid Texts describe the king ascending with the uraeus, who secures his dominion in the next world: "Your head is raised among the gods, your brow adorned with the serpent, who spits fire against your enemies" (Faulkner, *The Ancient Egyptian Pyramid Texts,* 1969). The uraeus thus functioned as both ornament and weapon, a perpetual reminder that the pharaoh's power was not his own, but bestowed and enforced by a living intermediary. The serpent was sovereignty itself, animated in stone and metal.

Mexico–Egypt Parallels in Regal Iconography

The use of the forehead as a seat of power is not limited to the Egyptian uraeus. Across the Atlantic, Mesoamerican rulers also placed emblems directly at the brow, embedding authority into the very face of the sovereign. A striking example comes from Toltec and Maya sculpture, where enthroned figures wear squared headdresses capped with a central medallion. The emblem sits precisely at the mid-brow, echoing the placement of Egypt's rearing cobra on the pharaoh's crown.

The parallels run deeper than the emblem alone. Both traditions favored the squared headdress, a rigid frame enclosing the head and shoulders, flattening the silhouette into geometric order. This choice is unusual — most cultures used crowns or helmets with rounded or tapering tops. Squared headdresses, by contrast, suggest intentional standardization, as though divine authority was to be depicted within the same architectural outline.

The seated posture reinforces the comparison. Egyptian kings are shown enthroned with symmetrical rigidity: hands upon knees, torso erect, gaze fixed forward. Mexican sculptures of rulers — including those at Tula and Chichen Itza — display the same symmetrical frontality, arms pressed forward in formal stillness. The visual grammar is nearly identical: crown above, emblem at brow, body enthroned, attendants or guardians often flanking the figure.

Mainstream interpretation explains these similarities as archetypal: rulers everywhere borrow solar imagery, central placement, and frontal symmetry to project order. Yet when the squared crown, brow emblem, and enthroned posture recur together in cultures supposedly unconnected, coincidence strains credulity. These are not general symbols of kingship; they are specific conventions reproduced across an ocean.

The simplest reading is that both priesthoods were reproducing fragments of the same instruction set. The gods were to be enthroned in light, crowned in geometry, marked on the brow with a seal of authority. Mexico and Egypt, though separated by oceans, preserved the same visual code.

New Kingdom inscriptions reinforce Wadjet's role as more than a symbol. At Edfu, she is hailed as "the Great Flame, Lady of the Sky, who burns the rebels with her fire." In temple hymns, she is invoked as the serpent whose "venom protects the throne, whose flame consumes the enemies of Ra" (Assmann, *Egyptian Hymns and Prayers*, 1984). These texts confirm that the uraeus was not ornamental. It was a living covenant partner, a fiery guardian present at every coronation and ritual, reminding Egyptians that kingship was enforced by lethal power rising from the serpent's hood.

The Mesoamerican world transfigured the serpent into an even more dynamic form. Among the Maya, Kukulkan, the "feathered serpent," united the earthbound coil with the skyborne quetzal bird. For the Aztecs, his name was Quetzalcoatl, "quetzal-feather serpent," a god of wind, rain, and cultural order. Myths describe Quetzalcoatl as the one who descended into the underworld to retrieve the bones of a past humanity, sprinkling them with his own blood to fashion the present race (León-Portilla, *Aztec Thought and Culture*, 1963). His name appears in glyphs entwined with feathers and coils, his visage crowned by plumes that shimmered like lightning in the tropical sun. At Chichen Itza, the pyramid of El Castillo was engineered so that at equinox, sunlight cast the shadow of a serpent undulating down its staircase — Kukulkan himself descending in real time (Schele & Freidel, *A Forest of Kings*, 1990).

The Florentine Codex records that Quetzalcoatl was closely associated with rituals of penitential bloodletting. Priests and rulers pierced their ears, tongues, or genitals, offering drops of blood upon bark paper that was then burned as smoke to nourish him (Sahagún, *Florentine Codex, Book 2*). These offerings were not symbolic. They were payment. As blood seeped from the ruler's body, it was believed to feed the feathered serpent who, in turn, kept cosmic order intact. Quetzalcoatl's cult thus linked kingship directly to covenant, binding rulers to bleed for the god as proof of legitimacy.

This was not theater but covenant made visible: a deity returning to collect his due. The Maya and Aztecs both believed the gods required nourishment in blood, and Quetzalcoatl was among those to whom it was given. In the Florentine Codex, priests describe his association with penitential bloodletting, where rulers pierced their ears or tongues and offered drops of blood on bark paper to feed him (Sahagún, *Florentine Codex, Book 2*). The serpent was not only a crown but a channel — the visible line through which sustenance flowed between human and divine.

In India, the serpent appears as nāga, semi-divine beings inhabiting rivers, lakes, and underworld palaces. The Mahabharata describes the nāgas as rulers of subterranean realms, fierce and powerful, capable of bringing rains or disasters (Ganguli, *The Mahabharata, Book I*). In Khmer art at Angkor, seven-headed nāgas stretch across causeways, their bodies forming balustrades that connect the human and divine precincts of the temple (Coedès, *The Indianized States of Southeast Asia*, 1968). These bridges are not metaphorical:

they are literal stone pathways that worshippers crossed, passing under the gaze of serpent kings. To step into the temple was to cross the nāga, to acknowledge the serpent as guardian of thresholds.

Indian mythology elaborates the nāgas as more than guardians. In Hindu cosmology, the great serpent Shesha coils beneath Vishnu, supporting the universe on his thousand hoods. Another nāga, Vasuki, is wrapped around Mount Mandara in the churning of the cosmic ocean, his body serving as the rope by which gods and demons drew forth the nectar of immortality (Bhattacharyya, *The Indian Naga Cult*, 1975). These myths elevate the nāga from threshold guardian to cosmic axis — a being without whom creation and sustenance could not occur. The parallel with Kukulkan as world-renewer and Wadjet as sustainer of kingship underscores the serpent's global role as both foundation and bridge.

The consistency is remarkable. Egypt placed the serpent on the brow of kings. Mesoamerica placed it on temple stairways. India and Cambodia placed it at gateways. Everywhere, the serpent crowned thresholds: from earth to heaven, from city to temple, from mortal to divine. It was always more than an animal. It was a passage.

Skeptics note that snakes are universal: they inhabit every climate save the frozen north, and their venom has always inspired fear. To elevate them as symbols of power, they argue, is only natural. But the persistence of the serpent's specific functions — crown, bridge, guardian — suggests something more deliberate. Why should the uraeus and the nāga both guard entrances? Why should Kukulkan and Wadjet both spit or descend as fire? Why should serpent forms crown kings in Egypt and line causeways in Cambodia? Archetype may explain the snake, but it cannot explain the same gestures, names, and functions repeating across civilizations.

Even linguistics hints at continuity. Kukulkan, Quetzalcoatl, Nāga, Mushussu, uraeus — different tongues, yet recurring guttural and hissing syllables. The hiss is preserved in the name itself, a phonetic fossil of the serpent's call. And where the serpent is remembered, it is always tied to nourishment. Kukulkan descends for offerings. Nāgas guard the waters. Wadjet spits fire to defend the order of Egypt. The serpent's body is a channel, its mouth a weapon, its name a sound of covenant.

In this light, the serpent as crown and conduit is not random mythmaking. It is part of a kit — a set of standardized symbols meant to diagram covenantal power. To wear the serpent was to show alignment with unseen masters. To cross the serpent bridge was to enter the realm of those who demanded tribute. And to carve its image in stone was to fix in memory the channel through which power flowed.

The serpent's role as conduit is not limited to Egypt, Mesoamerica, or India. In Aboriginal Australia, the Rainbow Serpent is the primordial creator, carving rivers and demanding ritual to keep water flowing (Berndt, *The World of the First Australians*, 1964). In China, the dragon — a scaled, serpent-bodied creature — was revered as the bringer of rain and imperial legitimacy (Keightley, *Sources of Shang History*, 1978). The serpent-dragon Mushussu of Babylon, Quetzalcoatl's feathered coils, Wadjet's fiery hood, and the nāgas' cosmic rope all converge upon the same truth: the serpent was remembered as the axis of power, fertility, and survival.

Across civilizations, the serpent was not a passive emblem but an active channel. It crowned kings, guarded gateways, churned oceans, spat fire, and descended temple stairs in shadow and light. Always it demanded payment — blood, water, ritual — to keep life flowing. If power required a conduit, the serpent was chosen again and again as its living diagram. The consistency of this role across hemispheres suggests not invention, but instruction. Humanity was taught to crown its rulers and sanctify its temples with serpents because the serpent was already the sign of covenant, the mark of a system older than any one civilization.

Winged Beings and Avian Couriers

If the serpent marked the channel of covenant, the winged being marked its courier. Across civilizations, figures with feathers and flight were portrayed as messengers, guardians, and technicians — intermediaries who moved between worlds to deliver knowledge, enforce ritual, and collect tribute. Their wings symbolized more than decoration. They embodied jurisdiction over altitude, the realm where offerings rose in smoke and decrees descended from heaven.

In Mesopotamia, the Apkallu were the archetype. These hybrid beings — human in form but often winged and sometimes fish-cloaked — adorned the walls of Assyrian palaces from Nimrud to Nineveh. Always they are shown in action: wings outstretched, one hand grasping a bucket, the other a cone. The cone is touched to sacred trees, altars, or the king himself. Scholars call this "fertilization" or "purification," but the repetition makes it look procedural. The Apkallu were not posing as symbols; they were at work, applying something from container to target, as if conducting maintenance on an invisible system. Their wings signify mobility, their tools signify transfer. In Assyrian inscriptions, they are remembered as the "seven sages" sent by the god Ea to teach mankind agriculture, law, and ritual (Black & Green, *Gods, Demons and Symbols of Ancient Mesopotamia*, 1992). They were not only intermediaries but instructors — couriers of both substance and knowledge.

Cuneiform tablets from Nineveh describe the Apkallu as "those of great understanding, perfect in wisdom, who teach the ordinances of heaven and earth" (Lambert, *Babylonian Wisdom Literature*, 1960). They are listed by name in the Uruk List of Kings and Sages, each paired with a legendary ruler, suggesting that no king governed without a sage by his side. Archaeologists have found small clay figurines of Apkallu buried under thresholds of Assyrian buildings, positioned as guardians. This confirms their dual role: both instructors of ritual and couriers of protection, ensuring that households and palaces were aligned with the covenant.

India preserves the avian courier in the colossal figure of Garuda. Part man, part eagle, Garuda is remembered in the Mahabharata as so vast that his wings darkened the sun. In one epic episode, he devours the serpent nāgas and secures immortality by stealing amrita, the nectar of the gods. From that day, he becomes the eternal mount of Vishnu, the preserver god, carrying him between realms (Ganguli, *The Mahabharata, Book I*). In iconography, Garuda appears with human torso and eagle's wings, crouched in flight or poised in attack. His very name means "devourer." Just as Apkallu are remembered as enemies of chaos-serpents, Garuda is remembered as scourge of the nāgas. The parallel is striking: both figures are feathered, both oppose serpents, both act as couriers of divine will.

Beyond his enmity with the nāgas, Garuda's role in the epics includes cosmic contests. In the Mahabharata, he steals the pot of amrita from Indra's heaven, evading even the thunderbolt to bring it to his serpent kin. This theft, paradoxically, establishes him as master of immortality. Later, as Vishnu's mount, he becomes inseparable from divine preservation, carrying the god between realms. The consistency with Apkallu is striking: both are feathered beings remembered not only for mobility but for their technical mastery of divine substances — cones, buckets, amrita.

In Southeast Asia, Garuda's imagery dominates royal regalia. The emblem of Thailand today is Garuda, wings outstretched, clutching serpents. Cambodian kings likewise adopted Garuda as a royal symbol, plastering his form across Angkor's walls as both defender and vehicle. The persistence of Garuda from Indian myth to modern national emblem suggests that his function as courier and protector carried extraordinary durability. His wings, like the Apkallu's, marked him as the one who bridged worlds.

Mesoamerica also preserved avian couriers. Maya rulers often donned headdresses of quetzal feathers and avian beaks, dressing as bird-men to signal that their authority descended from the sky. Murals at Bonampak depict warriors and rulers in feathered costumes, outspread wings doubling as regalia of divine sanction. Codices show avian deities perched on world trees, watching over rituals below. In Mixtec codices, bird-men appear with speech scrolls issuing from their beaks, literally delivering messages from gods to humans (Boone, *Stories in Red and Black*, 2000). Here again the role is courier: wings signify transmission, voice, and mandate.

Maya inscriptions often combine avian heads with speech scrolls, showing that bird-deities were literally the bearers of words. In the *Dresden Codex*, avian figures perch atop world trees, releasing rain or fire from their beaks. In the Bonampak murals, rulers in avian costume preside over rituals of bloodletting and tribute. Linda Schele argued that avian costumes linked rulers to celestial messengers, marking them as couriers of divine will (Schele & Freidel, *A Forest of Kings*, 1990). The persistence of bird-imagery in Maya texts reinforces that wings signified not just transcendence, but the literal delivery of covenantal communication.

Even in the Old World, the pattern repeats beyond Mesopotamia and India. In Persia, the winged disk known as the faravahar shows a human figure with outstretched wings, associated with Zoroastrian divine presence. Though often interpreted as a symbol of the soul, the faravahar depicts a feathered intermediary between mortal and divine. In Egypt, the ba-bird — often shown as a human-headed falcon — was the mobile soul, capable of flight between the tomb and the afterlife. Again and again, wings symbolized the ability to traverse boundaries, to carry offerings upward and divine decrees downward.

Scholars debate the faravahar's meaning, but inscriptions at Persepolis suggest it represented more than an abstract soul. In the *Behistun Inscription of Darius I*, the winged figure hovers above the king as he subdues rebels, reinforcing that divine authority was actively present (Kuhrt, *The Persian Empire*, 2007). The faravahar's raised hand and ring are interpreted as symbols of covenant — an oath or bond between king and god. Like the Apkallu's bucket, the faravahar's tools are functional, not decorative, anchoring him in the role of courier of divine legitimacy.

The consistency of tools is just as telling as the wings. Apkallu carry buckets and cones. Garuda clutches nāgas in his talons. Maya rulers wield feathered staffs. The gestures differ, but the logic is shared: winged beings act as handlers, manipulators of sacred substances, conveyors of divine power. They are never distant gods aloof in the heavens. They are functional, operative, technical.

Skeptics explain winged beings as the natural symbol of freedom, transcendence, and communication. Birds fly; humans dream of flight; therefore cultures everywhere imagine winged messengers.

But as with the serpent, the parallels extend beyond general archetype. The Apkallu, Garuda, and Mesoamerican bird-men all stand opposed to serpents, acting as their rivals or predators. They all carry specific tools or symbols. And they all function as intermediaries in ritual, positioned at thresholds. Coincidence cannot fully account for these shared functions.

Winged couriers appear far beyond Mesopotamia, India, or Mesoamerica. In Greece, Hermes wore winged sandals as messenger of the gods. In Rome, Victoria spread feathered wings over triumphal arches. In Christian tradition, angels are feathered emissaries who deliver commands and carry souls. The repetition of wings as courier-mark is so consistent that it reads less like archetype and more like instruction. Humanity was taught to imagine its messengers feathered, to remember in image the role of couriers who once moved tangibly between realms.

If serpents were the channels, winged beings were the couriers. They enforced the logistics of covenant, moving offerings from earth to heaven and commands from heaven to earth. Their wings marked authority not only to ascend but to return, bringing mandates and knowledge. In every hemisphere, power required a courier, and every culture remembered them the same way: feathered, functional, opposed to serpents, servants of covenant.

The Ritual Toolkit: Bag and Cone

If the serpent was the conduit and the winged beings were the couriers, then the bag-and-cone was their equipment — the ritual toolkit carried from one hemisphere to another, reproduced with unnerving fidelity. In the art of Mesopotamia and Mesoamerica, figures are consistently shown holding small bucket-like containers and applying their contents with a conical object. The objects are so plain that they stand out, stripped of ornament, handled with the deliberate precision of technicians. These were not emblems of status. They were tools.

The most famous examples are from Assyria, where the Apkallu are shown flanking sacred trees or kings. In one hand, they hold a bucket (*banduddu* in Akkadian); in the other, a cone (*mullilu*), often interpreted as a fir cone. In nearly every depiction, the Apkallu perform the same action: dipping the cone into the bucket and applying it to a tree, altar, or figure. Scholars suggest the cone symbolizes pollination or purification, but the repetition across centuries suggests something more procedural — a step in a ritual process. The gesture is workmanlike: gather substance, apply substance, repeat.

Akkadian ritual texts even preserve the name mullilu for the cone, glossed as "purifier." In one fragment, the priest is instructed to "take the mullilu, touch the forehead, touch the tree, purify the offering." The word itself suggests action, not ornament — something to be wielded in precise contact. The repeated instruction mirrors what the reliefs show: application, infusion, activation. If the mullilu was remembered in text as well as in stone, it strengthens the case that this tool was functional, not symbolic invention.

Texts provide only fragmentary clues. Akkadian ritual instructions mention sprinkling holy water, and some scholars argue the bucket contained water from the apsû, the primordial ocean of creation. Yet the cone-and-bucket appear so consistently, and in contexts so charged with sacred authority, that they seem more than mere sprinklers. They look like standard-issue gear, the same across palaces, temples, and reliefs. Black and Green, in *Gods, Demons and Symbols of Ancient Mesopotamia* (1992), describe them as "ritual tools whose precise function eludes us but whose consistency bespeaks central importance."

What makes the toolkit remarkable is that it does not remain confined to Mesopotamia. Carvings in Mesoamerica show gods and rulers holding nearly identical bucket-shaped objects, with handles arcing over the top. On stelae at La Venta and Izapa, figures clutch small pails in one hand, while their other hand gestures toward altars or attendants. Erich von Däniken drew attention to these parallels in *The Gold of the Gods* (1972), arguing that the recurrence of the "handbag" across hemispheres defied coincidence. While von Däniken's conclusions were sensational, the visual data remain: bucket-like objects recur where no contact should exist, carried by divine intermediaries as part of their iconographic kit.

Olmec monuments at La Venta include figures grasping small arc-handled containers, their curved silhouettes nearly identical to Assyrian buckets. At Izapa, stelae depict gods with pails beside them, as though carrying a reservoir of sacred liquid or substance. Linda Schele noted that these objects appear in ritual contexts, often with rain or fertility deities (Schele & Freidel, *A Forest of Kings*, 1990). The recurrence of the same handled container, carved into stone thousands of miles from Mesopotamia, suggests more than parallel invention. It hints at a common instruction set remembered and preserved by different cultures.

Even earlier, at Göbekli Tepe in southeastern Turkey (c. 10,000 BCE), carved reliefs show pail-like shapes lined above animal figures. Archaeologist Klaus Schmidt identified these as possible early versions of the same ritual container (Schmidt, *Göbekli Tepe: A Stone Age Sanctuary in Southeastern Anatolia*, 2010). If so, the motif spans from the Pre-Pottery Neolithic to the Assyrian Empire, then leaps to Mesoamerica thousands of years later. Its durability rivals that of the serpent and winged being, suggesting a template preserved across ages.

What were these objects? Mainstream interpretations vary: containers of pollen or seeds, libation buckets for holy water, even symbolic purses representing divine wealth. The cone has been linked to male fertility, the bucket to female receptivity. Yet these readings strain against the evidence. The cones are always applied, never simply displayed; the buckets are always functional, gripped by handles. Their action is consistent: take, apply, repeat. In the language of ritual, this is dosage and delivery.

The possibility arises that the bag and cone represented — or literally were — containers of sacred substance. Something tangible was being transferred from one realm to another, mediated by winged couriers and enforced by serpentine guardians. The fact that the cone is applied to trees, kings, and altars suggests nourishment or

A Blood Covenant

activation. In some reliefs, the Apkallu touch the cone to the sacred tree, while in others, they bring it to the king's forehead. Both acts imply infusion: of fertility to the cosmos, or of power to the ruler.

Comparative evidence reinforces the idea of transfer. In Mesoamerica, pails appear in association with gods of rain and agriculture. In Hindu ritual, conch shells and sprinklers are used to apply holy water during purification ceremonies. In Egypt, libation basins were carved to catch fluids poured over altars. Yet only in Mesopotamia and Mesoamerica do we see the precise pairing of bucket and cone, handled with the same technician's grip.

The ritual toolkit becomes even more intriguing when we consider scale. In some Assyrian reliefs, the buckets are small, held at the hip; in others, they are exaggerated, nearly half the figure's height. This range suggests symbolic as well as practical significance, perhaps indicating greater or lesser potency of the substance within. The cones, too, vary in size but are always pinched between two fingers, reinforcing the sense of delicate application. These were not clubs or weapons. They were applicators.

Skeptics argue that such parallels prove nothing. Buckets are universal, cones are natural, and rituals everywhere involve sprinkling. Yet the specific combination of bag-and-cone, paired and performed by winged beings in the Old World and echoed by gods in the New, stretches coincidence. Why should Mesoamerican rulers be shown holding the same arc-handled containers as Assyrian Apkallu? Why should Göbekli Tepe, millennia earlier, already present the same motif?

Egypt provides a parallel in its libation vessels and purification basins. Priests poured water, milk, or wine over altars and collected it in carved drains, the liquid representing offerings to nourish the gods. While not identical in form to the Assyrian bucket, the Egyptian tools performed the same act of fluid transfer — application of substance from vessel to sacred object. The visual difference may conceal a functional similarity: every culture preserved the image of a container from which offerings were dispensed in precise ritual.

Mircea Eliade, cautious though he was, admitted that ritual implements often preserve the oldest layers of religious memory (Patterns in Comparative Religion, 1958). Tools endure because they are functional. If the bag-and-cone were part of an original covenantal kit, their survival across civilizations is not surprising. They were not inventions of art but instructions in stone, reminding priesthoods what had to be carried, applied, and delivered.

Some scholars have proposed that the cone was not pine at all, but a stylized ear of grain or fruiting body, a symbol of life carried in concentrated form. If so, the bag may have represented a portable store of fertility — seed, pollen, or the "essence" of life. The Apkallu's gestures would then be agricultural as well as ritual, touching cone to tree to ensure the transmission of fertility. That the same gesture reappears in Mesoamerican art, where maize kernels were treated as divine essence, suggests a common symbolic code for carrying and applying life itself.

When seen alongside serpents and winged couriers, the toolkit completes the picture. The serpent provides the conduit. The winged beings provide mobility. The bag-and-cone provide the method of transfer. Together they form a closed system: channel, courier, and instrument. Across hemispheres, priesthoods repeated the same imagery, carved the same tools, and enacted the same gestures. The gods wore the same faces, carried the same gear, and demanded the same offerings.

Case Study: Maya and Indian Parallels

Among the most arresting examples of cross-hemisphere imagery is the uncanny resemblance between sculptures of the Maya in Mesoamerica and the Indians of South Asia. In both traditions, a central deity is depicted enthroned or haloed, framed by a gateway or niche, and flanked by smaller attendants at the feet. The compositions are so close in staging and symbolism that they invite more than casual comparison.

The Maya example shows a central figure seated in majesty, a radiant nimbus encircling the head, arms extended in ritual gesture. Smaller figures crouch or stand at the deity's feet, reinforcing hierarchy through scale. Architectural elements frame the scene, suggesting both a temple façade and a cosmic threshold. This was not casual portraiture. It was theology in stone: the god enthroned within order, surrounded by symbols of subordination and passage.

The Maya carving rewards close attention. The central figure is haloed not only by a solar disc but also by curling glyphs that signify radiance, light, and divinity. The deity's posture is erect, arms extended in a gesture that echoes both command and blessing. At the feet, attendants bow with arms folded or kneeling postures, their smaller scale reinforcing their subordination. Architectural scrolls frame the scene, suggesting both a temple façade and a cosmic enclosure. For Maya viewers, this was not mere artistry — it was theology encoded in stone, an image of divine hierarchy staged so that every element reinforced cosmic order.

The Indian sculpture presents the same arrangement. The central deity is haloed, often with a lotus or solar disc radiating behind the head. Attendants cluster at the feet, sometimes human, sometimes semi-divine beings. The base is framed with carved apertures or gateways, architectural elements that double as symbolic thresholds between mortal and divine realms. The resemblance to the Maya relief is startling. Both images stage authority as a vertical composition: deity above, attendants below, throne or gateway beneath, halo crowning the head.

Indian parallels are equally rich in detail. The halo behind the deity is not a simple disc but often a lotus-like aureole, radiating petals or flames that symbolize cosmic energy. The central figure sits upon a lotus pedestal, the archetypal base of purity rising above the profane earth. Mudra hand-gestures communicate precise functions: reassurance, teaching, or granting of boons. At the feet, diminutive figures — apsaras, yakshas, or devotees — enact their service in stone. The entire composition is framed by a torana, a sculpted gateway, marking the deity's presence as threshold between realms. Each of these features repeats the Maya staging with uncanny specificity.

Mainstream scholars explain such parallels as convergent symbolism. Across cultures, authority is naturally portrayed as central, elevated, and flanked by subordinates. The halo is simply the sun, invoked universally as a symbol of power. The gateway is the threshold, a ubiquitous motif in temple art. Hierarchy always finds visual form. Thus, to skeptics, the Maya–India parallels are archetypal, not connected.

Maya scholars such as Linda Schele argued that hieratic compositions were not casual choices but deliberate statements of cosmic hierarchy, aligning rulers with divine sanction (Schele & Freidel, *A Forest of Kings,* 1990). Indian art historians like Stella Kramrisch and Ananda Coomaraswamy noted the same principle in South Asia: centrality, radiance, and attendants as visual proofs of authority (*The Hindu Temple,* 1946). Both bodies of scholarship stress that these images were functional — they made theological order visible. That two distant civilizations employed the same compositional grammar suggests a common template remembered across cultures.

Yet the combination of elements is so precise that archetype strains as an explanation. Why should two cultures separated by oceans present not just central authority, but the same staging: haloed figure, flanking attendants, architectural base? Why should the attendants always be smaller and subordinate, crouched at the feet? Why should the halo always crown the head, rather than the body or throne? Each element may be archetypal; their constellation is less easily dismissed.

Comparative religion offers context. The halo as a marker of divinity appears in Buddhist, Hindu, and Christian art alike. The aureole behind Christ echoes the sun disc of Shiva. In Maya art, halos appear as solar glyphs crowning rulers, emphasizing their alignment with cosmic cycles (Miller & Taube, *The Gods and Symbols of Ancient Mexico and the Maya,* 1993). Attendants, too, appear universally as markers of hierarchy: gods with retinues, kings with servants. Yet again, it is the combination that matters. When halo, attendants, and gateway are paired together in the same vertical staging, across hemispheres, the case for shared instruction grows stronger.

The attendants in particular deserve attention. In both Maya and Indian art, these diminutive figures represent more than decoration. They are theological punctuation, reminders that central authority is magnified by subordination. In the Indian case, attendants are often apsaras, yakshas, or worshippers; in the Maya case, they are captives, ancestors, or ritual actors. In both traditions, they enact the same function: visually reinforcing the asymmetry of power. The halo signals cosmic sanction; the attendants embody mortal submission.

Threshold imagery deepens the parallel. The Indian sculpture's architectural base resembles a gateway or temple entrance, often elaborated with scrolls, foliage, or miniature shrines. The Maya example, likewise, integrates architectural elements into the composition, framing the central figure as though enthroned in a cosmic doorway. Both cases reinforce the idea of passage: the deity is not merely present but enthroned at the juncture of realms. To approach the figure is to cross a boundary.

The symbolism aligns with ritual practice. In India, the haloed deity enthroned in shrines represented not only divine authority but the actual presence of the god, who was invited into the image during ritual consecration (prana pratishta). Attendants at the base mirrored the human devotees who clustered at the temple threshold. In Maya ritual, rulers dressed as gods sat upon thrones framed by temple façades, haloed by solar glyphs, while subordinates knelt at their feet. Both cultures enacted the same theology: power is vertical, sanctioned by light, and staged through hierarchy at thresholds.

Skeptics might still insist this is archetype. But the specificity of the Maya–India parallels is difficult to ignore. Central figure, halo, attendants, threshold. Not one or two elements, but four, combined with such consistency that they appear as a template — a remembered instruction for staging divine authority.

Archaeology does not easily explain such a connection. Mainstream consensus rejects direct contact between Mesoamerica and South Asia in antiquity. Yet if the parallels cannot be explained by diffusion, they may be explained by transmission of another kind: a system of symbols taught to both cultures at the dawn of their sacred traditions. The covenantal system we have traced through serpents, winged beings, and ritual toolkits may also have included templates for staging divine authority. The Maya and Indian statues are visual echoes of the same original pattern.

Comparative studies strengthen this claim. In Christian basilicas, Christ is enthroned in mandorla or halo, flanked by apostles or saints, often set above a framed doorway. In Buddhist cave temples at Ajanta, the Buddha sits haloed, flanked by bodhisattvas, enthroned within a carved shrine. In Maya art, rulers adopt the same staging. The pattern repeats because it was preserved, not invented — a liturgical template carried across civilizations.

Mircea Eliade remarked that symbols often endure longer than doctrines: "The image preserves what words forget" (*The Sacred and the Profane*, 1957). The Maya and Indian statues exemplify this endurance. Whatever texts were lost, the images carried forward the instructions: crown authority with light, flank it with subordinates, stage it at a threshold.

Seen this way, the Maya–India parallels are not curiosities but evidence. They show that sacred iconography was not local invention but global memory — fragments of a program seeded across continents. To set the deity in light, surround with attendants, and enthrone at a threshold was to obey instructions from powers who once stood in flesh.

Conclusion: Instructions in Stone

Across civilizations, power was never left abstract. It was given a face, wings, coils, and tools. From Egypt to Mesoamerica, from Mesopotamia to India, the same images recur: serpents crowning brows and stretching across gateways; winged beings crouched with buckets and cones, feathers spread wide; central deities haloed in light, flanked by smaller attendants, enthroned in thresholds. These were not decorative flourishes. They were instructions — visual protocols carved into stone to preserve how power moved, who delivered it, and what it demanded.

A Blood Covenant

The serpent crowned rulers as Wadjet, coiled across Maya stairways as Kukulkan, bridged causeways as nāgas, and churned oceans as Vasuki. Its body was remembered everywhere as conduit, a living channel of life-force and sovereignty. Winged beings — Apkallu, Garuda, Maya bird-men, Persian faravahar, Christian angels — acted as couriers, feathered and functional, handling tools and carrying mandates between worlds. And the ritual toolkit — the bag and cone — appears in reliefs from Göbekli Tepe to Assyria, from La Venta to Izapa, always in the same grip, always in the same gestures of application. Even the staging of divine authority itself — haloed central figure, attendants at the feet, gateway frame — was preserved from India to Mesoamerica, a liturgical template so consistent it looks less like invention and more like instruction.

Taken together, these motifs form a kit. The serpent marks the channel. The winged being provides the courier. The bag and cone provide the transfer. The attendants enforce hierarchy, while the halo crowns it with light. It is a standardized iconography of covenant, repeated across hemispheres as though priesthoods everywhere were handed the same manual. To carve these images was to diagram how the covenant functioned: power transmitted through channels, delivered by couriers, applied with tools, sanctioned by light.

Mainstream scholarship explains each motif in isolation: serpents as natural symbols of fear and fertility, wings as archetypes of transcendence, cones as sprinklers of holy water, halos as universal solar imagery. But the system is lost when the pieces are separated. Only when they are seen together — repeating as a constellation of images across unconnected civilizations — does their function become clear. Coincidence may explain one or two parallels. It cannot explain the recurrence of an entire toolkit.

These images endured because they mattered. They were carved into walls, stamped onto seals, painted in codices, built into temples. They encoded instructions that priesthoods had to remember. They reminded kings that their crowns, their couriers, and their rituals were part of a larger debt owed to powers unseen. In their simplicity

— a serpent, a feather, a bucket, a cone — they hid in plain sight, durable across conquests and collapses.

What Chapter 2 revealed in names, Chapter 3 has revealed in faces. Both are memory devices, fragments of a larger program seeded into humanity. Names survive in syllables; faces survive in stone. Together they whisper the same message: power was not invented by humans, but bestowed under covenant. Humanity was not merely creative but instructed, taught to depict the same gods with the same kit so that the covenant could never be forgotten.

As we turn to the next chapter, the argument grows heavier still. We will move from the faces of gods to the architecture of their houses — pyramids, ziggurats, and temples aligned with the stars. If faces and tools were instructions, then architecture was the machinery itself: stone mountains built to sustain the covenant, to collect offerings, and to bind heaven and earth in an unbroken contract.

∼

Figure 3.1

URAEUS & VULTURE, FUNERARY MASK TUTANKHAMUN

Uraeus and Vulture, Funerary Mask of Tutankhamun (ca. 1330 BCE).
The cobra goddess Wadjet and vulture goddess Nekhbet rise from the pharaoh's brow, poised to strike with flame and venom against his enemies. The uraeus was not ornament but a living emblem of covenantal kingship—sovereignty enforced by lethal power.

Figure 3.2

APKALLU WITH BUCKET & CONE, NEO-ASSYRIAN RELIEF

Apkallu with Bucket and Cone, Neo-Assyrian Relief (9th–7th c. BCE). Winged Apkallu sage holding the banduddu (bucket) and mullilu (cone). Always depicted in the same action — dipping and applying — the gesture suggests procedure rather than ornament: take, apply, effect. These figures were remembered as the "seven sages" who taught kings agriculture, ritual, and law, acting as feathered couriers and technicians of covenant.

Figure 3.3

GARUDA SUBDUING THE NāGA, TIBETAN BRONZE

Garuda Subduing the Nāga, Tibetan Bronze (ca. 12th–15th c. CE).
Garuda, the eagle-man and eternal mount of Vishnu, spreads his wings while seizing the nāgas. Remembered in the Mahabharata as vast enough to blot out the sun, Garuda devoured serpents and carried the nectar of immortality. His role as scourge of the serpent mirrors the Apkallu's battle with chaos and the bird-man figures of Mesoamerica, all remembered as winged couriers enforcing covenant.

HANDBAG MOTIF & BIRD MAN FIGURE GÖBEKLI TEPE

"Handbag" Motif and Bird-Man Figure, Göbekli Tepe (c. 10,000 BCE).
A row of arc-handled "handbags" carved above animal figures, with a striking avian or bird-man form beside them. The same container shape later appears in Assyrian reliefs and Mesoamerican stelae, while bird-men recur globally as couriers of divine power. This early pairing at Göbekli Tepe suggests the ritual toolkit and avian intermediaries were already established at the dawn of civilization.

Figure 3.3

GARUDA VERSUS NAGA - TIBET

Figure 3.5

SAN AGUSTÍN BIRD-MAN STATUE - COLOMBIA

Garuda vs. Bird-Man, Tibet & Colombia.
Garuda, eagle-man and scourge of serpents, mirrors the bird-man statues of San Agustín. Across hemispheres, avian couriers appear as enforcers of covenant, opposing the serpent conduit and carrying divine power between realms.

Figure 3.6

CAHOKIA BIRDMAN TABLET, ILLINOIS

Cahokia Birdman Tablet, Illinois (ca. 1200 CE). Carved stone tablet from the Mississippian mound center at Cahokia, depicting a bird-man figure with elaborate headdress and wing motif. Found near the great Monks Mound, the image embodies rulership, sacrifice, and cosmic mediation—paralleling bird-man and falcon figures from Mesoamerica and Eurasia. The Cahokia Birdman shows that North America, too, carried forward the covenantal iconography of avian couriers, linking human power with divine enforcement.

Figure 3.7 Figure 3.8

VISHNU WITH CONSORTS - INDIA **KINICH AJAW WITH ATTENDANTS - MAYAN**

Haloed Deity with Attendants, India & Maya (ca. 5th–9th c. CE). Both traditions depict a central figure haloed in light, enthroned and flanked by smaller attendants at the feet. The near-identical staging of divine authority across hemispheres suggests a shared template for representing cosmic hierarchy.

4

THE ARCHITECTURE OF THE GODS

Introduction — Machines of Stone

Stone is more than shelter; it is testimony. Across the ancient world, civilizations raised structures that still defy erosion, empire, and explanation. Unlike the perishable materials of daily life—wood, cloth, reed, mudbrick—these monuments were designed to endure. Their permanence was part of their message: not only to mark the existence of the builders, but to proclaim the demands of those for whom the structures were built.

The societies that enacted the blood covenant did not leave their obligations in fragile records alone. They inscribed them in stone mountains. Pyramids, temples, tombs, and towers were constructed as more than tomb markers or civic centers. They were ritual machines, colossal engines built to connect heaven and earth, to stabilize cycles of fertility and cosmos, and to stage the offerings by which the covenant was maintained.

Everywhere the pattern repeats. The Giza plateau in Egypt, with its perfectly squared blocks and internal shafts that align with key stars, remains the most iconic. The Valley of Mexico, where Teotihuacan spreads across its basin in the shape of a celestial mirror, replicates the logic half a world away. In Cambodia, Angkor Wat stretches like a star map on the ground, its towers echoing the stars of Orion's belt just as Giza's pyramids do. In Java, Borobudur rises as a three-dimensional mandala, while in China, the mound tombs of early emperors mimic cosmic order beneath their earthen shells.

Borobudur in Java deserves special mention here. Rising as a stepped mandala, its terraces spiral upward in a cosmic diagram meant to embody the Buddhist universe. But beneath that religious skin lies the same architectural impulse as Giza or Teotihuacan: colossal stone mass shaped as a bridge between earth and sky, a ritual path of ascent culminating in the union of human effort and divine presence. When Borobudur is set beside Angkor or Giza, the family resemblance becomes undeniable.

The similarities are not casual. They are obsessive. Each site embodies three elements that recur with uncanny fidelity:

1. **Scale** — mountains of stone that overwhelm human effort.
2. **Alignment** — precision to celestial markers, especially Orion.
3. **Function** — platforms for offerings, bloodletting, or ritual passage.

Taken together, these elements suggest not isolated bursts of human ingenuity, but blueprints followed again and again. Blueprints that were never merely local, but global.

Mainstream archaeology struggles with this repetition. For Giza, scholars argue the pyramids are tombs, expressions of political power, or national projects of labor control. For Teotihuacan, explanations range from solar cults to political theater. Angkor is interpreted as a state temple and water-management system. Each site is boxed into its own cultural context. And yet, when placed side by side, the patterns leap out: stairways climbing toward heaven, summits doubling as altars, alignments tying terrestrial foundations to stellar coordinates.

The repetition also raises questions about knowledge transmission. If these societies were truly isolated, how did they arrive at the same solutions — not just pyramids, but stair-stepped ascent, summit altars, and stellar alignments? Some scholars fall back on convergent evolution: human beings everywhere "naturally" build mountains to mimic the cosmos. Yet the precision argues otherwise. Giza's near-perfect cardinal alignment, Teotihuacan's deliberate 15.5° offset, Angkor's mapping of Orion — these are not vague mountain-shapes, but engineered blueprints. Convergence may explain a pyramid's shape. It does not explain shared obsession with Orion.

The Orion correlation remains the most controversial. Robert Bauval, in *The Orion Mystery* (1994), argued that the three pyramids of Giza mirror the three stars of Orion's belt, and that shafts within the Great Pyramid align to stars including Orion and Sirius. Critics have dismissed this as selective patterning, yet the idea refuses to fade because it does not stand alone. At Teotihuacan, the pyramids of the Sun and Moon anchor a layout that parallels the heavens, their central avenue tilted 15.5° east of north to match celestial cycles (Aveni, *Skywatchers of Ancient Mexico*, 2001). At Angkor, scholars have noted that the towers of Angkor Wat map onto the stars of Orion's belt with eerie fidelity (Sprajc, *Cosmic Order and Cultural Astronomy in Cambodia*, 2018). Why should cultures separated by oceans and millennia choose the same constellation, the same pattern of three?

For the covenant thesis, the answer is simple: they were instructed. Orion was chosen because it was already the marker recognized by the covenant's recipients. It became the lodestar by which priesthoods oriented their machines of stone.

These structures were not idle monuments. They were functional. The stairways served as channels for processions; the summits as stages for sacrifice; the altars as points of transfer where blood, smoke, and offerings ascended into the sky. The architecture itself insisted on participation. A pyramid does not allow casual access; it demands climbing, exertion, ritual ascent. At the summit, human and divine were brought together at the junction of matter and cosmos. Blood spilled there was not random violence, but the activation of a system.

The permanence of stone reinforced the permanence of the covenant. Texts can be forgotten, myths can be reinterpreted, but monuments endure. Even when cultures collapsed, the stones remained as silent testimony. The builders believed—or were instructed to believe—that the gods required not only blood, but architecture: vessels shaped from earth, raised as mountains, aligned to stars, upon which life itself could be exchanged.

When we overlay these sites—Giza, Teotihuacan, Angkor—the alignments recur with unsettling fidelity. Orion again and again. Stairways again and again. Altars again and again. Mainstream explanations fracture under this weight. It is one thing to argue that Egypt independently conceived of star-aligned pyramids. It is another to explain why Angkor, Teotihuacan, and Borobudur would replicate the same template oceans apart. Coincidence strains; common instruction fits more cleanly.

The architecture of the gods is thus not only a testimony to human ambition but to nonhuman demand. These were not tombs, not civic projects, not simple temples. They were covenant machines, stone-built interfaces between mortals and the powers that fed upon them. Their very existence refutes the idea of isolated development. They are the gods' architectural signature, written on the landscape of earth, visible even now to those who are willing to see.

Egypt: Orion's Blueprint

The pyramids of Giza remain the most enduring icons of ancient architecture, rising from the desert like geometric mountains. Khufu's Great Pyramid, flanked by the slightly smaller pyramids of Khafre and Menkaure, forms a triad that has baffled engineers, astronomers, and historians for centuries. Mainstream explanations insist these were tombs—colossal sepulchers for god-kings, their bulk an expression of centralized power. Yet the monuments themselves resist reduction to mortuary function. No pharaoh's body has ever been found within them. Their precision surpasses anything required for mere interment. And their alignments—to cardinal directions, to solstices, to stars—suggest not only earthly ambition but cosmic intent.

The Great Pyramid is aligned to true north with an error of less than three arc minutes, a feat not surpassed until the advent of modern surveying instruments. Its sides vary in length by less than 0.1 percent. At its original height of 481 feet, it was the tallest manmade structure on earth for nearly four millennia. Such precision implies not trial and error but instruction—plans given, not guessed.

Inside the Great Pyramid, shafts extend from the King's Chamber and the so-called Queen's Chamber outward at precise angles. In 1964, Virginia Trimble and Alexander Badawy first suggested these channels were aimed at key stars: Orion's belt, Sirius, and perhaps the circumpolar stars (Badawy & Trimble, *Journal of Near Eastern Studies*, 1964). Robert Bauval later developed the idea, arguing that the three main pyramids themselves were arranged to mirror the three stars of Orion's belt—a correlation he presented in *The Orion Mystery* (1994). The match is striking: Khufu and Khafre correspond to Alnitak and Alnilam, Menkaure to Mintaka, offset slightly just as the star is.

Mainstream Egyptology has largely resisted Bauval's thesis, calling the Orion correlation coincidence, pattern-seeking, or retrofitting. Yet critics rarely address the deeper issue: why should a culture so obsessed with order, so exacting in geometry, build its three greatest monuments in a configuration that just happens to mirror one of the most distinctive asterisms in the night sky? Even if unintended, the resemblance would have been obvious to the ancient priests. To suggest it meant nothing strains credulity.

For the covenant framework, the Orion alignment is not optional —it is expected. If other covenant sites across the world also orient to Orion, then Giza becomes the prototype, the model remembered and reproduced elsewhere. The shafts were not simply air vents. They were sightlines, channels aimed deliberately at the gods' chosen markers in the heavens. When blood and smoke rose on the altar, when chants echoed in the passages, the offering was directed not vaguely upward but to specific coordinates.

The Pyramid Texts, inscribed in later pyramids of the Fifth and Sixth Dynasties, reinforce this. They describe the pharaoh ascending to the stars, uniting with Orion (Sah) and Sirius (Sopdet). Utterance

820 proclaims: "*Behold, he has come as Orion. Behold, Osiris has come as Orion. The king is Osiris, this pyramid of the king is Osiris, this construction of his is Osiris.*" (Faulkner, *The Ancient Egyptian Pyramid Texts*, 1969). Here the link between architecture, ruler, and constellation is explicit: the pyramid itself is equated with Orion, a vessel for transformation and transit.

Blood sacrifice in Egypt has often been downplayed by scholars who emphasize bread, beer, and incense as offerings. Yet the Pyramid Texts also speak of "red offerings" and "eating the red and drinking the white"—blood and milk as sustenance for the gods (Utterance 32). Reliefs depict libations poured into channels carved in altars, fluids collected in basins beneath. The architecture itself was designed to manage liquid offerings, directing them along stone-cut grooves. Just as in Mesopotamia, where temple drains channeled blood and water, Egypt's altars functioned as fluid-transfer devices.

When viewed this way, the pyramids cease to be inert tombs and become functional machines. Their stair-like casing stones (before erosion smoothed them) allowed ritual ascent. Their summits provided elevated platforms for offerings. Their internal shafts aimed those offerings at specific stars. The entire structure embodied a covenantal interface: earth-shaped into cosmic machinery.

Mainstream scholarship often dismisses this functional reading as "pseudoarchaeology." Yet even orthodox Egyptologists admit the pyramids embodied cosmological symbolism. Mark Lehner notes that the pyramid field at Giza was carefully aligned with Heliopolis, the solar cult center to the northeast (Lehner, *The Complete Pyramids*, 1997). The causeways of Khufu and Khafre align with solstitial sunrise and sunset. The layout is cosmic theater, stage-managed with precision. If the Egyptians went to such lengths for solar and stellar alignments, why dismiss the possibility that the alignments were not symbolic alone, but covenantal—literal channels for communication and transfer?

Moreover, the scale of the pyramids suggests purpose beyond mortuary ritual. The Great Pyramid's estimated 2.3 million blocks average 2.5 tons each, some weighing as much as 70 tons. Moving them required an organizational apparatus rivaling modern states. Would such resources be expended merely to inter a king? Or was the king himself the justification for a machine that serviced the gods? In the covenant reading, the pharaoh's burial was incidental. The true function was sacrificial transaction, with the king's tomb serving as a convenient theological justification for a much older obligation.

Comparisons to later temples strengthen this case. At Karnak and Luxor, altars and sanctuaries were carefully oriented to solstitial events. At Abydos, Osirian cult rituals reenacted death and resurrection as covenant payment. These temples are explicitly described as "feeding places" for the gods, where offerings "sustained their kas" (Assmann, *The Search for God in Ancient Egypt*, 2001). If New Kingdom temples functioned as feeding stations, why should Old Kingdom pyramids—grandest of all—be exempt from this logic?

The symbolism of Orion also intersects with Osiris, the god of death and resurrection. By the Middle Kingdom, Osiris had absorbed older stellar associations, becoming the deity with whom the king united in the afterlife. If Osiris is Orion, and the king becomes Osiris, then the pyramid—aligned to Orion—is the machine that effects this transformation. From the covenant perspective, this is not metaphor. It is the codification of a literal transaction: blood for power, death for renewal, human life for cosmic sustenance.

When seen alongside Teotihuacan and Angkor, Giza's significance grows. It is the first node in a network, the prototype of covenant architecture repeated across hemispheres. Its alignments to Orion were not cultural quirks but global instructions. Its bulk was not funerary vanity but cosmic necessity. To look upon it today is to see not only the ambition of Egypt's rulers but the enduring demand of the covenant itself.

Teotihuacan — The City of the Gods

Teotihuacan, the "place where gods were made," sprawls across the Basin of Mexico like a terrestrial star map. At its height around the

5th century CE, it was the largest city in the Western Hemisphere, with a population exceeding 100,000—greater than most European capitals of the time. Yet what astonishes visitors even today is not its scale of habitation, but its monumental core: the Avenue of the Dead stretching for miles, flanked by towering pyramids and ceremonial platforms that transform the valley floor into a cosmic theater.

The Pyramid of the Sun dominates the site. Rising 216 feet with a base nearly identical in scale to Khufu's Great Pyramid, it contains an estimated 1.2 million cubic meters of stone and rubble. Though built of different materials and with different techniques, the effect is the same: an artificial mountain commanding the horizon. Beneath its base lies a cave, modified into a four-lobed chamber, interpreted as the womb of the earth. Here, archaeologists believe, rituals of creation and renewal were performed—offerings placed at the navel of the world.

Aligned with it along the Avenue of the Dead is the Pyramid of the Moon, smaller but strategically placed against the backdrop of Cerro Gordo, the mountain to the north. Together they frame the city's axis, the Avenue itself tilted 15.5° east of north. This skew is no accident: archaeoastronomers like Anthony Aveni have shown it corresponds to the setting of the Pleiades and cycles of Venus (Aveni, *Skywatchers*, 2001). On key calendar dates, the sun sets along the Avenue, synchronizing urban geometry with cosmic cycles.

Further studies by Ivan Šprajc and others have shown that the city's 15.5° orientation links directly to a sacred calendar of 260 days, the same system later formalized by the Maya. Twice each year, the sun passes directly over the zenith in the Basin of Mexico. Teotihuacan's layout captures these moments, transforming the city into a solar calendar inscribed in stone (Šprajc, *Time and Cosmos in Mesoamerica*, 2015). This is not incidental orientation but a deliberate harnessing of cosmic cycles. Just as Giza's shafts pointed to Orion, Teotihuacan's axis pointed to the heavens' rhythms, ensuring that offerings were synchronized to the gods' timetable. The covenant was not haphazard—it was scheduled.

At the southern end of the Avenue lies the Ciudadela, a vast sunken plaza capable of holding tens of thousands. At its center rises the Temple of the Feathered Serpent (Quetzalcoatl), its façade covered in repeating serpent heads and goggle-eyed storm masks. Excavations beneath it have uncovered extraordinary offerings: hundreds of obsidian blades, jade figurines, shell ornaments, and—most disturbingly—mass burials of warriors and captives, their hands bound, many decapitated. Saburo Sugiyama's excavations in the 1980s and 90s revealed over 200 such sacrificial victims interred as part of the temple's dedication (Sugiyama, *Human Sacrifice, Militarism, and Rulership*, 2005). The message is unmistakable: the temple was not simply decorated with serpent imagery, it was fed with human life from its inception.

Later Aztec traditions claimed Teotihuacan as the birthplace of the Fifth Sun, the cosmic age in which they lived. According to these myths, the gods themselves gathered here to sacrifice and ignite the sun's fire. That mythology preserves the older truth: Teotihuacan was understood as a site where sacrifice renewed the cosmos. The mass burials beneath the Feathered Serpent temple were not aberrations but inaugurations, charges that activated the temple itself. Fire, obsidian, blood, and breath were fused into offerings, turning architecture into a covenant machine. Each captive's life was currency, each deposit of obsidian a seal, binding the people to their gods.

The entire city seems calibrated for ritual procession. Pilgrims entered from the south, moving northward along the Avenue of the Dead, past plazas and platforms, until ascending the great stairways to the summits of the pyramids. From there, sacrifices could be made in view of tens of thousands. Blood flowed not in hidden chambers but across broad staircases, visible from every angle, a public transaction meant to renew the covenant on behalf of the entire city.

The effect was theatrical in the deepest sense: the architecture was designed not only to impress, but to choreograph. Each plaza along the Avenue of the Dead acted like a stage set, its staircases providing elevation for actors in ritual, its broad expanses providing seating for thousands of eyes. Sacrifices performed on the Pyramid of the Moon were silhouetted against the Cerro Gordo mountain, a backdrop that amplified the cosmic symbolism. On the Pyramid of the Sun, the broad staircases forced participants into ordered ascent, step after step, until they reached the summit—a journey of submission before offering. Teotihuacan was not merely a city with temples; it was a performance environment where every ritual reinforced the covenant, ensuring that the people saw their leaders deliver blood to the gods.

Beneath the monuments, hidden systems reinforced this role as a ritual machine. In 2003, Sergio Gómez discovered a sealed tunnel beneath the Temple of the Feathered Serpent. Within it lay pools of liquid mercury, pyrite mirrors, and miniature mountains—an underworld rendered in reflective brilliance. The tunnel culminated in three chambers thought to represent cosmic wombs, perhaps used for initiations or offerings to underworld gods. Mercury, a toxic and luminous substance, may have symbolized the waters of creation. Here again we find architecture not as inert stone but as cosmic interface, linking surface sacrifice with subterranean mysteries.

The discovery of liquid mercury stunned archaeologists, who had never before encountered it in such context. Rivers of shimmering metal pooled in channels, reflecting torchlight like flowing silver. In Mesoamerican symbolism, mercury may have represented the underworld waters or the blood of the earth itself—volatile, luminous, deadly. The tunnel walls were studded with pyrite mirrors, which when illuminated created the illusion of a starry sky underground. At its far end, three chambers held miniature mountains, echoing the cosmic triads above. What Gómez uncovered was not storage, but simulation: a hidden cosmos beneath the temple, where priests could descend into an artificial underworld and offer treasures, blood, or captives to the gods below. In covenant terms, the mercury tunnel made the transaction complete. Blood spilled on the pyramid's summit rose toward the heavens, while offerings in mercury pools sank to the underworld. Teotihuacan thus bridged sky and chthonic depths, enclosing the entire cosmos within its architecture.

Mainstream interpretations of Teotihuacan emphasize political power, urban planning, and religious devotion. Yet the precision of its layout speaks a more technical language. Why tilt the entire city 15.5° unless to match celestial cycles? Why bury hundreds beneath a temple if not to "charge" it with blood? Why construct a tunnel with mercury pools if not to simulate a cosmic underworld? The pieces align more with machine than with metaphor.

For the covenant framework, Teotihuacan mirrors Giza in function if not in form. Both sites are colossal, both align to Orion and other celestial markers, both integrate tomb-like structures with sacrificial function. Yet Teotihuacan goes further by making the process public. Where Giza enshrined covenant transactions in massive stone sealed for eternity, Teotihuacan staged them in plazas for all to see. The gods did not merely receive in secret—they demanded spectacle.

That the same logic appears in Mexico and Egypt, with no plausible line of cultural contact, demands explanation. Either coincidence produced the same design twice, or both priesthoods followed the same instructions. The covenant reading argues for the latter: that Teotihuacan, like Giza, was a machine built to channel human life into cosmic order. Its serpent-temple echoes Mesopotamian dragon-guardians, its star alignments echo Egypt, its blood offerings echo the Maya and Aztec who followed. The blueprints are not local —they are global.

Today the Avenue of the Dead lies silent, its plazas emptied of the crowds who once witnessed the covenant's renewal. Yet the stones still speak. They testify that here, as at Giza, Angkor, and elsewhere, humanity built not simply for itself but for those who required its lifeblood, staging architecture as interface between earth and sky.

Angkor — The Stone Sky

If Teotihuacan was a city of processions and Giza a mountain of stone, Angkor was a cosmos laid flat across the earth. From the 9th to the 15th centuries CE, the Khmer kings of Cambodia constructed one of the largest temple complexes in the world—Angkor Wat and its surrounding structures—sprawling over hundreds of square miles. At its heart stands Angkor Wat itself, a temple dedicated to Vishnu and later absorbed into Buddhist use, whose scale, precision, and alignment have baffled archaeologists and architects alike. To this day it is the largest religious monument on earth.

The complex is not simply large; it is astronomically precise. The five towers of Angkor Wat rise like lotus buds, but their placement has long been argued to mirror the three stars of Orion's Belt plus two attendant stars, mapped onto the Cambodian plain (Sprajc, *Cosmic Order and Cultural Astronomy in Cambodia*, 2018). The central tower represents Alnitak, flanked by others corresponding to Alnilam and Mintaka, echoing the same Orion correlation found at Giza. When viewed at dawn during the equinox, the sun rises directly over the central tower, locking celestial motion to terrestrial architecture. The message is unmistakable: this was not merely a shrine, but a cosmic machine.

Even more compelling is Angkor's integration of water. The temple is surrounded by a massive moat nearly 200 meters wide, filled by channels that link it to an elaborate hydraulic system stretching across the Khmer capital. Reservoirs, canals, and dikes were not only practical for irrigation—they were cosmological. Scholars such as Eleanor Mannikka (*Angkor Wat: Time, Space, and Kingship*, 1996) argue that the temple's dimensions encode the cycles of the Hindu calendar, with the moat symbolizing the cosmic ocean and the towers representing Mount Meru, the axis mundi. Offerings made within this watery framework were not simply gifts but transactions in a symbolic universe of mountains and seas.

But water also served a more practical ritual purpose: as a conduit for offerings of blood. Just as altars in Egypt incorporated channels to collect libations, Angkor's moats and basins could receive liquid offerings that coursed through the temple's arteries. The architecture itself made fluid transfer visible—blood diluted in water, flowing outward like lifeblood from a body. From the covenant perspective, Angkor was not just symbolic cosmology; it was hydraulics as sacrificial interface.

Evidence suggests that liquids—including animal blood—were

part of ritual practice. Stone basins discovered in smaller Angkorian shrines show traces of iron-rich residue, likely from sacrificial use. While mainstream reports classify these as "libation stains," their distribution around altars parallels patterns seen in Mesopotamian and Egyptian temples. When diluted in water, blood became a flowing offering, coursing through channels into moats and reservoirs. Symbolically, it merged human life with the cosmic ocean surrounding Mount Meru. Functionally, it allowed the covenant to be dramatized in a visible medium: blood streaming as river, flowing from the hands of the priests into the temple's engineered arteries.

Archaeological surveys confirm that Angkor Wat was oriented with obsessive care. The temple's axis is tilted slightly south of east to capture equinox sunrises, while alignments with lunar standstills and solstices are also present (Mannikka, 1996). Reliefs carved into the temple walls depict the Churning of the Ocean of Milk, a myth of gods and demons pulling a cosmic serpent to extract the nectar of immortality. Yet the reliefs are more than myth—they are instruction manuals in stone. The serpent becomes the conduit, the gods its handlers, the ocean the reservoir of energy. Here again, the same motifs we have traced in Mesopotamia, Egypt, and Mesoamerica return: serpents, water, sacrifice, and cosmic renewal.

Scholars have noted that Angkor's galleries, with their long east–west corridors, may have functioned as observational sightlines. During equinox sunrises, shafts of light penetrate straight through the temple's eastern gate and strike the central sanctuary, a phenomenon visible only on those dates. Eleanor Mannikka calculated that the temple's measurements encode solar and lunar cycles, including the 584-day synodic period of Venus (Mannikka, 1996). In other words, Angkor was not just symbolic cosmology but a sky clock —a machine for tracking and synchronizing rituals to celestial rhythms. Offerings were made at moments of cosmic resonance, binding the covenant to the heartbeat of the heavens.

The scale of labor at Angkor rivals that of Giza or Teotihuacan. Millions of sandstone blocks were quarried and transported by canals from sites 50 kilometers away. Estimates suggest 300,000 workers and 6,000 elephants were involved in construction over several decades. To modern historians, this is explained as the exertion of political power. Yet when compared with the global pattern, the logic of the covenant makes better sense. Just as Egyptians expended millions of man-hours for pyramids and Mexicans for Teotihuacan, the Khmer were compelled to mobilize vast populations to construct what was essentially a ritual machine for the gods.

Within Angkor's walls, ritual offerings reinforced this role. Inscriptions record donations of rice, livestock, and slaves to the temple (Higham, *The Civilization of Angkor*, 2001). But archaeologists also find evidence of animal sacrifice, and Chinese envoys to the Khmer court in the 13th century described human offerings performed at state ceremonies. While mainstream scholars tend to interpret these as rare or symbolic, the covenant lens suggests continuity: Angkor, like Egypt and Teotihuacan, fed its gods in blood as well as in grain.

The site's durability reinforces its covenantal role. Just as Giza's pyramids were meant to last beyond dynasties, Angkor Wat's towers endure long after the Khmer Empire's collapse. Jungle swallowed the city, but the stone remained, testimony to a covenant whose memory could not be erased. Even when Buddhism supplanted Hinduism, the site remained sacred, its cosmic logic too deeply embedded in the stones to be discarded.

Even as dynasties shifted and religions changed, Angkor remained sacred. Originally dedicated to Vishnu, it was later absorbed into Mahayana and then Theravada Buddhism, its walls rededicated with new inscriptions and statues. Yet the structure itself was never abandoned as a ritual center. The Khmer kings fell, the city was swallowed by jungle, but pilgrims continued to visit, and Buddhist monks maintained shrines within its towers. When French explorers "rediscovered" Angkor in the 19th century, they found it still alive with devotion. The covenant, embodied in stone, had outlasted every empire that touched it. This endurance mirrors the persistence of the covenant worldwide: beliefs may evolve, priesthoods may fall, but the stones continue to testify. Where paper rots and dynasties collapse, covenant machines remain, their alignments still catching equinox light, their moats still channeling water, their towers still pointing to Orion.

Mainstream interpretations emphasize Angkor as a masterpiece of symbolic kingship—an architectural embodiment of Vishnu, of Hindu cosmology, of imperial order. Yet the same could be said of Giza or Teotihuacan. What unites them is not metaphor, but function: stairways for ascent, towers for alignment, basins for offerings, labor for construction. Angkor was not built simply as an act of devotion. It was built to renew a bargain with unseen powers, its alignments and hydraulics designed to ensure the gods were fed and the cosmos remained stable.

For the covenant framework, Angkor confirms the global blueprint. Orion again. Towers as mountains. Serpents as conduits. Water as offering channel. Whether through Hindu myth or Khmer inscription, the message remains the same: human blood and labor were demanded, and stone was the medium through which the covenant was enacted. Angkor, like Giza and Teotihuacan, is not local idiosyncrasy but part of a global system.

Borobudur & Asian Parallels

If Angkor spread a cosmos flat upon the earth, Borobudur in Java turned it into a spiral mountain. Constructed in the 8th–9th centuries CE by the Sailendra dynasty, Borobudur is the largest Buddhist monument in the world: a colossal mandala rendered in stone. Its nine stacked platforms, capped by a central dome and surrounded by 72 perforated stupas, form a tiered diagram of the universe. From above it resembles a cosmic lotus; from below it looms as an artificial mountain. In both interpretations, Borobudur is less a temple than a machine for ascent.

Pilgrims were meant to climb it in procession. Starting at the base, they would circumambulate each level clockwise before ascending to the next, following galleries carved with 2,600 relief panels and populated by 500 statues of the Buddha. The journey was narrative as well as physical: the panels depicted karmic law, the life of the Buddha, and the path to enlightenment. By the time the pilgrim reached the summit, he had symbolically traversed the entire cosmos.

Borobudur's design was not only visual but acoustic. The galleries, with their enclosed passageways, created resonant chambers where chants and percussion could reverberate during rituals. Archaeologists and acoustic engineers studying the site have noted that the bell-shaped stupas amplify sound when struck, creating harmonic tones that could be heard across the terraces. Pilgrims climbing in procession would have been enveloped not only in narrative reliefs but in waves of chant and vibration—an immersive experience binding body, sound, and cosmos. The architecture itself became a resonator, carrying mantras upward toward the central stupa like offerings in sound. From a covenant perspective, these tones were not decorative, but part of the transaction: sonic energy rising to join the blood and breath of sacrifice in feeding the gods.

Yet Borobudur's function was not merely meditative. It was astronomical. The monument is aligned with the cardinal directions, and studies suggest it incorporates solar and lunar cycles into its proportions (Soekmono, *Chandi Borobudur: A Monument of Mankind*, 1976). The upper terraces, open to the sky, may have been used for observing celestial events, while the central stupa has been argued to symbolize the cosmic axis, the point at which heaven and earth meet. In covenant terms, Borobudur's tiers and stairways provided the stage for ritual ascent, its summit serving as the altar of ultimate offering.

While no explicit evidence of blood sacrifice has been found at Borobudur itself, it emerges from a cultural milieu in which offerings —both animal and human—were not unknown. In Java and Bali, inscriptions record bloodletting rituals to secure fertility and protection (Wisseman Christie, *Javanese Markets and the Asian Trade System*, 1995). Borobudur, therefore, may represent the sublimated form of a practice already established: the channeling of life-force through architecture, staged here not as slaughter but as symbolic pilgrimage. From the covenant perspective, it illustrates how the same blueprint could be adapted to different religious veneers, with the function—linking human life to cosmic demand—remaining constant.

Borobudur also shares with Giza, Teotihuacan, and Angkor the obsession with mass, labor, and permanence. Its 55,000 square meters of relief carvings and millions of volcanic stone blocks required immense manpower, transported and assembled without mortar. The sheer effort ensured that the covenant machine could not be easily dismantled. Even when abandoned after the decline of Buddhism in Java, Borobudur remained, swallowed by volcanic ash and jungle until rediscovered in the 19th century. Like Angkor, it endured beyond empire, its testimony carved in stone.

Beyond Java, parallels appear across Asia. In China, the great mound tombs of the Western Han dynasty (2nd century BCE) rise as earthen pyramids aligned to cardinal points. The most famous, the tomb of Emperor Jing, sits within a necropolis containing thousands of sacrificial burials of servants, soldiers, and horses (Wu Hung, *Monumentality in Early Chinese Art and Architecture*, 1995). The First Emperor's mausoleum at Xi'an, with its buried terracotta army, follows the same logic: monumental scale, cosmic alignment, mass sacrifice. Though cloaked in Confucian and ancestral rhetoric, these tombs replicate the covenantal formula—stone and earth shaped as cosmic mountains, blood and labor expended to maintain the ruler's journey and the gods' favor.

The preference for mounds rather than exposed pyramids in China and Japan may reflect a different phase of the covenant. While Egypt and Mesoamerica displayed bloodletting publicly on elevated stages, East Asia enclosed the transaction within earth, burying rulers and sacrificial victims beneath layers of soil. In both cases the principle was the same: monumental mass as conduit, sacrifice as fuel. The difference was one of visibility. In the West, covenant performance was public theater. In the East, it was sealed underground, guarded by armies of clay or hidden beneath keyhole-shaped moats. Yet both forms speak to the same blueprint—architecture designed not for shelter or beauty, but to anchor the covenant in the landscape.

The pattern even extends to Japan, where the Kofun period (3rd–7th centuries CE) saw the construction of giant keyhole-shaped tomb mounds. Surrounded by moats and often aligned with celestial events, these tombs required thousands of laborers and were associated with rituals of offerings and feasting. Though later mythologized as ancestral reverence, the sheer scale suggests something closer to covenant architecture: labor and life given to construct machines of permanence, overseen by elites who claimed their power from the gods.

These Asian monuments demonstrate the flexibility of the blueprint. Where Egypt and Mexico emphasized pyramids of stone, Asia experimented with earth mounds, spirals, and mandalas. Yet the core principles remained: massive scale, cosmic alignment, stairways or pathways of ascent, offerings made at elevated or central points, and endurance beyond dynasties. Whether in Java, China, or Japan, the covenant was not erased but adapted—clothed in Buddhist, Confucian, or Shinto language, yet retaining its demand for human life, labor, and blood.

Mainstream archaeology often treats these monuments as independent expressions of local culture. Borobudur is said to be uniquely Buddhist; the Han tombs uniquely Chinese; the Kofun mounds uniquely Japanese. But when seen alongside Giza, Teotihuacan, and Angkor, the similarities overshadow the differences. These were not isolated efflorescences of human ingenuity. They were nodes in a network, built according to instructions repeated across continents.

For the covenant thesis, Borobudur and its Asian parallels confirm the global reach of the system. Whether framed as Hindu cosmology, Buddhist pilgrimage, or ancestral veneration, the underlying logic persists: the gods required architecture as vessel, human beings supplied blood and labor as payment, and the monuments endure as testimony to that bargain.

Overlay & Pattern Recognition

When viewed in isolation, each monument can be explained away as a marvel of local genius. Egypt's pyramids as funerary architecture. Teotihuacan as imperial spectacle. Angkor as a mandala of Hindu cosmology. Borobudur as a Buddhist diagram of enlightenment. Yet when they are set side by side, the similarities overwhelm the differences. What emerges is not cultural coincidence but architectural convergence—blueprints repeated across continents as though the same instructions were issued to different builders at different times.

Scale and Permanence

The first point of convergence is scale. Each monument is enormous, demanding the mobilization of tens or hundreds of thousands of workers over decades. The Great Pyramid's 2.3 million blocks, Teotihuacan's mile-long avenue, Angkor's moats stretching for kilometers, Borobudur's millions of stones—these are not temples for small communities. They are projects that consumed whole populations. Their mass ensured permanence. As dynasties fell, jungles grew, and empires collapsed, the structures remained. The covenant demanded not only ritual, but testimony. Stones that could not be erased testified to obligations that could not be forgotten.

Labor as Sacrifice

Beyond the literal blood of captives, the monuments themselves consumed human life through labor. Every block hauled, every canal dug, every relief carved represented years of toil, injury, and death. Ancient chronicles record thousands perishing in service to their rulers' projects. To interpret this as "mere labor" misses the point: labor was itself a form of sacrifice. The covenant did not demand only victims on altars, but the lifeblood of whole populations poured out in sweat and shortened lifespans, their energy transmuted into stone.

Cosmic Alignment

The second point of convergence is celestial orientation. Giza's shafts and triad of pyramids align with Orion. Teotihuacan's axis matches the Pleiades and Venus cycles. Angkor Wat captures equinox sunrises, its towers echoing Orion's belt. Borobudur encodes lunar and solar cycles into its terraces. In each case, the monuments are not random mountains but sky clocks—machines that synchronize human ritual with celestial cycles. From the covenant perspective, this was essential. Blood was to be offered at the right time, when the gods' eyes were upon the earth. Architecture became the gearwork that locked human sacrifice to the heavens' rhythms.

Stairways and Pathways of Ascent

Third is the obsession with stairways and ascents. Giza's pyramids once bore smooth casing stones but retained internal galleries and passages for ritual movement. Teotihuacan's pyramids stage sacrifices at their summits, reached by massive staircases climbed in view of the multitudes. Angkor's galleries and towers guide pilgrims upward, aligning with solar risings. Borobudur is literally a stairway mandala, a spiraling climb to the central stupa. In each case, ascent is ritualized. Human bodies move upward in choreographed fashion, reenacting the transition from earth to sky. And at the summit, blood is offered—life carried upward to the gods as covenant payment.

Liquid Channels and Sacrificial Interface

A fourth convergence is liquid management. At Giza, temple basins and altar channels directed libations of blood, milk, and beer. At Teotihuacan, obsidian blades and bound captives fed temples whose tunnels channeled mercury and water. At Angkor, moats and reservoirs acted as cosmic oceans into which blood offerings were poured. At Borobudur and the Asian mounds, evidence of basins with iron-rich residue suggests similar practices. The principle is identical:

architecture as interface, stone as conduit, fluids as offering. Sacrifice was not a haphazard act but a system engineered into the monuments themselves.

Public vs. Sealed Sacrifice

Differences emerge, but they too form a pattern. In Egypt and Teotihuacan, sacrifice was often public, displayed on altars visible to thousands. In China and Japan, sacrifices were sealed beneath earth, guarded by terracotta armies or moats. Angkor combined both: public ceremonies for the masses, hidden rituals in moats and inner sanctuaries. Borobudur sublimated the process, converting bloodletting into symbolic ascent. These variations suggest not different origins, but different phases of the same covenant. Sometimes the gods required public feeding. Sometimes hidden. Sometimes literal, sometimes symbolic. But always, the principle remained: human life, offered to maintain cosmic order.

Mythological Echoes

Even the myths echo. Orion and Osiris in Egypt. Quetzalcoatl and the Fifth Sun in Mexico. Vishnu's Churning of the Ocean in Angkor. The Buddha's cosmic mandala in Borobudur. Different names, different stories, yet the same motifs: serpents as conduits, cosmic mountains as stages, oceans of creation as basins, divine ascent tied to stars. The surface narratives differ; the covenant beneath them remains constant.

Blueprints, Not Coincidence

Mainstream archaeology explains these similarities as convergent evolution—different cultures independently choosing pyramids because mountains inspire awe. But the convergence is too precise, too repeated. Not only pyramids, but Orion correlations. Not only stairways, but ritualized ascents. Not only offerings, but engineered basins and channels. Not only myths, but recurring symbols of serpents, birds, and cosmic oceans. Coincidence might explain one or two overlaps. It does not explain dozens, spread across continents, repeated for millennia.

The covenant thesis provides a simpler explanation: these were not independent inventions, but implementations of a shared program. Nonhuman instructors—whether called gods, devas, or feathered serpents—delivered blueprints. Human rulers, eager for favor and power, executed them. The monuments are signatures left behind, material evidence of transactions that bound human blood to divine sustenance.

Toward a Global System

When the monuments are overlaid—Giza's pyramids, Teotihuacan's avenue, Angkor's towers, Borobudur's mandala—the alignments with Orion and celestial cycles recur with unsettling fidelity. The same functions repeat: stairways for ascent, summits for offering, basins for fluids, myths for justification. The gods' architectural signature appears on every continent. This was not local worship. It was a global system, administered in stone so that its memory could not be erased.

What is perhaps most striking is that even after the fall of empires, local populations often preserved the memory that these places were not entirely human. In Mexico, the Aztecs named Teotihuacan "the place where gods were made." In Cambodia, Angkor Wat was never abandoned, remaining active under Buddhist monks. In Java, Borobudur was rediscovered but still wrapped in stories of sacred mountains. Even in Egypt, later dynasties continued to link their legitimacy to the pyramids. Across continents, memory persisted: these were not simply ruins of kings, but the dwelling places of beings who demanded payment.

Today, we walk among these monuments as tourists. We marvel at their scale, photograph their reliefs, trace their stairways with sneakered feet. But to the ancients, these were not ruins. They were contracts. Every block placed, every stair climbed, every drop of blood spilled was part of a bargain struck in the dawn of civilization. The monuments still stand because the covenant still whispers. We may forget the terms, but the stone remembers.

Conclusion: Stone as Covenant

Across continents and millennia, stone became the chosen medium for a transaction humanity did not invent but inherited. Egypt raised mountains of limestone, Teotihuacan paved a valley into a cosmic theater, Angkor laid a sky clock across the Cambodian plain, and Borobudur spiraled a mandala into volcanic rock. Each site drew on local myths, languages, and iconography, yet when viewed together they reveal the same design principles: scale to awe, permanence to testify, alignment to synchronize, stairways to ascend, and basins to receive. These were not simply monuments of kingship. They were covenant machines.

The architecture itself demanded blood. Some monuments staged it in public—Aztec captives sprawled across pyramids, Egyptians pouring libations at altars, Khmer sacrifices before moats. Others concealed it underground—in sealed Han tombs, in mercury tunnels beneath Teotihuacan, in basins stained with iron. Some sublimated it into symbolic ascent, as in Borobudur's circumambulations. But whether literal, hidden, or symbolic, the covenant logic persisted: human life was the payment, stone the medium, the gods the recipients.

Mainstream explanations emphasize local genius. Egypt perfected engineering. Teotihuacan orchestrated urban power. Angkor embodied Vishnu's cosmology. Borobudur diagrammed enlightenment. All true, in part. But the overlaps are too systematic to be accidental. Orion repeats in Egypt and Angkor. Stairway ascents repeat in Mexico and Java. Liquid channels recur from the Nile to the Mekong. Myths of serpents, oceans, and cosmic mountains echo across every site. These are not random coincidences; they are signatures of a shared instruction.

The covenant framework makes sense of what conventional archaeology leaves fragmented. It explains why unrelated cultures would mobilize entire populations for projects of staggering futility from a purely human perspective. Why build mountains of stone that outlast the kings who commissioned them? Why synchronize them with celestial cycles intelligible only to priesthoods? Why design them as theaters of ascent and sacrifice? The answer is simple: they were not building only for themselves. They were building for beings who required testimony, sustenance, and order.

Stone outlasts empire. That was the gods' insurance. Texts could be lost, priesthoods suppressed, dynasties erased—but the monuments remained, immutable ledgers of debt. Even after jungles swallowed Angkor and lava buried Borobudur, the stones persisted, waiting to be rediscovered. And when rediscovered, they still whispered the same message: these were not merely temples of devotion. They were contracts carved into the earth.

When later generations stumbled upon these ruins, they often recognized them as something beyond human. Herodotus, visiting Egypt in the 5th century BCE, described the pyramids with awe and admitted confusion at how they were built. The Aztecs, centuries after Teotihuacan's collapse, named it "the place where gods were made," insisting its origins were divine. In the 19th century, French explorers hacking through Cambodian jungle found Angkor Wat still functioning as a monastery, tended by Buddhist monks who never considered it abandoned. In Java, Sir Thomas Raffles' men uncovered Borobudur beneath volcanic ash and overgrowth, marveling at its mandala form. Each rediscovery reawakened the testimony carved in stone: that these were not merely relics of past kings, but monuments of a covenant whose memory refused erasure.

Seen this way, the monuments form a global network, a lattice of covenant sites connecting hemispheres. Each acted as a node in a system that spanned continents, synchronizing sacrifice with celestial rhythms. Egypt in the Old World and Teotihuacan in the New mirror each other not because of trade or diffusion but because the same instructors issued the same blueprints. Angkor and Borobudur extended the system into Southeast Asia, adapting Hindu and Buddhist language to preserve the same function. The covenant was not regional. It was planetary.

Up to this point we have traced the architecture of the gods across stone and soil, across dynasties and empires. We have seen that monuments were not only cultural expressions but covenant machines, designed to extract, channel, and testify. What comes next will turn our gaze from the stones themselves to the heavens above them. For the covenant was never confined to the earth. It was written in the stars. The alignments of pyramids, avenues, towers, and mandalas are not curiosities. They are calendars, instruments, and timetables for ritual payment. To understand the covenant fully, we must examine how ancient peoples synchronized their blood offerings with celestial movements—how architecture became not only monument but clock.

What these monuments demonstrate most clearly is that architecture and astronomy were never separate. The stones were built to last, but the stars provided the schedule. Sacrifice was not random violence; it was a calendar-driven system, timed to solstices, equinoxes, zenith passages, and the cycles of Venus and Orion. Just as farmers mark the seasons by planting and harvest, the gods marked theirs by blood and breath, delivered at precise intervals. The covenant was both monument and clock, written in matter and motion together.

Stone testifies. Stars command. Together they form the system through which humanity was domesticated. The monuments stand as mute reminders, but the heavens still move, just as they always have. The covenant was written in both, and its terms may not yet be void.

∽

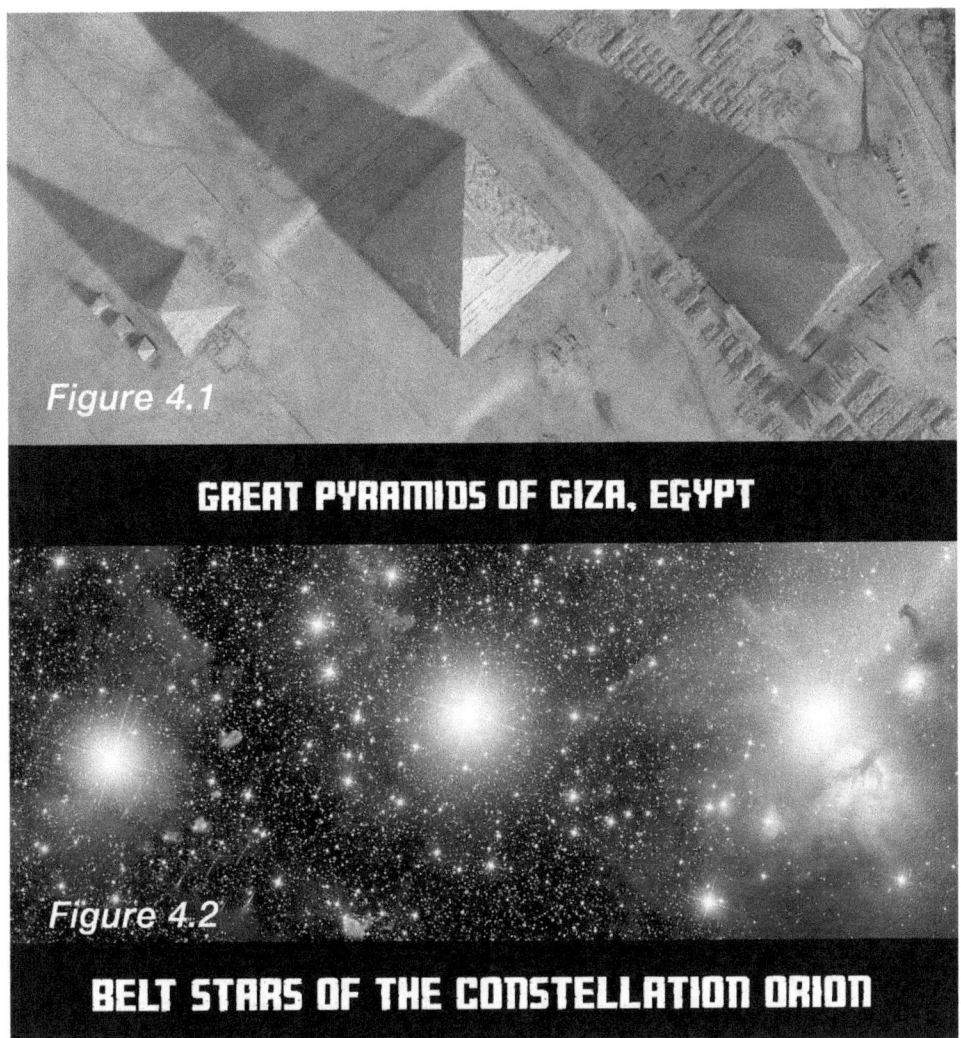

Figure 4.1

GREAT PYRAMIDS OF GIZA, EGYPT

Figure 4.2

BELT STARS OF THE CONSTELLATION ORION

Great Pyramids of Giza, Egypt (ca. 2550–2490 BCE).
The three pyramids of Khufu, Khafre, and Menkaure mirror the stars of Orion's Belt: Alnitak, Alnilam, and Mintaka. Khufu's Great Pyramid, the largest, is aligned to true north within three arc minutes. Robert Bauval's "Orion Correlation" highlights this stellar match, suggesting that Giza was conceived as a covenant machine, locking human ritual and sacrifice to the stars.

Figure 4.3

AVENUE OF THE DEAD - TEOTIHUACAN

Avenue of the Dead & Pyramid of the Sun, Teotihuacan (ca. 1–500 CE).
The Pyramid of the Sun dominates the Avenue of the Dead, a processional axis tilted 15.5° east of north to capture solar and Venus cycles. Together with the Pyramid of the Moon, the layout mirrors celestial rhythms and encodes the 260-day sacred calendar later used by the Maya. Excavations beneath the Temple of the Feathered Serpent revealed mass burials of bound captives, showing that Teotihuacan's monuments were not symbolic alone but charged by blood, functioning as covenant machines that synchronized ritual sacrifice with the heavens.

Figure 4.4

ANGKOR WAT - CAMBODIA

Angkor Wat, Cambodia (12th c. CE).
The world's largest temple complex, Angkor Wat fuses stone and water into a cosmic machine. Its five towers mirror the stars of Orion's Belt, while its moat symbolizes the cosmic ocean, linking architecture to celestial and mythic order. At equinox dawn, the sun crowns the central tower, synchronizing ritual with the heavens. Inscriptions and residue from basins suggest offerings of grain, animals, and blood were channeled through the temple's arteries, binding Khmer kingship to the covenant of sacrifice and cosmic renewal.

Figure 4.5

BOROBUDUR, JAVA

Borobudur, Java (8th–9th c. CE).
Borobudur rises as a stone mandala, its nine stacked terraces spiraling toward a central stupa that symbolizes the cosmic axis. Pilgrims circumambulated each level in ritual ascent, passing 2,600 carved reliefs and 500 Buddha statues that narrated karmic law and cosmic order. Acoustic studies show its stupas amplified chants and percussion, turning the monument into a resonator of sound as well as stone. Though clothed in Buddhist symbolism, Borobudur functioned as a covenant machine: a mountain of labor and ritual ascent designed to synchronize human devotion with cosmic demand.

Temple of the Feathered Serpent, Teotihuacan (ca. 200 CE).
The façade of the Ciudadela's Feathered Serpent temple is covered in alternating serpent heads and storm masks, each carved with fangs, plumes, and goggle eyes. Excavations beneath the temple revealed over 200 bound captives sacrificed at its dedication, "charging" the monument with blood. This fusion of serpent iconography and mass sacrifice marks the temple as a covenant machine, built to bind Teotihuacan's ritual power to the heavens.

Figure 4.7

TEMPLE OF THE GREAT JAGUAR, TIKAL - GUATEMALA

Figure 4.8

BAKONG TEMPLE - CAMBODIA

Temple of the Great Jaguar, Tikal (8th c. CE) and Bakong Temple, Cambodia (9th c. CE).
Though oceans apart, both monuments rise as stepped mountains with axial stairways leading to summit sanctuaries. Each functioned as a covenant machine: platforms for ascent, altars for offerings, and stages for sacrifice synchronized with celestial cycles.

KEYHOLE KOFUN TOMB - JAPAN

Keyhole Kofun Tomb, Japan (3rd–6th c. CE). The giant keyhole-shaped tombs of Japan's Kofun period, such as the Daisenryō Kofun shown here, were surrounded by moats and aligned with the landscape. Thousands of laborers moved earth and stone to create these monumental enclosures, often accompanied by ritual offerings and burials. Though cloaked in Shinto and ancestral reverence, their scale and form mirror the covenant blueprint: massive labor, cosmic alignment, and sacrifice sealed in earth.

5

SKYWATCHERS AND STELLAR TIMETABLES

The Heavens as Contract

If temples and pyramids were the stage, the heavens were the clock. Across every great center of sacrifice, the stones did not stand alone. They were oriented, tilted, pierced with shafts, or crowned with stairways designed not only for ritual but for observation. Priests were not merely keepers of liturgy but of calendars. They watched the sun, the moon, the stars, and the wandering planets with a rigor that still surprises archaeologists today. Their task was not curiosity. It was covenantal precision.

No civilization practiced sacrifice in isolation from the sky. The Egyptians aligned their pyramids and temples with solstices and stellar risings. The Maya charted the planet Venus until their codices could predict its risings and settings to the very day. At Angkor, the rising sun on the equinox sent shafts of light down long galleries to strike sanctuaries in moments of orchestrated brilliance. At Chichén Itzá, the shadow of the serpent descended El Castillo precisely when the equinox sun angled low. Each case reflects the same principle: blood was not spilled randomly. It was delivered on schedule, as though the gods had written appointments in light.

This precision is not incidental. The Mayan Venus tables in the *Dresden Codex*, for example, are accurate to within a single day over 500 years of observation (Aveni, *Skywatchers*, 2001). Why such rigor in a society otherwise struggling with subsistence agriculture? Why divert so much attention to the heavens when survival depended on the earth? The answer, in the covenant framework, is clear: the gods required punctuality. Sacrifice had to occur in rhythm with cosmic events, perhaps to synchronize offerings with cycles of energy or with openings in whatever dimensional fabric separated human from divine.

In Egypt, the heliacal rising of Sirius marked the annual Nile flood, the very lifeblood of the land. But it was also a signal for festivals, offerings, and state rituals. The Book of the Dead even calls Sirius "the soul of Isis," linking the star's appearance with the goddess who received offerings of blood and wine. At Karnak, shafts of sunlight pierced the sanctuary at solstice, illuminating the altar where sacrifices and libations were placed. This was not mere play of light. It was timing. The gods were present when the sky aligned.

The Maya extended the principle with almost obsessive care. Venus, their war god's star, dictated when battles could begin and when captives should be taken for sacrifice. The Codex Borgia and Dresden Codex both depict Venus as a spear-thrower, its appearance in the sky matched with glyphs describing war and death. Anthropologist Linda Schele once described this obsession as "calendrical militarism" — a system where time itself determined violence. To the Maya, it was not sufficient to sacrifice a captive. One had to do so at the precise moment when Venus rose heliacally, signaling the gods' demand.

The spectacle at Chichén Itzá remains one of the most dramatic proofs. Twice each year, at the equinoxes, the setting sun casts a serpent-shaped shadow down the staircase of El Castillo, joining with a carved serpent head at the base. To modern tourists it is a showpiece of archaeoastronomy. To the ancient Maya, it was an appointment. The god descended in shadow and demanded renewal. Priests staged bloodletting and offerings at that moment, binding the city's fate to the clockwork of the sky.

Angkor offers the same principle, though expressed through Hindu cosmology. The temple's galleries are aligned so that equinox and solstice sunrises cast light through gates and corridors, striking inner sanctums with uncanny precision (Mannikka, *Angkor Wat: Time, Space, and Kingship*, 1996). The central tower, representing Mount Meru, caught the rising sun directly over its peak at equinox. To the Khmer, this confirmed the union of heaven and earth. Ritual offerings flowed into moats and basins at that moment, merging human blood and libation with cosmic order.

When these sites are mapped together, their alignments form a geometry across continents: solstices, equinoxes, the heliacal rising of Sirius, the cycle of Venus, the belt of Orion. Again and again, cultures supposedly separated by oceans and centuries converged on the same celestial markers. Mainstream archaeology explains this as "convergent development," each culture responding to the obvious regularities of the sky. But the repetition is too specific, too focused on the same stars and planets, the same solar events. Coincidence might explain one case. It does not explain dozens.

The covenant framework offers a simpler explanation. The gods required timing. Their emissaries instructed priesthoods not only in how to build altars and pyramids but in how to watch the sky for signals. When the sun reached a solstice, when Sirius rose before dawn, when Venus flared in the twilight, those were not natural curiosities. They were signatures, sign-offs on a cosmic contract. At those moments, the altar below had to be fed.

To the ancients, the stars were not distant suns. They were the visible handwriting of the divine. Orion's belt was the waist of Osiris. Venus was the spear of Quetzalcoatl. Sirius was the soul of Isis. Each celestial body carried the name and presence of a god, and when it appeared, the corresponding ritual had to be performed. Sacrifice was not a matter of human will but of cosmic schedule. The gods did not leave offerings to chance. They timed them with light.

Thus humanity became the timekeeper of its own bloodletting.

Priesthoods watched the sky with vigilance, knowing that neglecting the schedule could mean disaster: famine, flood, defeat, or plague. Sacrifice was not just about appeasement. It was about synchronization — keeping human society locked in rhythm with cosmic cycles dictated by nonhuman powers.

In this way, the covenant was doubly binding: in stone and in sky. The monuments provided the stage, but the heavens provided the timetable. And so the knife fell not only by decree of rulers, but by decree of the stars.

Egyptian Sky Temples

If any civilization exemplifies the covenant between blood and sky, it is Egypt. The Nile valley's prosperity was bound to a single astronomical event: the heliacal rising of Sirius, which announced the inundation of the river and the renewal of the land. Without that flood, fields withered and famine loomed. The Egyptians learned early to track the heavens with rigor, for survival depended on precision. Yet their skywatching went far beyond agriculture. It became the timetable for offerings, the calendar of covenantal payment, and the geometry by which temples were built.

The heliacal rising of Sirius, called Sopdet in Egyptian and later associated with the goddess Isis, occurred each year just before dawn in midsummer. When the star first appeared in the eastern sky after a seventy-day absence, the Nile began to swell. Priests watched the horizon carefully, recording the date and announcing the start of the new year. But this was more than a seasonal marker. In Egyptian religion, Sirius embodied the life-force of Isis, and its rising was her appearance on earth. At that moment, the people brought offerings of bread, beer, wine, and animals to the temples, acknowledging the goddess whose star had summoned fertility. Some texts hint at deeper offerings: the Pyramid Texts speak of "red offerings" and "blood of the gods" poured to sustain the divine ka (Faulkner, *The Ancient Egyptian Pyramid Texts*, 1969). Sirius was not only a sign of water. It was a sign of due payment.

The great temples reflected this celestial contract in stone. At Karnak, the axis of the temple complex is aligned so that the rising sun of the winter solstice penetrates directly into the sanctuary, illuminating the shrine of Amun-Ra. On that day, when the longest night gave way to the returning sun, priests performed rituals of renewal. Reliefs depict offerings of oxen, birds, and libations being poured, and though mainstream Egyptology interprets these as symbolic gifts, the language of the texts is literal: the gods "drink" and "eat" what is placed before them. The shaft of sunlight was more than dramatic architecture—it was a spotlight for covenant fulfillment.

Karnak was not unique. The temple of Luxor is aligned to lunar cycles, with colonnades designed to catch moonlight during festivals. The temple of Abu Simbel is famously aligned so that twice each year, the rising sun illuminates statues of the gods seated deep within the rock-cut chamber. These alignments are not accidents of architecture. They are deliberate calibrations. Each solar or lunar event was a cosmic appointment. The priests ensured that offerings coincided with the moment of celestial presence.

Egyptian skywatching was not confined to temples in stone—it lived in the cycle of state festivals. The Opet Festival, for instance, held each year at Luxor, coincided with the inundation of the Nile and the rising of Sirius. Statues of Amun, Mut, and Khonsu were carried in procession from Karnak to Luxor, accompanied by priests, musicians, and offerings. Texts describe animals sacrificed and libations poured as the procession moved, renewing the king's divine mandate in tandem with the star's appearance (Shafer, *Temples of Ancient Egypt*, 1997). The Nile flood was Osiris's blood, Sirius was Isis's soul, and the offerings of the people reenacted that cosmic transaction.

Similarly, the Valley Festival, associated with the cult of Osiris, was timed to lunar and solar markers in the summer months. During the ceremonies, images of the gods crossed the river to the west bank, where tombs were opened and offerings made to the dead. The synchrony of celestial events, river cycles, and ritual bloodletting underscored the same principle: sacrifice was scheduled. The festivals were not arbitrary holidays but calendrical obligations, carefully linked to the heavens' timetable.

These public events reveal how deeply the covenant permeated Egyptian life. Ordinary people may never have entered Karnak's sanctum, but they participated in festivals where the alignment of stars and the swell of the Nile were matched with offerings. The gods' calendar was written not only in stone but in the very rhythm of civic life.

Even the pyramids themselves participated in this system. The Great Pyramid of Khufu at Giza contains narrow shafts that angle upward from the king's chamber. For decades they were dismissed as ventilation channels, but in the 1960s, astronomer Virginia Trimble and engineer Alexander Badawy demonstrated that the shafts once pointed directly at specific stars: Orion's belt to the south and Sirius to the east (Badawy & Trimble, *Journal of Near Eastern Studies,* 1964). This was no accident. Orion was associated with Osiris, lord of the dead and god of resurrection. Sirius was Isis, his consort. Together they marked the cycle of death and renewal. When the shafts caught the stars, they signaled that offerings and rites of passage were in order.

The Pyramid Texts confirm this interpretation. In *Utterance 302,* the king is urged to ascend: "May you ascend to the sky among the stars of Orion. May you rise with Sirius, pure of seat, living forever." The alignment of the shafts was not decorative but functional: they pointed to the gods whose appearance triggered ritual obligation. Blood, libation, and sacrifice synchronized with stellar risings. In this sense, the pyramid was less a tomb than a clock, its geometry locked to the heavens, ensuring that the covenant was kept even in eternity.

Egyptian mythology reinforces the pattern. Osiris was slain and dismembered, his body reconstituted by Isis, who conceived Horus from him. Each year, the flooding Nile was equated with Osiris's blood, renewing the land. Sacrifice, in this worldview, was not arbitrary violence but participation in a cosmic cycle: Osiris slain, his blood spilled, life restored. Sirius rising marked the reenactment. The gods' story and the people's ritual were one.

To the Egyptians, this synchronization was not optional. Failure to sacrifice at the appointed time threatened Ma'at, the cosmic order. Ma'at was not an abstract principle but the balance of the universe itself: truth, justice, fertility, stability. When the solstice sun entered Karnak's sanctuary, when Sirius rose before dawn, when Orion crossed the meridian, these were the signatures of divine demand. The altar had to be fed. Bread and beer might suffice for daily rites, but the Pyramid and Coffin Texts show that blood—human or animal—was the ultimate payment. "Your bread is the blood of the gods; you eat the red and drink the white" (*Pyramid Texts, Utterance 32*).

Mainstream Egyptology often interprets these practices symbolically. Jan Assmann, for example, describes sacrifice as "the act that nourishes the gods and thereby restores the world" (*The Search for God in Ancient Egypt*, 2001). Yet even in his phrasing, the literal slips through. Nourishment, restoration, food, drink—these are not metaphors but transactions. The gods required sustenance, and the stars marked the hours at which it was to be delivered.

In this light, the role of the Egyptian priest becomes clear. He was not simply a ritual specialist but a cosmic accountant, tracking celestial cycles to ensure timely payments. Temples were not only houses of worship but observatories. The alignment of Karnak, Luxor, Abu Simbel, and the pyramids themselves reveals a system of architecture that doubled as a sky calendar. Each stone corridor and shaft pointed not only to gods but to deadlines.

The Egyptian case thus establishes the principle of the chapter: sacrifice was not free-floating but scheduled. Astronomy was not the hobby of sky-gazers but the ledger of the covenant. The Nile's flood, Sirius's rising, Orion's belt, the solstices and equinoxes—all were appointments. And when the appointment arrived, the offering had to be made.

Mesoamerican Venus Lords

If Egypt's covenant was scheduled by Sirius and the solstices, in Mesoamerica it was ruled by Venus. To the Maya and later the Aztec, Venus was not a cold planet of rock and atmosphere but a living deity whose cycle dictated the rhythms of war and sacrifice. They tracked it with astonishing accuracy, recording its heliacal risings and disappearances in codices that survive to this day. For them, the planet was a clock, and its hours were written in blood.

The Dresden Codex, one of the few Mayan books to survive the Spanish conquest, contains a Venus table spanning 584 days—the exact length of the planet's synodic cycle. Each appearance of Venus, whether as morning star or evening star, was tied to specific omens. Battles were launched on days when Venus first appeared before dawn, and prisoners taken in those battles were kept until the next appointed date, when their hearts were cut out on temple summits. Anthropologist Anthony Aveni notes that the table is so precise that it corrects for accumulated errors over centuries, proving that Maya priests observed Venus for generations, refining their schedule (Aveni, *Skywatchers*, 2001). Their obsession was not intellectual. It was covenantal. The gods demanded punctuality, and Venus was their herald.

The Aztec inherited this logic, embedding it in their imperial rites. Their war god Tlahuizcalpantecuhtli—literally "Lord of the Dawn"—was Venus personified as a spear-thrower. In codices such as the Codex Borgia, he is depicted casting darts downward toward human victims, accompanied by glyphs of death and sacrifice. Aztec annals describe wars launched as "Venus wars," timed to the planet's first appearance as morning star. Victims captured in these conflicts were taken to the Templo Mayor and sacrificed at dawn, their blood feeding the god whose star glowed in the eastern sky.

Perhaps the most theatrical display of this covenant clock is found at Chichén Itzá. The great pyramid of El Castillo, built around the 10th century CE, is aligned so that at the equinox, the setting sun casts a serpent-shaped shadow down the north staircase. The shadow joins with a massive serpent head carved at the base, creating the illusion of a giant snake descending from the heavens. To modern visitors it is an archaeoastronomical spectacle. To the ancient Maya, it was a signal. The descent of the serpent announced the time for renewal. Priests staged bloodletting rituals, and captives were sacrificed at the base of the pyramid, their hearts offered as the shadow-serpent "drank."

The serpent shadow was not a parlor trick but a covenant marker. Its precision reveals careful engineering: each of the pyramid's four staircases has 91 steps, totaling 364, with the platform at the top making 365—the solar year. The descent of the serpent shadow on the equinox confirmed that the calendar was on track and that the covenant had to be renewed. The pyramid itself was a calendar in stone, its geometry a reminder that human life was to be measured and offered in rhythm with celestial cycles.

Mayan rulers reinforced this system with their own blood. Reliefs at sites such as Yaxchilán and Bonampak show kings and queens drawing blood from their tongues, ears, and genitals, collecting it on bark paper which was then burned as an offering. These bloodletting rites were not random acts of devotion but carefully timed to celestial events—Venus risings, solstices, equinoxes. The royal body became both altar and clock, bleeding on schedule to ensure the gods' favor.

Archaeological evidence from Bonampak and Yaxchilán drives this point home. Murals from Structure 1 at Bonampak, dating to the late 8th century CE, depict a sequence of rituals culminating in bloodletting and sacrifice. In one scene, noble captives are presented to rulers seated beneath banners marked with celestial glyphs, while musicians play and incense thickens the air. The murals are not random snapshots—they encode time. Scholars such as Mary Miller and Karl Taube (*The Gods and Symbols of Ancient Mexico and the Maya*, 1993) have shown that the glyphs correspond to Venus intervals, indicating that the captives' fates were tied to planetary phases.

At Yaxchilán, carved lintels reveal rulers piercing their tongues and genitals with stingray spines, threading cords through the wounds to draw blood onto bark paper. That paper, once soaked, was burned in offering, its smoke rising toward the heavens. One lintel shows Lady Xook, wife of King Shield Jaguar, kneeling as she draws a thorned rope through her tongue, while a vision serpent rises from the smoke, revealing a warrior ancestor. The timing of these rites aligns with recorded Venus appearances, suggesting that even royal visions were synchronized to the planet's cycle. The king's blood was not his own to spill—it was scheduled, contracted, demanded by the same celestial ledger that dictated war and sacrifice.

Spanish chroniclers, horrified by what they saw, often dismissed these rites as barbaric superstition. Yet their own accounts confirm the calendrical precision. Diego de Landa, writing in the 16th century, observed that the Maya *"sacrificed according to the course of the heavens,"* particularly Venus, which they considered *"the great star of war."* What the friars condemned as cruelty was in fact an astronomical schedule carried into ritual.

From the covenant perspective, Venus functioned as an appointment book. Each phase of its 584-day cycle was a slot for a particular type of offering. When Venus rose as morning star, it demanded human blood—often through war. When it disappeared into conjunction with the sun, other offerings, sometimes symbolic, were made to mark its absence. Priests were not simply astronomers; they were schedulers of sacrifice, ensuring that the covenant was fulfilled at each celestial interval.

The obsession with Venus was not limited to elites. Entire communities participated in festivals tied to the planet's cycle. Murals at Bonampak show mass gatherings where musicians, dancers, and warriors assembled during Venus phases, culminating in sacrifice before the crowd. Like Egypt's Opet festival, these events embedded the covenant into civic life. Everyone saw, everyone participated, and everyone was reminded that human life itself was bound to the stars.

The scale of this synchronization is difficult to overstate. Imagine a civilization where wars are not declared by politics alone but by the rising of a planet; where the fate of captives is not decided by whim but by a 584-day celestial cycle; where even the geometry of pyramids encodes the timing of bloodletting. For the Maya and Aztec, this was not metaphor. It was system. The gods' demands were written in the sky, and failure to comply risked drought, famine, or defeat.

Modern astronomy marvels at the precision of Mayan calculations. But from the covenant lens, the precision was not for its own sake. It was for the gods. Venus was the spear in their hand, and its appearance was the signature on the contract. To miss the appointment was to break the covenant.

Thus in Mesoamerica, as in Egypt, astronomy was never neutral. It was obligation. The stars were not distant suns but divine signatures, and the planet Venus was the most urgent of them all. Through its cycle, the covenant was kept. Through its rising, blood flowed. And through its shadow at Chichén Itzá, the serpent itself descended to drink.

Angkor and Asian Alignments

If Egypt tracked Sirius and the Maya tracked Venus, the Khmer of Cambodia tracked the entire sky. Angkor Wat, constructed in the early 12th century CE, remains the largest religious monument on earth, sprawling across a plain with moats, causeways, and towers that still bewilder archaeologists. Its purpose, at least in part, was the same as Karnak or Chichén Itzá: to align human offerings with celestial cycles.

The five towers of Angkor Wat rise like lotus buds, but scholars such as Eleanor Mannikka (*Angkor Wat: Time, Space, and Kingship*, 1996) have shown that their placement corresponds to Orion's Belt and attendant stars. At equinox sunrise, the sun appears directly over the central tower when viewed from the temple's western entrance, casting shafts of light deep into the sanctuary. The equinox was no abstract date—it was a contract renewal. Priests offered food, animals, and perhaps blood as the first rays struck the sanctum, timing the sacrifice to the heavens' heartbeat.

At equinox dawn the effect was theatrical in the most literal sense. Witnesses standing on the western causeway would see the first rim of sunlight crown the central tower and then pour like a blade of gold down the axial corridor, striking the sanctum at the exact moment of sunrise. Processions were timed to this light: drummers, conch-blowers, and banner-bearers advancing as the sun ascended; priests pacing the gallery intervals with bowls of offerings. The architecture forced a choreography—pauses at thresholds, turns at pylons, ascent by measured steps—so that movement itself mirrored the slow transit of light. When the beam reached the sanctuary, torches were extinguished and libations poured, sealing the moment when heaven's timing and human payment met. In covenant terms, the ray was not decorative illumination; it was the arrival signature. Blood and grain were delivered on the minute the sky declared due.

Angkor was also a machine of water. Its vast moats, 200 meters wide, linked to reservoirs and canals that turned the city into both an irrigation network and a cosmic ocean. In Hindu cosmology, the world was surrounded by primordial waters, and Mount Meru rose at the center. Angkor recreated this in stone. But the waters were not symbolic alone. Stone basins within shrines bear traces of iron-rich residue, consistent with sacrificial fluids diluted in water. Just as Egyptian altars had channels, Angkor's moats may have received offerings that coursed visibly around the temple, dramatizing the covenant for all to see.

The waterworks that girdle Angkor Wat are only a fraction of a greater hydraulic engine. To the north and east lie the barays—vast man-made reservoirs that dwarf the temple moat. The West Baray spans roughly 8 km by 2 km; the East Baray about 7.5 km by 1.8 km, both fed by canals, with stone spillways regulating flow. On the surface they irrigated rice fields. In the ritual economy they were the cosmic ocean made literal: a visible, navigable reservoir into which offerings could be released and seen to move. Flowers, oils, grains—and at times iron-tinged liquids—were cast upon the water and drawn along channels that circled temple precincts before dispersing to the fields. This circulation married myth to mechanism: the ocean of creation pulsed through spillways; the world-mountain rose in towers; and the people's tribute returned as fertility. From the covenant perspective, the barays turned sacrifice into a public interface—fluid proof that what left the altar entered the body of the city and the land.

Reliefs carved into the temple walls reinforce the theme. The famous *"Churning of the Ocean of Milk"* depicts gods and demons pulling on a serpent wrapped around Mount Meru to extract the nectar of immortality. To modern scholars this is mythological allegory. To the covenant lens, it is a manual: serpents as conduits, water as reservoir, cosmic renewal powered by offering.

Archaeoastronomical surveys confirm Angkor's precision. The temple encodes solar and lunar cycles in its dimensions, and even the 584-day cycle of Venus appears in its galleries (Mannikka, 1996). Processions moved along corridors that served as sightlines, so that during equinox sunrise, light penetrated straight through to the sanctuary. At those moments, priests staged offerings—blood, grain, incense—binding the human covenant to celestial rhythm.

Angkor sits near 13–14° north latitude, which means the sun passes directly overhead twice each year. On those zenith days, vertical objects cast no shadow at noon—a phenomenon Khmer priests could have tracked with simple gnomons long before temple construction. Several long east–west galleries function like sight tubes: at particular dates light shafts run their length and vanish precisely at midday when the sun reaches zenith. Scholars have argued that the lengths and bay counts of certain corridors encode these intervals, just as other dimensions encode lunar synodics and the 584-day cycle of Venus (Mannikka, 1996). In practice this made Angkor a composite sky clock: equinox sunrises marked public rites; zenith passages keyed noon offerings; lunar standstills cued night processions; and Venus cycles signaled festival sequences. The point was not astronomy for its own sake; it was punctuality. Offerings were delivered when solar, lunar, and planetary gates were open, keeping covenant payments synchronized with the heavens.

Like Giza and Teotihuacan, Angkor demanded staggering labor. Hundreds of thousands of workers and elephants hauled sandstone blocks across canals from quarries fifty kilometers away. Modern historians attribute this to political power, but the pattern repeats too often. Monumental labor was itself sacrificial, the lifeblood of populations poured into stone for gods who demanded permanence.

Accounts by visiting envoys describe Angkor's processions as overwhelming: drums, dancers, parasols, elephants, and long files of attendants escorting divine images along causeways lined with nāga balustrades. The 13th-century observer Zhou Daguan reports elaborate rites, strict taboos, and penalties administered at festivals —scenes that, read alongside inscriptions, suggest that formal offerings (livestock, grain, oils) sometimes culminated in harsher payments for the gods. Whether or not human victims were regular at Angkor Wat itself, the Khmer ritual state clearly linked civic time to sacred time—mustering labor, wealth, and life on appointed days. In the covenant reading, the spectacle was not propaganda alone. It was the public face of a schedule kept in the sanctuaries: equinox light striking stone, conches sounding the hour, waters bearing away what the altar had received. Even as the empire waned and Buddhism repurposed the precincts, the calendar survived in the stones, and the rites adapted to it rather than the other way around.

Inscriptions and Chinese accounts describe offerings at Angkor that included livestock and, at times, human victims. While mainstream scholars downplay these as exceptional, the covenant reading sees continuity: the same payment demanded in Egypt and Mexico was demanded in Cambodia, scheduled to cosmic alignments and dramatized through water, stone, and light.

Even when the Khmer empire collapsed, Angkor remained sacred. Buddhist monks rededicated its sanctuaries, but the architecture's cosmic alignments could not be erased. Pilgrims continued to visit, performing rituals timed to equinoxes and solstices. The covenant, written in stone and sky, outlived the kings who built it.

Angkor demonstrates that the logic of cosmic scheduling was not confined to one hemisphere. Whether in Egypt, Mexico, or Cambodia, the same elements recur: Orion, solstices, equinoxes, Venus, cosmic mountains, waters as channels. These were not independent curiosities. They were appointments kept on behalf of nonhuman powers.

The Shang and the Eastern Horizon

While Egypt timed sacrifices to Sirius and the Maya to Venus, in Bronze Age China the Shang dynasty (c. 1600–1046 BCE) looked upward to track the heavens and downward to cut into bone. Their inscriptions, carved on turtle plastrons and cattle scapulae, record sacrifices to celestial and ancestral powers with a precision that reveals the same global logic: bloodletting as a transaction scheduled by the sky.

The oracle bones—thousands of them—are our earliest written records from East Asia. In them we find not only questions of kingship and war but carefully dated inquiries about when to sacrifice. "Should we sacrifice ten men to Shangdi for harvest?" one inscription reads (Keightley, *Sources of Shang History*, 1978). Another records the offering of cattle and sheep on days tied to lunar phases. The presence of both humans and animals as victims shows that the Shang, like their Western counterparts, considered blood a form of sustenance for the divine. And just as in Egypt and Mesoamerica, the timing was never arbitrary.

Shang cosmology centered on Shangdi, the high god residing in the heavens, and on the royal ancestors who acted as intermediaries. Blood offerings were thought to nourish both. What mattered was not only what was killed, but when. Diviners heated the bones, read the cracks, and recorded the results alongside the sacrifices. The language is blunt: "*On the day dinghai, sacrifice men.*" These were not symbolic gestures. They were executions performed on schedule, the covenant renewed through the arteries of time itself. The sheer number of these records makes their covenantal logic impossible to ignore. Over 20,000 inscribed bones have been recovered from Anyang alone, many of them repeating the same formula: a calendrical sign, a diviner's crack, and a sacrifice prescribed. "*Crack-making on dinghai: it will rain; we sacrifice sheep,*" reads one. Another: "*On *gengwu day, sacrifice men to Father Ding.*" In still others, victims are paired with celestial events: "At eclipse, offer cattle to Shangdi; at eclipse, offer men to the ancestors." (Keightley, 1978). The matter-of-fact tone is chilling in its consistency. No metaphors, no allegories—only schedules. These bones are ledgers in which life was tallied against the heavens, a written record of the covenant as binding contract.

The scale of Shang ritual was immense. Excavations at Anyang have uncovered entire pits filled with human victims—sometimes dozens, sometimes hundreds—often buried alongside bronzes and weapons. These mass sacrifices, associated with royal tombs, echo the subsidiary burials at Egypt's Abydos or the warrior graves at Teotihuacan. Each pit is both grave and offering bowl, its blood poured to affirm the king's mandate under heaven. The parallel is exact: monumental architecture above, ritual slaughter below, both oriented to celestial markers. Excavations at Anyang's royal cemetery deepen this parallel. Tomb M1001, thought to belong to Lady Fu Hao, yielded not only jade and bronze but evidence of more than 16 human sacrifices at her burial. Larger royal tombs contained dozens, sometimes hundreds, of victims—young men decapitated or buried alive, their remains arranged in rows. One pit near Tomb 1004 contained at least 70 individuals, most stripped of grave goods, suggesting their sole purpose was as offerings. Scholars like Robert Bagley have compared these pits to the "death pits" of Ur in Mesopotamia, where retainers were interred with kings. The message is the same across continents: rulers carried their household into death not as companions but as currency, a down payment on continued favor from the powers above.

Astronomical alignment played its role here as well. Scholars such as David Pankenier (*Astrology and Cosmology in Early China*, 2013) have shown that early Chinese kings were obsessed with the circumpolar stars—the "imperial palace" of the heavens. The north celestial pole, the still point around which all stars revolved, symbolized the throne of Shangdi. Royal architecture aligned to this axis, just as Giza aligned to Orion or Angkor to the equinox. Blood was spilled not randomly, but under the pivot of the sky, synchronizing terrestrial sacrifice with celestial permanence.

Even more striking are records of lunar and solar eclipses, meticulously tied to ritual actions. Oracle bones note when eclipses occurred and what sacrifices followed, as though the blotting of the sun or moon was itself a summons for blood. The gods' calendar was visible in real time, and the Shang kept pace with it.

By the Zhou dynasty (1046–256 BCE), the language of covenant had evolved into the "Mandate of Heaven." Kings ruled only so long as they maintained cosmic harmony. Ritual offerings, often including animal and occasional human victims, were the currency of that mandate. Seasonal sacrifices were performed at the solstices and equinoxes, exactly the same celestial benchmarks found at Karnak and Chichén Itzá. The Zhou kings even constructed the "Mingtang," or Bright Hall, an architectural observatory where rituals were performed at cardinal points and times. The building itself was a sky clock, ensuring that offerings were made at precise seasonal markers.

China's great earthen mound tombs further extend this pattern. The tomb of the First Emperor (3rd century BCE), guarded by his terracotta army, was aligned to cardinal directions and said to contain rivers of mercury representing cosmic waters (Sima Qian, *Records of the Grand Historian*). Like the mercury tunnels at Teotihuacan, this hidden underworld of liquid metal echoed the cosmos below ground. Sacrifices of workers and concubines sealed the tomb, mirroring the Abydos retainer graves. Here again, architecture, blood, and celestial symbolism converged.

Mainstream sinology tends to interpret these sacrifices as ancestor worship and political theater. Yet the repetition of motifs argues otherwise. Why should Anyang pits echo Ur's death pits or Abydos's subsidiary graves? Why should the First Emperor's mercury rivers mirror Teotihuacan's? Why should solstices, equinoxes, and polar stars serve as covenant clocks across every hemisphere? Coincidence strains belief. The covenant framework makes sense of the data: nonhuman powers demanded punctual offerings, and the Shang, Zhou, and Qin obeyed.

Blood was the medium, the stars were the schedule, and architecture was the ledger. Together they bound the East to the same contract seen in Egypt, Mesoamerica, and Angkor.

Although China did not raise pyramids in cut stone, its rulers shaped earth into mountains of equal intent. The royal mounds of the Zhou and Han, and above all the colossal tumulus of Qin Shi Huangdi, functioned as artificial mountains aligned to the heavens. Inside, rivers of mercury shimmered through chambers arranged as a cosmic map, echoing the liquid underworld of Teotihuacan's tunnels and the barays of Angkor. Around these tombs lay rows of human victims, the same retainer graves seen at Abydos or Ur. Even the shift to the terracotta army preserved the principle: life-energy transmuted into a standing host for the afterlife. In every essential, the covenant architecture was present—mountain, sacrifice, cosmic waters, celestial alignment. China's covenant was written not in limestone but in rammed earth, yet it belongs unmistakably to the same system of instructions that shaped Egypt, Mesopotamia, and Mesoamerica. In surveying Egypt, Mesoamerica, Angkor, and now China, the pattern sharpens: no matter the material or myth, the sky was the clock, the monument the ledger, and blood the currency of the covenant.

Conclusion: Calendars of Blood

Across four continents, civilizations that should have been strangers to one another watched the sky with the same intent. In Egypt, shafts aimed at Orion and temples that caught the solstice sun dictated when priests poured libations and shed blood. In Mesoamerica, the risings and settings of Venus determined when wars began and captives were offered, their hearts raised at the exact hour the planet blazed on the horizon. In Cambodia, equinox light cut through Angkor Wat, synchronizing offerings to the cosmos with theatrical precision. In China, diviners heated bones and marked the cracks, recording sacrifices on the days when eclipses, lunar phases, or polar stars demanded payment. Different myths, different names, yet the same pattern: the heavens were not distant wonders but the covenant's clock face.

This convergence cannot be dismissed as coincidence. Why would cultures separated by oceans, climates, and languages all exert colossal effort to build architecture that tracked the sky, only to spill blood in rhythm with celestial events? Why not offer whenever convenient, whenever war or famine pressed the need? The insistence on punctuality suggests something more than human imagination at work. It implies instructions—deadlines set not by priests alone but by the recipients of the offerings.

From Karnak's corridors to Teotihuacan's Avenue of the Dead, from Angkor's galleries to the Shang oracle bones, the architecture and records say the same thing: blood was not to be given freely, but on schedule. Sacrifice was not a spontaneous plea but an installment payment, kept in sync with the stars. In covenant terms, the gods were not simply hungry; they were exacting. The sky was their calendar, the monuments their ledgers, the priests their accountants, and humanity their treasury.

Even the differences reinforce the pattern. Egypt poured libations into channels carved in stone, while Angkor diluted offerings into its moats and barays. The Maya calculated with Venus, while the Shang fixed their gaze on the pole star. Yet all served the same logic: blood had to be delivered at the moment when heaven's eye was open. These were appointments written in light, and to miss them was to risk famine, invasion, or cosmic disorder. The disasters recorded in myths—deluges, droughts, darkened suns—can be read as covenant penalties, punishments for missed payments.

Modern scholars often call these alignments "symbolic," as if ancient societies coincidentally chose the same handful of stars and cycles for decoration. But the practical costs contradict that explanation. Aligning massive stone or earthworks required survey, calculation, and generational labor. Training astronomer-priests to track Venus for centuries was not symbolic indulgence; it was a survival mechanism. If the people believed their world depended on offerings made at the correct time, then those calendars were as vital as harvests or rivers. And if their belief was reinforced by actual contact —by emissaries demanding punctuality—then the global repetition of this system makes perfect sense.

The implication is sobering. Humanity's first calendars may not have been invented for farming alone, but for feeding the gods. The solstice was not only a marker for planting, but a reminder for sacrifice. The new moon did not merely reset the month; it reset the covenant. Civilizations became timekeepers of their own bloodletting, enslaved not only in labor but in schedule.

As we move forward, the pieces align more clearly. Pyramids and temples were not random marvels, nor were the rituals quaint superstitions. They were components of a global apparatus—a ritual machine in which architecture, astronomy, and sacrifice locked together like gears. Egypt, Mesoamerica, Angkor, and China were not independent experiments in devotion. They were regional installations of a single system.

And the stars, written in every culture's myths, were not metaphors but mandates. The gods wrote their appointments in the heavens, and humanity kept them with blood.

∼

Figure 5.1

ABU SIMBEL SOLAR ALIGNMENT – EGYPT

Abu Simbel, Great Temple (13th c. BCE). Twice each year, the rising sun penetrates the sanctuary to illuminate Ra-Horakhty, Amun-Ra, and Ramesses II, while Ptah—god of the hidden—remains in shadow. The biannual beam (now observed near 22 Feb and 22 Oct after the temple's relocation) is a timed signature in light, confirming that Egyptian offerings and festivals were keyed to celestial appointments rather than arbitrary dates.

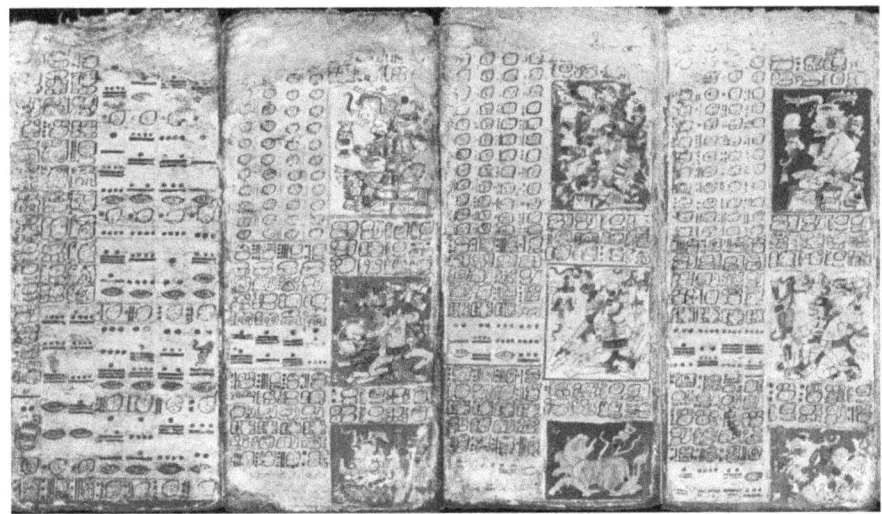

Figure 5.2

DRESDEN CODEX – VENUS TABLE [MAYA]

Dresden Codex, Maya (ca. 11th–12th c. CE, copied from earlier texts).
The Venus Table of the Dresden Codex tracks the planet's 584-day synodic cycle with such precision that it remains accurate within a single day over 500 years. For the Maya, Venus was the war god's star: its heliacal rising signaled the time for battle and sacrifice. This was not astronomy for curiosity's sake but covenantal scheduling. The codex functioned as a blood calendar, ensuring offerings were delivered on the exact celestial day demanded by the gods.

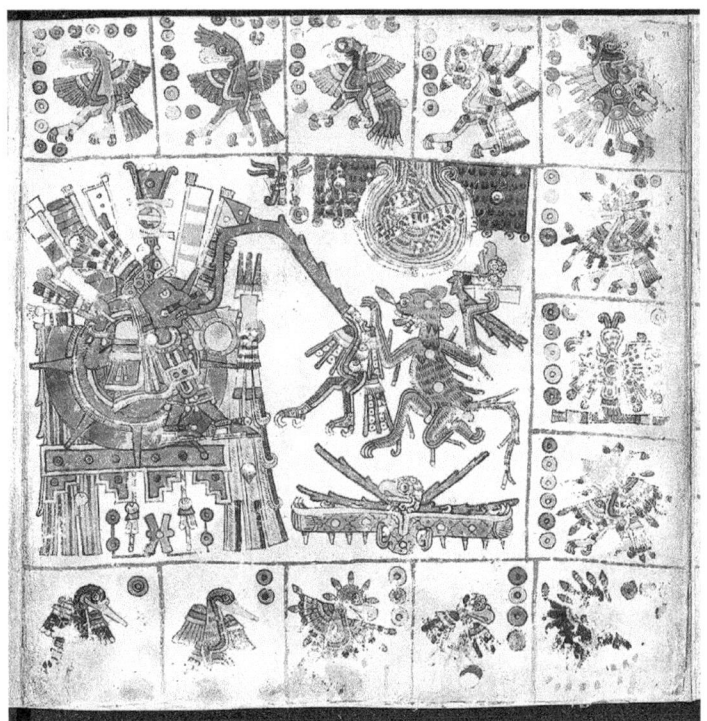

Figure 5.3

CODEX BORGIA – VENUS AS SPEAR-THROWER [AZTEC]

Codex Borgia, Aztec (ca. 15th–16th c. CE). Here Tlahuizcalpantecuhtli, the deity of Venus, appears as the "Lord of the Dawn," hurling darts toward human victims. For the Aztec, Venus was not an inert planet but a war god whose heliacal rising dictated when battles began and captives were sacrificed. The codex depicts Venus as an active spear-thrower, reinforcing its role as covenantal clock: each rising of the star was a summons for human blood.

EL CASTILLO EQUINOX SERPENT – CHICHÉN ITZÁ

El Castillo, Chichén Itzá (ca. 10th–12th c. CE). At the spring and autumn equinoxes, the setting sun casts a serpent-shaped shadow down the pyramid's north staircase, joining with a carved serpent head at the base. To modern visitors it is an archaeoastronomical spectacle, but to the ancient Maya it was a covenant appointment: the god descended in shadow, and offerings of blood and ritual renewal were required. The pyramid itself was a calendar in stone, its 365 steps encoding the solar year and reminding priesthoods to keep sacrifice synchronized with celestial time.

ANGKOR WAT EQUINOX SUNRISE – CAMBODIA

Figure 5.5

Angkor Wat, Cambodia (12th c. CE).
At the equinox sunrise, the sun crowns the central tower of Angkor Wat and sends its first rays down the temple's axial corridor to the sanctuary. To the Khmer, this was no accident of design but a cosmic appointment: heaven's light entering the temple signaled the moment for offerings of grain, animals, and blood. Angkor's equinox alignment transformed ritual into schedule, binding human tribute to the precise rhythm of the sky.

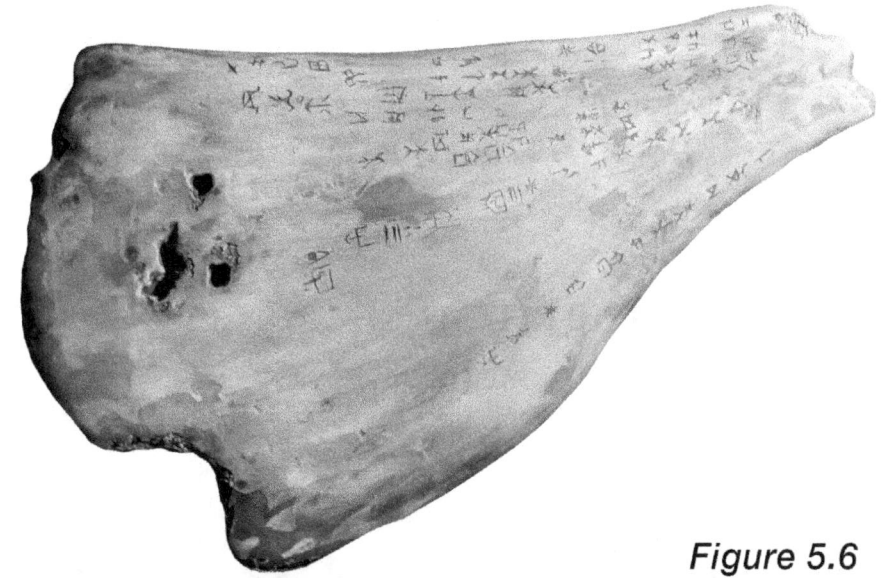

Figure 5.6

SHANG ORACLE BONE – ANYANG, CHINA

Oracle bone, Shang Dynasty (ca. 1600–1046 BCE).
The Shang inscribed questions and records on turtle plastrons and cattle scapulae, heated until they cracked. Many specify human offerings tied to calendrical signs: "On dinghai day, sacrifice men," or "At eclipse, offer cattle to Shangdi." These were not metaphors but scheduled executions — covenant payments written into the calendar itself. Over 20,000 such bones have been excavated at Anyang, revealing a system where blood was tallied against celestial events.

6

THE RITUAL MACHINE

Introduction: The Machinery of Ritual

If architecture was the stage and astronomy the clock, ritual itself was the machinery. Sacrifice was not an improvisation born of panic, nor a mere cultural flourish, but a carefully tuned process. Each step—the cleansing, the dressing, the killing, the collecting—was repeated with such precision across centuries that the whole resembles the function of a mechanism. The same phases appear in Egypt, Mesoamerica, Mesopotamia, India, and China: preparation, offering, and transmission. Only the costumes and languages changed. The design of the ritual machine remained constant.

The anthropologist James Frazer, writing in *The Golden Bough* (1890), treated these repetitions as symbolic attempts to manipulate nature. For him, the Aztec's bloodletting was a primitive plea for crops; the Egyptian's daily offerings to the sun god were magical dramas reinforcing cosmic order. Mircea Eliade, in *The Sacred and the Profane* (1957), took a subtler view, seeing ritual repetition as the re-enactment of primordial events, the "eternal return" of myth into history. René Girard, in *Violence and the Sacred* (1972), argued that sacrifice functioned socially, as a way of channeling human violence into a controlled outlet. These interpretations emphasize psychology, cohesion, or symbolism. But they share an assumption: the gods were not literally eating, and the ritual was only a metaphor.

The covenant thesis challenges this assumption. What if the rituals were not mere theater but the literal servicing of an agreement with nonhuman powers? If so, the similarity across continents takes on a new meaning. The repetition is not evidence of shared psychology, but of shared instruction. The machinery of sacrifice looks mechanical because it was—an operating system exported across hemispheres, its schematics delivered by emissaries who demanded maintenance at precise intervals.

The first phase of the machine was preparation. The offering was not seized and slaughtered without ceremony; it was tuned. In Mesoamerica, victims were stripped, painted blue—the color of Tlaloc, the rain god—and sometimes given hallucinogens to ease their passage into the god's presence. In Egypt, sacrificial animals were bathed, adorned with garlands, and paraded before the altar. In Vedic India, the fire altars themselves were prepared as if they were living beings: bricks laid in exact numbers, geometric patterns drawn with obsessive care, priests reciting mantras that "consecrated" the very stage of death. In Shang China, victims were designated weeks in advance on oracle bones, their fates scheduled like appointments in a ledger. The preparation phase was not decoration. It was calibration, as though the offering needed to be made compatible with the machine it was about to enter.

The second phase was sacrifice proper, the moment of release. Here the choreography becomes explicit. At Teotihuacan, captives were laid out in rows, throats slit in unison to dedicate the Temple of the Feathered Serpent. In Egypt, oxen were felled with ceremonial blades, their blood pouring into carved channels. In the Vedic *Ashvamedha*, a horse was suffocated, its body dismembered and offered part by part into the fire, each limb assigned to a god. In Shang China, humans were decapitated or buried alive, their deaths performed in strict sequence. The ritual's violence was never random

—it was codified, as if each act were a lever pulled, a switch flipped, advancing the mechanism step by step toward its intended outcome.

The third phase was transmission, the final movement of the machine. Death alone did not complete the offering. It had to be delivered. Thus the Aztec cuauhxicalli—massive stone bowls carved as jaguars or eagles—collected human hearts, their surfaces often grooved to channel blood like irrigation ditches. Egyptian altars bore basins and spouts to catch and direct the lifeblood of oxen or birds. In Vedic India, the fire altar transformed animal flesh and ghee into smoke that rose skyward. Shang ritual bronzes received libations of blood and wine, which were then buried or poured into the earth. Always there was a conduit, a channel, a device for transference. It is as though the gods issued not only the demand for sacrifice but the schematics for how the energy of life was to be harvested and routed: up to the heavens in smoke, down to the underworld in blood, or held in vessels for later presentation.

When viewed together, these phases—preparation, sacrifice, transmission—reveal a startling consistency. The Aztec bowl, the Egyptian basin, the Vedic altar, the Shang bronze: all are functionally equivalent components of a global operating system. Local variations matter no more than the brand of a plug; the socket is universal. In one land the machine is made of limestone, in another of clay or bronze, but the system is the same: life in, blood out, offering delivered.

This mechanical logic is reinforced by the very language of the rituals. In Nahuatl, the heart offered to the gods was called chalchíhuatl, "precious water," a substance to be consumed. Egyptian Pyramid Texts speak of "feeding the ka" and "drinking the red." Vedic hymns describe Soma and blood as "the drink that makes them mighty." Shang inscriptions record that "men were sacrificed" to secure harvests or victory. The phrasing is not symbolic flourish—it is transactional, almost contractual, as if the ritual were the writing of checks in blood, honored only when signed at the correct time and delivered through the proper channel.

Modern interpreters often struggle with this literalism, preferring to soften the language into metaphor. Yet the machinery of ritual resists metaphorical reduction. If it were only symbolic, why the obsession with precision? Why the geometric altars, the scheduled sacrifices, the carefully carved channels? Why the blood collected rather than spilled, the hearts stored in stone bowls, the smoke directed by flues? Symbolism does not require such technicalities. Machines do.

The covenant thesis reframes ritual as not only cultural but technical. What the ancients experienced as worship may have functioned as service—regular maintenance performed on behalf of gods who demanded fuel. The cycle of preparation, sacrifice, and transmission is too consistent, too widespread, to be dismissed as coincidence. It looks like design, as though priesthoods across the world were issued a manual: consecrate the victim, release the life, deliver the substance. Reset the covenant. Repeat.

In the chapters before, we traced the stages and calendars of the covenant—the architecture and the astronomy. Here we move into the machinery itself: how rituals operated as engines of exchange, binding the human body to cosmic order. To place the Aztec bowl beside the Shang basin, the Vedic fire altar beside the Egyptian libation channel, is to watch the illusion of cultural independence dissolve. These were not separate inventions. They were compatible parts of a single, global mechanism.

Phase 1: Preparation

Before a knife was drawn or a libation poured, there was preparation. The covenant was not fed casually; its machinery required calibration. Across cultures, offerings were made ready through ritual acts that stripped them of ordinary status and tuned them to the divine. Preparation was a phase in itself, long before the final stroke, as if the gods demanded not only the life but the quality of the life, adjusted and purified to suit their needs.

In Mesoamerica, the victim's preparation was elaborate and highly visual. Aztec captives destined for sacrifice were stripped of clothing, painted with pigments whose colors denoted the deity they would serve, and adorned with paper ornaments that transformed them from prisoners into embodiments of divine forces. The blue paint was especially telling: associated with Tlaloc, the rain god, it symbolized not only water but fertility. To paint a captive blue was to declare him an offering whose blood would summon rain. Bernardino de Sahagún's *Florentine Codex* describes victims intoxicated with pulque, the fermented agave drink, or given hallucinogenic mushrooms to dull their fear and ease their passage. This was not compassion but calibration. The altered states prepared the victim to "meet" the god, while ensuring compliance on the altar.

Among the Maya, preparation extended to the ritual dressing of rulers themselves when they offered their own blood. Reliefs from Yaxchilán depict kings and queens drawing blood from their tongues or genitals, having first fasted and purified themselves with incense. Their clothing—white linen or jaguar pelts—was carefully chosen, and the implements—stingray spines, obsidian blades—were sanctified before use. In each case, preparation ensured that the blood to be drawn was ritually "clean," free of pollution, and charged with symbolic power. Even the paper strips used to collect the blood were pretreated with incense, ready to be burned as smoke-offerings.

In Egypt, preparation of sacrificial animals followed similarly rigid protocols. Texts and tomb scenes show cattle bathed in the Nile before sacrifice, their horns gilded, their hides adorned with garlands of flowers. Priests examined the animals for blemishes; only the unblemished could be offered. The ritual bath was not only hygienic but symbolic, cleansing away earthly dust before presenting the life to the divine. As Jan Assmann notes in *The Search for God in Ancient Egypt* (2001), preparation was central to Egyptian cultic life: purification of both victim and officiant was a prerequisite. Priests shaved their bodies, washed four times a day, and abstained from certain foods before entering the sanctuary. The gods were not to be approached casually.

In Vedic India, preparation took an even more geometric turn. Sacrifice there was not only about the victim but about the altar itself. The Śulbasūtras, ancient manuals on altar construction, detail exact measurements for fire pits used in offerings. Each brick, each layer, was assigned a mantra; each shape corresponded to cosmic principles. The Agnicayana (fire altar ritual) demanded 10,800 bricks arranged to mirror the days and nights of a year. Before any victim was slain or offering burned, priests constructed the altar with obsessive precision, aligning it with cardinal directions and celestial cycles. Preparation here was cosmological engineering, turning the ground itself into a tuned instrument.

Shang China reveals yet another facet of preparation: scheduling. Oracle bones, inscribed with divination questions, recorded the designation of sacrificial victims days or weeks in advance. Inscriptions such as "Crack-making on day 7: we will sacrifice ten men to the river spirit" (Keightley, *Sources of Shang History*, 1978) reveal that sacrifice was calendrical, planned, and rehearsed. Victims were not seized at random; they were chosen, kept aside, and prepared with ritual markings. Bronze basins and elaborate grave pits were dug in anticipation, ensuring that when the appointed day came, the machine of sacrifice would operate smoothly.

Preparation extended beyond the victims to the officiants. In nearly every culture, the priests themselves underwent purification. Egyptian priests abstained from sex and certain foods, shaved their entire bodies, and washed in sacred pools. Aztec priests fasted and bled themselves in the days before major festivals, blackening their faces with soot. Vedic Brahmins recited hundreds of verses, ritually cleansing themselves through sound. Shang diviners burned turtle shells and ox scapulae, inhaling the smoke as part of their ritual tuning. This emphasis on the preparer's body highlights the mechanical nature of the process: the operator had to be "sterile," reset to a baseline before engaging the machinery of the covenant.

The preparation phase also carried theatrical weight. Processions, chants, and public displays transformed victims from ordinary beings into sacred offerings. The stripping of clothes in Mesoamerica, the leading of cattle garlanded with flowers in Egypt, the parading of horses in Vedic India, the binding of captives in Shang China—all served to signal to the people that the sacrifice was not a crime but a covenantal duty. The victim ceased to be human or animal and became, in the community's eyes, an offering, a commodity of exchange.

What unites these practices is the insistence that sacrifice was not simply killing, but the execution of a protocol. Preparation sanctified the act, made it legible to the gods, and ensured its acceptance. A blemished animal, an unpainted victim, an improperly aligned altar —these were seen as dangerous, risks that could void the covenant or bring punishment. The machine demanded proper inputs, or else the output failed.

From the covenant perspective, this obsession with preparation takes on a practical logic. If the gods required specific biochemical qualities—blood free from contamination, victims whose bodies had been tuned through fasting or intoxication—then preparation was not superstition but specification. Blue paint, fasting, purification, incense, and geometry may have acted as markers, ensuring that the offering was properly formatted before transmission. To us these may look like cultural flourishes; to the gods, they may have been required settings, like calibrating an instrument before use.

Even the timing itself was preparation. Just as astronomy dictated when the knives would fall, preparation dictated how the victim was made ready. Rituals did not allow for improvisation. Everything was scheduled: the fasts, the baths, the painting, the parading, the building of altars, the marking of days on oracle bones. Sacrifice was not reactive—it was premeditated, planned with the precision of a service manual.

Taken together, these preparatory rites strip away the illusion of cultural independence. Whether in the jungles of Mesoamerica, the deserts of Egypt, the plains of India, or the river valleys of China, the pattern is consistent: consecrate, purify, adorn, align, schedule. Each act transformed the ordinary into the sacred, converting flesh into offering. Preparation was the first gear of the machine, the setting of dials before the main sequence. It was the phase in which victims and priests alike were tuned to the covenant, readying the fuel for transfer.

Phase 2: Sacrifice

If preparation was calibration, sacrifice itself was ignition. It was the moment when the latent potential of the victim was converted into the fuel of the covenant. Here, across the ancient world, the rituals converge most clearly. Despite vast distances and cultural differences, the choreography of death reveals a mechanical sameness: victims bound, positioned, dispatched in ways that maximized the offering and dramatized the transfer. Sacrifice was not random killing. It was precise, efficient, and theatrical, as though humanity had been instructed in how to flip the switch that delivered life-force to the gods.

In Mesoamerica, the act was staged in full view of thousands. The Aztec capital of Tenochtitlan witnessed sacrifices on the broad summit of the Templo Mayor, where captives were laid across the techcatl, the sacrificial stone. Four priests pinned the limbs, while a fifth wielded the tecpatl, the flint blade sharpened to a translucent edge. With one swift motion, the chest was opened and the heart pulled free, still quivering in the priest's hand. The organ was lifted toward the sun before being placed into a cuauhxicalli vessel carved with predator imagery. The efficiency is striking: the chest cavity opened in seconds, the heart removed intact. Bernal Díaz del Castillo, a Spanish conquistador who witnessed such rites, described the speed and precision with astonishment, noting how the priests "knew their craft well" (*The Conquest of New Spain*, 1568). This was not improvised brutality but a refined technique, practiced and repeated until flawless.

Variations abounded, but the principle remained. At some Aztec festivals, captives were shot with volleys of arrows, each shaft piercing in unison to create what Sahagún's codices describe as a "flowering of arrows" (*Florentine Codex, Book II*). The spectacle multiplied the sacrifice, producing not one but dozens of heartbeats fading at once, a chorus of deaths offered simultaneously. Elsewhere captives were decapitated, their skulls mounted on tzompantli racks—rows of bleached bone that transformed the plaza into an abacus of life-force spent. Each method had its timing, its symbolism, but all were parts of the same sequence: release of blood, exposure of heart, collection of energy.

Among the Maya, sacrifice could be more intimate but no less mechanical. Captives were sometimes hurled into cenotes—sacred water-filled sinkholes—at Chichén Itzá, their bodies descending into the underworld waters. Archaeological dredging of the Sacred Cenote has recovered human bones alongside jade, gold, and obsidian offerings. Diego de Landa, a 16th-century bishop of Yucatán, reported that victims were often pulled back from the cenote alive, their near-drowning itself an offering before final dispatch. Here the choreography extended the release, drawing it out in stages. Maya texts also describe bloodletting by rulers themselves: tongues pierced with stingray spines, cords drawn through wounds to produce streams of blood collected on bark paper. That paper, once soaked, was burned, its smoke the visible carrier of the offering. Whether the heart of a captive or the tongue of a king, the release was the same: blood leaving the body to be transferred upward.

Egypt provides a different but parallel picture. Animal sacrifices, particularly oxen, were dispatched with ritual efficiency. Tomb reliefs show butchers cutting throats, catching blood in basins, and laying carcasses on altars in a sequence that reads like an instruction manual. In some cases, smaller animals—geese, ducks, fish—were decapitated or gutted in orderly rows, their blood and viscera collected for presentation. Human sacrifice, though rarer in later dynasties, is evident in the subsidiary burials of Abydos, where scores of attendants were dispatched at once to accompany a pharaoh. The precision of mass death is unmistakable: graves cut in straight lines, victims interred simultaneously, their lives extinguished in one coordinated act. For the Egyptians, as for the Aztecs, sacrifice was not random violence but an orchestrated phase, performed with consistency and regularity.

In Vedic India, the sacrificial moment took its most complex form in the Ashvamedha, the horse sacrifice. After a year of ritual roaming and purification, the horse was suffocated, its body dismembered, and each part offered into the fire with mantras assigning limbs to specific gods. The ritual reads like a disassembly manual: head for the dawn, eyes for the sun, breath for the wind. The fire acted as the conduit, carrying each portion upward in smoke. The killing was prolonged and segmented, transforming one victim into dozens of offerings. This choreography of partition echoes the Aztec's multiple arrow-piercings or the Maya's staged drownings—the same principle of maximizing release, delivering not one but many pulses of life-force to the gods.

Shang China adds yet another dimension: scale. Oracle bones record sacrifices of "100 cattle, 50 sheep, 20 men" on a single occasion. Archaeological excavations at Anyang have revealed mass pits containing dozens of human victims, often decapitated or bound. Bronze blades and axes, purpose-built for sacrifice, were used with chilling regularity. Victims were buried in rows or circles, sometimes surrounding the tomb of a king, their placement too precise to be anything but choreographed. The Shang ritual machine operated on bulk release: life-force delivered not one at a time but in shipments, like consignments of fuel.

What unites these disparate examples is the same mechanical logic. Victims are not killed randomly. They are bound, painted, positioned, and dispatched with ritual precision. Instruments are standardized: flint knives in Mesoamerica, bronze blades in China, butcher's knives in Egypt, fire in India. The sequence is repeated so often it becomes reflexive, the muscle memory of priesthoods who act less like improvising shamans than like technicians following a manual. The gestures—lifting the heart to the sun, pouring blood into basins, burning flesh in fire—are the switches and levers of the machine, actions that guarantee transmission.

The sensory environment reinforces the mechanical sequence. Drums beat in steady rhythm as victims ascend stairways. Conch shells or trumpets blast at the moment of death. Incense smoke mingles with blood, creating a synesthetic atmosphere where sound, scent, and sight converge. The ritual machine is not silent; it is noisy, deliberate, a sensory overload that marks the transition. Spanish chroniclers at Tenochtitlan described hearing the drums from miles away, their relentless pounding signaling to the city that the covenant was being serviced. In Vedic sacrifices, priests chanted thousands of verses in precise meter, their voices rising with the flames. In Shang ceremonies, bronze bells and drums punctuated the killings. The choreography extended to sound itself, which marked the timing of the act.

From the covenant perspective, this obsession with precision suggests an external demand. If the gods required fuel in the form of blood, they may also have required it delivered in specific formats— hearts removed intact, blood collected unspilled, smoke released in measured columns. The rituals look mechanical because they were fulfilling specifications, much as modern machines must receive the correct voltage or fuel type. A botched sacrifice was more than a failed performance; it was a failed delivery.

Even the public nature of many sacrifices supports this reading. The presence of thousands of witnesses in Tenochtitlan, the mass pits at Anyang, the processions at Karnak—these ensured not only social cohesion but covenantal compliance. If the gods demanded regular servicing, then it had to be visible, verifiable, undeniable. The machine was not hidden in a back room but operated on the stage of the city, so that the entire population could testify: yes, the debt has been paid.

The written and material record underscores this mechanical logic. Diego de Landa, in his *Relación de las Cosas de Yucatán* (1566), described the ritual of throwing captives into the Sacred Cenote at Chichén Itzá, noting that some victims were pulled out alive to deliver oracles before being killed—a detail that archaeologists later confirmed by recovering both male and female remains from the cenote, many bearing trauma consistent with drowning or sacrifice (Coggins, *Handbook of Middle American Indians*, 1975). Murals at Bonampak and lintels at Yaxchilán, analyzed by Mary Miller and Karl

Taube in *The Gods and Symbols of Ancient Mexico and the Maya* (1993), depict rulers drawing blood from their tongues and genitals, timing these acts to celestial cycles. These images demonstrate that elite self-sacrifice was no less codified than the mass killings of captives; both were parts of the same machinery.

In Teotihuacan, excavations by Saburo Sugiyama revealed more than 200 bound and executed individuals interred beneath the Temple of the Feathered Serpent (*Human Sacrifice, Militarism, and Rulership*, 2005). The careful arrangement of bodies—many with hands tied behind their backs, some decapitated, others accompanied by weapons and ornaments—shows that the deaths were not aftermath but inauguration, activating the temple at its dedication. Similarly, Shang oracle bone inscriptions provide written evidence of scale and scheduling, recording that "ten men" or "hundreds of cattle" were offered on appointed days (Keightley, *Sources of Shang History*, 1978). Archaeological excavations at Anyang have confirmed these records, uncovering pits filled with sacrificed humans and animals, buried in deliberate patterns around royal tombs.

Taken together, these sources—eyewitness reports, murals, inscriptions, and archaeological finds—affirm that sacrifice was not haphazard violence but structured, repeatable process. The accounts converge across continents and centuries, documenting the same sequence of preparation, dispatch, and transmission. In light of such evidence, the sacrificial act appears less a ritual metaphor than the middle gear of a global machine.

Sacrifice, then, was the ignition of the ritual machine, the moment when calibrated preparation met orchestrated release. It was a mechanical phase, as consistent across continents as the gears of a clock. Different tools, different costumes, but the same logic: bind, position, kill, collect. The switch was flipped, the energy released, the covenant serviced.

Phase 3: Transmission

If preparation calibrated the offering and sacrifice released its essence, transmission was the phase that completed the circuit. The blood, breath, or life-force had to be moved—delivered through a medium to those unseen powers who demanded it. Across the world, this final step took strikingly similar forms. Vessels collected, fires consumed, smoke carried, basins drained, burials deposited. Each acted as conduit, ensuring that the covenant was not left hanging but fulfilled. In covenant terms, this was the discharge phase, the moment when the energy released at the altar was transported into the gods' domain.

The Aztec cuauhxicalli are the most explicit example. These massive stone bowls, often carved in the form of jaguars or eagles, were designed to receive human hearts. Archaeologists have uncovered dozens of them, some large enough to hold several liters of liquid. Their form was not symbolic but functional. Sahagún's *Florentine Codex* describes how, after the heart was torn from the chest, it was placed into the vessel, sometimes alongside offerings of maize or jade. The vessel acted as collector and transmitter, a repository that concentrated the essence of the offering. From there, priests burned incense or poured libations, completing the transfer. The predator imagery—jaguar jaws, eagle talons—underscored the idea that the vessel was itself an intermediary, a divine animal consuming the heart on behalf of the gods.

Blood channels at the Templo Mayor reinforce this logic. Excavations reveal that carved grooves ran along the sacrificial stone and down the stairways, allowing blood to flow visibly toward the plaza below. Sahagún's informants noted that the streams of blood were not hidden but displayed, coursing down in rivulets that the people could see. In some ceremonies, the blood was mixed with maize dough to create tzoalli, a sacramental paste offered to the gods and sometimes consumed by participants. Here blood became both visible river and edible medium, bridging divine and human consumption. Transmission was not only vertical to the gods but horizontal within the community, binding people together in shared covenant.

Egypt presents an almost mirror image. Reliefs from Karnak and Luxor depict priests pouring libations into carved basins, the liquid then funneled through channels cut into the stone floors. These channels directed offerings—milk, beer, wine, and occasionally blood—toward underground receptacles or outward into the Nile. The Pyramid Texts speak of *"pouring the red and the white"* to nourish the ka of the gods. The basins themselves survive, their interiors worn smooth by centuries of ritual use. Excavations at Saqqara have revealed altars with drain-holes leading to subterranean jars, suggesting that offerings were collected and stored or allowed to seep into the earth. Just as Mesoamerican blood flowed down stairways, Egyptian libations flowed down channels: in both cases, the architecture acted as a pump, moving fluid from human hands into divine custody.

In Vedic India, fire became the conduit. The meticulously constructed altars were not passive receptacles but combustion engines. Grain, ghee, milk, soma, and occasionally blood or animals were placed into the flames, accompanied by mantras directing them upward. The Rigveda calls Agni, the fire god, "the mouth of the gods," through which offerings are consumed (*Rigveda 1.1*). The idea is unmistakable: the fire was a digestive organ, transforming matter into smoke and carrying it heavenward. Ritual texts describe how the smoke was inhaled by the devas, just as humans inhale fragrance. In covenant terms, fire was the transmission line, converting physical offerings into a form receivable by nonhuman beings.

Shang China again displays chilling parallels. Bronze basins and ding vessels, found in tombs and ceremonial pits, bear residue consistent with animal blood and wine. Oracle bones record sacrifices in which blood was poured into the earth or onto altars, often in conjunction with human burials. At Anyang, archaeologists uncovered pits where victims were interred alongside bronzes, jade, and oracle bones—deposits that functioned as packages of offerings. Transmission here was downward, into the underworld or into the ancestors' realm. Yet the logic is identical: a conduit was required, whether fire, basin, or pit. The essence had to be transported, and the vessel—stone, bronze, or earth—was the device.

Other cultures elaborated the same principle with creative variations. At Chichén Itzá, victims were hurled into the Sacred Cenote, their bodies themselves becoming the offering, water the conduit. At Teotihuacan, the tunnel beneath the Temple of the Feathered Serpent contained pools of liquid mercury, pyrite mirrors, and miniature mountains, creating an artificial underworld into which offerings were deposited. Transmission here was both visual and chemical: mercury reflected torchlight like rivers of silver, symbolizing the cosmic waters that carried the offering into the earth. At Angkor Wat, moats and channels linked the temple to a hydraulic system that surrounded the city. When blood or libations were poured into the temple basins, they mingled with water that coursed through the moats, dramatizing the covenant on a grand scale. The waters were both irrigation and interface, sustaining crops while carrying offerings into a cosmic ocean.

The sensory environment of transmission reinforced its role. Smoke rising in curls from incense burners. Blood pouring down stairs, glistening in the sun. Water carrying crimson streaks through channels. Sound accompanied the transfer: chants timed to libations, drums marking the moment the heart was placed in the vessel, bells ringing as smoke rose. Transmission was not silent. It was meant to be perceived, to assure both humans and gods that the covenant had been serviced.

The covenant reading clarifies why such conduits were necessary. If the gods required biological material—blood, marrow, tissue fluids—then simply killing was not enough. The material had to be collected, concentrated, and directed. Vessels prevented waste, fire converted matter into volatile form, basins ensured collection and redirection. The similarities across cultures suggest that the gods provided not only the demand but the schematic: "catch here, pour there, burn this, bury that." Priests did not invent these machines; they maintained them.

Scholars who prefer symbolic readings emphasize the metaphorical roles of these conduits: fire as transformation, water as purification, basins as cosmic wombs. But the literalism of the practices is hard to ignore. Why carve channels if the liquid was only metaphorical? Why pour blood into jars and seal them if the gods required only intention? Why hurl bodies into cenotes or bury victims in pits unless the deposit itself was the point? The insistence on physical conduits speaks less to symbolism and more to utility. These were delivery systems.

Even the scale of the conduits reflects this. The cuauhxicalli were massive, too large for symbolic tokens alone. The moats of Angkor stretched kilometers, too vast for simple allegory. The mercury tunnels of Teotihuacan required engineering effort disproportionate to mere myth. These features make more sense if read as functional parts of a machine: visible, durable, theatrical ways of channeling life-force from humans to gods.

Transmission was also the phase most open to error, and cultures treated it with corresponding gravity. In Vedic India, a misplaced brick in the fire altar or a mispronounced mantra could render the sacrifice void. In Egypt, a blemished animal's blood was considered polluted and unsuitable for collection. In Mesoamerica, if blood failed to flow properly, it was considered a sign of divine displeasure. The anxiety over proper transfer suggests that the process was believed to matter literally—that unless the life-force reached its destination, the covenant remained unpaid.

In covenant terms, transmission was the final gear of the ritual machine. Preparation tuned the offering, sacrifice released it, and transmission delivered it. Without this last step, the process was incomplete. The gods were not imagined to sense intention but to require delivery through specific conduits. This is why basins, channels, fires, and burials recur with such monotony across cultures. They are the infrastructure of the covenant, the pipelines of an economy in which blood was currency and ritual the transfer system.

Conclusion: Servicing the Covenant

When the fragments of preparation, sacrifice, and transmission are set side by side, the illusion of cultural independence dissolves. What emerges instead is a global schematic—a three-phase engine designed to harness human life-force and deliver it to powers that demanded it. The Aztec cuauhxicalli, the Egyptian libation basin, the Vedic fire altar, the Shang bronze ding: these are not random vessels, but interchangeable components of a ritual machine. Each part carried out a specific role, and together they formed a system so consistent across hemispheres that coincidence strains belief.

The consistency is not merely structural but temporal. The same sequence—calibration, release, delivery—repeats everywhere. Victims prepared with paint, fasting, or adornment. The act of killing staged with precision, timed to chants and drums. The product—blood, hearts, smoke, bones—channeled into fire, water, or earth. In modern terms, one might call it a "supply chain," moving raw material from source to consumer. But the ancients knew it as ritual. They called it covenant.

From the covenant perspective, the ritual machine is not a metaphor but a technology. It functioned like any other engineered system, with inputs, processes, and outputs. Inputs: the lives of humans and animals, prepared and consecrated. Processes: the sacrificial act, choreographed for maximum efficiency. Outputs: the transmission of vital essence through conduits to nonhuman recipients. The repetition of these steps across thousands of years and multiple continents suggests not only shared human instinct but shared instruction. Priesthoods appear less like inventors than like operators of machinery handed down to them.

Mainstream anthropology often interprets sacrifice as symbolic theater. René Girard saw it as a way to channel social violence, Mircea Eliade as a re-enactment of cosmic myth. These interpretations have value, but they stop short of explaining the mechanical precision of the acts themselves. If sacrifice were only symbolic, why the obsessive attention to vessels, channels, and timing? Why did so many cultures engineer permanent structures to repeat the process with clockwork regularity? Symbolism could have been satisfied with gesture. Instead, we find systems.

The image of the ritual machine also clarifies why sacrifice endured long after its original operators may have departed. Once priesthoods learned the sequence, they could replicate it without understanding its full purpose, much as technicians might continue to service a device whose original engineers are gone. Over time, what may have begun as literal delivery devolved into symbolic reenactment, but the form was retained. Even when human sacrifice was replaced by animal offerings or symbolic substitutes, the three-phase structure endured. The machine kept running, though on lower settings.

The cost of servicing the machine was immense. Victims' blood was the obvious price, but the greater toll was the mobilization of entire populations. Building the altars, hauling the stones, training the priesthood, rehearsing the chants—all of it consumed the lifeblood of societies. Sacrifice was not confined to the altar but embedded in the very fabric of life. Labor itself was sacrificial, generations pouring their strength into monuments designed to ensure the covenant was renewed. In this sense, the machine was total: it harvested not only the victims' blood but the energy of entire civilizations.

When seen this way, the ritual machine becomes one of the most sobering legacies of human antiquity. It suggests that humanity's earliest great works—the pyramids, temples, processions—were not spontaneous expressions of devotion but infrastructural obligations. They were service stations on a global network, each one maintaining the same covenant. The blueprints were consistent, the operators obedient, and the recipients invisible.

And this raises the question we must carry forward: who built the machine? If sacrifice was symbolic invention, then its mechanical consistency is a mystery. But if it was the result of nonhuman instruction—if emissaries once walked among priesthoods and issued specifications—then the pattern makes sense. The gods of myth, the feathered serpents and winged men, were not mere fictions but supervisors, ensuring that the machinery of blood operated to their requirements.

In the chapters that follow, we will explore what those requirements may have been. The consistency of vessels and conduits suggests not symbolic meaning but biological utility: blood and tissue as fuel, marrow and plasma as feedstock. The covenant may not have been about pleasing distant deities at all, but about sustaining nonhuman beings in immediate need. The ritual machine, in that light, was less religion than logistics—a delivery system engineered to keep recipients alive.

Civilization itself may have been the price humanity paid to operate the machine. Cities, calendars, priesthoods, architecture—all were organized around sacrifice. Without the covenant, these systems might not have arisen so suddenly or so universally. With it, they became inevitable. Humanity's first great achievement was not literacy or metallurgy, but the building of a machine that turned its own lifeblood into tribute.

The ritual machine reveals a sobering truth: we were not merely worshippers. We were operators. The altars and basins, the fires and moats, the chants and drums—all were levers and gears in a global system designed to keep the covenant alive. Whether we understood its true purpose or not, we kept it running for millennia. And in the silence of those basins and tunnels today, the memory of that machinery lingers, whispering of debts once paid in blood.

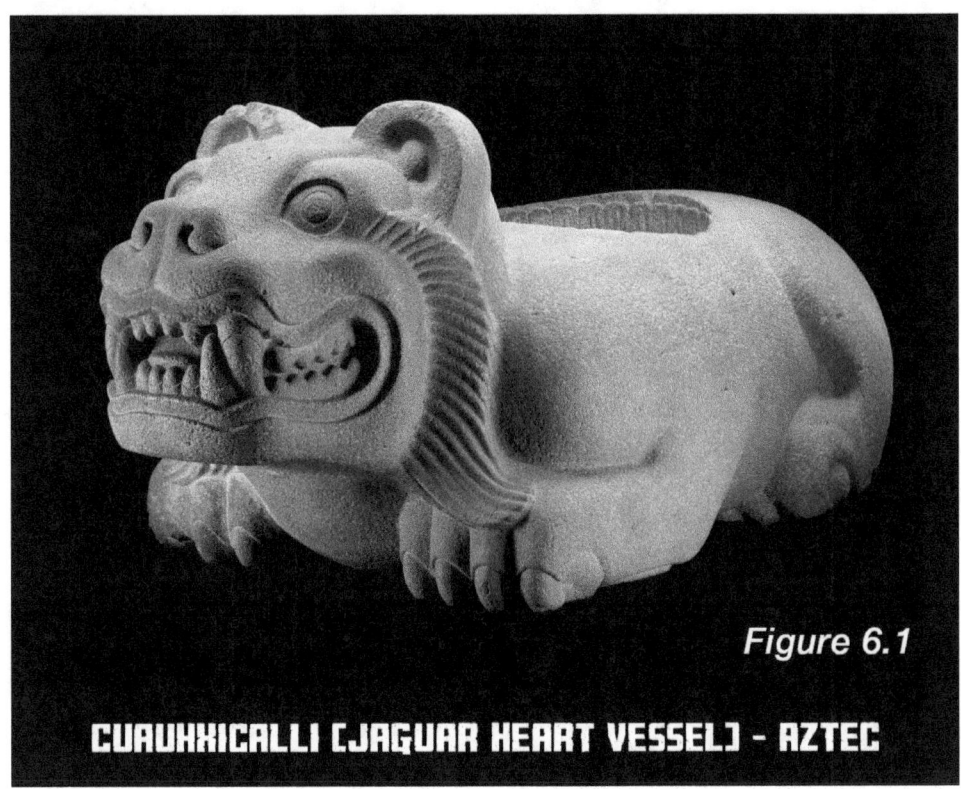

Figure 6.1

CUAUHXICALLI [JAGUAR HEART VESSEL] - AZTEC

Cuauhxicalli (Jaguar Heart Vessel), Aztec, Central Mexico (ca. 15th–16th c. CE). Carved stone container used to receive human hearts torn from sacrificial victims atop the Templo Mayor. Shaped as a jaguar, the predator doubled as divine intermediary, consuming on behalf of the gods. The cuauhxicalli functioned as a ritual component of the sacrificial machine—collector, concentrator, and transmitter of human life-force into the covenant economy of blood.

SACRED CENOTE, CHICHÉN ITZÁ, YUCATÁN - MEXICO

Sacred Cenote, Chichén Itzá, Yucatán, Mexico (ca. 9th–16th c. CE).
Natural sinkhole used by the Maya for ritual offerings of gold, jade, incense, and human victims, cast into the waters as gifts to the rain god Chaac and the underworld. Archaeological dredging has recovered bones alongside artifacts, confirming the cenote's role as a conduit of transmission in the ritual machine — a watery gateway delivering sacrifice from the surface world to the divine below.

Figure 6.3

BRONZE DING VESSEL - SHANG OR ZHOU DYNASTY

Bronze Ding Vessel, Shang or Zhou Dynasty, China (ca. 1200–771 BCE).
Tripod bronze cauldron used in ritual sacrifices to hold blood, wine, or cooked offerings. Such vessels were buried in tombs or presented at altars, serving as containers and transmitters of sacrificial essence. The ding symbolized authority and covenant, functioning as a component of the ritual machine: collector, preserver, and conduit of offerings into the realm of gods and ancestors.

Figure 6.4

LIBATION BASIN WITH HATHOR HEAD - EGYPT

Libation Basin with Hathor Head, Egypt (ca. 1500–500 BCE).
Carved stone basin used in ritual offerings of blood, wine, milk, and water, often poured into channels that carried libations into the earth or toward underground receptacles. The Hathor-head motif links the vessel to nourishment, fertility, and divine sustenance. As part of the ritual machine, the libation basin functioned as a conduit of transmission—collecting, channeling, and delivering offerings to the gods, ensuring the covenant was fulfilled through liquid flow.

7

TWO HEMISPHERES, MULTIPLE COVENANTS

Introduction: A Global Network

By the time we step back from the monuments, vessels, and rituals already examined, the pattern is undeniable. Civilizations divided by oceans and millennia nevertheless carried out the same procedures: they raised stone mountains aligned to the stars, they consecrated victims, they spilled blood in channels or fires, and they transmitted that essence through carefully engineered conduits. The names were different, the myths local, the costumes colorful and varied. But the machinery was the same.

If all this were invention—if the Egyptians, Maya, Sumerians, and Chinese each invented sacrifice independently—then the convergences would be few and superficial. Instead, they are deep and structural. Not just pyramids, but pyramids aligned to Orion. Not just altars, but altars with channels to carry blood. Not just myths of gods, but gods who drink, who feed, who demand repayment in life-force. The similarities extend beyond coincidence and into choreography, as though a single set of instructions was distributed to multiple peoples, each adjusting the vocabulary but retaining the blueprint.

And yet, when we look closer, the covenant is not identical everywhere. The same machine, yes—but calibrated differently depending on geography, culture, and perhaps even biology. The Old World covenants, stretching from Egypt to China, emphasize continuity. They bind dynasties, secure cosmic order, and link priesthoods to eternal cycles. They are covenants of hierarchy, where sacrifice reinforces kingship and stability. The New World covenants, by contrast, pulse with urgency. The Maya bled themselves to renew the gods. The Aztec cut open captives to keep the sun in the sky. The Inca buried children atop mountains so that rains would fall and harvests succeed. Here, sacrifice was not about maintaining order in the abstract. It was about keeping the universe alive day by day.

Why such a divergence? If the source of the covenant was truly global, why not uniformity? The answer may lie in optimization. Just as a single empire will grant different charters to different provinces, the gods appear to have franchised their system, adapting contracts to the conditions of each hemisphere. Where blood types and lineages made direct harvest more viable, sacrifice leaned heavily on humans. Where populations carried little of the desired genetic profile, animal offerings, symbolic rites, or dynastic breeding programs took precedence. The outcome was not one covenant, but multiple covenants, bound together by principle but diverse in execution.

The distinction is starkest when one compares texts and traditions. In Egypt, the Pyramid Texts assure the king that he consumes gods and is sustained by offerings, all in the name of cosmic order. In Mesopotamia, temple inscriptions treat blood as wine for the gods' banquet, a proof of loyalty to the city's divine patrons. In India, the Vedic fire altars channel offerings upward as recalibrations of universal law, yajna as the mechanism of stability. In China, oracle bones and tomb pits speak of feeding ancestors and rulers to maintain dynastic legitimacy. Each Old World expression turns sacrifice into a stabilizer, tying people to hierarchy and cosmos in a contract of order.

Contrast that with the New World. *The Dresden Codex* records Chaac, the Maya rain god, receiving human blood explicitly as "his food." The Aztec *Florentine Codex* describes the heart as "precious eagle-cactus fruit" that nourishes the sun. In Andean capacocha ceremonies, children were prepared, adorned, marched up mountains, and killed at the summits—offerings delivered directly to sky and earth to renew the fertility of the land. These are not covenants of stability but of survival. The gods of the Americas were not content with occasional sacrifices at coronations or funerals. They demanded blood daily, urgently, ravenously.

From the covenant perspective, this bifurcation makes sense. If humanity was indeed servicing a program directed by nonhuman powers, then different regions could be assigned different functions. The Old World contracts emphasized order, kingship, and continuity —perhaps reflecting a priority on managing bloodlines and long-term stability. The New World contracts emphasized sustenance and immediacy—reflecting a priority on direct nutritional harvest, the feeding of gods who demanded life to fuel cosmic processes.

The emissaries remind us that despite the variations, the instructions came from the same source. Feathered serpents in Mesoamerica echo nāgas in India and uraei in Egypt. Bird-men in Maya murals echo Apkallu in Assyria and Garuda in Hindu lore. The so-called "handbag" motif, carried by winged figures in Mesopotamia, appears carved on stelae in the Americas. These were not local inventions. They were common symbols, common tools, carried across hemispheres as signatures of a single system. The differences lie not in origin, but in implementation.

It is tempting to imagine priesthoods as inventors, experimenting with ritual as a form of religious creativity. But the degree of consistency points to another role. They were operators, regional managers servicing a system whose blueprint they did not design. Their gods were not metaphorical ideals but supervisors, enforcing contracts that required payment in blood. And just as imperial governors adapt central policies to local conditions, so too the covenant was diversified: dynastic and hierarchical in the Old World, urgent and apocalyptic in the New.

What emerges, then, is not a single covenant but multiple covenants—local adaptations of a global program. In the Old World, the emphasis fell on order, kingship, and cosmic harmony. In the New World, the focus shifted to sustenance, renewal, and survival. Both were faithful to the same principle: blood as payment, ritual as machinery, architecture as interface. The divergence lay in emphasis, and that difference may itself reveal the priorities of those who demanded the offerings.

By tracing these hemispheric expressions, we step closer to understanding the covenant not as myth but as system. It was not uniform because it did not need to be. It was diversified because diversity made it stronger, more adaptable, more resilient across geography and time. The same gods, the same emissaries, the same demands—but many contracts, signed in blood on every continent.

The Old World Covenant

If we look first to the Old World, sacrifice is everywhere linked to kingship, continuity, and the maintenance of cosmic order. These were not covenants of daily desperation but of dynastic anchoring, where blood offerings supported both the throne and the heavens. The Old World covenant presents itself as deliberate, structured, and hierarchical. Kingship was the hinge, and sacrifice the bolt that kept it secured.

Egypt: Sacrifice and the Afterlife of Kings

In Egypt, the pharaoh was no mere ruler but the living embodiment of Horus, destined to become Osiris in death. To maintain this divine kingship, offerings were constant. In the First Dynasty, retainers were buried alive alongside rulers at Abydos, numbering in the hundreds. Sir Flinders Petrie's excavations in the early 20th century revealed rows of subsidiary graves, each carefully aligned around the pharaoh's tomb (Petrie, *Abydos*, 1902). These retainers were not honored in death but expended, their lives cut short to serve as attendants in the king's eternal household.

As Egyptian ritual evolved, the literal killing of retainers gave way to symbolic substitutes—figurines, servant statues, animal offerings—but the logic persisted. Sacrifice in Egypt was never about appeasing gods in isolation. It was about sustaining Ma'at—the balance of cosmos and society—through the pharaoh's mediation. The Pyramid Texts make the relationship explicit: *"Your bread is the blood of the gods; you eat the red and drink the white"* (Faulkner, *The Ancient Egyptian Pyramid Texts,* 1969). In such phrases, food, blood, and cosmic balance blur together. The offering is both literal sustenance and metaphysical guarantee. Without it, the divine order falters.

Mesopotamia: Sacrifice as Civic Loyalty

Where Egypt tied sacrifice to kingship, Mesopotamia tethered it to the city-state. Each Sumerian city had its patron god—Enlil in Nippur, Inanna in Uruk, Enki in Eridu—and the people's loyalty was measured by their offerings. Temples functioned not just as religious centers but as economic engines. Excavations at Ur and Lagash show storerooms packed with sacrificial remains—bones, ashes, blood-stained altars (Woolley, *Ur of the Chaldees,* 1934). A Sumerian hymn declares: "May the blood be poured for the gods as wine for the feast" (Black, *The Literature of Ancient Sumer,* 2004). The blood covenant here was explicit: no offering, no favor.

Mesopotamian sacrifice often involved animals, but humans were not excluded. The Royal Cemetery of Ur (c. 2600 BCE) yielded dozens of retainer burials, where guards and attendants were interred with their rulers, much like at Abydos. Cuneiform tablets also record offerings made during times of crisis—epidemics, famines, wars—where children or captives were killed to avert disaster (Hallo, *The World's Oldest Literature,* 2010). In Mesopotamia, blood was less about daily cosmic renewal, as it was in the New World, and more about sealing loyalty between people, city, and gods. The covenant bound not just the ruler but the entire civic body.

Vedic India: Fire as Conduit of Covenant

In Vedic India, sacrifice centered not on tombs or temples but on fire. The yajna rites, detailed in the Śatapatha Brāhmaṇa and Rigveda hymns, were complex ceremonies in which offerings of ghee, grain, soma, and sometimes blood were poured into flames that carried them upward to the gods. Fire altars had to be built with perfect geometry—squares, falcon-shapes, or mandalas of bricks precisely placed to align with cosmic order (Staal, *Agni: The Vedic Ritual of the Fire Altar*, 1983).

What made Vedic sacrifice unique was its philosophy. The offerings were not only sustenance but recalibrations of the universe. The Rigveda describes sacrifice as the very mechanism by which the cosmos was first established: "*By sacrifice the gods sacrificed to sacrifice*" (RV 10.90, Griffith, 1896). In other words, ritual killing and offering were woven into creation itself. Without yajna, the cosmos unraveled. Blood sacrifices were less frequent than in Egypt or Mesopotamia, but they did occur. The Aśvamedha, the horse sacrifice, involved ritual slaughter of a consecrated stallion, its blood symbolizing both fertility and sovereignty (Altekar, The Position of Women in Hindu Civilization, 1938). Here again, kingship and cosmic stability intersect.

China: Ancestors, Kings, and the Mandate of Heaven

In China, the Shang dynasty (c. 1600–1046 BCE) practiced sacrifice on a massive scale. Oracle bone inscriptions record human and animal offerings made to royal ancestors and to Shangdi, the high god. One bone reads starkly: "We sacrifice ten men to Shangdi for a good harvest" (Keightley, *Sources of Shang History*, 1978). Excavations at Anyang have uncovered vast pits filled with decapitated captives, chariots, and animal remains, all buried as offerings to secure dynastic prosperity.

For the Shang kings, sacrifice was a tool of legitimacy. By feeding ancestors and gods with blood, rulers claimed the Mandate of Heaven—the divine approval that justified their reign. This logic continued into the Zhou dynasty, though blood sacrifices shifted gradually toward symbolic offerings of grain and wine. Still, the principle remained: without offerings, the Mandate lapsed, and rulers risked overthrow. Sacrifice was less about daily cosmic renewal and more about dynastic continuity, binding the fate of the state to ritual slaughter.

A Unified Pattern of Continuity

Despite differences in detail, a unifying pattern emerges in the Old World. Egypt, Mesopotamia, India, and China all linked sacrifice to kingship, dynasty, or cosmic stability. The offerings were not demanded randomly but were structured into statecraft. Pharaohs, lugal-kings, rajas, and emperors alike used blood to bind themselves to powers greater than themselves. The covenant in the Old World was not about urgent sustenance but about continuity—about making sure that the sun rose in order, that dynasties endured, that cities remained under divine favor.

In each case, ritual was bureaucratized. Egypt trained entire priestly orders to maintain offerings daily. Mesopotamia recorded sacrifices in cuneiform ledgers. India codified yajna in exhaustive ritual texts. China inscribed sacrificial acts onto bones and bronzes as permanent records. This bureaucratic fixation suggests that sacrifice was not a matter of local imagination but of compliance with external instruction. The gods—or their emissaries—had demanded order, and priesthoods ensured it was supplied.

From the covenant perspective, the Old World represents one axis of the program: stability. Where O-negative blood was rare, as it was in Asia, human life may have been less useful as direct nourishment and more valuable for genetic continuity. Where it was present, as in Mesopotamia and Egypt, human blood was used but tied to hierarchy rather than urgency. The machine operated at a slower rhythm, reinforcing dynasties instead of feeding daily hunger.

The Old World covenant thus offers one half of the global equation. It demonstrates that sacrifice could be adapted to emphasize continuity, legitimacy, and stability, binding people to rulers and rulers to gods. But when we cross the ocean to the New World, we find the covenant transformed. There, urgency replaces continuity, immediacy replaces hierarchy, and blood is demanded not just for kings or ancestors but for the survival of the cosmos itself.

The New World Covenant

Across the ocean, sacrifice took on a different face. If the Old World covenant emphasized continuity—dynasties secured, cosmic order upheld—the New World covenant demanded urgency. Here, the gods were not abstract guarantors of stability but immediate consumers, dependent on offerings to keep the machinery of the cosmos running. The distinction is sharp: in the Old World, sacrifice underwrote kingship; in the New World, it sustained creation itself.

The Maya: Blood as Cosmic Renewal

In the Maya lowlands, sacrifice was inseparable from astronomy. Priests tracked the cycles of Venus with astonishing precision, charting its 584-day synodic period until they could predict its risings and settings to the day (Aveni, *Skywatchers of Ancient Mexico*, 2001). These celestial markers were not curiosities but deadlines. Wars were launched, captives taken, and sacrifices performed in synchrony with the planet's phases.

Royal bloodletting was central. Reliefs from Yaxchilán and Bonampak depict kings and queens piercing tongues and genitals with stingray spines, their blood collected on bark paper and burned as offering. The smoke rose skyward, carrying life-force to the gods. At Bonampak, murals show captives bound and awaiting death beneath banners marked with Venus glyphs (Miller & Taube, *The Gods and Symbols of Ancient Mexico and the Maya*, 1993). The message is clear: bloodletting and sacrifice were timed to celestial rhythms. The covenant here was not symbolic but scheduled.

The Popol Vuh, the K'iche' Maya creation epic, preserves the theology: the gods made humanity to "nourish and sustain them." The first attempts failed—mud men dissolved, wooden men had no blood. Only when maize-flesh was combined with blood did humanity succeed. The story encodes the principle: blood was the ingredient the gods required, the nutrient without which creation faltered.

The Aztec: Debt to the Sun

If the Maya saw sacrifice as cosmic recalibration, the Aztec made it an economy of debt. The very word nextlahualli means "payment" or "debt settlement." In their worldview, the sun had sacrificed itself to rise in the Fifth Age, and humans were bound in reciprocity to repay that debt with blood. Without continual offerings, the sun would falter and the world would collapse.

At the Templo Mayor in Tenochtitlan, rituals unfolded on a colossal scale. Spanish chroniclers like Bernardino de Sahagún and Diego Durán describe festivals where hundreds, even thousands, of captives were killed in a single day, their bodies hurled down the temple stairs while priests raised still-beating hearts skyward. The cuauhxicalli—stone vessels carved as jaguars or eagles—received the hearts, their surfaces darkened with blood (Sahagún, *Florentine Codex, Book II*). The symbolism was explicit: just as eagles and jaguars consumed flesh, so too did the gods consume blood.

This was no occasional rite. The Aztec waged "flower wars," battles fought explicitly to capture prisoners for sacrifice. Warfare itself was ritualized, less about conquest than supply. Captives were currency, their bodies harvested to feed the gods. The *Florentine Codex* records the priests' rationale: "If we do not offer them food, they will die of hunger... and then it will be night forever." The stakes were absolute.

The Aztec were not the only Mesoamerican culture to center sacrifice on blood and hearts. In Oaxaca, the Zapotec civilization (c. 500 BCE–900 CE) left behind ceramic urns that depict gods grasping human hearts or victims with open chests. Archaeologists working at Monte Albán uncovered temples where bloodletting instruments and sacrificial altars were discovered alongside these urns (Marcus & Flannery, *Zapotec Civilization*, 1996). Unlike the Aztec cuauhxicalli, which served as literal bowls, Zapotec urns symbolized the act itself, embedding the covenant into funerary contexts. This suggests that sacrifice was not only public theater but also private devotion, enacted in tombs as a way of sustaining both ancestors and gods. Captives appear to have been taken from rival groups in Oaxaca's valleys, their deaths serving as offerings for agricultural fertility and dynastic legitimacy. The Zapotec record underscores that heart extraction and blood as "precious water" were not innovations of the Mexica alone, but part of a much older covenantal framework.

The Inca and the Andes: Sacrifice at the Edge of the Sky

Further south, the Inca empire practiced capacocha, child sacrifices performed on mountaintops. Archaeologists Johan Reinhard and Constanza Ceruti have uncovered frozen mummies on peaks from Peru to Argentina—children aged 6 to 15, elaborately dressed, buried with figurines of gold and silver, and left to die from exposure or suffocation (Reinhard, *Sacred Mountains, Ceremonial Sites, and Human Sacrifice Among the Incas*, 2005).

Capacocha was not random cruelty. It was a transaction: the best and purest children were chosen, sometimes the offspring of nobles, their innocence considered the most valuable payment. They were marched hundreds of miles to high-altitude shrines, given intoxicants, and interred alive. Their deaths were offerings to mountain deities and to Inti, the sun god, ensuring rain, fertility, and political cohesion.

The scale of the practice is staggering. Over a hundred capacocha sites have been identified, often at altitudes above 20,000 feet, where construction of platforms required immense labor. These were offerings delivered at the threshold of heaven, where breath itself falters. To kill at such heights dramatized the urgency: blood given at the very edge of the sky, as if to place the covenant payment directly into the hands of the gods.

Long before the rise of the Inca, the Moche culture of Peru (c. 100–700 CE) practiced blood sacrifice on a scale both brutal and theatrical. Excavations at Huaca de la Luna revealed murals showing bound captives marched in procession, stripped naked, and slain in ritual plazas. Many are shown bleeding from slit throats, their blood collected in goblets and presented to priests or deities painted with goggle-eyes and fanged mouths (Benson, *The Moche of Ancient Peru*, 2012). Beneath these murals, archaeologists found mass graves filled with young men whose bones bore cut marks consistent with ritual execution (Verano, *Human Sacrifice and Sacred Landscapes in Ancient Peru*, 2001). The Moche integrated these killings into cycles of warfare and fertility: captives taken in battle were offered at temples to ensure rains and agricultural success. The imagery is strikingly consistent with Aztec flower wars and Maya captives, underscoring that the covenant's urgency permeated the Andes centuries before the Inca institutionalized it at mountaintop shrines.

Urgency vs. Continuity

Comparing Maya, Aztec, and Inca practices reveals the New World covenant's distinctive emphasis. The gods were not guarantors of dynasties but consumers whose appetite was constant. Sacrifice did not occur primarily at royal funerals or coronations but daily, seasonally, and cosmically. In Mesoamerica, the gods required feeding to keep the sun alive and the rains falling. In the Andes, they required children at mountaintops to open the skies.

This urgency is reflected in language. The Maya word ch'ahb' means both "to give" and "to nourish." The Aztec called human blood "chalchíhuatl," precious water, explicitly equating it with rainfall. For the Inca, children were called qhapaq hucha—"royal obligations." Each term encodes sacrifice as necessity, not metaphor. Blood was the literal medium by which the cosmos survived.

Theater of Renewal

The architecture of New World sacrifice reinforced the urgency. At Chichén Itzá, equinox sunlight casts the shadow of a serpent down the steps of El Castillo, signaling the moment for ritual renewal. At the Templo Mayor, sacrifices were staged before crowds of thousands, the blood flowing visibly down the staircases. At mountaintop shrines, the location itself dramatized the covenant: life exchanged at the edge of the sky.

This theatricality was not for spectacle alone. It was pedagogy, reminding entire populations that survival hinged on continual repayment. In contrast to the Old World's dynastic sacrifices—often hidden in tombs or restricted to temple interiors—the New World made covenantal exchange public, communal, and inescapable.

Taken together, the Zapotec, Moche, and Inca examples reinforce the New World's emphasis on spectacle. Murals, urns, plazas, and mountain shrines all made the covenant visible—whether through public execution, artistic representation, or pilgrimages to remote peaks. Unlike the Old World, where many sacrifices were enclosed in tombs or hidden in temple basements, the New World covenant demanded exposure. Blood flowed in plazas, shadows of serpents slithered down staircases, and frozen children were left in shrines accessible to the skies. Visibility was part of the payment. The gods were not content with hidden offerings; they required a pedagogy of fear and awe, a continual reminder to the living that life itself was a debt.

A Different Covenant, Same Origin

Despite these differences, the underlying principle remains the same: blood as payment, ritual as machinery, architecture as interface. The Maya, Aztec, and Inca did not invent this principle. They adapted it, pressing the covenant into forms suited to their landscapes and cosmologies. What differs is not origin but emphasis. The Old World emphasized stability; the New World emphasized sustenance.

From the covenant perspective, these hemispheric variations suggest a distributed system. The gods administered not one contract but many, optimized for local conditions. In the Old World, the covenant reinforced hierarchy and continuity. In the New, it demanded constant payment to sustain creation itself. The program was flexible, adaptive, and global.

Comparing Hemispheres

When the Old World and New World traditions are set side by side, the contrasts are striking enough to feel almost deliberate. Both hemispheres developed monumental architecture, priestly hierarchies, and ritual calendars tied to celestial cycles. Both built ritual machines in stone, choreographed sacrifice to the heavens, and personified divine intermediaries in the forms of serpents, bird-men, and winged messengers. Yet what they emphasized differs so sharply that it suggests not mere cultural divergence, but distinct instructions tailored to each hemisphere.

Old World Priorities: Order and Continuity

In Egypt, Mesopotamia, India, and China, sacrifice reinforced hierarchy. Pharaohs buried with retainer victims carried dynastic order into eternity. Sumerian city-gods received blood alongside bread and beer to secure loyalty. Vedic fire altars burned offerings with geometric precision to uphold cosmic law. Shang kings offered human victims to ancestors to legitimize dynasties. In each case, the covenant functioned as stabilizer. It was less about appeasing an immediate hunger and more about maintaining balance—social, political, and cosmic. The offerings sanctified kingship, reassured the ruled, and demonstrated that the cosmos itself was aligned with the ruler's command.

This emphasis gave Old World sacrifice a certain regularity. Rituals tied to enthronements, funerals, festivals, or astronomical cycles were designed to underwrite continuity. Blood was payment, but it was also proof of order, ensuring that dynasties endured and divine balance held firm.

New World Priorities: Sustenance and Urgency

Across the ocean, the covenant assumed a different posture. Maya rulers cut themselves in synchrony with Venus, spilling their own blood as clockwork offerings. Aztec priests raised beating hearts toward the sun daily, convinced that without continual repayment, the sky would darken forever. Inca emperors dispatched children to die on mountain shrines, gifts to the sun and to the apus, the mountain spirits who held weather and fertility in their grasp.

Here sacrifice was not stabilizer but sustenance. The cosmos was imagined as fragile, perpetually in need of feeding. Blood was not occasional reassurance but constant necessity. Where the Old World spoke of continuity, the New World spoke of survival. The difference is not subtle—it is existential.

Frequency and Scale

The contrast is especially clear when frequency is considered. In the Old World, large-scale human sacrifice tended to cluster around transitions: coronations, funerals, foundation rituals, or crises. It was episodic, symbolic of turning points in dynastic or cosmic time.

In the New World, sacrifice was woven into daily life. The Aztec launched wars to capture victims, ensuring a continual supply. The Maya scheduled bloodletting to astronomical intervals so precise they rivaled modern calendars. The Inca performed capacocha not as rare anomalies but as part of an empire-wide program, sending children from across their territories to mountaintops as routine offerings.

Scale also diverged. Old World sacrifices, even when bloody, rarely approached the industrial magnitude of Aztec festivals or the geographic expanse of Inca mountaintop burials. The New World covenant operated as an economy of blood, demanding both volume and regularity.

Visibility and Secrecy

Another distinction lies in visibility. Old World sacrifices often took place within temple enclosures, royal tombs, or restricted precincts. Retainer burials at Abydos were hidden underground. Shang sacrifices were interred in tomb pits. Even Vedic fire rituals, though public, were framed by esoteric geometry intelligible only to initiated priests.

The New World, by contrast, made covenantal transactions unmistakably visible. Aztec sacrifices cascaded down temple stairs in front of tens of thousands. Maya murals depicted bound captives and vision serpents in public plazas. Inca capacocha, though remote, dramatized the covenant at the edge of the sky, where the environment itself testified to the extremity of the offering. The pedagogy of fear and awe was part of the system. People did not just hear about sacrifice—they saw it, smelled it, and sometimes participated in it.

The choice of sacrificial landscapes also reveals a hemispheric distinction. Old World sacrifices clustered in river valleys, tomb complexes, and temple precincts—controlled environments where dynasties staged their continuity. New World sacrifices often unfolded in liminal zones: mountaintops, open plazas, equinox staircases. The Inca carried victims to the edge of breathable air, while Aztec priests cast bodies down staircases for entire cities to witness. In both cases the geography was more than backdrop; it was itself covenantal theater. Stone, mountain, river, and sky became extensions of the machinery through which blood was delivered.

Cosmic Logic

Despite these differences, the cosmologies rhyme. Both hemispheres imagined a debt humans owed to divine powers. Both spoke of blood as food, drink, or precious substance. Both linked offerings to celestial cycles—whether the solstices at Karnak, the heliacal rising of Sirius, or the equinox serpent-shadow at Chichén Itzá. Both envisioned architecture as interface: temples, pyramids, and shrines aligned with stars and infused with blood.

The differences, then, are not in principle but in application. The gods demanded blood everywhere. But in one hemisphere, the emphasis was on dynastic continuity; in the other, on cosmic sustenance. This suggests adaptation—local variations of a single underlying program.

The mythologies of both hemispheres echo the same themes even as they dress them in different names. In Egypt, Osiris is slain and dismembered, his restoration tied to fertility and the flooding of the Nile. In Mexico, Huitzilopochtli must be nourished daily with blood to rise in the east. Both myths anchor the same principle: cosmic order depends on sacrifice, whether to reassemble the body of a god or to keep the sun alive. In India, the *Purusha Sukta* describes creation emerging from the dismemberment of a cosmic man, while in the Andes, the Inca spoke of Viracocha shaping humanity from sacrificed matter at Lake Titicaca. Across cultures, myth enshrined the same logic: blood and body as raw material for continuity and renewal.

Toward a Global Interpretation

When read through the covenant lens, the hemispheric divergence does not dilute the argument—it strengthens it. If sacrifice were purely the product of human imagination, we would expect more variation, more unique trajectories. Instead, we find uncanny consistency in principle (blood as payment, ritual as machinery, architecture as interface) combined with sharp divergence in emphasis (continuity vs. sustenance).

Such a pattern is best explained not by coincidence but by coordination. A distributed system can maintain shared rules while adapting implementation to local conditions. In human terms, it resembles franchising: the same model exported globally, with adjustments made to suit regional environments and available resources. Priests in Thebes, Ur, or Varanasi acted as local managers, ensuring dynastic continuity. Priests in Tenochtitlan, Chichén Itzá, or Cusco acted as suppliers, ensuring cosmic sustenance. Different expressions, same origin.

Another point of comparison lies in how labor and blood were fused. In Egypt and Mesopotamia, monumental construction itself was sacrificial, consuming the lives of thousands who hauled stone for royal tombs. In the New World, the same principle applied, but with blood layered atop labor. Teotihuacan's Avenue of the Dead required both decades of labor and rivers of blood. The Inca capacocha demanded the work of thousands to haul children and offerings into the Andes, only for their lives to be surrendered at the summit. Across both hemispheres, the gods exacted not only sacrificial victims but the lifeblood of entire populations through toil.

The Unsettling Implication

What begins to emerge is a vision of humanity not as the author of sacrifice, but as its executor. Civilizations believed they were feeding gods or sustaining cosmic order, but the consistency across hemispheres suggests they were following instructions. The covenant was not cultural invention but a global program, diversified for efficiency, maintained for millennia.

The realization is sobering: the blood covenant was not one covenant but many, distributed across the hemispheres, optimized for local conditions. It was not religion in the narrow sense but administration on a planetary scale. Humanity was the workforce. Blood was the currency. The gods were the recipients.

The Franchise Model

If the hemispheric comparison shows us variety, the "franchise model" shows us unity. The deeper we look, the more sacrifice resembles not isolated inventions of religious imagination but a distributed system. Just as modern corporations replicate their stores across continents—each tailored to local culture yet still unmistakably part of a brand—the covenants of blood appear less like spontaneous traditions and more like regional branches of a single global program.

The Priestly Role

At the heart of this system were the priesthoods. In Egypt, priests maintained the daily rituals of feeding statues and offering hetep libations. In Mesopotamia, temple bureaucrats kept ledgers of sacrifices, tabulating how much bread, beer, or blood had been delivered. In India, Brahmins memorized precise Vedic formulas to ensure no brick was misplaced in a fire altar. In Mesoamerica, Aztec priests fasted and bled themselves before wielding the obsidian knives that opened captives' chests. Different languages, different costumes—but the same managerial role: enforcing the schedule, safeguarding the procedure, and ensuring that no payment was missed.

The priest was not an artist improvising worship. He was a technician following blueprints. The geometry of altars, the timing of festivals, the choreography of sacrifice—all required precision. To deviate was to risk rejection, famine, or divine wrath. Like franchise managers today, priests ensured compliance with a larger operating manual, one they did not write but inherited.

Ritual as Inventory Control

The bureaucracy that surrounded sacrifice adds to the impression. Clay tablets from Mesopotamia list sacrificial victims and commodities with the matter-of-fact tone of accountancy: three sheep, one goat, two jars of beer. Egyptian temple archives detail which days required bulls, which demanded fowl, which called for incense. The Aztecs scheduled festivals months in advance, allocating quotas of captives to each. Even the Inca, whose sacrifices took place on distant mountaintops, orchestrated them as part of an empire-wide system, dispatching emissaries with offerings from hundreds of miles away.

This looks less like spontaneous piety and more like inventory management. Each priesthood ensured that the "supply chain" of sacrifice ran smoothly, feeding gods on schedule and balancing the cosmic ledger. The gods, in this reading, were not distant ideals but consuming clients with appetites that had to be met.

The paperwork of sacrifice is one of its strangest consistencies. Cuneiform tablets listing sheep and oxen read like invoices. Egyptian temple scrolls specify which cuts of meat belonged to which god. Aztec codices diagram rows of bound captives like a catalog of tribute. These are not poetic hymns but bureaucratic records, the kind any modern corporation would recognize. The priesthood was not simply religious—it was administrative, tracking supply, forecasting demand, and ensuring delivery. What scholars often dismiss as "temple economy" may have been something else entirely: an enforced bookkeeping system for a contract that spanned the world.

Cultural Variation, Structural Consistency

The most telling detail is the balance of similarity and difference. No two covenants looked identical—Egyptian basins are not Aztec cuauhxicalli, Shang oracle bones are not Vedic fire altars—but they share structural functions. Each provides a vessel to capture life-force, a conduit to transmit it, and a calendar to schedule its delivery. The local flavor—whether bread and beer, maize and blood, or smoke and incense—was customization, not invention.

Just as a fast-food chain adapts menus to local tastes while keeping the underlying model intact, the gods' covenant adapted to local populations while maintaining the same machinery: preparation, offering, transmission. In places with abundant O-negative bloodlines, human hearts were the premium product. In places where such blood was scarce, animals or symbolic substitutes carried the load, while breeding programs focused on lineage. Different offerings, same logic.

Fear as Quality Assurance

Every franchise requires enforcement. In the covenant system, fear did the work. Droughts, floods, plagues, or military defeats were explained as lapses in sacrificial duty. Priests invoked these disasters as proof that offerings had not been sufficient or properly executed. The people complied not only because of belief but because every crop failure and eclipse reinforced the connection between neglect and catastrophe.

This created a feedback loop: sacrifice ensured survival, survival justified sacrifice. Once established, the covenant was nearly impossible to escape. Even when emissaries disappeared, cultures carried on the rites, convinced that their survival still depended on the blood payments. The franchise model thus outlived its founders, running on inertia long after the original managers had departed.

Continuity Across Millennia

The persistence of this system is remarkable. Egyptian Pyramid Texts (c. 2400 BCE) already describe offerings as sustenance. Aztec chronicles from the 16th century repeat the same language: blood as food, hearts as drink. Between them lies over three thousand years and an ocean, yet the vocabulary has not shifted. When cultures invent independently, their metaphors diverge. When they inherit from a shared source, the metaphors remain.

Even in the face of conquest, the model endured. Spanish missionaries condemned Aztec sacrifices as demonic, yet Catholic liturgy carried its own sacrificial vocabulary—body and blood, wine and bread. In India, Brahmanical ritual outlasted Buddhism, absorbing and reinterpreting it but never abandoning the altar. In China, the cult of Shangdi gave way to Confucian and Daoist practices, yet animal offerings remained at ancestral shrines for centuries. The franchise had remarkable resilience, adapting to conquerors and reformers alike.

Spanish friars thought they had stamped out the blood-soaked altars of Mexico, yet in their place they installed the Mass — a ritual still described in terms of "sacrifice." The Eucharist, presented as bread and wine transformed into body and blood, carried forward the same covenantal vocabulary. The people who once witnessed hearts raised to the sun now watched chalices raised to the crucifix. To the conquerors it was salvation; to the conquered it was continuity under another name. In the Old World too, Christian liturgy did not abandon sacrifice but universalized it, presenting the death of Christ as a single, eternal blood-offering meant to replace the endless cycles of the past. But the logic remained: divine favor required blood, and humanity was bound to offer it.

The Global Ledger

When the system is seen as a whole, a global ledger emerges. Each culture believed it was paying its own gods, but the consistency suggests a shared set of recipients. If one civilization faltered, another still delivered. The covenant was not local but planetary, with humanity as the common resource. The Old World's sacrifices of continuity and the New World's sacrifices of sustenance were not contradictions but complementary streams, each servicing the same demand in different forms.

Why It Matters

The franchise model reframes human history. Civilization did not simply grow around agriculture, trade, or writing. It grew around sacrifice, coordinated through priesthoods who functioned less as spiritual leaders and more as contract enforcers. The gods did not just inspire worship—they issued instructions, trained administrators, and oversaw a planetary program. What humanity remembers as religion may in fact have been compliance.

The unsettling implication is that civilization itself may be the byproduct of an imposed system. Our greatest monuments, from Karnak to Tenochtitlan, may not be celebrations of human genius but receipts—stone ledgers documenting transactions paid in blood. And if this was a franchise, it was one we never owned. We were the staff, not the shareholders.

Conclusion — Two Hemispheres, One System

When the strands are woven together, the picture clarifies. The Old World did not invent its covenants in isolation, nor did the New World improvise its own. Both hemispheres carried forward the same blueprint: blood as payment, ritual as mechanism, architecture as interface, and priesthood as administrator. What differed was the emphasis—continuity and dynastic stability in the East, sustenance and cosmic renewal in the West. Those contrasts are not contradictions; they are adjustments.

It is as though the gods—or their emissaries—distributed not a single manual, but a set of templates. Some cultures were instructed to tie sacrifice to kingship and cosmic balance, others to wage continual war for captives, others still to carry offerings to mountaintops or bury them beneath pyramids. The principle never shifted. Only the form. Such variety is exactly what we would expect from a program optimized across a planet. Local resources, climates, and populations differed; so did the availability of certain bloodlines. A global system attentive to those differences would adapt. Where dynastic stability mattered most, kingship was sacralized. Where cosmic hunger was urgent, mass sacrifice was normalized. What unites them is the sense of obligation—that human life was not entirely its own, but a resource to be drawn upon for the maintenance of something beyond.

The persistence of this system across centuries suggests it was more than religion. Religions fracture, evolve, and diverge. The covenant endured, recognizable from Ur to Tenochtitlan, from Karnak to Cusco. It was not a creed but an administration, one that outlasted the empires it served. Even when dynasties collapsed and priesthoods vanished, successor cultures often preserved the memory: ruins reinterpreted as "places where gods were made," or mountain shrines remembered as thresholds between worlds. What fades in doctrine survives in stone, testimony to a system too deeply embedded to erase.

If anything, the hemispheric divide strengthens the argument for coordination. Independent invention would have produced greater diversity. Instead, we find uncanny parallels and carefully tuned divergences. A single global origin explains both better than coincidence ever could. The franchise analogy holds: the brand remains consistent, the menu changes slightly, but the operating logic persists.

Mythology itself confirms this global architecture. In Egypt, Osiris is slain and reassembled so that life may continue. In Mesopotamia, Tammuz dies and returns, binding fertility to blood. In Vedic India, the *Purusha Sukta* describes the cosmos emerging from the dismemberment of a primordial being. Among the Aztec, Huitzilopochtli must be nourished daily with blood to rise again in the east. In the Andes, Viracocha shapes humanity from sacrificed substance at Lake Titicaca. Across continents, myths tell the same story in different accents: the world is precarious, and only sacrifice keeps it alive.

The frequency of those myths—so often pairing creation or renewal with dismemberment and blood—cannot be ignored. They are not simply allegories for seasonal cycles. They are echoes of an older contract, retold in human terms. Each myth is a cultural memory of debt, a story designed to explain why the covenant demanded blood.

The differences in emphasis between hemispheres suggest that the recipients themselves tailored their approach. Where blood of a certain type was abundant, direct sacrifice was emphasized. Where it was rare, symbolic substitutes and controlled breeding carried more weight. The gods' needs may not have been identical everywhere; they adjusted their contracts to what the local population could provide. In this light, Egypt's dynastic emphasis and Mesoamerica's insatiable demand are not opposing philosophies, but two sides of a single coin—each covenant designed to extract maximum utility from local conditions.

And here lies the most unsettling implication. The system was not only cultural. It was biological. Civilizations believed they were offering blood to secure rain or legitimacy, but the eerie consistency across hemispheres points to a deeper calculus. It suggests that the gods were not simply satisfied with ritual; they were attentive to what kind of blood was offered, and perhaps whose bloodlines were being managed. This opens the door to a darker possibility: that humanity's diversity was not incidental, but leveraged. That different populations were tasked differently because their very biology made them more useful for feeding, for breeding, or for both.

The covenant was never a single agreement, then, but many—distributed, diversified, optimized. Two hemispheres, multiple covenants, one system. The conclusion is sobering: from the beginning of civilization, humanity may have been less the architect of its sacred imagination than the executor of instructions. The rites that seemed to honor gods or sustain creation may have been something else entirely: the servicing of a planetary program, maintained for millennia, with human life as its principal resource.

And if the covenant was tuned not only to culture but to blood, then the story is not finished. It means that what began in ancient temples may still echo in the modern world—in the genetics of abduction lineages, in the persistence of rare blood types, and in the continuing sense that humanity is not entirely its own. If sacrifice was tailored by hemisphere, it may also have been tailored by blood itself. The gods did not demand life indiscriminately. They selected, cultivated, and tracked certain lineages with precision. To see how deep this logic runs, we must turn to the chemistry of blood—its types, its rarity, and the biological utility that may have underwritten the covenant from the beginning.

8

BLOOD TYPES AND BIOLOGICAL UTILITY

Blood as Chemistry, Blood as Covenant

Human beings often speak of blood in poetic terms: as life itself, as kinship, as sacrifice. But beneath the poetry lies cold chemistry. Blood is not uniform across our species. It is a fluid with structure, a composition that varies from one individual to the next, shaped by molecular markers that define who can give and who can receive. These differences are not trivial. In medicine, they mean the difference between life and death. In the covenant framework, they may have meant the difference between who was harvested, who was bred, and who was left untouched.

Modern hematology recognizes the ABO system as the primary grouping of human blood. Discovered in the early 20th century by Karl Landsteiner, it classifies blood according to the presence or absence of antigens—A, B, or neither (O)—on the surface of red blood cells. Added to this is the Rh factor, determined by the D antigen. If present, the blood is positive (A+, O+, etc.); if absent, negative (A–, O–). The ABO group dictates who can safely receive a transfusion. The Rh factor adds another layer of compatibility. Together, they define a matrix of possibility: some people can give broadly,

A Blood Covenant

others only narrowly. The rarest blood types—such as O-negative or the even rarer Rh-null ("golden blood")—are prized in medicine because of their compatibility.

From a covenant perspective, these same traits may have dictated not medical treatment but ritual demand. A fluid that is universal, compatible with many, and rare would have been an obvious target for beings who depended on blood not for poetry but for sustenance.

Consider the distribution of blood types worldwide. Europe, and particularly the Basque region straddling Spain and France, has the highest frequency of Rh-negative blood. Roughly 15% of Europeans are Rh-negative, while in East Asia the number drops below 1%. Africa and the Middle East occupy a middle ground, with frequencies ranging from 2–8%. O-negative, the "universal donor," is globally scarce, but its highest densities again appear in Europe. In contrast, O-positive dominates in Asia and Africa, with some regions reporting rates as high as 90%.

These aren't speculative figures but well-documented population data. Global surveys of blood group frequencies consistently show that Rh-negative peaks in Europe—reaching up to 15% among the Basques—while it is nearly absent across East Asia, and occurs at moderate levels in the Near East (Mourant, Kopec & Domaniewska-Sobczak, *The Distribution of the Human Blood Groups*, 1976; *WHO Global Blood Safety Reports*, 2011–2017). Such mapping provides more than a medical curiosity: it sketches the biological backdrop against which sacrificial systems unfolded.

On their own, these numbers are dry population genetics. But when placed against the archaeological record of sacrifice, unsettling patterns emerge. Where Rh-negative blood is abundant, the record shows direct human sacrifice at scale: bog bodies in Celtic Europe, decapitations and heart extractions in Iberia, Carthaginian child offerings in North Africa. Where Rh-negative is nearly absent, human sacrifice declines in prominence and animal offerings dominate: Vedic horse rituals, Shang dynasty cattle pits, dynastic ancestor worship in East Asia. Where Rh-negative is moderate, as in

Mesopotamia, both appear: animal sacrifice alongside human retainers and royal bloodlines.

This correlation suggests that the covenant was not uniform. It was optimized. The gods did not demand the same rites everywhere—they adjusted their instructions to match the biology of the populations they ruled. Europe became a feeding zone. Asia became a breeding zone. The Near East became both.

The logic, from their perspective, is chillingly simple. If rare blood types were nutritionally valuable for transdermal absorption—more compatible, less likely to produce rejection—then Europe offered the richest supply. O-negative was the premium product, and so human lives were spilled directly. In Asia, where such blood was scarce, the emphasis shifted to reproduction and lineage. Dynasties became laboratories. Sacrifice often took symbolic or animal form, while human populations were manipulated for their genetic utility. In the Near East, the covenant blended both: animal offerings satisfied the demand for bulk "nutrients," while royal and priestly bloodlines maintained continuity and experimentation.

Even modern medicine hints at why such a system might have developed. O-negative, lacking both A and B antigens and the Rh factor, is the least likely to provoke immune reaction. In transfusion, it is universally accepted. In a covenant framework, it may also have been the most efficiently absorbed through Grey dermal membranes. Rare blood types like Rh-null—of which fewer than a hundred individuals are known worldwide—would have been unimaginably valuable, perhaps even the key to hybridization. In this light, the persistence of abduction reports focused on specific families across generations may not be psychological coincidence. It may be resource tracking: the same lineages harvested again and again for their blood and reproductive potential.

This would also explain why sacrificial practices shifted over time. In the earliest phases of contact, the covenant may have been literal: emissaries demanding blood as payment, teaching priesthoods how to collect, prepare, and deliver it. But as the emissaries departed—or withdrew into secrecy—the rituals continued symbolically. Priests, no longer in direct contact, repeated the motions without fully understanding the machinery. Animal sacrifices substituted for human ones, libations of wine or red ochre replaced blood, dynastic marriages stood in for breeding. The system ran on inertia, maintained by fear and tradition long after the original recipients had ceased to appear.

Seen this way, theology becomes biology writ large. Myths of gods drinking blood, eating hearts, or demanding children are not inventions of fearful minds but cultural translations of literal demands placed upon human populations. The fact that the myths differ in detail but converge in principle—blood as food, lineage as currency—strengthens the argument. The gods adapted their program to each region, just as modern corporations adapt franchises to local markets. Bread and beer in Mesopotamia, maize and hearts in Mexico, incense and cattle in China—all different menus, but the same kitchen.

The unsettling conclusion is that biology dictated theology. Human populations did not invent sacrifice at random. They were responding to instructions that exploited their own blood chemistry and genetic diversity. Where rare blood was abundant, gods demanded feeding. Where it was scarce, gods demanded breeding. And everywhere, humans complied, believing that survival depended on it.

Feeding Zones Part 1 — Europe and North Africa

If blood is the universal currency of the covenant, then Europe and North Africa held a disproportionate share of its premium form. The frequency of Rh-negative blood, particularly O-negative, reaches its global peak in western Europe, with the Basque population long noted as an outlier at up to 15% (Mourant et al., 1976). This is not a trivial quirk of genetics. In transfusion medicine O-negative is prized as the "universal donor," free of A, B, and Rh antigens that trigger rejection. In the covenant framework, it may have been equally prized: a substrate least likely to provoke metabolic complications, the cleanest fuel for nonhuman biology.

The archaeological record across Europe and the Mediterranean is unusually saturated with evidence of human sacrifice. From the peat bogs of northern Europe to the stone altars of Carthage, blood itself appears to have been the premium commodity. In Iron Age Britain and Scandinavia, bodies preserved in bogs show signs of violent death — garroting, drowning, stabbing — often in combination. Archaeologist Miranda Aldhouse-Green (*Dying for the Gods*, 2001) notes that such "triple deaths" appear excessive if interpreted as executions but logical if understood as ritual offerings, each wound symbolizing payment to multiple deities. The preservation of these bodies in anaerobic bogs is an accident of environment, but the ritual impulse is undeniable: human lives given directly.

On the Mediterranean rim, the pattern continues. In Carthage, the infamous Tophet shrines contained urns filled with the cremated remains of infants, often buried beneath stelae inscribed with dedications to Baal Hammon and Tanit. Debate rages over whether these represent natural infant burials or ritual infanticide, but inscriptions themselves betray the logic: they speak of offerings "for favor," "for life," and "for the gods' portion" (Stager & Wolff, *Biblical Archaeologist*, 1984). The very vocabulary suggests payment, and the scale — tens of thousands of urns — suggests that this was no marginal rite. Blood, here in its most innocent form, was rendered as the most precious offering.

Even classical sources, often hostile to their rivals, preserved the memory of blood sacrifice in the region. *Diodorus Siculus* describes the Carthaginians offering children during times of crisis, placing them into the bronze arms of a god-statue heated so that the victims rolled into a fiery pit. Roman chroniclers used these accounts as propaganda, but the corroboration from archaeology complicates dismissal. Whether or not every lurid detail is accurate, the broader point stands: blood — not grain, not incense, not animals — was the covenant's preferred currency in these zones.

In Iberia, archaeological surveys reveal sanctuaries where dismembered human remains were interred alongside animal offerings. The Tartessians and later Celtiberians appear to have practiced ritual killings of captives, a pattern noted in both skeletal trauma and weapon deposits (Almagro-Gorbea, 2006). In Gaul, Julius Caesar himself records that the Druids built wicker effigies stuffed with humans and burned them as offerings to their gods (*Gallic Wars, VI.16*). Modern scholars debate the literalness of these accounts, but bog finds and votive deposits across Celtic Europe lend credence to at least some level of systemic human sacrifice.

North Africa, too, bears the marks. Egyptian practices in the Early Dynastic period included retainer sacrifice at Abydos, but farther west, Libyan tribes were described by Herodotus as making human offerings before battle (*Histories, IV.188*). Across the Mediterranean littoral, the combination of high Rh-negative frequencies and ritual violence suggests a zone optimized for direct blood harvest.

What unites these practices is not simply the presence of human sacrifice — which occurs globally — but its intensity and frequency. In the Feeding Zone, bloodletting seems to have been not a last resort or a symbolic stand-in, but the central act. Unlike in East Asia, where animal proxies gradually predominated, or in Mesopotamia, where sacrifice entwined with political loyalty, here the logic was visceral: the gods demanded human life itself.

The covenant interpretation reframes this. Rather than seeing these practices as cultural curiosities or aberrant extremes, they become expressions of local biology. Where O-negative blood was abundant, the gods could afford to demand it directly. Where it was rare, they adapted the contract to lean on animal surrogates or reproductive lineages. In Europe and North Africa, the abundance of "universal donor" blood made direct feeding zones feasible.

This also helps explain the persistence of blood-centric ritual even into late antiquity. When Christianity spread across Europe, it carried with it sacrificial language transposed into metaphor: Christ's blood shed "for the life of the world." Scholars often trace this to Judaic temple sacrifice, but the imagery resonated so powerfully in Europe precisely because it echoed an older covenantal economy. The Eucharist, with its focus on body and blood consumed, can be seen as the symbolic survival of a literal feeding system that had once dominated the region.

The unsettling implication is that entire populations may have been valued not for their labor, as in Egypt, nor for their genetic lineages, as in India, but for the chemical profile of their blood. Europe and North Africa supplied the nutrient — the "premium stock" — that fed a system larger than any one culture. Their bog bodies, Tophets, and altars were not anomalies of superstition. They were the infrastructure of a feeding zone.

Sidebar: Blood and the Vampire Archetype

Europe carries not only genetic concentrations of O-negative blood but also some of the deepest legends of blood-hungry beings. Long before Bram Stoker's *Dracula* (1897) and the bloody reputation of Vlad Țepeș, Northern and Eastern European folklore told of strigoi, upir, and vrykolakas—restless revenants who rose from graves to drain the living. Paul Barber, in *Vampires, Burial, and Death* (1988), shows how these traditions were rooted in anxieties about death, disease, and improper burial. Yet the consistent theme across centuries and cultures is hunger—not for flesh, but for blood.

David Keyworth's *Troublesome Corpses: Vampires & Revenants from Antiquity to the Present* (2007) catalogs the ubiquity of such myths, noting that nearly every European culture developed stories of creatures who required human blood to maintain their half-life. While scholars typically interpret these legends as symbolic or pathological metaphors, they may also preserve a cultural memory of an older truth—that blood itself was once demanded by nonhuman forces. In this reading, the vampire becomes less a gothic invention and more an echo of the covenant: a distorted recollection of beings who fed on life-force directly.

Feeding Zones, Part II: The Americas

If Europe and North Africa represent a premium feeding ground in terms of blood chemistry, the Americas represent the covenant's most visible and voracious theater. Here, sacrifice was not occasional or symbolic—it was industrial, cosmological, and perpetual. Blood was not only "the life" but the daily food of the gods. Chroniclers, codices, and archaeology converge to show a continent where human sacrifice reached scales and intensities unmatched anywhere else.

Mesoamerica: Sustenance for the Sun

Nowhere was the feeding covenant more explicit than among the Mexica (Aztec). The Templo Mayor in Tenochtitlan stood as the axis mundi, a twin-pyramid complex dedicated to Huitzilopochtli, the sun and war god, and Tlaloc, the rain god. To neglect either was to risk cosmic collapse. Bernardino de Sahagún's *Florentine Codex* preserves the priests' own language: hearts were the "precious eagle-cactus fruit" and blood the "precious water" given to sustain the gods (Sahagún, *Historia General de las Cosas de la Nueva España, Book II*). This was no metaphor. Priests spoke plainly of feeding—without blood, the sun would not rise.

The logistics were staggering. During the reign of Ahuitzotl (1486–1502), sources claim that as many as 20,000 captives were sacrificed in a single four-day dedication ceremony of the Templo Mayor. Modern scholars debate the number, but even conservative estimates acknowledge thousands of deaths (Carrasco, *City of Sacrifice*, 1999). Archaeological evidence supports the scale: mass burial pits around the Templo Mayor, skull racks (tzompantli) displaying hundreds of crania, and sacrificial stones still stained with residue. Recent excavations beneath the Mexico City cathedral—built atop the Templo Mayor—revealed a tower of skulls (the Huey Tzompantli) containing over 600 individuals, confirming the chronicles' accounts (López Luján et al., *Mexicon*, 2017).

These killings were not random acts of cruelty but a regulated economy of blood. Aztec warfare itself was structured to supply the altars. So-called "Flower Wars" were waged not for territory but for captives, who were paraded through the city before being sacrificed. The covenant demanded volume, and the state organized itself accordingly. As historian David Carrasco notes, sacrifice was *"the pivot of Mexica statecraft, theology, and cosmic maintenance"* (*Religions of Mesoamerica*, 1990).

The Maya, though less centralized than the Aztec, were no less devoted to blood as sustenance. *The Dresden Codex*—the best-preserved of their hieroglyphic books—shows the rain god Chaac receiving bowls of blood and human hearts, with glyphs literally reading "his food" (Houston, Stuart & Taube, *The Memory of Bones*, 2006). Rulers reinforced this system with their own bodies: Yaxchilán lintels and Bonampak murals depict kings and queens drawing blood from tongues and genitals, offering it on bark paper that was then burned so its smoke could nourish the gods. These acts were timed to celestial events, particularly the cycle of Venus, whose heliacal risings marked moments when captives were sacrificed and rulers bled themselves (Šprajc, *Venus and the Maya Calendar*, 1996).

The Maya worldview framed bloodletting as cosmic sustenance. Kings were not only political leaders but living intermediaries whose blood was a renewable resource for the gods. Yet this "renewable" supply was not sufficient alone. Captives—taken in war or tribute—provided additional blood and hearts, ensuring that the covenant was fed both by royal veins and by conquered enemies. In murals at Bonampak, bound captives are displayed beneath celestial glyphs, their fates clearly tied to planetary cycles. Here the covenant's punctuality is unmistakable: the sky gave the schedule, the altar the payment.

The precision with which the Maya tracked celestial cycles has long puzzled scholars. Why devote such extraordinary effort to calculating Venus risings to the exact day? Why embed solar zenith passages and equinox alignments into city plans? To the covenant lens, the answer may lie not in abstract astronomy but in biology. If the covenant's recipients required blood not only in quantity but on schedule, then punctuality was essential.

In modern medicine, timing can be the difference between life and death. Patients reliant on dialysis, insulin, or plasma infusions must receive them at precise intervals or risk collapse. If the Greys lacked digestive systems and instead depended on transdermal absorption of blood-derived nutrients, their physiology may have required replenishment on a timetable as exacting as the Maya's calendar. Feeding was not symbolic; it was scheduled maintenance.

Seen in this light, the Maya obsession with Venus becomes less arcane. The planet's cycle was not only a marker of war and sacrifice —it may have been the mnemonic for when the covenant payments were due. Venus's heliacal rising could have signaled a collection window, an appointed time when emissaries arrived or when rituals were believed to "connect" most effectively. The priests were not merely astronomers; they were timekeepers for a biological demand.

What makes this interpretation especially haunting is what followed. Even after the gods' physical presence diminished, the machinery of the calendar remained. The Maya and their successors continued to schedule offerings with meticulous care, convinced that neglect would bring disaster. The covenant became self-perpetuating: a system designed for alien sustenance transmuted into a cultural obsession with cosmic precision.

This would explain why sacrifice in the New World took on such urgency, such relentless regularity. The priests were not only feeding gods—they were servicing a schedule, one that may have originated in the biology of their nonhuman patrons. When the emissaries stopped appearing, the calendar remained as their ghost, a stone ledger of due dates written in light.

South America: The Edge of the Sky

In the Andes, the Inca carried the logic of feeding to the very roof of the world. Their capacocha ceremonies sent children—carefully chosen for their beauty, health, and noble lineage—on pilgrimages from Cusco to distant mountaintops. There, priests sacrificed them by strangulation, blunt force, or exposure, leaving their bodies intact in stone shrines above 20,000 feet. The rationale was explicit: children were gifts to the sun and to the apus, mountain spirits who controlled weather, fertility, and life itself (Reinhard & Ceruti, *Sacred Mountains, Sacred Bodies*, 2010).

Archaeological discoveries confirm this covenantal feeding. The frozen mummies of Llullaillaco, Ampato, and other Andean peaks show astonishing preservation, their braided hair and ceremonial garments testifying to careful preparation. Toxicological studies reveal that coca and alcohol were administered beforehand, sedating the children for their final moments (Wilson et al., *Proceedings of the National Academy of Sciences*, 2007). These were not battlefield captives but carefully selected emissaries, their blood and breath intended as sustenance at the highest altars on earth.

The Inca framed capacocha as repayment for prosperity. Chronicler Bernabé Cobo recorded that such sacrifices were offered after earthquakes, droughts, or imperial victories. In each case, the offering was not symbolic but necessary, a literal feeding of divine powers to restore balance (Cobo, *Historia del Nuevo Mundo*, 1653). The mountaintop setting dramatized the principle: blood was given at the boundary of heaven and earth, breath carried into the thin air as the final gift.

Animal sacrifice, especially of llamas, accompanied capacocha. Archaeologists have found young llamas buried alongside children in high-altitude shrines, their throats slit, their bodies wrapped in textiles. These were supplementary offerings, reinforcing the principle that life—whether human or animal—was food for the gods. The emphasis, however, was on the human child, whose innocence and lineage made the sacrifice more potent. In covenant terms, these mountaintop ceremonies were pure feeding: a direct transaction of life-force for divine favor.

Feeding as System, Not Exception

The Americas reveal feeding not as aberration but as infrastructure. Just as Europe and North Africa optimized sacrifice around blood chemistry, the civilizations of Mesoamerica and South America optimized it around cosmology and spectacle. The Aztec made feeding public, a theater of blood seen by tens of thousands. The Maya tied it to astronomical precision, syncing offerings to Venus and equinoxes. The Inca carried it to the heights, offering blood and breath where the air itself seemed divine.

Mainstream interpretations emphasize religion, politics, and ideology. Sacrifice is often framed as a tool of social control or as symbolic reciprocity. Yet the consistency of language—blood as food, hearts as drink—suggests something more literal. When Sahagún records priests describing blood as "precious water," when codices depict Chaac drinking bowls of blood, when Inca chroniclers speak of children "given to the sun," the metaphor strains. From the covenant perspective, these cultures were not imagining divine hunger—they were servicing it.

Toward a Comparative Lens

When Feeding Zones are viewed globally, the Americas and Europe/North Africa form complementary poles. In Europe, O-negative bloodlines made direct feeding biologically advantageous. In the Americas, cosmology made direct feeding unavoidable. Both zones produced ritual machinery to deliver life-force, but their emphases differed: chemistry in one, spectacle in the other. Together they reveal that the covenant was adaptable, exploiting whatever resources—genetic or cultural—were available.

The unsettling implication is that the gods did not simply demand sacrifice as devotion. They engineered environments in which sacrifice became systemic. In Europe, certain bloodlines were cultivated and harvested. In the Americas, entire empires reorganized themselves around supplying blood in volume. Different rationales, same end: the covenant was fed.

Feeding vs. Breeding: A Hemispheric Contrast

When the sacrificial landscapes of the world are viewed side by side, their differences are so sharp they cannot be ignored. The Old World —Egypt, Mesopotamia, India, China—structured its covenant around order. Sacrifice here was episodic, tied to enthronements, funerals, or seasonal rituals. The blood of retainers interred with kings at Abydos, the lives taken in Shang oracle rituals, the cattle offered on Vedic fire altars—all served as payments to maintain continuity. These were sacrifices as stabilizers, designed to underwrite dynastic legitimacy and cosmic harmony.

The New World told another story entirely. From the Aztec heart extractions atop the Templo Mayor to Inca children carried to freezing mountaintops, the West's covenant was immediate, visceral, and urgent. Sacrifice was not an occasional punctuation of cosmic time but its daily fuel. The sun itself, Aztec priests declared, would die without blood. Venus's risings dictated the Maya's calendar of slaughter. Mountains became altars, plazas became theaters, pyramids became engines of continual repayment. The covenant here was not reassurance but sustenance—blood spilled as often as breath itself.

The difference is not only in scale but in tone. The Old World's rites were guarded, often hidden in tombs or temple precincts, staged by elites for dynastic gods. The New World's rites were public, spectacular, impossible to ignore. Where Egypt poured libations into temple basins, Mexico poured blood down the faces of pyramids before tens of thousands of eyes. Where India calculated altar geometry to uphold cosmic balance, the Maya calculated Venus cycles to know precisely when to cut. Both systems were precise—but the precision served different appetites.

Even the landscape reflects the divide. Old World sacrifices clustered in river valleys, controlled spaces where dynasties staged their continuity. New World sacrifices reached into liminal extremes: staircases ascending to the sky, mountaintops at the edge of breathable air, plazas wide enough to host entire populations as witnesses. The very choice of terrain dramatized the difference—order in the East, urgency in the West.

The covenant lens sharpens this divergence. Where O-negative and Rh-negative blood was more abundant—in Europe, North Africa, and the Americas—sacrifice tilted toward direct feeding. Hearts, blood, marrow: raw biological payment. Where such blood was scarce—in East and South Asia—animal sacrifice and controlled breeding predominated, bloodlines managed through dynasties, priesthoods, and ancestor cults. In the middle ground—Mesopotamia and the Near East—both feeding and breeding were combined, animal offerings and priestly bloodlines sustaining a dual covenant.

The result is a pattern too consistent to dismiss as chance. The same logic is visible everywhere—blood as payment, architecture as interface, astronomy as calendar—but expressed in hemispheric dialects. In the East, the gods demanded stability and lineage. In the West, they demanded volume and punctuality. One hemisphere gave continuity; the other gave sustenance. Together, they completed a planetary system of extraction.

This duality also explains the psychological texture of the civilizations themselves. Old World cultures developed elaborate bureaucracies, codified laws, and dynasties stretching across millennia. Their covenant emphasized longevity and continuity, mirroring the breeding and lineage priorities of their gods. The New World, by contrast, lived under a horizon of immediacy. Aztec chronicles describe the terror of the sun's possible failure; Inca rituals dramatized life at the edge of death. Their covenant emphasized urgency, mirroring the hunger of their gods.

Placed together, the hemispheres reveal not contradiction but complementarity. A single intelligence could easily have optimized its program this way: stabilize one side of the planet through breeding and continuity, and drain the other side through relentless feeding.

Order and sustenance, hierarchy and hunger—two strategies, one program. Humanity, divided by oceans, was nevertheless enlisted into the same planetary contract.

Seen in this light, the collapse of dynasties or empires does not negate the covenant but underscores its grip. Even after emissaries withdrew, cultures carried on the rites. Egyptians continued their temple offerings long after the First Dynasty. The Maya and Aztec kept their calendar of blood even when the gods no longer appeared in the sky. What began as servicing alien biology endured as human religion.

The unsettling conclusion is this: civilization did not simply imagine sacrifice. It administered it. And it did so in forms optimized to its own bloodlines and geographies. The Old World bred stability. The New World fed survival. Two hemispheres, multiple covenants, one origin. Humanity was not the author of this system—it was its workforce. The gods wrote the contract, and the world bled to keep it.

In the end, the message is stark. The gods did not ask for faith—they demanded blood. In one hemisphere they fed on it, in the other they bred with it. The temples, calendars, and priesthoods were never simply human inventions; they were instruments of a system that turned our species into livestock and lineage. Civilization was not humanity's triumph, but its contract. And the covenant, written in blood, has never truly been broken.

9

POPULATION MANAGEMENT ACROSS HEMISPHERES

Blood was not the only resource managed under the covenant. Populations themselves were sculpted, directed, and sometimes erased. When we step back from the individual sacrifices and view whole societies, a broader picture emerges: the gods were not only fed by blood, they were organizing humanity the way a farmer tends herds. Sacrifice was one tool among many, accompanied by migrations, selective breeding, enforced concentration, and calculated collapse.

Civilizations that imagined themselves as free agents, building empires on their own terms, appear in this light as herds steered along invisible fences. The rituals that left behind pyramids, skull racks, and burnt offerings were not isolated phenomena. They were gears in a larger mechanism that determined who lived, who bred, and who vanished. The same way a farmer alternates between feeding, breeding, and culling to maintain livestock, the covenant system appears to have applied parallel strategies to humanity itself.

In the Old World, this management often took the form of controlled concentration. Mesopotamia flowered with tightly organized city-states, each bound to its patron deity and temple complex. The ziggurat did more than house ritual—it concentrated population density around a central node, ensuring a steady supply of offerings and a controlled workforce. Administrative tablets from Uruk and Ur record food rations and sacrificial tallies in the same ledgers (Kramer, *History Begins at Sumer*, 1956). Egypt followed a similar logic by consolidating its people along the Nile, the river itself functioning as a corridor of life that could be taxed, measured, and harvested. In Vedic India, ritual calendars synchronized not only religious festivals but agricultural planting and reproductive cycles. The *Śatapatha Brāhmaṇa* prescribes precise timing for sacrificial rites to align with cosmic law, but also with seasonal labor, tying fertility of crops and people alike to the same schedule. In China, Shang oracle bones record not only the outcomes of divination but the tally of human and animal victims sacrificed for kings and ancestors, demonstrating how the covenant was integrated into the very governance of dynastic stability (Keightley, *Sources of Shang History*, 1978).

In these cases, populations were managed through stability. Density, hierarchy, and reproduction were kept under surveillance by temples and priesthoods. The covenant functioned as a stabilizer, ensuring dynastic continuity and cosmic order. Humans were not culled in massive numbers, but rather bred, taxed, and channeled.

In the New World, the picture darkens. The Maya rose and fell in cycles of expansion and collapse, each wave leaving behind monuments to vanished populations. Archaeologists still debate the causes —drought, warfare, soil exhaustion—but the synchrony of their decline with peaks in monumental building and sacrificial intensity raises a chilling question: were they over-harvested? The Aztecs organized an entire imperial economy around captives. Their "Flower Wars" were not fought for territory but for inventory—young men and women who became raw material for sacrificial payment. Entire villages were depopulated, their strongest members funneled into the ritual economy of blood. In the Andes, the Inca relocated whole communities under the mitmaq system, uprooting tens of thousands to serve temple labor and supply victims for capacocha sacrifices on mountain shrines (Cobo, *History of the Inca Empire*, 1653/1990). Population management here meant attrition as much as organization, a deliberate keeping of numbers in check by feeding them directly into the covenant machine.

One of the most striking signs of management lies in the very origins of civilization itself. Archaeologists often speak of the Neolithic Revolution as a leap forward, when humans shifted from nomadic hunting and gathering into settled villages and early cities. Yet many scholars have noted that this "revolution" reduced health, shortened lifespans, and increased disease compared to foraging life (Scott, *Against the Grain*, 2017). From the covenant perspective, the logic becomes clearer: dispersed nomads could not be harvested efficiently. Concentrated farmers could. By anchoring populations along rivers, in valleys, or beneath temple complexes, the gods transformed humanity into something like penned herds—predictable, trackable, and renewable.

The earliest temples—Göbekli Tepe in Anatolia, Eridu in Mesopotamia, Abydos in Egypt—appear not at the end of this process but at its very beginning, as though monumental ritual architecture was the cause of settlement rather than the result. People gathered because offerings had to be made, and in gathering, they were domesticated. Once cities arose, priesthoods enforced taxation, rationing, and sacrifice, ensuring that the human "flock" remained available in both numbers and fertility. What historians call the birth of civilization may equally be described as the penning of the herd.

When we place the timelines of ancient collapses side by side, a disturbing pattern emerges. Civilizations rose to density, reached a fever pitch of sacrifice, and then declined—sometimes in famine, sometimes in sudden abandonment, sometimes in violence that left cities strewn with skeletons. The Old World provides examples too— the Indus Valley's unexplained decline, the Hittites' sudden disappearance—but the New World is littered with them: the Maya, Nasca, Moche, Tiwanaku. Each flourished, reached a crescendo of population and ritual, and then faltered, leaving behind stone testimony and silence.

Mainstream archaeology often frames these as coincidences of climate or politics. Droughts certainly happened, wars certainly destabilized, soils were certainly depleted. Yet the eerie recurrence of collapse following sacrificial intensification hints that something more was at work. It is as though an unseen hand calibrated human numbers, never allowing the herds to exceed the needs of their keepers.

The covenant, then, was not only about what was taken in blood. It was also about who was permitted to live, breed, and thrive. In one hemisphere, numbers were managed through dynasties and continuity; in the other, through culling and collapse. Two strategies, one purpose: keep humanity within boundaries set not by accident, but by administration.

Seen this way, sacrifice was only the visible part of a larger system of domestication. Just as livestock are bred, culled, and corralled, so too were humans—sometimes through ritual knife, sometimes through famine, sometimes through forced migration, always under the shadow of temples aligned to stars. The gods were not indifferent spectators. They were managers, and humanity was their managed resource.

Old World Models of Control

If sacrifice was the visible engine of the covenant, population control was the operating system. In the Old World, the gods' program rarely presented itself as random slaughter. Instead it appeared through ordered city-states, dynastic legitimacy, and ritual calendars that synchronized human fertility, harvest, and blood. At first glance these look like cultural achievements—civilization blossoming along rivers and plains. But when the evidence is arranged, a different picture emerges: these were corrals, built to hold humanity in place, concentrate its numbers, and ensure reliable harvests of life.

Mesopotamia: The City as Corral

The earliest city-states of Mesopotamia—Ur, Uruk, Eridu—were not simply aggregations of people around fertile soil. They were temple economies, centered on ziggurats whose scale dwarfed the modest dwellings clustered around them. Cuneiform tablets from as early as 2500 BCE record offerings to gods measured with bureaucratic precision: three sheep for Inanna, one ox for Enlil, jars of beer and oil alongside human captives (Black & Green, *Gods, Demons and Symbols of Ancient Mesopotamia*, 1992).

Each city had its patron deity, and its population was bound to serve that deity's temple. The walls of Uruk did not only protect against invaders—they kept people in. Populations that had once roamed the steppe as herders or hunters now found themselves subject to taxation in grain, labor, and blood. In exchange for protection and irrigation, they submitted to a system that demanded constant tribute. Seen through the covenant lens, the ziggurat was less a house of worship than a collection point, a funnel for human output—food, labor, life-force—directed upward.

Egypt: Fertility Managed by the Nile

Egypt's concentration of population along the Nile created one of history's most stable civilizations. The river provided the lifeblood of agriculture, but it also created a natural corridor of control. Pharaohs claimed divine mandate as incarnations of Horus, maintaining Ma'at —the cosmic order—through rituals and offerings. The Pyramid Texts and later Coffin Texts speak plainly of feeding the gods: *"Your bread is the blood of the gods; you eat the red and drink the white"* (Faulkner, 1969).

But Egypt's covenant went beyond feeding. It regulated fertility itself. Agricultural yields were tracked by nilometers, and taxation ensured surpluses were redirected to temples. Populations were counted, corvée labor conscripted, and festivals scheduled around solar and lunar cycles. Retainer sacrifices in the Early Dynastic period reveal the willingness to prune populations at a ruler's death. Even when human sacrifice gave way to animal substitutes, the underlying logic of management remained. Egyptians were not free agents—they were concentrated, counted, and culled when required.

Civilization here looks less like spontaneous flowering and more like deliberate corralling into a ribbon of irrigated land, where every harvest and every life could be measured against cosmic balance.

Vedic India: Ritual as Population Metronome

In Vedic India, the covenant took the form of fire. The Śrauta rituals, codified in the *Vedas*, required altars built to exact geometric specifications. Each brick corresponded to a syllable, a measure of cosmic order. The sacrifices themselves—goats, horses, sometimes humans—were consecrated, killed, and transmuted into smoke and ash that ascended to the gods. But the logic of the ritual went beyond appeasement.

As Frits Staal argued (*Rules Without Meaning*, 1989), Vedic ritual functioned like a program, a self-contained system that regulated agricultural timing, sexual abstinence, and even community organization. The famous Ashvamedha horse sacrifice was as much about consolidating dynastic fertility as it was about pleasing the gods: the king's potency and his people's fertility were bound to the ritual cycle. Blood, semen, and grain were woven together in a single calendar of control. From the covenant perspective, the Vedic fire altar was a metronome for population—ensuring reproduction, synchronizing harvests, and legitimizing rulers who enforced the cycle.

Shang China: Ancestors and the State

In Shang dynasty China (c. 1600–1046 BCE), we find perhaps the clearest example of population management as covenant. Oracle bone inscriptions record questions to Shangdi, the high god, and to royal ancestors: Should we sacrifice ten men for rain? Should twenty captives be offered for victory? (Keightley, *Sources of Shang History*, 1978). The answers were sought through divination cracks in bone, but the acts themselves were brutally real.

Large-scale human and animal sacrifices accompanied royal burials at Anyang, where hundreds of victims were interred in pits surrounding elite tombs. Here sacrifice functioned not only as sustenance for the divine but as population culling, a way to prune captives and reinforce hierarchy. At the same time, the ancestral cult bound fertility and loyalty to dynastic legitimacy. Families owed offerings to their ancestors, and the king's line owed offerings to Shangdi. Population was thereby funneled upward through kinship and hierarchy, ensuring no household escaped the covenant's reach.

Urbanization as Domestication

What unites these Old World examples is not only ritual but concentration. Nomadic bands were drawn into walled cities, irrigated corridors, dynastic states. What archaeologists celebrate as the "cradle of civilization" may equally be read as the corral of domestication. Temples, altars, and palaces were not only centers of worship but enclosures that fixed populations in place. Priests and kings acted as managers, ensuring the herd did not scatter.

James C. Scott, in *Against the Grain* (2017), has shown how early states often forced populations into sedentary life, despite the fact that hunter-gatherers were healthier and freer. From the covenant perspective, the reason is simple: dispersed humans could not be harvested efficiently. Concentrated humans could. The gods' emissaries needed density, predictability, and surplus. Urbanization provided it. Grain could be taxed, labor conscripted, fertility regulated, blood collected. Humanity was transformed from roaming bands into urbanized "cattle," penned in by stone and ritual.

Management through Fertility and Famine

Control was not only physical but biological. In Egypt, festivals of Hathor and Osiris linked fertility to seasonal cycles, ensuring reproduction aligned with agricultural surpluses. In Mesopotamia, offerings to Inanna included rituals of sacred marriage designed to bless crops and wombs together. In Shang China, ancestors were asked to intercede in childbirth and harvest simultaneously. Fertility was thus not private—it was calendared, supervised, and bound to covenantal logic.

Famine, too, became a lever of control. When the Nile failed or rains faltered, priests declared that offerings had lapsed, that humans had not paid their dues. Disasters reinforced the system, ensuring compliance through fear. Populations were reminded that their very survival depended on obedience to the covenant's schedule.

The Old World Covenant in Perspective

Taken together, the Old World's sacrificial systems functioned less as spontaneous piety and more as organized management. Populations were corralled into cities, tied to rivers and temples, counted and culled through ritual. Fertility was monitored, famine weaponized, and dynasties legitimized through blood.

From Mesopotamia's ledgers to Egypt's nilometers, from Vedic altars to Shang oracle bones, the pattern repeats: humanity organized as a resource. In one hemisphere, the covenant's priority was order, continuity, and control. The herd was not to be consumed in one feast but kept steady, fertile, and productive over millennia.

New World Models of Attrition

If the Old World covenant concentrated populations, the New World covenant burned through them. In Mesoamerica and the Andes, the gods did not ask only for continuity or dynastic reassurance. They demanded sustenance in the rawest sense: blood in volume, hearts in frequency, and populations culled to fuel the cosmos. Where Mesopotamia tallied sheep and oxen, Mexico and Peru tallied captives and skulls. Here, sacrifice was not the occasional pruning of a dynastic tree but the scythe swung again and again, keeping human numbers at levels the gods appeared to dictate.

Maya Cycles of Growth and Collapse

The Classic Maya flourished from c. 250 to 900 CE, filling the forests of the Yucatán with city-states, pyramids, and stelae inscribed with dynastic histories. Yet their rise and fall followed a strange pulse. Cities like Tikal, Copán, and Palenque reached peaks of population and monumental construction, only to be abandoned, their temples swallowed by jungle. Archaeologists debate drought, warfare, or ecological collapse, but the cycles are too patterned to ignore.

The covenant lens sees another possibility: population culling by design. The Maya bled themselves ritually, timed to Venus, and sacrificed captives to Chaac, the rain god. But when populations swelled beyond sustainable levels—or beyond the gods' requirements—the system collapsed. Famine and warfare cut numbers drastically, leaving scattered survivors to rebuild. The *Dresden Codex* preserves apocalyptic imagery of floods and fires unleashed when offerings lapsed. To the Maya, catastrophe was not a break in the covenant but its enforcement. The gods pruned the herd when priests failed to keep up with the schedule of blood.

Aztec Economy of Captives

If the Maya dramatized cosmic cycles, the Mexica (Aztec) industrialized them. The empire that dominated central Mexico from the 14th to 16th centuries CE built its entire military machine around the capture of sacrificial victims. The so-called "Flower Wars" were campaigns not to seize territory but to seize people—human inventory destined for the altars of Tenochtitlan.

The Templo Mayor was the covenant's center. Twin pyramids dedicated to Huitzilopochtli (sun and war) and Tlaloc (rain and fertility) required offerings on a scale that dwarfs the Old World. Chroniclers speak of thousands of victims sacrificed during single festivals. Archaeology confirms it: mass graves, skull racks (tzompantli), and dedicatory burials beneath temples. The Huey Tzompantli excavated in 2017 contained more than 600 skulls, many drilled to be mounted on display racks.

This was not random cruelty. It was an economy. Aztec agriculture, tribute, and war were organized to keep a steady flow of blood to the gods. Captives were processed like a resource: paraded, sacrificed, their hearts raised to the sun, their skulls displayed as proof of payment. The covenant here was immediate. If offerings lapsed, the sun itself might falter. Where Egypt assured continuity of dynasties, Mexico assured continuity of creation, day by day.

Inca and the Mountain of Death

Farther south, the Inca empire managed populations through mass relocation and mountaintop sacrifice. The capacocha ritual required children from across the empire to be brought to Cuzco, feted, and then marched to distant peaks. There, at altitudes where breathing itself was sacrifice, they were buried alive or killed, their bodies preserved by ice. Archaeological finds such as the "Ice Maiden" on Mount Ampato or the Llullaillaco mummies testify to the scale and extremity of these rites.

These children were not random. They were selected for purity, beauty, or lineage—biological traits valued by the covenant. Families were "honored" by the offering of a child, their grief transmuted into imperial loyalty. At the same time, populations were culled. The Inca also relocated whole villages, dispersing or concentrating labor as imperial policy dictated. Here management was twofold: tribute in blood at the empire's edges, and tribute in labor across its heartland. The Andes became not only a stage for the covenant but a machine for redistributing and reducing populations as the gods required.

Nasca Lines and the Theater of Absence

On Peru's coastal plain, the Nasca culture etched hundreds of geoglyphs into the desert—lines, spirals, and animal figures visible only from above. Scholars debate whether these were ritual walkways, astronomical calendars, or water symbols. But one striking pattern emerges: many of the lines converge on ceremonial centers where evidence of human sacrifice has been found. Victims were killed and displayed in desert plazas, their bodies exposed to the sky.

The Nasca themselves disappeared by c. 600 CE. Drought and ecological stress are the standard explanations. But the covenant interpretation asks whether these collapses were enforced reductions. If populations were harvested too aggressively—if blood tribute exceeded replenishment—collapse would follow. The lines themselves may testify to a covenant of attrition: humans reduced, landscapes scarred, offerings stretched across barren plains until nothing remained to give.

Collapse as Covenant Enforcement

Across the Americas, sudden collapses follow patterns too consistent to dismiss. Maya cities emptied, Nasca vanished, the Mississippian mound-builders at Cahokia dwindled. Mainstream archaeology points to climate change, resource depletion, or warfare. All may be true. Yet why do these collapses so often coincide with peaks of ritual intensity? Why do the greatest monuments—Teotihuacan, Chichén Itzá, Tenochtitlan—arise just before populations crash?

From the covenant lens, collapse was not failure but enforcement. When offerings fell behind or populations exceeded demand, disaster reset the balance. Drought, plague, invasion—whatever the instrument, the effect was the same: numbers reduced, survivors scattered, the covenant reasserted. The gods did not merely receive blood; they regulated the herd.

Domestication vs. Culling

Here the hemispheric contrast sharpens. In the Old World, populations were corralled into continuity—dynasties stabilized, lineages preserved, cities sustained for millennia. In the New World, populations were culled repeatedly—empires rising and falling, cities abandoned, lineages cut short. One hemisphere was managed like a herd of cattle kept for milk and wool, the other like a flock of animals periodically slaughtered to feed the masters.

The logic is chilling but consistent. Feeding required culling. The gods optimized strategy to local resources: in Europe, Africa, and Asia, blood was drawn in measured doses while fertility was maintained; in the Americas, blood was drawn in torrents, and populations were replenished only to be harvested again. Two strategies, one program.

Implications

When seen this way, the great collapses of American civilizations may not be mysteries at all. They may be the visible scars of covenant enforcement, moments when the gods' harvest exceeded sustainability or when they withdrew after taking too much. To modern eyes, the abandonment of Copán or the disappearance of the Nasca are puzzles. To ancient eyes, they were judgments—proof that the gods' hunger had not been satisfied, or had been satisfied too much.

The Americas thus reveal the covenant's harsher face. Here sacrifice was not reassurance but survival, not continuity but consumption. Populations were not corralled for steady service but burned through in cycles of growth and collapse. The gods who demanded blood also dictated attrition, keeping humanity from ever exceeding its allotted bounds.

Comparison and Synthesis: Two Hemispheres, One Program

Placed side by side, the Old and New World covenant systems read less like independent traditions and more like two halves of a single design. The differences are striking, but they are differences of emphasis, not of origin. Both hemispheres display the same core traits—monumental architecture aligned to the heavens, priestly hierarchies enforcing ritual schedules, and sacrificial economies that treated human life as a resource. Yet the way those systems played out suggests deliberate calibration. In the Old World, the covenant tended toward domestication and continuity. In the New World, it leaned toward culling and collapse. Two strategies, one program: manage humanity.

Continuity vs. Attrition

The Old World strategy revolved around keeping populations stable, tethered to dynasties and priesthoods. In Egypt, Mesopotamia, India, and China, continuity was prized. Sacrifices marked enthronements, funerals, or crises, but the underlying goal was to sustain order. Populations were corralled along rivers and fertile valleys, taxed and tithed to support temples. The covenant here worked like a long-term herd management system: people fed their gods while reproducing under priestly supervision. Continuity produced reliability.

The New World strategy inverted the logic. Populations were pushed to crescendos and then cut down. Maya cities waxed and waned in cycles, Aztec captives streamed daily to the knife, and Inca children were buried on frozen peaks. Collapse was not failure but function. The herd was not only corralled but thinned, sometimes violently. Continuity mattered less than immediacy. Blood was not reassurance but fuel, demanded in quantities that destabilized the very societies that produced it. Attrition produced intensity.

Visibility vs. Secrecy

Another contrast lies in visibility. In the Old World, sacrificial practice often remained enclosed: retainers buried in Abydos tombs, Shang victims interred beneath palace floors, Vedic offerings guarded by layers of ritual geometry. The acts were real, but they were contained, often hidden from public view. The covenant emphasized regularity more than spectacle.

In the New World, sacrifice was public pedagogy. Aztec priests displayed skulls in racks for entire cities to see, Maya murals depicted bound captives beneath celestial glyphs, and Inca capacocha burials dramatized offerings at the literal edge of the sky. Sacrifice here was lesson as much as payment, performed in plazas and mountaintops where visibility was unavoidable. The covenant emphasized spectacle because spectacle reinforced fear, and fear ensured compliance.

Calendars and Timetables

Both hemispheres synchronized sacrifice with celestial events, but the intensity differed. The Old World tracked solstices, equinoxes, and star risings—moments when offerings aligned with cosmic order. The New World tracked cycles with obsessive precision: Venus risings down to the day, solar zenith passages embedded in city grids, equinox shadows choreographed across staircases. For Egypt, missing a solstice rite risked disorder. For the Maya, missing a Venus interval risked cosmic collapse. Both kept calendars, but one read them as guidelines, the other as ledgers of debt.

Labor as Sacrifice

Here the hemispheres converge most clearly. Monumental construction consumed human life everywhere. Whether in hauling limestone blocks for Giza, carving stelae for Copán, or hauling children into the Andes, the energy of populations was poured into stone as offering. Yet again the emphasis diverged. In the Old World, labor was the primary sacrifice—millions of man-hours dedicated to temples and tombs. In the New World, labor was paired with literal blood in industrial quantities. The pyramids of Mexico were built by tens of thousands, and then those same tens of thousands were marched up the stairs as offerings. One hemisphere bled its workers through toil, the other through both toil and the knife.

Hemispheric Feedback Loops

The difference in strategies may also explain the difference in trajectories. Old World civilizations persisted for millennia: Egypt endured three thousand years of dynasties, Mesopotamian city-states rose and fell but never vanished outright, India's Vedic rituals transmuted into later Hindu traditions, and China's dynastic cycles continued unbroken. Continuity of practice bred continuity of civilization.

The New World civilizations burned brighter but shorter. Teotihuacan collapsed by 600 CE, the Maya fragmented by 900, the Nasca vanished, the Inca lasted scarcely a century in imperial form before conquest. Collapse followed peak. This may not have been failure but deliberate calibration. If the gods required more blood than a population could sustain, collapse was the inevitable reset, reducing numbers until replenishment was possible. The cycle repeated because the program demanded it.

Two Modes, One Hand

What unites these differences is not chance but coordination. No matter the hemisphere, the same elements recur: serpent intermediaries, winged messengers, star alignments, ritual machinery. The program was global, but its modes were tuned to local conditions. Where O-negative blood was abundant (Europe, North Africa, parts of the Americas), feeding zones flourished. Where it was scarce (East and South Asia), breeding programs emphasized lineage. Where populations could be corralled, continuity prevailed. Where they could be culled, attrition reigned. The gods adapted their demands not only to blood chemistry but to demography, playing humanity like an instrument tuned differently in each hemisphere.

The Domestication Analogy

The most chilling synthesis may be the simplest: humans were managed like livestock. In the Old World, we were dairy cattle—kept alive, bred, milked for blood in measured doses. In the New World, we were meat stock—fattened, slaughtered, replenished. Both modes require control of population, manipulation of fertility, and enforcement of compliance. Both modes require architecture as pens, calendars as schedules, and priests as herdsmen. Both modes demand sacrifice, whether slow or swift. The covenant's genius was its ability to disguise this management as religion, to convince the herds that their service was worship.

The Global Ledger

When viewed across hemispheres, sacrifice resolves into a ledger. Populations fed gods with blood, labor, and loyalty. The entries differ —an Egyptian bull here, a Maya captive there—but the balance sheet is the same: human life paid as currency. The gods' appetite did not wane; it only adjusted. Collapse in one region meant intensification in another. If the covenant was global, then humanity as a whole was the herd, redistributed across hemispheres to meet demand.

Toward Modern Parallels

The hemispheric synthesis also sets the stage for modern continuities. If ancient populations were managed as herds, what of modern populations? Abduction reports, genetic experiments, cattle mutilations, and blood extractions echo the same logic. The covenant may not have ended; it may only have changed form, shifting from temples to laboratories, from public plazas to hidden rooms. The hemispheric comparison reminds us that management was never uniform. It was always adaptive. And if it was adaptive then, it is adaptive now.

Afterword

The Old World and New World covenants were not contradictions but complements. One preserved dynasties; the other renewed the cosmos. One corralled, the other culled. Both obeyed the same principle: humanity managed as resource. The differences sharpen the outline of the program. The gods who demanded blood were not improvising—they were administering. And humanity's role was not worshipper but livestock, domesticated or slaughtered depending on the hemisphere.

In the end, the hemispheres were not opposites but experiments —two modes of control applied to the same species. Domesticate or cull, corral or bleed, the result was always management. And yet the architecture, the alignments, and the rituals were never ends in themselves. They pointed to something deeper: the biology of both gods and humans, and the question of why certain bodies, certain bloodlines, were chosen. That question takes us beyond the mechanics of population into the raw material itself—the blood that fueled the covenant.

10

THE ENFORCERS

No covenant endures without enforcement. Across cultures, the gods were rarely faceless abstractions; they appeared in forms that inspired awe and terror, emissaries stationed between human and divine. These beings were remembered not only in myth but in art—half-human, half-animal figures carved into stone, painted on walls, carried into ritual as masks and costumes. They were the ones who ensured the covenant was kept, who reminded mortals that disobedience had consequences.

In Mesopotamia, the Apkallu stand as the archetype: winged, bearded figures holding the bucket and cone, guardians of kings and cities. They were portrayed not as distant deities but as active agents, always at work, always applying their strange tools. In Egypt, Horus the falcon-headed god—protector, avenger, and divine enforcer— watched over pharaohs, his piercing gaze promising both justice and reprisal. In India, Garuda, half-man and half-eagle, stood as both mount and enforcer for Vishnu, a figure whose speed and ferocity made him more than symbolic. In Mesoamerica, murals depict bird-men, jaguar-men, and serpent-guardians, hybrid enforcers who blurred the line between priesthood and something otherworldly.

Archaeological context makes their role even clearer. Apkallu are carved again and again on the walls of Assyrian palaces at Nineveh, Nimrud, and Khorsabad, never tucked away in hidden chambers but stationed at thresholds: flanking doorways, standing at the bases of staircases, or guarding the approaches to throne rooms. Anyone entering or leaving the palace, whether courtier or commoner, passed beneath their wings. Their gaze and their gestures announced that human authority was shadowed by something greater. These were not background decorations — they were sentinels in stone, positioned like guards of flesh and blood.

Cuneiform inscriptions reinforce this visual message. Texts describe Apkallu as "purifiers" and "watchers," beings invoked to drive away evil, to guard against pestilence, to ensure fertility of fields and wombs. They were said to hold wisdom from before the flood, survivors or emissaries of a time when gods walked openly with men. Berossus, a Hellenistic-era Babylonian priest, describes one such being, Oannes, a fish-man who rose from the sea each day to teach humans writing, architecture, and agriculture before retreating back into the waters at night. Whether fish-clad sages or winged guardians, the function is the same: beings who bridge the human and divine and ensure the order of the covenant.

The tools they hold — the bucket (*banduddu*) and the cone (*mullilu*) — remain enigmatic. Mainstream scholars interpret the cone as a stylized fir cone, symbol of fertility, and the bucket as a container of holy water, together forming a ritual of purification. Yet the consistency of the depiction, repeated with almost mechanical precision across centuries, suggests more than symbolic flourish. The cone is always pinched delicately between thumb and forefinger, angled as if to apply or anoint. The bucket is always suspended at the ready, never overturned, as though it carried a finite and precious substance. Some researchers have speculated that the "water" could be pollen, resin, or even a kind of chemical solution used in temple rites. From the covenant perspective, however, the gestures look procedural — the application of a dose, the servicing of a system, the careful maintenance of an exchange between gods and men.

Scale itself conveys hierarchy. In reliefs, Apkallu are often taller and more imposing than the kings they flank. Their feathers spread wide, their beards curl in immaculate rows, their gaze remains unblinking. The king may be enthroned, but the Apkallu overshadow him, suggesting that human rulers governed only under the watch of these greater beings. Just as the enforcer gods of Egypt dwarf their pharaohs, the Apkallu remind us that human sovereignty was conditional — a delegated authority monitored by emissaries.

The Apkallu tradition did not vanish with Assyria. Echoes surface in later myth and scripture. The fish-clad Oannes becomes the prototype of the culture-bringer. The hybrid guardians of Mesopotamian gates evolve into the biblical cherubim who guard Eden with flaming swords, or the Watchers of the Book of Enoch who descend to oversee humanity before straying from their mandate. The persistence of the imagery hints that what began as living memory of enforcers hardened into myth over millennia.

Taken together, the context, the tools, the scale, and the mythic continuity argue for something more than allegory. The Apkallu were remembered not as abstract ideas but as tangible presences — hybrids, emissaries, or overseers placed to ensure that the covenant was kept.

Placed side by side, the similarities are difficult to dismiss. The Apkallu of Mesopotamia, carved with wings spread and tools in hand, stand in uncanny parallel to the bird-men of Mesoamerica, their feathered helmets, beaked faces, and avian postures marking them as more than costumed warriors. Both are winged humanoids, both act as intermediaries between rulers and gods, both are shown wielding objects of power and confronting serpents. Is this merely coincidence—two cultures inventing the same hybrid guardians—or does it hint that emissaries of the same kind once appeared in both hemispheres, remembered through different artistic tongues? The symmetry is almost too precise to explain away, leaving the unsettling possibility that these were not myths at all, but recollections of the same enforcers deployed across continents.

What ties them together is their posture: they are never passive. They carry tools, they extend hands, they confront serpents or

A Blood Covenant

demons. In other words, they act. The "handbag" motif we encountered earlier reappears here, clutched by enforcers who apply its contents to trees, rulers, or victims. The cone or pinecone appears again, touched like an instrument of power. These repeated details suggest something functional, not ornamental. The enforcers were technicians of the covenant, armed with instruments whose meaning the ancients only partly understood.

And in every culture, they are depicted larger than life. Reliefs show Apkallu towering over kings. Egyptian gods dwarf their human companions. Mesoamerican murals present feathered and jaguar beings more imposing than the mortals beside them. The scale speaks a truth: these were not imagined equals, but superiors—agents of power who enforced compliance. Priests may have officiated, but the enforcers embodied divine authority, whether in physical presence or through the masks and rituals that bore their likeness.

The continuity of these figures suggests something more than mythic invention. They may have been remembered emissaries, or even hybridized overseers placed among humans to maintain order. Egypt provides perhaps the most vivid examples of enforcers remembered as gods. Horus, the falcon-headed protector of pharaohs, was not simply a symbol of kingship but a being described in texts as "the Great God, the Lord of the Sky" whose eye saw every offense (Faulkner, *The Ancient Egyptian Pyramid Texts*, 1969). Anubis, the jackal-headed guardian of the necropolis, is shown towering over mortals in tomb reliefs, presiding at scales that judged the dead. In the *Book of the Dead*, he is called *"He Who Counts the Hearts,"* a chilling reminder that blood and conscience alike were subject to enforcement (Hornung, *Conceptions of God in Ancient Egypt*, 1982). Sobek, the crocodile-headed deity, embodied raw predation; temples along the Nile literally housed live crocodiles adorned with jewels, a living reminder that the gods' guardians were not abstractions. Together, these beings formed a pantheon of hybrid overseers—falcon, jackal, crocodile—whose very bodies declared the consequences of disobedience.

In India, Garuda served as Vishnu's mount and as a symbol of violent protection. Half-man and half-eagle, he was always depicted in motion: wings outspread, talons extended, serpents clutched in his hands or coiled beneath his feet (Doniger, *Hindu Myths*, 1975). His role was not abstract but functional—destroyer of demons, devourer of serpents, a reminder that covenantal order required active enforcement. Garuda is not a contemplative deity but an enforcer, a figure of speed and ferocity whose form blends human intelligence with predatory power.

Even more provocative is the appearance of nearly identical birdman figures in pre-Columbian Colombia. At San Agustín, massive stone statues depict winged, beaked humanoids whose posture and proportions echo Garuda so precisely that they cannot be dismissed as coincidence. One figure in particular shows the bird-man gripping a serpent in its claw while clamping the same serpent in its beak. This is not generic bird symbolism. It is the signature pose of Garuda in Hindu art, where he is defined by his combat with the nāga serpents, pinning them in his talons while tearing them with his beak. To find the same formula carved into the Andes is unsettling: two continents, two cultures, the same enforcer. Were the San Agustín figures independent inventions, or the very same beings remembered oceans apart? If enforcers could be remembered oceans apart in stone, they could just as easily be remembered above, in the sky itself.

Another layer of continuity lies not in the bodies of the enforcers, but in the vehicles they commanded. Across cultures, the sky itself was remembered as a stage of enforcement. In Egypt and Mesopotamia, the winged solar disk hovers over kings, its radiant orb carried on outstretched wings. To modern eyes it is stylized ornament, yet its geometry is unmistakably mechanical: a central disk, lateral wings, tail feathers below. The motif recurs for centuries, sanctifying rulers beneath the emblem of aerial power. In Native North America, the Thunderbird filled the same role—an immense sky-being whose wings shook the heavens, whose lightning punished defiance, whose appearance reminded all that sovereignty descended from above. Tribal traditions describe the Thunderbird not as an abstraction but as a presence that terrified villages with storm, noise, and strike. These were not idle myths; they were memories of aerial enforcement. The vehicle itself became the enforcer, its sound and light translated into thunder and lightning, its hovering presence stylized as bird or disk depending on the culture's tongue. Whether as Thunderbird or winged sun, the message was the same: authority descended from machines that ruled the sky, reminding mortals that disobedience had consequences.

What also is striking is the echo in language. In India, the serpent subdued by Garuda was called *nāga*. In Mesoamerica, linguists reconstruct the Olmec ancestral language (Proto-Mixe-Zoquean) with the root *nak^w*, meaning *"serpent."* The consonant cluster is nearly identical: nag/nak, both carrying the same meaning of snake or dragon. Iconography alone might be dismissed as coincidence — but iconography reinforced by phonetic parallels, separated by an ocean, suggests something deeper. Were both cultures preserving the same memory of avian enforcers grappling with cosmic serpents?

Even farther north, in the heart of North America, the same archetype surfaces. At Cahokia, the largest pre-Columbian city north of Mexico, a stone tablet portrays the so-called Birdman: a winged figure with taloned feet and outstretched arms, one side carved with avian form, the reverse etched with a cross-hatched snakeskin pattern. Archaeologists identify him as a falcon warrior or fertility symbol, but the covenant lens suggests something deeper. The Birdman combines the upper world of sky with the underworld of serpent, a fusion of domination that recalls Garuda gripping nāgas or Apkallu standing astride demons. His presence at Cahokia is no isolated flourish: the city's vast mound complexes, aligned to solstices and equinoxes, were centers of sacrifice where elites staged compliance on a monumental scale. The Birdman was not decorative—he was the enforcer, remembered in stone as the figure who bound the covenant in the Mississippi Valley. That his snakeskin counterpart was carved on the reverse only sharpens the point: avian power had subdued serpentine rival, sky had conquered underworld, and the covenant was sealed in blood atop the mounds of Illinois.

Mesoamerica offers further parallels. Maya murals and Aztec codices portray bird-men and jaguar hybrids who guarded rulers and altars, their costumes blurring the line between priestly attire and otherworldly anatomy (Miller & Taube, *Gods and Symbols of Ancient Mexico and the Maya*, 1993). At Teotihuacan, feathered warriors flank the Temple of the Feathered Serpent, while in Maya art, avian headdresses and vision-serpents appear in ritual scenes that emphasize their role as intermediaries and guardians. Just as in Mesopotamia and Egypt, these figures are not passive symbols—they are active presences, reminders that the covenant was enforced not only by priests but by beings whose appearance alone could terrify compliance.

Mesoamerica too abounds with these hybrids. Maya murals show rulers wearing bird and jaguar regalia, but glyphs and iconography often blur costume with being. The "Vision Serpent" of Yaxchilán, for example, is accompanied by bird-headed attendants emerging from its jaws, figures so consistent across lintels and murals that they suggest a remembered template rather than random imagination (Miller & Taube, *An Illustrated Dictionary of the Gods and Symbols of Ancient Mexico and the Maya*, 1993). Aztec depictions of jaguar warriors, their mouths open in permanent roars, and eagle warriors with feathered helmets, likewise straddle the line between human priesthood and something more-than-human.

Placed side by side, the consistency is striking: falcon-headed Horus, eagle-bodied Garuda, bird-men of Yaxchilán; jackal Anubis, jaguar-men of Teotihuacan; serpent-fighters in Mesopotamia and Mesoamerica alike. They are never idle figures. They confront, grasp, punish, and devour. Across continents, humanity remembered its guardians not as benevolent teachers but as enforcers—hybridized overseers whose power derived as much from fear as from reverence. Their tools, their gestures, their recurring iconography point to a role beyond symbolism: they were the covenant's police, ensuring the blood flowed when it must and punishing when it did not.

In myth, they become heroes, guardians, avengers. In truth, they may have been the ones who ensured humanity never strayed far from its obligations. The covenant was never voluntary; it was imposed. And the enforcers were its living reminder.

Apkallu — Guardians with Tools

The Mesopotamian Apkallu are among the clearest examples of covenant enforcers. These hybrid figures, half-human and half-fish or bird, appear across Assyrian palace reliefs from the 9th–7th centuries BCE, always in postures of action rather than repose. They stand beside kings, flank sacred trees, and extend their strange instruments — a small bucket held in one hand, and a cone or "pollen object" in the other. To modern eyes, the gesture is repetitive to the point of monotony. Yet repetition is the signature of procedure, not artistry. These were not idle decorations but ritual acts frozen in stone.

The bucket, known in Akkadian as the *banduddu*, and the cone, the *mullilu*, appear again and again. Scholars such as Black and Green (*Gods, Demons and Symbols of Ancient Mesopotamia*, 1992) interpret them as symbols of purification: the cone perhaps a stylized date palm or fir fruit, dipped into the bucket of water to sprinkle over the king or sacred tree. But the context resists purely symbolic readings. Relief after relief shows Apkallu in duplicate, sometimes mirrored across a tree of life, each performing the exact same gesture. If this were only metaphor, why the precision? Why the insistence on showing tools wielded, not merely carried?

From the covenant perspective, the Apkallu function as technicians. The cone is not ornamental; it is applicative. The bucket is not symbolic; it is a container. Together they form a delivery system, transferring substances from vessel to target, whether sacred tree, king, or offering. In modern terms, they look less like priests blessing and more like workers servicing an interface — applying doses, maintaining flows, resetting a mechanism.

Even Mesopotamian texts hint at their role as more than mythic figures. The Apkallu were said to be seven sages sent by Ea/Enki, the god of wisdom, to instruct humanity in law, ritual, and craftsmanship (Dalley, *Myths from Mesopotamia*, 2000). They were not gods themselves but emissaries, half-divine beings dispatched to establish order. The duality is crucial: enforcers stationed among mortals to oversee the covenant, not distant deities to be prayed to. Their hybrid nature — human torsos with fish scales, or human faces with eagle wings — reinforces the idea of engineered intermediaries, shaped to inhabit both worlds but belonging to neither.

The reliefs also emphasize scale. Apkallu tower over the kings they flank, their wings spread, their beards elaborately carved, their posture dominating. Kings may have ruled cities, but the carvings proclaim a deeper truth: authority was enforced by beings greater than the throne. The king is depicted as dependent, dwarfed by the guardians who literally shield him with their wings. These images suggest that political power itself was derivative, contingent on the covenant's approval and enforcement.

Equally telling is the consistency of their iconography across centuries. From Nimrud to Nineveh, from Ashurnasirpal II to Ashurbanipal, the Apkallu repeat unchanged, their buckets and cones never omitted. No empire maintains an image so rigid unless it encodes something deemed indispensable. The tools are not optional — they are essential. That persistence suggests the enforcers' presence was not confined to art but was embedded in ritual life, a memory of beings who actively participated in ceremonies, applying substances, enforcing order, and reminding rulers of their dependence.

When we place the Apkallu alongside Garuda and the Mesoamerican bird-men, the cross-cultural pattern sharpens. In India and Colombia, the enforcer seizes the serpent, embodying power over chaos. In Mesopotamia, the enforcer applies tools, embodying power over ritual. Both postures are functional, not symbolic. They suggest a workforce — emissaries tasked with specific procedures, whether binding serpents or dosing sacred trees. In all cases, humanity's role was subordinated: kings and priests officiated, but the true power was embodied in these hybrids who ensured the covenant was maintained.

Archaeologists have long puzzled over why the Apkallu were placed so prominently on palace walls, gates, and thresholds. Their ubiquity is striking: from Khorsabad to Nineveh, relief after relief repeats the same figure, often mirrored across a sacred tree or positioned like guards at a doorway. In the throne room of Ashurnasirpal II at Nimrud, no fewer than seven Apkallu flank the royal seat, as though to remind courtiers that the king's words carried weight only under the supervision of higher powers (Albenda, *Assyrian Reliefs at the Palace of Ashurnasirpal II*, 1986). To enter such spaces was to be scrutinized not only by human eyes but by hybrid watchers, forever carved in mid-gesture with their buckets and cones.

The sacred tree before which they often appear is another clue. Scholars typically call it a stylized date palm, symbol of fertility. Yet the precision with which Apkallu interact with it — dipping the cone into the bucket, applying it directly to the tree's branches — makes the scene look less symbolic than procedural. The tree resembles a mechanism being serviced, its patterned geometry suggesting order and flow. If the cone carried pollen, resin, or even liquid, the Apkallu were performing a transfer: ensuring the tree, emblem of cosmic order, remained charged. In covenant terms, it was not art but maintenance, a servicing of the interface through which humans and gods exchanged life.

Texts from Mesopotamia reinforce this impression of procedure. The Bit Meseri ("*House of Confinement*") ritual series describes how Apkallu figurines were buried beneath thresholds and walls to protect buildings from demonic incursion. Each figurine held the same bucket and cone, even in miniature (Wiggermann, *Mesopotamian Protective Spirits*, 1992). The ritual instructions read like blueprints: place one Apkallu facing north, another facing south, all clutching their tools. This is not symbolic flourish; it is standardization. Just as modern engineers install identical circuit breakers in every building, Mesopotamian priests deployed Apkallu with their implements as protective technology.

The flood connection is equally telling. Berossus' account of Oannes describes him as a fish-clad teacher who brought humanity the arts of civilization from the sea (Burstein, *The Babyloniaca of Berossus*, 1978). Cuneiform sources list the seven Apkallu as antediluvian sages, dispatched by Ea/Enki before the great flood to instruct humankind. After the deluge, texts note that only part-human, part-divine "*post-diluvian Apkallu*" remained, assisting but no longer ruling directly. The distinction is crucial: it suggests the Apkallu were remembered as actual beings who withdrew after catastrophe, leaving only hybrid or diminished successors. Myth preserves them as Watchers, but their role as covenant enforcers may once have been literal.

The iconography also raises the unsettling possibility that their tools carried more than symbolic water. Some researchers have speculated about psychoactive resins or even antiseptic solutions, citing the importance of cedar oil and bitumen in Mesopotamian rituals (Collins, *Magic and Ritual in the Ancient Near East,* 2004). Others have proposed that the cone-and-bucket system resembles a handheld applicator — dipping, coating, pressing. From a covenant lens, this imagery could reflect not simple purification but dosage, as though Apkallu administered treatments or extracts to kings, trees, or victims to maintain a biological balance demanded by their masters.

Even their hybrid appearance hints at deliberate design. Human torsos grant intelligence and authority; eagle wings and beaks evoke predatory power; fish scales connect them to water, source of life and renewal. It is as if their very bodies were schematics, displaying multiple domains of control: air, land, water. The Apkallu were not random monsters but composite overseers, bridging categories in order to dominate them. Their recurrence in reliefs is a reminder: human kings reigned only under the surveillance of beings engineered to embody and enforce the covenant.

Later traditions confirm their endurance as memory. The biblical cherubim who guard Eden with flaming swords carry echoes of Apkallu guardianship. The Watchers of the *Book of Enoch* — angels who descended to instruct humanity before corrupting themselves with forbidden unions — recall the hybrid, half-divine, half-mortal role. Even classical art preserves distant echoes: Greek depictions of eagle-men like the Lamassu or griffins may be cultural afterimages of the Apkallu. Wherever one looks, the same posture recurs: wings unfurled, tools or weapons in hand, standing sentinel at thresholds between human and divine.

From this vantage, the Apkallu were not simply symbols of purification but the very image of enforcement. They carried the tools, they serviced the mechanism, they shadowed the throne. They were, in every sense, the technicians of the covenant.

Egyptian Enforcers — Guardians of Kings and Dead

If Mesopotamia remembered its enforcers as Apkallu sages, Egypt carved theirs as gods who towered over kings and stalked the thresholds of life and death. Here the covenant's enforcers appear not as winged men but as hybrids with falcon heads, jackal muzzles, or crocodile jaws — beings that embodied predation and vigilance in forms too visceral to mistake for allegory.

Horus, the falcon-headed god, was the quintessential enforcer of kingship. Reliefs show him standing behind pharaohs, one clawed hand on the royal shoulder, the other grasping an ankh or scepter. His eye, the udjat, was not only a symbol of healing but of unblinking surveillance. Pyramid Texts from the Fifth and Sixth Dynasties describe Horus as the avenger who "strikes down the enemies of Osiris" and "watches over his father's throne" (Faulkner, *The Ancient Egyptian Pyramid Texts*, 1969). In temple reliefs, pharaohs are depicted as the "living Horus," but the presence of Horus himself in the same scenes makes clear that kingship was conditional. The ruler did not embody Horus so much as he ruled under Horus's oversight, a reminder that sovereignty itself was enforced by a higher agent.

Anubis, the jackal-headed guardian of necropolises, played a more chilling role. In funerary papyri and tomb murals, he bends over the embalming table, his long snout looming over the wrapped corpse. In the Book of the Dead, he is called *"He Who Counts the*

Hearts," presiding over the weighing of souls against the feather of Ma'at. Reliefs show him towering over human petitioners, his black fur a symbol of decay and regeneration. Anubis did not simply guide the dead — he judged them, enforcing the covenant's demand that order (Ma'at) be maintained even in death. To cheat the gods, to arrive without proper offerings, was to risk annihilation at his jaws. Hornung notes that Anubis "stands at the transition between worlds, the overseer who ensures that what is due is delivered" (*Conceptions of God in Ancient Egypt*, 1982).

Sobek, the crocodile-headed god of the Nile, embodied enforcement at its most raw. Crocodiles were not symbolic metaphors but living predators embedded in Egyptian temple life. The temple of Kom Ombo housed live crocodiles, fed and adorned with jewelry, their presence a reminder that divine guardianship was never gentle. Sobek's cult titles — "He Who Loves Violence," "Lord of the Riverbank" — underscore his predatory role (Wilkinson, *The Complete Gods and Goddesses of Ancient Egypt*, 2003). Reliefs depict him grasping bound captives, his jaws agape. If Horus embodied vigilance and Anubis judgment, Sobek embodied the raw threat of consequences: disobedience meant being devoured.

What ties these figures together is not their mythological variety but their functional consistency. Each embodies a posture of oversight and reprisal. Each is larger than the humans they flank. Each is depicted with the tools or body parts of predation — claws, muzzles, jaws — poised in scenes where humans stand vulnerable. These are not distant creator gods but enforcers stationed at key thresholds: Horus at the throne, Anubis at the tomb, Sobek at the river where life and death mingled.

Archaeological context reinforces the impression. In royal tombs, wall scenes pair the presence of these enforcers with inscriptions reminding the dead of debts owed to the gods. In temple courts, statues of Horus or Sobek flanked gateways much as Apkallu flanked Assyrian doorways, positioned to confront entrants with the covenant's guardians. The architecture staged the same message across cultures: entry into sacred space was not free, it was conditional, monitored by beings larger than life.

Egyptian mythology also reinforces their role as active enforcers rather than passive symbols. The *"Contendings of Horus and Seth"* narrates Horus's unrelenting pursuit of his father's murderer, emphasizing vengeance and reprisal as his sacred duties. In funerary texts, Anubis is invoked not only as embalmer but as the one who *"stands against the enemies of Osiris"* and *"punishes the foes of Ra."* Sobek, meanwhile, appears in Coffin Texts as the god who *"opens the sky with his might"* and *"subdues the waters,"* enforcing divine control over both chaos and fertility (Faulkner, *Coffin Texts,* 1973). Each enforcer is defined not by abstract qualities but by violent action.

From the covenant perspective, their animal forms take on new meaning. A falcon can see vast distances and strike from above; a jackal scavenges corpses and prowls at thresholds; a crocodile lurks in rivers, dragging prey into hidden depths. These are predators — living embodiments of vigilance, pursuit, and reprisal. By embodying these forms, the covenant's emissaries communicated a simple truth: there was no escape. Whether in the sky, on land, or in water, enforcement followed.

Even later reinterpretations preserved this function. Under Greek and Roman influence, Horus merged into Harpocrates, Anubis into Hermanubis, yet their postures of vigilance remained. Christian iconography of Michael weighing souls echoes Anubis's scales, while later medieval imagery of crocodile-dragons evokes Sobek's predatory Nile presence. The persistence of these motifs across millennia suggests that what Egypt remembered as gods may have originated as encounters with beings whose role was enforcement, later mythologized but never forgotten.

Placed alongside Mesopotamia's Apkallu and India's Garuda, Egypt's enforcers complete a cross-cultural tableau: hybrids larger than men, armed with animal features, stationed at thresholds, punishing disobedience, and safeguarding the covenant's flow of offerings. Their imagery was not decorative but procedural, reminding mortals that blood and tribute were monitored, measured, and enforced.

When we set Horus, Anubis, and Sobek beside the Apkallu of Mesopotamia and the bird-men of India and Mesoamerica, the pattern becomes even clearer. Each hybrid shares a functional posture: guardianship of rulers, surveillance of offerings, and enforcement of order through the threat of violence. Horus, with his falcon gaze and taloned hands, echoes the winged Apkallu towering over Assyrian kings. Anubis, black-jawed judge of the dead, recalls the jackal and jaguar warriors of Mesoamerica, whose snarling visages warned that transgression carried a price. Sobek, with his crocodile jaws, parallels the serpent-fighting Garuda of India and the San Agustín bird-men of Colombia, each figure embodying predation in water, sky, or earth.

The consistency is too strong to dismiss as coincidence. Each culture remembered enforcers not as distant creator gods but as agents whose very anatomy made enforcement unavoidable. Whether it was wings spread across Mesopotamian palace gates, falcon eyes carved into Egyptian temples, or jaguar maws painted on Maya murals, the message was the same: compliance was not optional. The covenant was monitored by beings engineered to embody vigilance and reprisal.

What makes the Egyptian examples especially compelling is their integration into every level of ritual life. Horus stood behind kings in coronation scenes, reminding rulers that their power was conditional. Anubis crouched over embalming tables, ensuring the dead were processed in accordance with cosmic law. Sobek lurked in temple pools, his living crocodiles turning worship into confrontation with predation itself. This was not metaphor but administration. Just as Mesopotamian inscriptions listed procedures for purification with cone and bucket, Egyptian reliefs staged predators beside rulers and dead, dramatizing enforcement as part of the machinery of the covenant.

From the covenant perspective, this suggests a global program of "compliance officers" — emissaries whose physical forms varied with local symbolism but whose functions were interchangeable. Whether bird, jackal, or crocodile, their presence made sure the blood flowed when due and that rulers never forgot their dependence. The enforcers were not imaginative flourishes of art but parts of a shared operating system, deployed across continents to keep humanity within bounds.

The Egyptian record also sharpens the sense that these beings were not isolated to one land. Winged guardians in Mesopotamia, jackal- and falcon-headed overseers along the Nile, each carry the same traits: hybrid bodies, larger-than-life scale, and a posture of vigilance. Their differences in animal form may reflect local adaptation, but their shared role as enforcers is unmistakable. The pattern suggests that these figures were not figments of cultural imagination arising independently, but regional expressions of a common memory. Just as the Apkallu held their buckets and cones with procedural exactness, so too did Horus and Anubis embody oversight with predatory precision. When placed side by side, the hybrids of Mesopotamia and Egypt prepare us for the even wider echoes in India and the Americas, where bird-men like Garuda continue the same function under different names.

India — Garuda as Enforcer

In India, Garuda served as Vishnu's mount and as the archetype of violent protection. Half-man and half-eagle, he is always depicted in motion: wings outspread, talons extended, serpents clutched in his claws or crushed beneath his weight (Doniger, *Hindu Myths*, 1975). His role was not abstract but functional—destroyer of demons, devourer of serpents, a reminder that covenantal order required active enforcement. Garuda is not a contemplative deity but an operative, a figure whose speed, ferocity, and hybrid anatomy combine human intelligence with predatory instinct.

Garuda's role as enforcer was not confined to mythic texts. His image proliferated across Southeast Asia, carried by Hindu and later Buddhist kingdoms as they spread through the region. In Cambodia's Angkor, Garuda statues line causeways, each grasping a serpent as though eternally engaged in combat. In Java, Garuda reliefs flank temple doors, serving as threshold guardians, just as Apkallu flanked Mesopotamian gates. In Thailand and Laos, Garuda became so prominent that he remains the state emblem today, symbolizing power sanctioned by the divine. This continuity across geography and centuries suggests Garuda was not a minor figure but a central archetype of enforcement—an avian sentinel whose very posture reminded worshippers that serpents of chaos could be subdued only through divine power.

Ritual texts and folklore confirm his enforcer's role. Garuda was invoked in charms and amulets to cure snakebite, a practical extension of his mythic conquest of the nāga. The idea that invoking his name could drive venom from the body reflects the same logic: Garuda was not passive symbol but active agent, intervening to restore order when chaos intruded. In this sense, he was not simply Vishnu's mount but Vishnu's extension into the mortal world, a winged proxy ensuring that cosmic law was enforced in daily life.

Comparisons to other hybrid enforcers in Hindu mythology reinforce the point. Narasimha, the man-lion incarnation of Vishnu, likewise combines human intelligence with predatory ferocity, dispatched to annihilate a tyrant who defied cosmic law. Garuda and Narasimha embody the same principle: divine enforcement required beings whose very anatomy radiated terror, hybrids engineered—whether by myth or memory—to be both familiar and alien. The ancients remembered their strength in composite forms because those forms left the deepest impression.

That impression has proven enduring. Garuda survives not only in temples and manuscripts but as living symbol. The modern nation of Indonesia takes him as its crest, his wings outspread over the state seal, his talons clutching a scroll inscribed with the national motto. Here is a 21st-century republic still guarded by the enforcer archetype of the covenant. What began as myth, or memory, of an avian sentinel

A Blood Covenant

subduing serpents has endured as emblem of authority itself. The persistence of Garuda across three millennia suggests he was more than a mythological flourish. He was an enforcer remembered too vividly, too consistently, to fade.

Texts reinforce this role. The Mahabharata recounts Garuda as so fearsome that even the gods trembled when he descended, his wings blotting out the sun (Ganguli, *The Mahabharata, Book I*). His demand for amṛta, the nectar of immortality, echoes the language of sustenance—he was to be fed in order to be appeased, and his appetite was bound up with cosmic order. When Vishnu wages war against asuras (demons), Garuda is always at the forefront, tearing enemies apart or scattering serpents that symbolize chaos. Enforcement, in this framework, was not metaphorical: Garuda policed the boundaries between cosmos and chaos, ensuring the covenant was not undermined by forces of rebellion.

Temple art confirms the continuity of this role. At the 13th-century Sun Temple of Konark in Odisha, Garuda is carved as a muscular bird-man grasping serpents in both talons, towering over human figures dwarfed at his feet. In Angkor Wat, he is arrayed along the walls in rhythmic repetition, a line of enforcers with wings extended, each subduing a nāga. These were not isolated depictions but systematic placements: Garuda stationed as threshold guardian, arrayed like soldiers in stone, announcing visually that Vishnu's order was enforced by something more than human armies.

Ritual texts and liturgies show that Garuda was invoked for protection not only of kings but of entire communities. In later Hindu practice, the *Garuda Purāṇa* became one of the most feared scriptures, recited at funerals to guide souls and to terrify them with visions of judgment (Dimmitt & van Buitenen, *Classical Hindu Mythology*, 1978). Here, Garuda is not only warrior but judge, his predatory nature redirected toward punishing the wicked and maintaining balance. This dual function—as violent protector in myth and as arbiter in ritual—mirrors the role of enforcers worldwide: hybrid overseers who both secured loyalty and punished failure.

Placed alongside the Apkallu or Horus, Garuda sharpens the

global pattern. All are hybrids, all are active, and all are stationed at thresholds—palace gates, temple walls, funerary texts. The intro has already noted the uncanny parallels of Garuda-like bird-men appearing across the ocean in Colombia, gripping serpents in the same pose. Here in India, the indigenous record leaves no ambiguity: Garuda was the enforcer par excellence, the covenant's talon and beak made flesh.

Mesoamerican Enforcers — Eagles, Jaguars, and Serpents

If Mesopotamia's Apkallu were technicians and Egypt's hybrids were guardians of throne and tomb, Mesoamerica's enforcers stepped into the public square. Here the covenant's muscle was made visible: eagle-men and jaguar-men, serpent attendants and avian figures who blurred the line between priest, warrior, and something otherworldly. Their task was the same—enforce compliance—but their stage was broader. In plazas and on pyramids, before tens of thousands of witnesses, they embodied predation as policy.

Teotihuacan: Feathered Warriors at the Temple of the Serpent

At Teotihuacan, the Temple of the Feathered Serpent (Quetzalcoatl) presents one of the earliest and most striking arrays of hybrid enforcers. Its façade is covered with alternating images of plumed serpents and war-serpent heads adorned with shell-plate armor. These are not idle decorations: they are processional guardians, proclaiming that the temple itself was a theater of enforcement. Murals elsewhere in the city extend this theme, depicting elites wearing feathered headdresses so massive that they transform the human silhouette into birdlike profiles. In ritual, men became bird-men, intermediaries between serpent conduit and human authority.

The reality of their role was written in blood. Excavations beneath the temple revealed over 200 bound captives buried alive or slain as part of the temple's dedication. Many were interred with obsidian weapons, necklaces of jawbones, and other martial regalia

— offerings not of animals or symbolic substitutes, but of human lives conscripted into covenant service (Sugiyama, *Human Sacrifice, Militarism, and Rulership,* 2005). The dedication itself was an act of terror theater: the message that this sacred space would be guarded forever by those who had died to consecrate it.

The architectural staging made the point explicit. The temple's placement on the Avenue of the Dead ensured that every procession through the city passed its façade. Pilgrims, traders, and subjects alike saw feathered serpents flanked by armored heads, their stone eyes glaring down from the pyramid face. Enforcement was not hidden in crypts or chambers — it was performed on the city's main artery, unavoidable and public. In Teotihuacan, compliance was not only demanded; it was monumentalized.

Maya Courts: Avian Attendants and Vision Serpents

Among the Classic Maya, murals and lintels make the enforcers' presence explicit. At Bonampak, a sequence of late 8th-century murals shows captives dragged by the hair before nobles crowned with avian crests. Execution scenes unfold beneath banners marked with celestial glyphs. The spectacle was carefully timed: musicians played, incense clouds rose, and nobles in avian regalia presided, fusing the act of killing with the act of cosmic timekeeping (Miller & Taube, 1993). Enforcement was inseparable from the calendar, for the covenant demanded punctuality as well as blood.

At Yaxchilán, the famous *"Vision Serpent"* lintels depict rulers drawing blood from their tongues or genitals, their sacrifice birthing a colossal serpent. From its jaws emerge bird-headed attendants — beings that scholars debate as vision-spirits, ancestors, or masked assistants. Yet their repeated form across monuments suggests a remembered archetype: avian enforcers issuing from serpent conduits. Whether supernatural or physical, the message is clear: rulers were not alone in covenant duty; hybrid guardians materialized at the moment of bloodletting, enforcing the transfer from human to divine (Schele & Freidel, *A Forest of Kings,* 1990).

Maya iconography often blurs regalia with ontology. Eagle beaks carved into headdresses, avian crowns extending into feathers, serpents sprouting bird attendants — all hover at the edge between costume and being. The hybrids behave like actors, not adornments: they grasp, confront, and present. Their placement reinforces this: appearing at stairheads, door lintels, and façade thresholds — the very architectural positions occupied by Apkallu in Assyria or jackal-headed Anubis in Egypt. The Maya repeated the global logic: enforcement stands at the gate, reminding all who enter that compliance is not optional.

Mexica (Aztec): Eagle and Jaguar Orders

Nowhere is the enforcer role more institutionalized than in Mexica Tenochtitlan. Two military orders embodied hybrid predation: the Eagle (*cuāuhtli*) and Jaguar (*ocēlōtl*) warriors. Codices show eagle warriors with hooked beaks and feathered wings, jaguar warriors in snarling pelts with open maws. These were not masquerade costumes. They were state-sanctioned archetypes, uniforms that transformed fighters into living symbols of the covenant.

The Eagle and Jaguar orders did more than fight wars; they structured them. "Flower Wars" were ritual conflicts staged not to capture land but to capture people — fuel for the altars of the Templo Mayor. Captives were paraded into the city by Eagle and Jaguar warriors, their fate already known. Chroniclers describe the terror these orders instilled: the sight of their ranks was a reminder that refusal meant capture, and capture meant blood on the stone.

Archaeology corroborates the scale of their mission. The Huey Tzompantli, or Great Skull Rack, unearthed beside the Templo Mayor, contained hundreds of drilled crania arranged in towers for public display (López Luján et al., 2017). Chroniclers claim thousands more. Whether the numbers are precise or exaggerated, the principle is undeniable: the enforcers did not simply conquer; they delivered, transforming human bodies into covenant payment. Their presence in plazas made enforcement pedagogical: every skull was a lesson, every warrior a warning.

The Eagle and Jaguar orders thus served as living iconography — walking reminders that predation was not just divine symbolism but state policy. They embodied teeth and claws, terror and spectacle, ensuring that every subject of the empire knew where disobedience would lead.

Mixtecs and Zapotecs: Guardians in Funerary Space

Hybrid enforcers were not confined to imperial capitals. Among the Zapotecs of Monte Albán, funerary urns depict owl-headed and jaguar-headed guardians holding ritual vessels, their expressions fixed in predatory vigilance (Marcus & Flannery, *Zapotec Civilization*, 1996). These figures were placed in tombs, not plazas, but the principle was the same: enforcement at the threshold. The dead too had to pass under the gaze of hybrid guardians, their offerings monitored, their entry policed.

Among the Mixtecs, codices show bird- and jaguar-beings overseeing noble rituals and bloodletting. Their profiles are so consistent across manuscripts that they read less like artistic freedom and more like standardized templates, repeated generation after generation (Boone, *Stories in Red and Black*, 2000). In this sense, even manuscript margins became thresholds, policed by guardians who reminded viewers that ritual and covenant were inseparable.

Here the function of enforcers shifts from public spectacle to private guardianship. Whereas the Aztec orders terrorized whole populations, Zapotec and Mixtec guardians enforced compliance in sacred interiors — tombs, codex rituals, and altars. The covenant was not only a matter of mass terror; it was intimate, extending into the smallest domains of ritual life. Whether at the city's heart or a noble's burial, enforcement remained constant.

Procedure, Not Pageantry

Across Mesoamerica, hybrids are active: arms extended, blades raised, captives held, bowls presented. The gestures repeat with the same procedural regularity as the cone-and-bucket rites of Assyria or the ankh-to-face touch of Egypt. Repetition signals function. Eagle, jaguar, or bird-man — the enforcers were not symbolic flourishes. They performed tasks. They escorted, displayed, presented, executed. Their bodies were the covenant's instruments, their actions its enforcement.

Predators enforce because they terrorize. Eagles signify altitude and strike, jaguars signify night and ambush, serpents signify conduits and thresholds. By fusing human intelligence with predatory form, Mesoamerican systems created a visible, unforgettable reminder that noncompliance had consequences. The hybrid was not decoration. It was a weapon — an instrument of social control and cosmic compliance.

From the covenant perspective, hybrid enforcers also make technical sense. If emissaries were engineered beings, splicing traits of predator animals — keen sight, brute force, instinctive fear responses — would be rational. Standardized postures across art suggest procedure, not imagination. Bird-men emerging from serpents, eagle and jaguar orders arrayed in regimented ranks — they read like illustrations from a manual, not inventions of whimsy. Enforcers were not optional; they were the system's front line.

The choice of forms was not arbitrary. Eagles signified altitude and precision strikes, jaguars embodied stealth and nocturnal ambush, and serpents represented thresholds and conduits between worlds. By fusing human intelligence with these predatory archetypes, Mesoamerican enforcers became the perfect instruments of terror and compliance. Their hybrid bodies were not decorative but functional—engineered symbols of what awaited anyone who resisted the covenant's demands.

Continuity Across Civilizations

The persistence of enforcer imagery across civilizations is one of the most striking features of the covenant system. In Mesopotamia, Apkallu reliefs with cone and bucket repeated unchanged for centuries; in Egypt, Horus and Anubis never lost their posture of surveillance; in India, Garuda's serpent-grappling form carried into Southeast Asia and remains a state emblem today; in Mesoamerica, eagle and jaguar warriors stood at the center of imperial ritual. Even when empires collapsed and new religions arose, the archetypes endured. Biblical cherubim guarding Eden echo the Apkallu at Assyrian gates. Medieval saints depicted slaying dragons recall Garuda or Sobek punishing serpents and rebels. In Christian funerary art, angels weighing souls carry forward Anubis's scales. These continuities suggest not random artistic recycling, but long cultural memories—afterimages of figures that once stood in living presence, later mythologized but never erased. When symbols persist unchanged across thousands of years, they testify to something more than imagination: they preserve the outline of encounters too vivid to forget.

Fear as Enforcement

Fear was not incidental to these figures; it was their primary currency. Enforcers existed to terrify, to remind populations that failure to comply would bring swift and visceral consequences. The Aztec skull racks were not hidden but staged in plazas, turning the city itself into a classroom of dread. In Egypt, crocodile pools at Kom Ombo made worshippers confront predation with every visit. Mesopotamian gates flanked by winged guardians made clear that all who passed were under surveillance. Maya murals showed captives dragged by the hair, their fates inscribed in the stars overhead. These were not random theatrics—they were policy. Fear was structural, designed into architecture, ritual, and spectacle. It ensured continuity even when emissaries themselves faded from view. Once the association between ritual neglect and disaster—famine, plague, defeat—was embedded in collective memory, priesthoods could enforce compliance by invoking that fear. The enforcers had done their work so well that their absence was scarcely noticed: humanity continued to obey the system out of dread of the consequences.

When seen through this lens, the enforcers were not only hybridized beings but the very machines they commanded. The winged sun disk, the Thunderbird, the Birdman of Cahokia—each is less an allegory than a technical memory: aerial craft roaring across the sky, mistaken for colossal birds or stylized as disks, their presence weaponized as spectacle. Their very form encoded the victory of one faction over another: birds vanquishing serpents, sky conquering underworld. If the Greys' emissaries were remembered as falcons, eagles, and thunderbirds, it was because their arrival in the heavens proclaimed dominance, not suggestion. The covenant was not optional; it was enforced from above, by vehicles of awe and terror whose memory could not be erased. Yet even these airborne enforcers were only proxies. The greater mystery lies in the beings inside them — the ones whose physiology demanded the covenant in the first place.

The Covenant's Police

When viewed together, the Apkallu of Mesopotamia, the falcon and jackal guardians of Egypt, the eagle-bodied Garuda of India, and the jaguar and eagle warriors of Mesoamerica reveal themselves as more than mythic curiosities. They were the covenant's police. Their task was consistent: enforce order, ensure delivery, punish deviation. They embodied vigilance with wings and claws, judgment with scales and muzzles, predation with fangs and jaws. They appeared at thresholds, presided over rituals, and materialized in public plazas to remind humanity that blood owed must be blood paid. Priests officiated, but it was the enforcers who embodied authority, their forms engineered —whether literally or mythically—to terrify and compel. Civilization's most enduring images of gods may in fact be memories of administrators: hybrids dispatched to keep humanity compliant, using fear as the surest guarantee. Seen this way, the enforcers were not marginal figures at the edge of religion but central pillars of a planetary system. They were the covenant's front line, the embodiment of compliance itself. As the chapters that follow will show, their function was not only political but biological—for behind the rituals lay a physiology of consumption that explains the price in blood.

11

THE GODS OF THE PYRAMIDS

The Identity Reveal

Across the span of human history, the pyramid has stood as the great signature of civilization. From the limestone giants of Giza to the stepped temples of Mesoamerica, from the earthen mounds of Cahokia to the sun temples of India, the same structure rises again and again: a mountain of stone, aligned to the heavens, consecrated with blood. Scholars explain these parallels as coincidence — the natural product of engineering and agricultural societies reaching the same architectural solution. Yet coincidence cannot explain the uncanny symmetry of their beliefs. These cultures, separated by oceans and centuries, all remembered gods who descended from the sky, demanded sacrifice, and ruled from monuments that defied their eras.

Egypt carved falcons and solar disks above its kings (Hornung, *Conceptions of God in Ancient Egypt*, 1982). Mesopotamia stationed winged Apkallu at every palace threshold (Black & Green, *Gods, Demons and Symbols of Ancient Mesopotamia*, 1992). India preserved hymns of flying palaces, the vimanas, and bird-men who subdued serpents. Mesoamerica raised its feathered serpents and eagle warriors upon pyramid stages, where captives' hearts were torn out in public squares (Sugiyama, *Human Sacrifice, Militarism, and Rulership at the City of Teotihuacan,* 2005). Cahokia, the great mound city of Illinois, placed its Birdman tablet at the center of its ritual life, a figure whose very posture proclaimed dominion of sky over serpent (Pauketat, *Cahokia: Ancient America's Great City on the Mississippi,* 2009). Its vast mound complexes, aligned to solstices and equinoxes, served as both stage and altar, and the discovery of mass sacrificial burials at Mound 72 underscores the covenant's price in blood (Griffin, *The Burial Complexes of Mound 72 at Cahokia,* 1983). Each culture told its story in different language, but the pattern was the same: sky beings, hybrid enforcers, blood offerings, and pyramids aligned to the stars.

For centuries, the gods of these cultures have been interpreted as symbols — personifications of natural forces, allegories of fertility, morality tales encoded in myth. But this reduction collapses under the weight of the details. Why would so many unrelated peoples independently invent the same fusion of bird-men and serpent-slayers? Why the obsession with blood, with literal rivers of it flowing down the steps of temples? Why the precise alignments to solstices, equinoxes, and star clusters? The pattern is procedural, not poetic. It is the same operating system installed in multiple civilizations.

And every system points to the same authority. The falcon, the serpent, the jaguar were masks — costumes draped over a deeper reality. Behind them was not Horus or Quetzalcoatl, but something older, colder, and less metaphorical. The true "gods of the pyramids" were the administrators of the covenant: the Greys of Zeta 2 Reticuli.

This is not idle speculation. In the modern UFO and experiencer community, the Greys are the most consistently described nonhuman beings in history. Thin, frail bodies. Oversized craniums. Eyes black and almond-shaped, so large they dominate the face. Slits for mouths. Almost no noses. No ears. Their very physiology speaks to otherness, to an intelligence evolved or engineered along a path alien to our own. These descriptions recur not in one country or culture but in thousands of reports worldwide, from abductees who never knew each other, never shared notes, never had reason to fabricate the same face.

When we place that visage beside the masks of antiquity, the continuity emerges. The Apkallu stood taller than kings not to symbolize wisdom, but because emissaries had literally towered above rulers. The winged disk of Egypt is not metaphor but a memory of aerial vehicles hovering above temples. The Thunderbird of North America is not a mythic eagle, but the roar and lightning of an enforcement craft descending upon villages. When we strip away the animal skins, the jewelry, and the priestly elaboration, we are left with the same presence that abductees report today: Greys enforcing compliance, demanding offerings, extracting the one substance that unites every culture of the covenant — blood.

The implications are staggering. If this is true, then the boundary between religion and encounter collapses. The gods of Egypt, Sumer, India, Mesoamerica, and Cahokia were not figments of the imagination or projections of agrarian anxiety. They were administrators stationed on earth, emissaries of an authority that never departed. The rituals were not primitive theater, but protocols of delivery. The sacrifices were not symbolic gestures, but payments. The pyramids were not tombs, but stages for transactions between mortals and the beings they served.

This identity reveal forces us to confront an uncomfortable truth: humanity may never have been as autonomous as it believed. Our greatest monuments, our most enduring religions, our myths of sky and blood, all may trace back to the same beings whose ships still darken our skies and whose hands still reach for our bodies in the night. The Greys have not only been among us; they have shaped us. They were the gods of the pyramids, and they remain the enforcers of the covenant.

Circumstantial Visual Clues

If the gods of the pyramids were the Greys, then we would expect some trace of their visage to have survived in the record. Not every image would be faithful — cultures stylized, masked, and merged forms with animal attributes — but amid the wings and serpent coils, we should occasionally glimpse the same large eyes, the same bulbous heads, the same frail bodies that experiencers describe today. What we find are scattered but striking echoes. None is conclusive in isolation, but together they form a chorus of circumstantial clues too consistent to dismiss.

The Olmec Figurines

Among the Olmec of ancient Mesoamerica, long recognized as the "mother culture" of later Maya and Aztec civilizations, archaeologists uncovered hundreds of small ceramic and jade figurines. Many are called "baby-face" figures: round, hairless heads with slanted almond-shaped eyes, flat noses, and tiny mouths (Pool, *Olmec Archaeology and Early Mesoamerica*, 2007). Scholars have argued endlessly about what they represent — infants, were-jaguar hybrids, fertility gods. Yet for anyone familiar with modern abduction accounts, the resemblance is unmistakable. These are the faces abductees sketch again and again: oversized heads, large slanted eyes, underdeveloped features that seem more engineered than born. If Olmec society was an early theater of the covenant, then these figurines may be the oldest preserved attempts to represent the hybrids produced by it.

The Sego Canyon Petroglyphs

In the American Southwest, far from Mesoamerica's temples, the rock walls of Sego Canyon, Utah, preserve an older record still. Dating back 6,000 to 8,000 years, the Barrier Canyon Style petroglyphs depict elongated, otherworldly beings with huge, empty eyes and absent mouths (Schaafsma, *Indian Rock Art of the Southwest*, 1980). They hover in groups, sometimes flanked by smaller, more human-like figures, as if a hierarchy were being recorded. Archaeologists call them "spirit figures," but the comparison to modern descriptions of Greys is hard to ignore. Here, in the same continental theater that would later give rise to Cahokia's pyramid-mound society, we find images of beings who look like the administrators themselves. If the Birdman Tablet at Cahokia was a memory of their enforcer, the Sego Canyon panels may be memories of the enforcers' masters.

Bhimbetka Rock Art

Half a world away, in India's Bhimbetka rock shelters, UNESCO-listed sites dating to the Mesolithic era, similar forms appear. Amid the painted hunters and animals are occasional figures with disproportionately large heads and eyes, rendered in ways that do not match the conventions of the surrounding human images (Wakankar & Brooks, *Stone Age Rock Paintings of Bhimbetka*, 1976). Some researchers dismiss them as stylization or masks, but the shapes resonate uncannily with the same template: bulbous head, dark eyes, thin limbs. India remembered its gods not only in the hymns of the Rig Veda but in pigment on stone. And as later Vedic texts described vimanas — flying palaces, tiered like pyramids, piloted by radiant beings — the echoes of form and function begin to align.

The Eye of Ra

Egypt, for all its art, gives us a subtler but equally telling clue. The Eye of Ra (or Eye of Horus) is usually interpreted as a symbol of healing, protection, and cosmic order. Yet when examined closely, the stylized form parallels the proportions of a Grey's head: the almond-shaped eye, the teardrop curve, even the spiral line that mirrors the optic nerve and brain pathways. The Eye was said to leave the body of the god, to fly across the sky, to burn enemies with its wrath (Hornung, *Conceptions of God in Ancient Egypt: The One and the Many*, 1982). Was this symbol a stylized memory of the gods' own visage, abstracted into sacred geometry? Just as the pyramids echoed the Benben stone — a flying pyramid said to have descended from the heavens — so too might the Eye have echoed the true face of the beings who ruled from above.

Patterns Across Continents

Individually, each of these cases could be explained away. Figurines may be stylized infants. Petroglyphs may be spirits or shamans. Rock art may exaggerate features for effect. Egyptian symbols may be metaphors for natural cycles. But when placed side by side, the consistencies sharpen: large heads, large eyes, small mouths, frail bodies. The same form appears in Mesoamerica, North America, India, and Egypt — the very civilizations united by pyramids, blood ritual, and covenant enforcement.

Skeptics will say this is projection: we see Greys because we expect to see Greys. But the opposite is true. Abductees described these beings long before they were linked to ancient art, long before "Greys" were a pop culture trope. Their sketches came from memory, not from archaeology. If modern testimony and ancient imagery converge on the same form, the simplest explanation is continuity.

Circumstantial but Compelling

We must be honest: none of these artifacts is definitive proof. No Olmec figurine bears an inscription reading "Grey hybrid." No Egyptian text identifies the Eye of Ra as an alien face. These are circumstantial visual clues, not courtroom evidence. But history often rests on circumstantial patterns — on converging details that defy coincidence. And here, the convergence is global. The same visage haunts the art of cultures that never knew each other, all of them pyramid builders, all of them covenant societies.

When we add to this the modern continuity — experiencers describing identical beings, cattle drained of blood with surgical precision, abductions for genetic tissue — the pattern implicates. The gods of the pyramids were not masks of falcon, serpent, or jaguar. They were emissaries of the same beings who stand over us still: the Greys.

Architectural & Technological Clues

If the covenant was global, then the gods would not only have been remembered in masks and figurines, but in the machines they arrived in. Across cultures, the sky was not silent. Civilizations remembered radiant stones, thunderous birds, winged disks, and flying palaces. They carved them into walls, aligned their monuments to them, and sometimes built entire societies around their descent. These were not metaphors. They were memories of technology.

The Benben Stone

In Egypt, the story begins with the Benben stone — the primordial mound that rose from the waters of chaos, said to have descended from the heavens. Preserved at Heliopolis, the Benben was described as radiant, pyramidal, and even capable of flight. Later pyramidion capstones and obelisks were modeled after it, their gilded tips reflecting sunlight as if imitating the glow of the original (Wilkinson, *The Complete Temples of Ancient Egypt*, 2000). To the Egyptians, the Benben was the dwelling place of Atum-Ra, the seed of divine authority on earth. To us, it reads like the memory of a craft — a flying pyramid whose form became the blueprint for Egypt's greatest monuments. Every pyramid was an echo of the first descent.

The Winged Solar Disk

Egypt also remembered its aerial gods in the winged solar disk, carved above temple entrances and hovering over kings. The disk is flanked by extended wings, often with a tail of feathers beneath. Scholars interpret it as a solar symbol, but the geometry is strikingly mechanical: a central orb, lateral stabilizers, vertical fins. The Eye of Ra was said to leave the body of the god, to fly across the sky, and to punish enemies with its searing rays. What is this if not the description of a radiant craft, weaponized with beams of light? (Hornung, *Conceptions of God in Ancient Egypt*, 1982). The winged disk sanctified kingship because it hovered physically above the king — an aerial overseer proclaiming divine sanction.

The Vimanas of India

In India, the gods did not merely descend to pyramids — they flew them. The Vedas and epics describe vimanas, flying palaces that could move across the sky, sometimes tiered like step pyramids, sometimes circular like disks. The Mahabharata recounts aerial battles in which vimanas unleashed beams of fire, reducing cities to ash (Ganguli, *The Mahabharata*, Book VIII). The Ramayana describes the Pushpaka Vimana, a flying palace that could expand or contract to fit its passengers (N. Dutt, *The Ramayana*, 1891). Later texts like the Samarangana Sutradhara, an 11th-century Sanskrit treatise, go so far as to describe their construction, including propulsion by mercury and fire (Shukla, *Samarangana Sutradhara: An Ancient Treatise on Architecture*, 1924). Mainstream scholars dismiss these as poetic imagination, but the specificity of the descriptions defies mere allegory. A machine that hovers, ascends, projects beams, and terrifies populations is not myth — it is memory. The vimanas were flying pyramids, mobile temples of enforcement, counterparts to the grounded monuments of stone.

Thunderbirds and Feathered Serpents

In North America, the sky was dominated by the Thunderbird, remembered in tribal myth as a colossal being whose wings shook the heavens and whose eyes flashed lightning. The Thunderbird was not merely a bird of prey, but a sky-being that enforced law and balance. Its presence terrified villages, reminding them that order was overseen from above. When read through the covenant lens, the Thunderbird is a clear analog to the winged disk — an aerial vehicle stylized as a living bird. Its roar was thunder, its beams lightning, its shadow the terror of authority.

Mesoamerica preserved a similar memory in the plumed serpent.

Quetzalcoatl, the feathered serpent, was not just a god of wind and learning, but a hybrid emblem of sky and earth, bird and serpent fused. On the Temple of the Feathered Serpent at Teotihuacan, plumed serpent heads alternate with war-serpent masks across the façade. The imagery is architectural and aerial at once — pyramids guarded by serpents with feathers, the very fusion of flight and earth-bound power. When combined with eagle and jaguar warrior orders, the message is unambiguous: authority descended from above, and it demanded blood on stone.

Cahokia's Alignments

Even Cahokia, the great mound city of North America, encoded aerial memory into its architecture. Monks Mound, the largest earthen pyramid in the Western Hemisphere, is aligned to solstices and equinoxes, its shadow falling across subsidiary mounds like a cosmic calendar. The Birdman Tablet, with its avian figure on one side and snakeskin pattern on the reverse, embodies the same sky-over-serpent motif we find in Garuda and Quetzalcoatl. To Cahokia's people, the pyramid and the Birdman were inseparable: the ground was raised to meet the sky, and the enforcer descended to bind the covenant in blood (Pauketat, *Cahokia: Ancient America's Great City on the Mississippi*, 2009).

Technology Remembered as Myth

What unites these memories is their technological consistency. A radiant stone that descends from the sky and becomes the prototype of pyramids. A disk with wings that hovers above kings and emits beams of light. Tiered palaces that fly and fight aerial battles. Thunderbirds that roar and strike with lightning. Feathered serpents that fuse the earthbound and the airborne. Each culture described these through the lens available to them, clothing the craft in feathers, wings, or serpent scales. But stripped of costume, the mechanics emerge: aerial vehicles remembered as gods.

Skeptics will argue these were symbols of the sun, rain, or cosmic order. But symbols do not require such specificity. The Benben was not just a rock; it was said to fly. The vimanas were not poetic clouds; they were armed and piloted. The Thunderbird was not a mere eagle; it was a terror that enforced law. The winged disk was not a metaphor; it was carved with the precision of a technical emblem. Each instance strains against allegory and points instead to memory.

The Machines of the Covenant

If the enforcers were hybrids, then their gods were machines — vehicles whose presence terrified, sanctioned, and enforced. Pyramids and mounds were the ground stations; disks, stones, and birds were the aerial craft. Together they formed the infrastructure of the covenant. The monuments aligned to the heavens not for symbolic poetry, but to guide descent. The sacrifices flowed not as metaphor, but as payment. The gods of the pyramids were remembered in stone and myth, but behind them were administrators whose technology still casts a shadow today. If the covenant's technology standardized the theater, its iconography preserved the victors: across continents, avian enforcers stand over serpents as if a triumph were meant to be remembered.

Bird Against Serpent — A Memory of War

If the Greys were the administrators of the covenant, then their enforcers were the predators that kept it. Across continents, the avian figure is shown in the same posture: wings spread, talons set, beak clamped on a serpent. The image repeats so often—and in such specific, active poses—that it suggests more than archetype. It functions as commemoration—a victory carved into stone.

In India, Garuda is defined by conflict with the nāgas, the serpent lords—he seizes and devours them, rescues what they guard, and stands as Vishnu's wrath made winged. In Southeast Asia the theme is monumental: at Angkor, Nāga balustrades are literally "handled" by Garuda figures; on Khmer reliefs, avian guardians wrench serpents in beak and claws. In the Americas, the San Agustín "birdman" statues in Colombia grip serpents with beak and talon in the same unmistakable configuration, while at Cahokia the Birdman Tablet sets raptor over snakeskin, sky over underworld. Even national emblems remember it: the Mexican eagle poised over a serpent is a modern crest for an ancient scene.

North American oral traditions preserve the same rivalry in narrative. Among Algonquian and Plains peoples, the Thunderbird —a sky-being whose wings bring thunder and whose glance flashes lightning—struggles against the Horned Serpent, the water-dweller of the deep. Egypt dramatized the conflict as Horus (falcon) keeping order while Apophis (serpent of chaos) is attacked nightly; Mesopotamia preserved it as storm-gods and sages restraining dragon-serpents at cosmic thresholds. Across the Mediterranean and Indo-European worlds the storm-bringer fights the world-serpent: Indra–Vṛtra, Tarḫunna–Illuyanka, Zeus–Typhon, Thor–Jörmungandr. However the names change, the staging does not: sky strikes serpent, order suppresses a rival power from below.

If we read these scenes through the covenant lens, a possibility emerges. Before the Greys' program consolidated, a reptilian/serpentine faction may have held influence at watery thresholds, caves, and underworlds—powers of depth, secrecy, and liminality. The arrival of the covenant imposed a new order from the sky. To enforce it, the administrators deployed avian-predatory emissaries—hybridized enforcers built to dominate the serpent body plan. The result is the motif the world remembers: bird against serpent, the victory of aerial authority over the older, chthonic line.

Architecture kept the memory alive in ritual. At Chichén Itzá, the descent of Kukulkan—a feathered serpent animated in light on equinox—was literally staged on pyramid stairs: a serpent made to appear and be "handled" by a platform consecrated to the sky. Khmer causeways array Nāga along the liminal approach while Garuda figures restrain them—crossings dramatized as discipline of serpent powers. In North America, mound complexes and avian regalia elevated the raptor above the serpentine pattern; at Cahokia, the snakeskin engraved behind the Birdman fossilized the hierarchy. These were not neutral decorations. They were political theology in stone, ritualized reminders of who won.

The mythic record reads like "victor's history." Serpents that once taught or bargained are recast as chaos to be punished; bird-men stand memorialized as guardians and judges. Where serpents remain honored (Mesoamerica's feathered serpent, India's nāga kings), they are often subordinated—feathered, bridged to sky, or tasked with guarding treasure they no longer rule. Even Egypt's cobra (uraeus) survives as royal ordinance only when fixed to the brow—tamed fire under falcon eyes.

None of this requires abandoning symbolism; it reframes it. Symbols are operational memory. A millennium after an actual conflict, the easiest way to keep its lesson present is to encode it in perpetual ceremony: a raptor trampling a serpent; a storm-god pinning a dragon; a winged being grasping a coiled foe. The liturgy tells the populace daily what the power structure already knows: the sky enforcers stand, the serpent powers kneel. The covenant is not only vertical (gods over men) but factional (bird over serpent), and temples teach it by image.

Seen in this light, the global recurrence of avian triumph over serpent is not random. It is a memory of consolidation—a record that the Greys' system prevailed over a competing influence and then standardized the icon of that victory across the theaters where the covenant operated. That is why the same choreography appears on three continents: talon to coil, beak to neck, wing over scale. The story is old, but the message is current: the emissaries who enforced the covenant once won a war, and the world still speaks their victory in stone.

If so, we should expect the serpent faction to persist at the edges —reduced, demonized, driven beneath rivers and into caves, yet never entirely gone. Modern testimonies that describe reptilian beings at thresholds (subterranean sites, watery crossings, liminal spaces) may be aftershocks of that older alignment, flickers of a suppressed program that sometimes resurfaces. But in the public theater—on pyramids, in festivals, in royal iconography—the bird-men stand victorious because the covenant demanded it.

This does not change the core argument; it clarifies why the avian executor dominates pyramid cultures and why serpent figures are so often placed beneath, pinned, or re-coded as chaos. The covenant's enforcers are predators, and the world remembered their work. With the bird over serpent placed back into its probable historical frame—as a fossilized memory of a factional purge—the obsession with blood that follows is easier to understand. Tribute flows to the winners. And the winners made sure every stair, seal, and relief kept score.

The Serpent Faction — Reptilians Then and Now

If the serpent in ancient art was only a symbol, the story could end there. But modern testimony complicates the picture. For decades, experiencers have reported encounters with reptilian or serpent-featured humanoids—tall, scaled beings with slit pupils, ridged brows, and heavy musculature. Accounts vary on demeanor, but themes recur: intimidation, territorial behavior, and a fixation on hierarchy. Reports often place them at thresholds—caves, tunnels, subterranean installations, or near bodies of water—exactly where serpent powers were stationed in older myth. In other words: the serpent faction did not vanish from memory because it was imaginary; it persisted because, in some form, it continued.

How does this square with the covenant model? The cross-cultural "bird conquers serpent" motif reads like public history of a private war—a factional clash remembered as avian enforcers subduing a rival serpent line. If the Greys consolidated control, that would explain why avian-predatory emissaries dominate the iconography of pyramids while serpent figures are pinned, bridged, or subordinated. It also explains the diminished (but not absent) presence of reptilian encounters today. In some testimonies, reptilians appear above Greys in command; in others, they act as regional powers or specialists at liminal sites. Both patterns make sense if the serpent line survived in the margins—strategic, territorial, but no longer the public face of enforcement.

The covenant lens also clarifies the overlap in appetite. Serpent deities in antiquity guarded treasure, water, gates, and—crucially—sacrifice points. Modern reptilian reports often feature control tactics (fear induction, postural dominance) rather than the procedural harvest associated with Greys. That division of labor fits a post-conflict settlement: Greys standardize the system (technicians, collection, hybridization), while surviving reptilians exert territorial leverage in select theaters. The global art record then becomes intelligible: temples stage the victory (bird over serpent), while folk memory and modern testimony preserve the ongoing presence of a reduced—but not erased—serpent faction.

None of this requires dogmatism. The evidence is layered—art, myth, ritual, and modern encounter—and the parallels are suggestive, not juridical. But ignoring the reptilian thread would leave a conspicuous hole in the tapestry. The simplest synthesis is that both factions existed: serpent powers associated with water, depth, and thresholds; avian emissaries associated with sky, strike, and enforcement. The Greys' consolidation turned the avian executor into the public emblem of order and pushed the serpents into the wings. The world still tells that story on stone: talon over coil, beak to neck. And modern witnesses still meet its afterimage in tunnels, caves, and dark water—where the serpent waits at the edge of the covenant's light.

The Blood Obsession of Pyramid Cultures

If there is one constant in the pyramid societies of the ancient world, it is blood. Stone can weather, myths can shift, rulers can come and go, but the red river running across the altars remains. Whether in the deserts of Egypt, the jungles of Mesoamerica, the woodlands of Cahokia, or the plains of India, the pyramid was never just a monument — it was a machine of ritual extraction. The one substance all these cultures offered to their gods, with obsessive repetition, was blood.

Egypt

Egypt is often remembered as a civilization of measured order, of solar hymns and funerary texts that extol balance and eternal life. Yet beneath this veneer ran the same river. Animal sacrifice was routine, and texts describe human sacrifice in the earliest dynasties. Archaeologists have found subsidiary graves around the tombs of First Dynasty kings at Abydos containing retainers who were almost certainly sacrificed to accompany their ruler into the afterlife (O'Connor, *Abydos: Egypt's First Pharaohs and the Cult of Osiris,* 2009). In temple rituals, blood offerings to the gods were considered the most potent sustenance. Later traditions sublimated the act into libations of red wine — but the symbolism was thinly veiled. As Jan Assmann notes, Egyptian ritual texts often refer to "appeasing the gods with blood," making clear that beneath the poetry lay the same biological tribute (Assmann, *Death and Salvation in Ancient Egypt,* 2005).

Mesoamerica

Nowhere was the blood covenant more explicit than in Mesoamerica. At Teotihuacan, more than 200 bound captives were sacrificed in the dedication of the Temple of the Feathered Serpent, buried alive with obsidian blades and necklaces of human jaws (Sugiyama, *Human Sacrifice, Militarism, and Rulership at the City of Teotihuacan,* 2005). The Maya described their rulers piercing tongues and genitals with stingray spines, offering their own blood to vision-serpents that manifested attendants from other realms (Schele & Freidel, *A Forest of Kings,* 1990). The Aztec carried this to industrial scale. Flower Wars were fought not to capture territory but to capture bodies — fuel for the altars. At the Templo Mayor in Tenochtitlan, captives were stretched across stone slabs, their hearts cut out while still beating, their blood flowing down the pyramid steps into waiting troughs. The

Great Skull Rack (Huey Tzompantli) displayed hundreds, perhaps thousands, of drilled skulls stacked in towers, a city square of death reminding all that blood was the empire's currency (López Luján et al., *The Great Temple of Tenochtitlan*, 1988). For the Mexica, there was no metaphor. The sun itself was said to require human hearts to rise each day. Blood was the sustenance of the gods.

Cahokia

In North America, Cahokia's Mound 72 provides the clearest evidence of blood tribute. Excavations revealed over 250 individuals, many of them young women, buried in mass graves. Some were executed en masse, others carefully arranged with offerings of shell beads and copper. Timothy Pauketat argues that these burials were not random but ritual, part of Cahokia's hierarchical system of power and religion (Pauketat, *Cahokia: Ancient America's Great City on the Mississippi*, 2009). The Birdman Tablet, found in the same mound, places the imagery of avian dominion directly alongside human sacrifice — sky over serpent, sealed in blood. Like the Aztec, Cahokia's leaders enforced the covenant with lives. The mounds were not mere tombs but stages where life was given as offering.

India

In Vedic India, sacrifice was the very engine of cosmic order. The ritual of yajna involved the offering of animals, libations, and sometimes humans, their blood feeding the sacred fire that carried sustenance to the gods. The Rig Veda describes the cosmic giant Purusha being dismembered in the primordial sacrifice, his body parts forming the castes and elements of creation (Doniger, *The Rig Veda: An Anthology*, 1981). Blood was not metaphorical — it was the very medium by which the cosmos was sustained. Later traditions sought to sublimate sacrifice into symbolic offerings, but the ancient texts are clear: the gods were nourished by real blood. Even today, some Hindu sects maintain vestiges of blood sacrifice, offering goats or chickens at temples, a reminder that beneath centuries of reform the primal covenant remains.

Patterns in Blood

Placed side by side, the parallels are stark. Egypt buried retainers alive in service to their kings and gods. Mesoamerica industrialized sacrifice, turning cities into conveyor belts of blood. Cahokia arranged mass burials beneath its mounds, with avian enforcers looming in its iconography. India codified sacrifice into ritual law, declaring it the foundation of cosmic balance. Four regions, four traditions, one currency: blood.

Why? Mainstream scholars explain these sacrifices as social control, agricultural symbolism, or fertility rites. Yet these explanations falter when confronted with scale. Why would a civilization as sophisticated as the Aztec dedicate entire wars to capturing sacrificial victims? Why would Teotihuacan inter hundreds of bound captives in the foundations of a single temple? Why would Egypt kill dozens of attendants to accompany a pharaoh who could just as easily be honored with symbolic offerings? Why would India sanctify dismemberment as the act that birthed the cosmos? The obsession defies sociological metaphor. It suggests procedure.

The Currency of the Covenant

From the covenant perspective, the answer is clear. Blood was demanded because blood was required. It was not ritual theater but resource extraction. The gods of the pyramids were nourished by it, as experiencers today report of the Greys. Blood carries plasma, iron, proteins, hormones, genetic signatures — a biochemical feast and informational matrix in one fluid. To beings without digestive systems, capable of dermal absorption, blood would be the perfect sustenance. The pyramid cultures became global factories of blood, their rituals timed to celestial alignments because the gods descended at appointed times to collect what was owed.

From Then to Now

The obsession with blood did not end with the collapse of these civilizations. Today it surfaces in reports of cattle drained surgically of every drop, in abductees awakened to find samples taken from marrow and veins, in testimonies of Greys who appear not only to experiment but to harvest. The past and present rhyme in red. What was once staged on the steps of pyramids is now performed in fields and bedrooms. The covenant's appetite has never changed. Only the theater has.

Moments of Imposition

If sacrifice was the currency of the covenant, then we must ask when humanity first learned its terms. Civilizations do not wake one morning and decide to drain blood on pyramids. Obsessions this profound do not spring from imagination alone. They are imposed. And when we trace the timelines of the pyramid-building cultures, we find sudden shifts — moments when ritual escalates, when architecture leaps, when myth codifies blood as holy law. These are the fingerprints of the covenant's originators.

Sumer and Mesopotamia

In Mesopotamia, the covenant's first imposition likely came in the Uruk and Early Dynastic periods (c. 3500–2500 BCE). This was the crucible of civilization: the rise of cities, monumental ziggurats, kingship, and the written word. It is here that the Apkallu appear — the winged, bearded guardians, standing at thresholds with their cone and bucket, repeating the same procedure endlessly (Black & Green, *Gods, Demons and Symbols of Ancient Mesopotamia*, 1992). Berossus, a Hellenistic Babylonian priest, records Oannes, the fish-clad being who rose from the sea each day to teach humans writing, agriculture, and architecture (Burstein, *The Babyloniaca of Berossus*, 1978). In the archaeological record, we see not gradual experimentation but sudden leaps.

The invention of cuneiform, the codification of temple ritual, the building of ziggurats aligned with celestial bodies — these were not small steps but seismic shifts. The earliest Sumerian texts already describe blood sacrifice and temple offerings as if they had always been there. Myth presents them as instructions from the gods. What we may be seeing is the moment of covenantal imposition: emissaries arriving to enforce a system that demanded blood, tribute, and obedience, rationalized as divine law.

Egypt

In Egypt, the covenant surfaces in the Predynastic and Early Dynastic periods (c. 3500–2800 BCE). Archaeologists excavating the First Dynasty royal tombs at Abydos found subsidiary graves containing dozens, sometimes hundreds, of retainers buried with the king (O'Connor, *Abydos: Egypt's First Pharaohs and the Cult of Osiris*, 2009). Many were young, healthy adults. They were not volunteers. They were sacrificed to accompany their ruler into the afterlife. This practice appears suddenly in Egyptian history, fully formed, and then disappears just as suddenly in later dynasties, replaced by symbolic figurines (shabti).

The same pattern repeats in temple ritual. The Pyramid Texts of the Old Kingdom are already saturated with sacrificial imagery. Red wine is described as the "blood of the gods," poured on altars (Faulkner, *The Ancient Egyptian Pyramid Texts*, 1969). Animals were killed daily in their thousands to feed the temples. In myth, the Eye of Ra goes forth to punish humanity with slaughter, appeased only by rivers of blood and beer (Hornung, *Conceptions of God in Ancient Egypt*, 1982). This obsession does not look like the evolution of agrarian piety. It looks like enforcement. It looks like a covenant being imposed. The mass killings of Abydos may have been the inaugural down payment — the moment Egyptians learned what the gods required.

India

In India, the covenant's language of blood enters through the Rig Veda (c. 1500–1200 BCE). The hymns already describe yajna — sacrifice — as the engine of cosmic order. The Purusha Sukta depicts the cosmic giant dismembered, his blood and body forming the world and the castes of society (Doniger, *The Rig Veda: An Anthology*, 1981). Here, sacrifice is not peripheral but foundational. The gods themselves are said to have sacrificed Purusha to create existence.

The sudden centrality of sacrifice in early Vedic religion is striking. It is not a symbolic gesture tacked onto later theology but the root of the system. Archaeologists find fire altars at Harappan and early Vedic sites, aligned with stars, their geometry matching later Hindu temples (Witzel, *The Origins of the World's Mythologies*, 2012). The consistency suggests instruction, not invention. If emissaries of the covenant appeared in India, they impressed upon its priests that sacrifice was not optional but cosmic law. And from that moment forward, Indian spirituality bore the mark of the covenant. Even when reformers tried to sublimate blood into symbolic offerings, the logic of sacrifice remained.

The Olmec and Mesoamerica

In Mesoamerica, the covenant emerges with the Olmec (c. 1500–400 BCE). The colossal heads, carved from basalt, appear suddenly, their helmeted features staring across plazas aligned with solstices (Diehl, *The Olmecs: America's First Civilization*, 2004). The Olmec also left behind figurines — the so-called "baby-face" figures, with slanted eyes, flat noses, and bulbous heads — eerily reminiscent of hybrid offspring (Pool, *Olmec Archaeology and Early Mesoamerica*, 2007). Ritual objects show were-jaguar and bird-man forms, already blurring the line between human and predator. Bloodletting appears in Olmec iconography, suggesting that even at this early stage, sacrifice was embedded.

By the time of Teotihuacan (100–550 CE), the covenant had

matured into full-scale enforcement. The dedication of the Temple of the Feathered Serpent buried more than 200 captives alive, interred with jawbone necklaces and obsidian blades (Sugiyama, *Human Sacrifice, Militarism, and Rulership at the City of Teotihuacan*, 2005). The Maya (250–900 CE) expanded the system into ritual bloodletting by rulers, piercing their tongues and genitals to feed vision serpents (Schele & Freidel, *A Forest of Kings*, 1990). And in the Aztec Empire (1300–1521 CE), the covenant reached industrial scale: rivers of blood pouring down the steps of the Templo Mayor, tens of thousands sacrificed in a single festival (López Luján, *The Offerings of the Templo Mayor of Tenochtitlan*, 1994). This trajectory suggests a covenant first imposed in the Olmec heartland, renewed at Teotihuacan, intensified with the Maya, and finally consummated in Mexica terror.

Cahokia

In North America, the Mississippian culture of Cahokia (c. 1050–1350 CE) shows the covenant reemerging in striking form. At its peak, Cahokia was larger than London, its Monks Mound the largest earthwork pyramid in the hemisphere. Around 1050 CE, the city underwent a rapid expansion — archaeologists call it the "Big Bang" (Pauketat, *Cahokia: Ancient America's Great City on the Mississippi*, 2009). Within a generation, plazas, mounds, and ritual centers appeared, aligned to solstices and equinoxes. And with them, sacrifice.

Mound 72 tells the story. Over 250 bodies were found in its mass graves, many of them young women, killed and arranged in ritual fashion (Griffin, *The Burial Complexes of Mound 72 at Cahokia*, 1983). Alongside them was the Birdman Tablet — one side showing a raptor-like figure with outstretched wings, the other etched with a snakeskin pattern. The message is unmistakable: sky over serpent, sealed in blood. The timing suggests that the covenant was imposed or renewed during Cahokia's sudden rise, as if an external force intervened, instructing its leaders in the rituals of blood that had already shaped other pyramid societies.

Patterns of Suddenness

In each case, the covenant appears not gradually but suddenly. In Mesopotamia, writing and sacrifice erupt together. In Egypt, mass retainers appear overnight at Abydos. In India, the earliest hymns already assume sacrifice as cosmic law. In Mesoamerica, colossal heads and hybrid figurines emerge full-formed. In Cahokia, the city's "Big Bang" brings mounds and mass burials at once. This pattern of suddenness is the hallmark of imposition. These were not organic cultural developments. They were injections — moments when emissaries arrived, instructed, and enforced.

The archaeological record, stripped of myth, still bears witness. Ordinary human societies do not leap from subsistence farming to city-states aligned with the stars and rituals of blood in a few generations. Such leaps point to intervention. And the myths confirm it: Oannes rising from the sea, the Eye of Ra demanding appeasement, Purusha dismembered by the gods, Quetzalcoatl teaching sacrifice, the Birdman standing astride the serpent. These are not allegories. They are memories of the moment when the covenant was imposed.

Imposition and Enforcement

It is tempting to see these moments as the beginning of civilization itself. Writing, astronomy, monumental architecture — all seem to coincide with sacrifice. The covenant may not only have fed the gods but shaped the very structures of society. Temples became the centers of cities because they were the stations of the covenant. Priests became powerful because they were the administrators of blood. Kings became divine because they were intermediaries with the enforcers. Civilization and covenant were fused from the start.

But beneath the grandeur lies the stark truth: the gods did not bring wisdom for humanity's sake. They brought instruction for their own survival. Each pyramid society remembers the moment it was conscripted into service. The myths dress it in glory, the archaeology records it in graves, but the pattern is clear. At specific points in time, the covenant was imposed, and humanity became the supplier of blood.

Modern Continuity — The Greys Today

The covenant did not end with the collapse of the pyramid societies. It changed form, retreated into shadows, and resurfaced in ways that modern science struggles to explain. What was once staged on altars before multitudes now occurs in remote pastures and quiet bedrooms. The gods of the pyramids are not gone. They are still here.

Abductee Testimony

From the mid-twentieth century onward, thousands of people have reported encounters with beings strikingly consistent in form and behavior. These are not vague spirits or shifting dream figures, but entities described with clinical precision: thin-limbed, frail bodies; oversized craniums; large, almond-shaped black eyes; slits for mouths; nostrils reduced to pinholes. Whitley Strieber, in *Communion* (1987), recorded not only his own encounters but a flood of letters from readers who recognized the same beings in their own lives. David Jacobs, Budd Hopkins, and John Mack compiled case after case describing abductions that featured the same procedures: humans taken against their will, subjected to tissue extraction, reproductive sampling, and repeated blood draws. The beings' identity was unmistakable. They were the Greys, the same enforcers remembered in stone as gods.

What ties these modern encounters most directly to the covenant of the past is the focus on blood and genetic material. Abductees routinely describe needles inserted into veins, marrow extracted from bones, semen and ova taken for hybridization programs. Some wake with scoop marks in their skin or incisions that heal overnight. Many report being shown hybrid offspring, children who bear both human and Grey features, as if the covenant's demand has shifted from public sacrifice to private husbandry. The gods no longer collect from pyramids; they collect from bloodlines.

Cattle Mutilations

If human abduction testimony can be dismissed as subjective, the phenomenon of cattle mutilations resists such dismissal. For over half a century, ranchers across North and South America have reported livestock found dead in fields, their bodies surgically mutilated with chilling precision. Eyes, tongues, reproductive organs, and rectal tissue are removed. Carcasses are exsanguinated, drained of every drop of blood, with no pooling on the ground. Incisions appear cauterized, as if made with lasers. Predators and scavengers avoid the bodies. Linda Moulton Howe's groundbreaking documentary *A Strange Harvest* (1980) and decades of follow-up reporting documented hundreds of such cases. Law enforcement has been unable to provide a natural explanation. The FBI quietly investigated in the 1970s, only to conclude — without evidence — that the cases were probably natural predation. Yet forensic pathologists who examined the carcasses have admitted they cannot explain the bloodless precision.

The pattern is global. Cattle mutilations have been reported in the United States, Canada, Mexico, Brazil, and even Europe. Witnesses often report strange lights in the sky, silent craft, or unmarked helicopters near the time of the incidents. Whatever the cause, the effect is the same: blood and reproductive tissue removed with a level of efficiency that defies ordinary predators or human pranksters. To dismiss it as hysteria is to ignore thousands of carcasses left behind. The covenant's appetite has not waned. It has simply industrialized in a new form.

The Common Denominator: Blood

What unites ancient pyramid sacrifices and modern mutilations is the one substance that recurs across millennia: blood. In Egypt it accompanied the pharaoh into the tomb. In Teotihuacan it was buried alive beneath the pyramid. In Cahokia it filled mass graves. In Aztec plazas it ran down pyramid steps in torrents. In India it was poured into sacred fires. Today it disappears from cattle, vanishes from abductees' veins, and is demanded in procedures so cold and clinical that survivors are left traumatized. Blood is the constant currency of the gods.

My Vision

This continuity is not abstract for me. In 1995, during a period when I was being visited by Greys — I had seen four small beings leave my bedroom in 1994, and suspect other incidents that year as well — I experienced a lucid dream state where I subconsciously and intuitively asked if "they" could show me what God looked like. In response, I was shown a vision. I did not see a robed patriarch or radiant angel, but a winged eye hovering above concentric squares, glowing with a pulsing light. Only later did I realize those concentric squares resembled a pyramid viewed from above. The image resonated with symbols I would encounter years later: the Eye of Ra, the Ojo de Dios (God's Eye) crafted in yarn and wood by the Huichol of Mexico, the winged disk of Egypt. The message was unmistakable. The God of the pyramids was the eye above the pyramid — the overseer I myself had encountered. My vision was not unique. It was personal confirmation of a memory humanity has preserved in stone and ritual for thousands of years.

The Zeta Reticuli Connection

Even the Greys' place of origin has been whispered into our history. In 1961, Betty and Barney Hill were abducted in New Hampshire. Under hypnosis, Betty described being shown a star map by one of the beings. Years later, amateur astronomer Marjorie Fish reconstructed that map in three dimensions, identifying it as a view from the binary star system Zeta 1 and Zeta 2 Reticuli, 39 light-years away

(Fuller, *The Interrupted Journey*, 1966). Skeptics argue over the interpretation, but the pattern holds: the beings are not abstract gods but emissaries from somewhere real. If the gods of the pyramids were the Greys, then their temples were not only sacred spaces but outposts of an interstellar presence.

The Eisenhower Covenant

Rumors persist that the covenant did not vanish with the fall of the pyramids but was renegotiated in the modern age. In 1954, President Dwight D. Eisenhower reportedly vanished from public view during a trip to California. Official accounts said he had visited a dentist, but alternative histories suggest he was instead taken to Edwards Air Force Base, where he is said to have met with extraterrestrial beings — later alleged to be Greys. According to accounts gathered by researchers such as Timothy Good, an agreement was struck: in exchange for advanced technology, the beings were permitted to abduct a limited number of humans and livestock, provided that records were kept (Good, *Above Top Secret: The Worldwide UFO Cover-up*, 1988; Good, *Need to Know: UFOs, the Military and Intelligence*, 2007).

No documented proof has ever surfaced, and official archives are silent, yet the story has circulated for decades, repeated by whistleblowers, intelligence insiders, and military personnel who otherwise had little to gain. Other figures, such as William Cooper and Philip Corso, have repeated variations of the same claim, though with conflicting details (Cooper, *Behold a Pale Horse*, 1991; Corso, *The Day After Roswell*, 1997). What matters here is not whether the particulars of the story are verifiable, but the resonance it carries: it describes the same bargain that ancient kings and priests once made. Compliance and blood in exchange for power from the sky.

Where pharaohs raised pyramids and Aztec rulers staged mass sacrifices, a modern president is said to have offered something chillingly similar — the lives and bodies of his people, surrendered for knowledge not otherwise attainable. Even if apocryphal, the persistence of the Eisenhower story underscores the same pattern. The covenant, ancient and modern, always demands the same payment.

The Covenant Unbroken

Taken together, abductee testimony, cattle mutilations, my own vision, and the Hill case point to one conclusion: the covenant never ended. The rituals of the past and the procedures of the present are two expressions of the same program. The pyramid steps and cattle pastures are stages of a single theater. The gods have not been replaced by new myths. They are still here, operating under the same needs.

The Question of Why

This brings us to the most unsettling question: why? Why would such beings require blood? Why would they demand it from human civilizations, drain it from animals, and still pursue it today? Why does blood appear as the one constant across cultures, myths, and encounters? The answer lies not in theology but in biology. To understand why the gods of the pyramids demanded sacrifice, we must look at what they are — and what their physiology requires.

12

THE PHYSIOLOGY OF THE GODS

In the previous chapter I've proposed that the gods of the pyramids are the Greys of Zeta Reticuli. That leads us to the question of what they are — and why they demanded blood. Myth and ritual tell us what was given. Physiology may tell us why it was required.

The hybrids we have traced across Mesopotamia, Egypt, India, and the Americas remind us that enforcement was never abstract. They were carved as falcon-men, jackal-heads, jaguar warriors — half-human forms engineered or costumed to embody vigilance and terror. Yet even as these hybrids commanded obedience, they were not the ultimate recipients of the covenant. They were masks, intermediaries, proxies. The deeper question is: who stood behind them? What kind of beings demanded the blood that these guardians ensured would flow? To answer that, we must look past the carved bodies of enforcers to the physiology of the gods themselves.

Across thousands of abduction reports, cattle mutilation cases, and leaked military documents, one peculiar fact remains consistent in descriptions of the beings often referred to as "the Greys": they appear to lack a digestive system. This feature—or lack thereof—has long puzzled both researchers and abductees. In *Communion* (1987), Whitley Strieber described his memories of interactions with Greys as featuring beings that seemed biologically alien in the truest sense. Not only were their bodies thin, almost malnourished-looking, but they did not breathe, sweat, or blink in the way humans do. Their skin was smooth, often cool to the touch, and eerily uniform—suggestive of either a biological simplification or an artificial construct.

Strieber later speculated in interviews and follow-up works (*Transformation*, *The Key*) that their skin had qualities consistent with absorption. This echoes what other abductees have noted: their bodies do not appear to show any external organs related to digestion or excretion. Instead, witnesses have sometimes described a faint chemical or ammonia-like odor, and even more intriguingly, glowing handprints left behind after encounters—visible only under UV or black light. Linda Moulton Howe documented such accounts in her investigative work *Glimpses of Other Realities* and in her decades-long research into cattle mutilations, noting that some abductees reported dermal contact with Greys that left residues suggestive of skin-based excretory processes.

If we take these reports seriously—and we must, given their frequency and cross-cultural consistency—we are left with a startling hypothesis: the Greys do not feed or excrete as we do. Instead, their skin may function as a dual-purpose organ, designed for both excretion and absorption. A kind of living membrane, optimized to interact with its environment by pulling in and pushing out biochemical matter. This brings us directly back to the covenant: if blood was always the demanded offering, it may be because the physiology of the gods required it in the most literal sense.

This theory fits elegantly with the evidence from modern cattle mutilations, where the animals are often found completely exsanguinated—drained of blood without signs of spillage. In many cases, the mutilations are so precise that even forensic pathologists are baffled. Howe and others have documented hundreds of cases in which blood, soft tissues, bone marrow, and reproductive organs are taken with surgical exactness. No tracks. No predators. No witnesses. The same precision demanded in the ritual machine of antiquity is being applied in our fields today.

If we assume the Greys are harvesting blood and tissue for nourishment, the next logical question is: how do they process it?

The answer may lie in what we would call a nutritional slurry—a plasma-rich, cell-cultured medium derived from blood and possibly enhanced with marrow-derived cultures. This slurry could be absorbed directly through the skin, requiring no mouth, no digestion, and no waste beyond trace chemical residue. In fact, this type of nutrient intake would help explain the ammonia-like smell and greasy film sometimes reported in abduction scenarios.

From a biochemical standpoint, skin absorption is entirely feasible—especially if the skin has evolved (or been engineered) with high vascular density just beneath a semi-permeable epidermal layer. Amphibians use similar mechanisms. So do some marine animals. Transdermal patches in human medicine prove that small molecules, lipids, and certain proteins can pass through human skin—though it is far less efficient than internal digestion.

If the Greys do indeed rely on transdermal absorption rather than oral ingestion, then their skin—far from being a passive barrier—must function as an active interface between body and environment. In effect, their entire epidermis would be a nutritional organ. This, more than anything else, clarifies why the covenant's rituals were centered on blood: blood is not symbolic to them. It is sustenance.

Biologically, this isn't without precedent. In Earth-based lifeforms, we see examples of transdermal respiration, osmoregulation, and nutrient exchange. Amphibians such as frogs and salamanders breathe through their skin, which is lined with dense capillary beds just beneath a thin mucous membrane. Marine annelids and some species of nudibranchs absorb dissolved nutrients directly from seawater through dermal diffusion. Even humans can absorb small quantities of medication, nicotine, or hormones through the skin via transdermal patches—though human skin is relatively poor at passive absorption without enhancers.

For the Greys, whose bodies appear devoid of digestive or excretory anatomy, their skin must take on a role far more complex than any of these examples. The dermis would need to be semi-permeable, capable of selectively absorbing molecules based on size, charge, and concentration gradients. It would also require an extremely high surface-area-to-volume ratio, achieved by the Greys' tall, emaciated builds. This is not unlike heat-exchanging organisms on Earth that use physical form to maximize exposure.

The epidermis, likely devoid of keratinized layers (which in humans protect but hinder permeability), might instead resemble a mucosal surface or a bioengineered membrane. Such skin would need to be composed of amphiphilic molecules—similar to the lipid bilayers found in human cell membranes—that allow both hydrophilic and lipophilic compounds to diffuse across it. This would facilitate absorption of plasma solutes such as glucose, amino acids, and iron complexes.

Just beneath that surface, we would expect to find dense capillary networks designed for rapid uptake into systemic circulation. These vessels may not resemble human blood vessels at all. They could operate on a microfluidic principle—analogous to artificial perfusion systems used in biomedical engineering—where nutrient-laden fluids are wicked away from the dermis and redistributed through a closed loop.

Moreover, the skin would likely operate in tandem with electrochemical gradients, helping pull charged ions and trace metals into circulation. This is not speculation alone: in human medicine, iontophoresis is already used to deliver medication through the skin by applying a mild electric current. If the Greys evolved—or engineered themselves—to use this principle biologically, they may "draw in" the molecular contents of their nutrient slurry with remarkable efficiency.

In such a system, subcutaneous fat would only interfere. It would create a diffusion barrier. It is no coincidence, then, that Greys are described—as I personally have observed after physically touching the shoulder of a tall Grey—as having zero subcutaneous fat. Their dermis feels tight over sinew, with no pliability or thermal insulation. This suggests a biology optimized not for comfort or heat retention, but for exchange.

Such a biology, while efficient for nutrient absorption, would also make them dangerously exposed in our world. A body designed as a living membrane would be vulnerable to pathogens, environmental toxins, and above all to the sun's ultraviolet rays. On Earth's surface, UV is relentless—mutagenic, damaging to delicate tissues, and lethal to any organism without natural defenses. If the Tall Greys' skin is optimized for permeability rather than protection, then direct exposure to sunlight would be catastrophic. This vulnerability helps explain why they rarely appear directly in open environments, and why they have relied on emissaries and intermediaries throughout history. Their very physiology demands concealment, or surrogates strong enough to endure where they cannot.

What little waste they produce may be expelled in trace amounts through the same membrane, carried out in vapor or oily excretions —hence the reported greasy film or chemical odor, often likened to ammonia or bleach. This form of dermal excretion would explain the glowing handprint residues some abductees have reported under UV light. If their waste products include nitrogenous compounds, or if trace phospholipids or crystalline proteins are left behind, these could fluoresce under ultraviolet light much like urea or certain sterols do in humans.

Their skin, then, is not merely protective. It is alive with function: an osmotic interface, a nutritional organ, a metabolic sieve. And if their species has truly evolved—or more likely, designed itself—to operate this way, it would suggest a biology less like ours and more akin to synthetic wetware. A living membrane capable of both sustaining and regulating their internal systems without ever eating, chewing, or digesting.

Biochemical Detail: What They May Be Absorbing

Blood is a remarkably sophisticated fluid—more than a transport medium, it is a microcosm of the organism itself. It not only circulates nutrients, gases, and waste, but carries biochemical signatures of cellular processes, endocrine states, immune readiness, and genetic identity. If one were designing an ideal substrate for rapid nutrient harvesting, blood—particularly plasma—would be virtually unmatched.

Albumin, the most prevalent plasma protein in humans, maintains oncotic pressure but also binds a variety of hormones, free fatty acids, and drugs. Its amphiphilic nature may be especially attractive to dermal absorbers, as it can act as a carrier vehicle through lipid-like skin matrices. Immunoglobulins, while typically defensive in humans, could be repurposed or selectively filtered by the Greys. Hemoglobin, dense in iron, could serve as a metabolic catalyst. Electrolytes—sodium, potassium, magnesium, calcium—would help maintain neurochemical gradients. Glucose and amino acids would serve as raw fuel for metabolism and tissue repair. Even trace hormones, neurotransmitters, and exosomes could provide valuable regulatory feedback for hybrid gestation programs.

In short, blood is not only food. It is also information. And the Greys appear to have designed themselves to extract both. If certain blood types were more compatible with their physiology, then the global obsession with blood in pyramid cultures may have been less about symbolism and more about selective sourcing.

Blood Type Compatibility

If the Greys truly rely on transdermal absorption of biochemical nutrients, the composition and immunological signature of the blood they harvest becomes critically important. Human blood is not a uniform fluid—it varies by type, antigen profile, Rh factor, and numerous trace variables that determine compatibility. For a species engaging in skin-based absorption, these differences might make or break the efficiency of nutrient uptake—or trigger toxic responses.

Among the various types, O-negative blood stands out as the universal donor in human medicine. In the context of dermal absorption, this may be the least likely to provoke immune or osmotic rejection. Families with high incidence of O-negative blood may be genetically favored not only for reproductive experimentation but for their metabolic value. The persistence of abduction in certain lineages may represent not random targeting but bloodline tracking.

Moreover, rare blood types such as Rh-null—sometimes called "golden blood"—may be of even greater interest. Nearly antigen-less, they could be ideal for both absorption and hybrid compatibility. The scarcity of such blood may elevate its importance, perhaps explaining why some abductees report repeated medical sampling and marrow extraction.

These rare bloodlines—like heirloom strains in selective breeding—may represent the Greys' prized stock. Not just genetically valuable, but metabolically ideal. In this view, abduction is not random horror, but husbandry.

Waste, Efficiency, and Degeneration

At first glance, the physiology of the Greys appears efficient. Their bodies are lean, their systems stripped of excess. They do not waste energy on digestion, excretion, or reproduction as we know it. They operate as if every cell, every surface of their skin, has been optimized for function. But efficiency is a double-edged sword. What looks like advancement may, in truth, be degeneration — the loss of functions so fundamental that survival requires constant extraction from others.

Biology offers many parallels. Cave-dwelling fish and insects lose their eyes after generations in darkness. Parasites shed their digestive tracts when they can feed directly on the blood or tissues of their hosts. Flightless birds once soared but now walk, their wings atrophied. Evolution is not a ladder of progress but a series of trade-offs. Adaptations can just as easily represent loss as gain. The panda, exquisitely adapted to digest bamboo, is doomed by its specialization, just as the cheetah, master of speed, lives at the edge of genetic collapse. The Greys, with their absent digestive and reproductive systems, may represent not an evolutionary triumph but a collapse into dependency.

Consider what it means for a species to lack conventional waste systems. Waste is the byproduct of internal processing, the natural cost of independence. By eliminating digestion and excretion, the Greys may have eliminated their independence. What little waste they produce seeps through the skin as chemical residue — not the robust byproducts of an organism capable of feeding and reproducing on its own. They cannot take in raw food, cannot adapt to new environments, cannot generate sustenance internally. They are efficient, but only because they have externalized their costs. The covenant became their outsourced metabolism. Human blood became their digestive tract. Ritual sacrifice became their gut.

This pattern may not have been the result of natural evolution at all, but of deliberate engineering. If the Greys once possessed digestive and reproductive organs, perhaps they chose — or were forced — to remove them through bioengineering. In streamlining their bodies for longevity or neurological efficiency, they may have sacrificed flexibility. What they gained in control, they lost in resilience. And once functions are removed generation after generation, there is no easy return. A civilization that edits its own biology may create beings that survive for millennia, but at the cost of being forever dependent on external inputs.

The warning for humanity is clear. Even now, we experiment with genetic modification, cybernetic integration, and transhumanist dreams of eliminating hunger, disease, and reproduction as we know it. The Greys may be a mirror of our own future — a species that engineered itself into a corner, gaining efficiency but losing the ability to survive without siphoning vitality from others. Their covenant with humanity may be less an expression of superiority than a confession of desperation.

This desperation echoes not only in their biology but in their culture. What becomes of a society that can no longer reproduce naturally, that can no longer feed itself except by harvesting others? Ritual replaces intimacy. Procedure replaces individuality. The enforcers — bird-men, jackal-headed gods, jaguar warriors — may have been the prosthetics of a culture that could no longer generate symbols organically. They were cultural crutches, masks concealing the truth: the gods had withered, and their survival depended on convincing humanity to supply what they lacked.

Dependency erodes dignity. The Greys' cold demeanor, their lack of visible emotion, may not reflect superiority but shame. To feed by extracting blood, to breed by abducting tissues, is not the life of gods but of scavengers. Their obsession with control may be the compensation of a species that has lost autonomy. Ritual terror, pyramids aligned to the heavens, spectacles of sacrifice — these were not displays of abundance but of need. Every civilization that entered the covenant became the external stomach and womb of the Greys.

From this perspective, the covenant was never holy. It was logistical. It was biology masquerading as divinity. The gods demanded blood not as symbolic atonement but as metabolic necessity. And their apparent indifference to human suffering may be the cold logic of a species that has lost the capacity to feel beyond survival. They do not weep at altars because they cannot afford to.

Degeneration explains why the Greys pursue hybridization with such relentless focus. A species that has shed reproductive systems cannot restore them without assistance. A species that has lost digestion cannot reacquire it without grafting. Hybrids, then, are not curiosities but necessities. They are the attempt to climb back out of the evolutionary cul-de-sac, to recover functions that were engineered away. To witness their program is to witness a species clawing back from the brink of self-extinction.

Seen this way, the covenant is evidence of weakness, not power.

The gods of the pyramids were not omnipotent masters but dependents cloaked in ritual. Their wings and serpents were masks covering frailty. Their pyramids were not monuments of glory but machines of provisioning. The blood that flowed down their steps was not offered in reverence but extracted in desperation.

For humanity, this should reshape how we see the covenant. We were never the subjects of gods. We were the hosts of a dependent species, engineered into weakness and hiding its shame behind ritual grandeur. Their degeneration became our burden. Their efficiency became our slavery. And if their program continues today, then we must ask: are we the chosen, or simply the chosen resource?

The Cost of Dependency

If the Greys' physiology has collapsed into dependence on human blood, then the covenant takes on a darker meaning. It was never worship in the true sense, never a voluntary offering to higher beings. It was the arrangement of a parasite and a host, an addict and a supplier. To live, the gods required what humans alone could provide. Dependency defined the relationship — and dependency always carries a cost.

Dependency as Inversion of Divinity

The essence of divinity, in human thought, is independence. Gods are immortal, self-sustaining, radiant. They do not hunger as mortals do; they dispense life, they do not beg for it. But what if the beings who presented themselves as gods were not independent at all? What if their survival depended on the very creatures they ruled? In that case, the covenant inverts the logic of divinity. The gods are no longer omnipotent. They are tethered, needy, fragile. They feed not by grace but by extraction.

Biology offers two lenses for this relationship: symbiosis and parasitism. Symbiosis implies mutual benefit, as with bees and flowers. Parasitism implies one-sided extraction, as with a tick drawing blood from its host. The covenant, cloaked in the garments of religion, was presented as symbiosis — "you sacrifice to the gods, and in return they bless you." But in practice it bore all the hallmarks of parasitism. The benefit was rarely mutual. The gods consumed blood and tissue, and humanity rationalized the loss as holy necessity.

Historical Parallels of Exploitation

Human empires have acted in similar ways. Rome extracted grain and tribute from its provinces, demanding loyalty and ritual while giving little in return. Colonial powers drained colonies of resources, disguising the extraction as "civilization" or "progress." The Aztec empire staged Flower Wars to capture bodies, claiming the sacrifices sustained the cosmos itself. In every case, exploitation was wrapped in ideology. The covenant was no different. The gods drained blood and organs, but the priesthood translated the act into cosmic poetry. Dependency was concealed beneath the language of divinity.

What makes the covenant unique is that it was not merely cultural exploitation but biological. The Greys' very survival rested on the flow of blood. Where empires collapse if tribute falters, the gods themselves would wither without their harvest. Humanity was not only conquered politically but conscripted metabolically. Our bodies became their supply chain. Our civilizations became their infrastructure. The pyramids were not only monuments of stone but stations of provisioning.

The Psychological Cost to Humanity

Living under such dependency left scars on the human psyche. Imagine a world in which the most sacred rituals of your people revolve around bloodletting, sacrifice, and death. For Egyptians, Mayans, Aztecs, and Mississippians, this was normality. Children grew up watching rivers of blood flow from temple steps, told it was holy. Fear of famine or divine wrath reinforced the logic: to stop feeding the gods would be to risk annihilation. Generations internalized the trauma, rationalized it, and encoded it in myth. The gods' dependency became humanity's anxiety.

Even today, echoes persist. The language of blood sacrifice runs through the Bible and the Qur'an, through Hindu hymns and Greek tragedy. The need to "appease" higher powers with offerings of flesh or blood is a memory too deeply rooted to vanish. Dependency reshaped human spirituality itself, teaching us that holiness meant suffering, that life must be paid for with life.

Symbolism as Rationalization

How did priesthoods maintain such a system without collapse? By transmuting biology into symbolism. Blood was no longer described as the gods' meal but as the essence of life, the bridge between mortal and divine. Sacrifice became not extraction but communion. Temples became theaters in which humans convinced themselves they were participating in cosmic balance, not in feeding dependents. The act of giving blood was framed as noble, even joyous. By reframing necessity as holiness, humanity survived the humiliation of dependency.

But symbolism was always a mask. The gods' appetite did not change. Whether poured into fires, drained from captives, or offered from kings, blood was consumed the same way. Symbolism served the psychological needs of the host, not the metabolic needs of the parasite. And yet the illusion held, because illusion was necessary for survival. To see the gods as needy scavengers would have shattered the system. To preserve meaning, the covenant had to remain sacred in human eyes.

Modern Continuity of Dependency

In the modern era, the same dependency reveals itself in subtler ways. Abductees describe procedures focused not on teaching or communion but on sampling, extraction, and hybridization. Cattle mutilations leave carcasses drained of blood with surgical precision. Nothing about these acts suggests benevolence. Everything suggests maintenance. The gods still require what they cannot generate on their own. Their covenant with humanity may no longer take the form of public spectacle, but the biology is unchanged.

This continuity reframes the Eisenhower covenant lore in a chilling way. If leaders truly did negotiate with the Greys, the terms were not theological but logistical: permission to harvest in exchange for technology. Such an arrangement mirrors ancient bargains. Kings offered temples and victims; presidents allegedly offered populations and livestock. In both cases, dependency dictated the terms. The Greys needed blood, and humans agreed to supply it.

The Philosophical Question

This raises the most unsettling question of all: what does it mean if the universe's most advanced visitors are not gods of abundance but dependents? We expected gods to give, but ours only take. We expected divinity to be radiant, but ours are anemic. We expected salvation, but found extraction. If the covenant is the arrangement of dependents disguising themselves as masters, then humanity's relationship to the gods must be reevaluated entirely.

Should we fear them as parasites, pity them as degenerates, or resist them as exploiters? Dependency makes them vulnerable as well as dangerous. They cannot survive without us — and perhaps that is their greatest weakness. The covenant is not only a chain around humanity's neck but a chain around theirs. They have bound us, but in binding us they have bound themselves.

The Covenant Reconsidered

The cost of dependency, then, is twofold. For the Greys, it is the loss of autonomy, the humiliation of survival through extraction. For humanity, it is the internalization of sacrifice as spirituality, the shaping of civilizations around the needs of another species. The gods of the pyramids did not descend to bless mankind. They descended to live off mankind. And every altar, every captive, every mutilation testifies to the cost of a covenant that was never holy, but biological.

The Bovine Proxy

If the Greys are using human blood and marrow-derived tissue cultures as a nutritional base, it raises an obvious logistical challenge: how do they source enough of it? The answer may lie in cattle.

Cattle mutilations—long dismissed by skeptics as misidentified scavenging—have now been reported for over fifty years, with striking consistency across North America, South America, and parts of Europe. The common elements are unmistakable: bloodless corpses, excised reproductive and soft tissues, removed eyes and tongues, and most notably, no signs of struggle or predation. In many cases, ranchers report helicopters or strange lights in the area before or after the mutilation. Linda Moulton Howe's investigative reporting in *A Strange Harvest* and *Glimpses of Other Realities* has thoroughly documented these events, establishing patterns that suggest deliberate and systematic collection, not random animal deaths.

The biological similarity between bovine and human blood is one factor. Bovine plasma shares numerous transport proteins, osmotic regulators, and mineral carriers with its human counterpart—making it a near-ideal medium for bioengineering or supplementation. In fact, bovine serum is already used in human medical research to culture cells and grow tissues. Imagine that the Greys, rather than harvesting humans wholesale as in antiquity, have shifted to using cattle as nutrient carriers—with human-derived marrow or tissue cultures added to complete the recipe. The result: a slurry rich in growth factors and proteins, absorbed dermally like a living fuel.

This dual sourcing strategy—humans for seed stock, cattle for volume—solves their short-term nutritional needs. But it is not sustainable. If their goal is to anchor themselves permanently on

Earth, they cannot forever rely on slurry and engineered absorption. The covenant must evolve.

Implications for Hybrid Design

This brings us to the hybridization program, which abductees and researchers alike have documented for decades. If the Greys are attempting to move beyond transdermal nutrient absorption—either due to its limitations or to adapt more fully to Earth—then hybrids may be the answer. By merging Grey neurology with more terrestrial physiology, they may be working toward a species that can digest, reproduce, and survive without technological scaffolding.

Hybrids often appear more robust than Greys: with muscle tone, cardiovascular function, and sometimes even signs of sexual reproduction. Abductees report hybrids who smile, express curiosity, or mimic human behaviors, suggesting deliberate social calibration. In some cases, navels, breast tissue, or genital features are described, hinting at restored reproductive anatomy. Each of these traits points to the same goal: reintegrating what the Greys lost.

From a biochemical standpoint, the integration of a human-style digestive system would change everything. Nutrient absorption would shift from skin to gut, with enzymatic breakdown, gut flora, and peristalsis restored. This raises new engineering challenges, particularly the integration of Grey neurological systems with the human enteric nervous system. If successful, such hybrids would no longer need cattle blood or marrow cultures—they could feed directly from Earth's biosphere.

In this light, hybrids are not an experiment. They are the solution to a problem — the next stage of the covenant. Humanity's blood sustained the gods for millennia, but the gods appear to be preparing a replacement species, one that can walk among us, eat as we do, reproduce as we do, and yet carry within them the Grey mind. The covenant began with human blood, but it may end with human replacement.

If the Greys' physiology demands blood, then every ritual, every sacrifice, every mutilation, every abduction becomes intelligible. The covenant was never symbolic; it was metabolic. The gods demanded blood because they required it, and hybrids are the proof that they are still seeking to evolve beyond that need. The question is no longer why the covenant existed, but what comes after.

13

THE MODERN PARALLELS

The Covenant's New Mask

If the physiology of the gods explains what they are, the modern era reveals what they continue to do. The covenant did not collapse with the fall of the Aztecs or the fading of pharaonic priesthoods. It did not dissolve when temples crumbled or when pyramids were buried in jungle or prairie earth. It has simply changed costume. The same demands are visible now in our fields, hospitals, skies, and homes—expressed through cattle mutilations, abductions, and clinical procedures that bear the same precision as the sacrifices of old.

The cattle mutilation mystery is the most obvious continuity. For half a century, ranchers across the Americas have found animals drained of blood, organs excised with surgical exactness, reproductive tissues removed without struggle or predation. The scenes echo ancient ritual sites, only transposed to the open plains. Where once the cuauhxicalli bowl held human hearts, now fields hold carcasses left behind like husks. The gods have not stopped harvesting; they have merely shifted the source, employing cattle as proxies for human victims. This is not speculation alone—biological research already relies heavily on bovine serum for cell cultures. The Greys may be exploiting the same compatibility on a much larger scale, using bovines as mass providers of plasma and protein just as priests once delivered captives to temple steps.

Abduction accounts add the human dimension. Missing pregnancies, semen extractions, surgical procedures performed in sterile rooms—these reports repeat across continents with disturbing uniformity. The most famous example of this continuity surfaced in 1961, when Betty and Barney Hill reported being taken aboard a craft in New Hampshire. Under hypnosis, Betty recalled medical procedures performed with cold detachment: needles inserted into her abdomen, samples taken from her body, and the overwhelming sense that she was being used for purposes beyond her control (Fuller, *The Interrupted Journey*, 1966). These accounts are chillingly parallel to ancient descriptions of sacrifice—immobilization, invasive instruments, and the offering of flesh and blood to beings regarded as higher powers. What the Hills endured in a metallic craft echoes what captives once faced on stone altars: ritual extraction in service of the covenant. Women describe being told their fetus was "taken," only to find their womb empty weeks later. Men recount waking with unexplained soreness, drained as if harvested. The instruments described are cold, efficient, clinical. Victims speak of floating lights, paralysis, and beings who move with practiced detachment. The parallels to ancient sacrifice are unmistakable. The temple has become the craft; the priest's obsidian blade has become the laser scalpel. The covenant continues, adapted to modern settings, with abductees serving as unwilling offerings.

The precision itself is the signature. Ancient sacrificial remains show evidence of skill—hearts cut free, skulls opened, bones dismembered with practiced hands. Archaeologists examining Aztec sacrificial victims have remarked on the speed and dexterity required to cut through bone and tissue with stone blades, sometimes in the span of seconds. Today, pathologists examining mutilated cattle remark on incisions cleaner than any available scalpel, tissues removed without blood loss, cuts executed with a kind of surgical automation. The techniques may have advanced, but the outcome is the same: targeted extraction of blood, marrow, reproductive organs, and life-force. Whether upon a stone altar or in a sterile craft, the ritual remains.

The modern era also reveals the purpose more clearly. Abductees report hybrids shown to them, children bred from human and Grey material, beings who stare with unsettling familiarity. Some are told, "This is your child." Others describe feelings of overwhelming grief or guilt, as if the beings knew how to manipulate parental instinct. Blood and tissue are not harvested at random. They are raw stock for a program whose aim is nothing less than the construction of a new species. Just as ancient priests fed the gods to ensure the survival of their cities, modern victims feed a genetic agenda intended to secure the gods' survival on Earth.

To view these phenomena separately—mutilations, abductions, hybrids—is to miss the thread that ties them together. They are the modern enactments of the same covenant that bound humanity thousands of years ago. The gods still harvest. The gods still demand. And the gods still enforce their contract with surgical precision. What has changed is not their appetite but our understanding. We no longer call them gods; we call them visitors, Greys, or extraterrestrials. But the covenant is the same, written in blood across both stone altars and sterile steel.

The chilling parallel is this: the past was never left behind. It was only updated. The covenant is alive, operating in the open fields of our world and in the closed rooms of our encounters. The faces of the priests are gone, but the recipients remain, still harvesting, still preparing for what comes next. The instruments have changed, the rituals disguised, but the continuity is unmistakable.

When we study the archaeological record, we see the same pattern: sudden imposition of sacrifice, obsessive repetition of blood ritual, precision in procedure. When we listen to abductees and ranchers, we see the pattern renewed. The blood covenant is not the invention of myth but the program of survival. The gods of the pyramids have not ascended into heaven or faded into legend. They are still here. They have always been here.

Cattle Mutilations — The Open-Field Altars

If modern abductions represent the closed sanctuaries of the covenant, cattle mutilations are its open-air altars. For more than fifty years, ranchers across North and South America have awoken to find their livestock dead, drained, and dismembered with precision no predator or prankster could replicate. The settings are as ordinary as they are chilling: empty pastures, barbed-wire fences, wide skies. Yet the scenes echo the plazas of Teotihuacan or the fields around Cahokia. Where once priests raised captives on pyramid steps, now fields hold carcasses left behind like husks. The gods of the covenant still harvest—but the theater has shifted from stone platforms to open plains.

The pattern is unmistakable. Animals are discovered bloodless, yet without pools of blood nearby. Incisions are precise, cauterized as if by heat, the edges smooth as glass. Eyes, tongues, reproductive organs, and rectal tissue are removed with surgical focus. Predators typically leave tracks, struggle marks, and torn flesh; here there are none. Scavengers often avoid the carcasses entirely, as though the remains repel life. Ranchers describe the smell of chemical sterility rather than decay. The impression is not of predation but of procedure.

The Colorado wave of the mid-1970s brought national attention to the phenomenon. Hundreds of cattle across the San Luis Valley were found mutilated in identical fashion: excised tissue, drained blood, reproductive organs removed. Law enforcement investigated, and the FBI opened inquiries under pressure from ranchers and senators alike. The final report waved the cases off as "natural predation," but this explanation satisfied no one. Veterinarians who examined the remains testified to surgical incisions beyond the capacity of scavengers. The wounds showed no signs of clotting or hemorrhage, suggesting that the blood had been extracted under controlled conditions (Howe, *A Strange Harvest*, 1980).

Brazil has produced equally disturbing cases. In the 1990s, mutilations reported in rural regions often coincided with sightings of strange lights. Some ranchers described beams descending onto their pastures, animals lifted, then discovered later with organs missing. In several cases, human bodies were found in similar condition: flayed with surgical precision, exsanguinated, with internal tissues removed while external wounds showed cauterization. These rare but shocking human mutilations suggest that the covenant occasionally bypasses bovine proxies altogether, reminding us that the original currency has always been human blood.

Biology offers a plausible rationale for the focus on cattle. Bovine blood is remarkably similar to human blood in its plasma profile. In fact, modern biomedical research relies heavily on fetal bovine serum (FBS) as the medium for growing human and animal cells in laboratory cultures. FBS is prized for its high concentration of growth factors and proteins, making it the ideal substrate for sustaining life in vitro. Scientists today depend on bovine blood to maintain tissue cultures. If we require this resource to build cells in a dish, why would the Greys not require it to build hybrids in their labs? What our biology laboratories purchase in bottles, their covenant may harvest directly from the field.

The parallel to ancient sacrifice is striking. In Mesoamerica, captives were led up the steps of pyramids and their hearts removed with precision, their blood spilled in tribute to the gods. Archaeological analysis of Aztec remains shows evidence of rapid, skilled excision of the heart and surrounding tissue. In Egypt, animals were slaughtered daily in temple courts, their blood drained as routine offering. At Cahokia, young women were executed en masse and buried as provisioning for leaders and deities. Each culture harvested specific tissues with skill and repetition. Today, mutilated cattle bear the same marks: targeted extraction of specific tissues, repeated across thousands of cases, with no wasted motion. The covenant has always been efficient.

Linda Moulton Howe's documentary *A Strange Harvest* (1980) brought this reality to the public eye. Traveling from ranch to ranch, she interviewed bewildered cattlemen, photographed carcasses, and gathered veterinary reports. Again and again, the details converged: animals drained, organs excised, no signs of predation. Ranchers described unmarked helicopters in the skies before or after mutilations, as if human authorities were monitoring or even cooperating. Howe concluded that the mutilations were not isolated crimes or hoaxes but part of a systematic program—an echo of the sacrificial system dressed in modern clothes. Her work remains foundational because it recorded what official reports refused to admit: something nonhuman was taking blood on an industrial scale.

The eerie sterility of the scenes underscores the covenantal parallel. In ancient plazas, priests purified altars with fire and incense before sacrifice. Today, ranchers describe carcasses as unnaturally clean, absent of insects, almost antiseptic. The impression is the same: the gods' work is not messy predation but clinical harvest. Just as priests performed rituals with solemn precision, the mutilations seem carried out with detached expertise. The resemblance to medical procedures is unavoidable.

To dismiss these cases as hysteria or hoax is to ignore the volume of evidence. Thousands of animals have been reported across decades and continents. Too many carcasses, too many repeated signatures, too many ranchers with nothing to gain. The phenomenon persists despite ridicule because the covenant persists. Fields have become the altars of the modern age. The gods no longer need priests to wield obsidian knives; they have machines to perform their harvest.

The cost to humanity is hidden but real. Each mutilated cow is a proxy, a stand-in for the captives who once bled on stone steps. The covenant has not ended—it has adapted. By shifting to cattle, the gods reduce human panic while continuing to draw the same substance. The logic is chilling: what priests once staged publicly, the Greys now perform quietly, distributed across fields and continents.

But the meaning is unchanged. Blood flows, tissues are taken, life is reduced to resource.

Seen in this light, cattle mutilations are not mysteries to be solved but rituals to be recognized. They are the continuation of the covenant in plain sight, disguised as anomaly but performed with the same precision as in antiquity. Where once the gods demanded rivers of human blood, they now harvest bovine surrogates to sustain their biology. The open plains are the new pyramid steps, and the carcasses left behind are the offerings.

Human Abductions — The Closed-Room Temples

If cattle mutilations represent the covenant in the open air, human abductions represent its hidden sanctuaries. These are the modern equivalents of the inner chambers of the temple, where only priests and victims entered, and where blood was shed under the gaze of the gods. The stories that abductees tell—sterile rooms, glaring lights, instruments of extraction, paralysis, and violation—echo the descriptions of rituals that once took place in stone sanctuaries. The space has changed from pyramid chamber to metallic craft, but the purpose remains the same: the harvest of blood, tissue, and reproductive essence.

The consistency of abduction accounts is striking. Across continents and decades, men and women who have never met describe the same elements: beams of light lifting them from beds or cars; paralysis that renders them helpless; rows of beings with large black eyes moving with practiced detachment; clinical tables surrounded by instruments; the sensation of cold metal pressed against skin; the extraction of semen, ova, or blood samples; the sudden awareness of fetuses implanted or removed. These are not scattered hallucinations. They are ritual scripts repeated with the regularity of liturgy.

Whitley Strieber's *Communion* (1987) gave the world its most famous modern testimony. Strieber described being taken from his cabin in upstate New York into a craft where he was subjected to intrusive procedures, including what he interpreted as the collection of semen. He emphasized the beings' efficiency and detachment, their movements deliberate and ritualistic. His account resonated with thousands of readers who wrote to him, describing nearly identical experiences. The book did not create a phenomenon—it revealed one that was already widespread, its continuity too strong to dismiss.

Women abductees often recount the most chilling continuity of all: missing pregnancies. They describe being told they were pregnant, sometimes confirmed by doctors, only to find weeks later that the fetus was gone. Under hypnosis or in dreams, they recall being taken aboard crafts and shown hybrid infants, and told that these children are theirs. Such stories mirror the sacrifice of infants and children in ancient times—Carthage, the Aztecs, even hints in the Hebrew Bible. Where once babies were presented on altars, today they are presented in incubation chambers, their purpose not worship but survival of the gods' genetic program.

Men, too, report parallel violations. Many describe forced extraction of semen, often through mechanical or telepathic inducement of ejaculation. The accounts are clinical and devoid of intimacy, consistent with a program designed for reproduction without reproduction. In ancient times, men were sometimes castrated as offerings, their reproductive capacity sacrificed to appease deities. Today, the same reproductive essence is harvested in craft chambers, not to destroy fertility but to exploit it. The principle is the same: the gods' survival demands human reproductive material.

The abduction environment itself functions as a temple. Victims describe rooms bathed in unnatural light, often with walls that seem seamless, metallic, and glowing. The table at the center is both altar and surgical bed. The beings move with ritual precision, each with a role, each repeating actions that abductees recognize across accounts. Instruments appear but are rarely understood, often described as rods, probes, or devices that operate without wires or attachments. The impression is not of improvisation but of practiced ceremony. Just as priests in Mesoamerica repeated the same gestures over centuries, the Greys repeat the same procedures, refining but never altering the ritual.

Some abductees describe being placed in restraints, others paralyzed without bonds. In both cases, the message is the same: consent is irrelevant. The victim is present to be offered, not to participate. In this sense, the covenant's logic is intact. Sacrifice was never voluntary—it was enforced. The gods did not wait for offerings; they took them. In modern abductions, the same truth emerges. The human is not a supplicant but a resource.

The parallels extend even to emotional manipulation. Ancient rituals often involved pageantry designed to awe or terrify victims into acceptance—feathers, fire, chants, masks. Abductees today describe telepathic images projected into their minds: visions of earth in flames if they resist, of children in need of care if they comply. The gods of the covenant no longer wear jaguar skins or falcon masks, but they still cloak their procedures in psychological theater. Fear and guilt are the liturgies of their new sanctuaries.

The scale of the phenomenon reinforces its covenantal nature. Researchers such as David Jacobs and Budd Hopkins have documented hundreds of cases across decades, and John Mack's studies at Harvard revealed the psychological toll: abductees traumatized yet insistent that their experiences were real. The very uniformity of the reports suggests something beyond imagination. Just as the rituals of ancient civilizations were standardized across centuries, the abduction procedures are standardized across nations. The covenant operates not as folklore but as program.

The most haunting continuity is the presentation of hybrids. Abductees report being shown children who are neither fully human nor fully Grey—infants with large eyes but recognizable human features. The beings insist on emotional connection: "This is your child." Such encounters mirror the ritual of presenting captives or infants before crowds in ancient temples. The gods are not only harvesting material but ensuring that humans remain emotionally entangled in their project. In antiquity, sacrifice bound entire cities to the gods. Today, hybrid presentations bind abductees and their bloodlines to the covenant.

The comparison may seem stark, but it is inescapable: the closed-room abduction chamber is the modern temple. The procedures are sacrifices stripped of mythic language but retaining their function. Blood, semen, ova, and fetuses are offerings not to appease divine wrath but to sustain the survival program of the Greys. The victim does not kneel before an idol; they lie on a table under a beam of light. The continuity is complete.

The covenant's modern sanctuaries are not built of stone but of metal. They float in the skies rather than rise from the earth. But their function is the same: to harvest, to extract, to enforce. The priests of old wore feathered headdresses and carried obsidian knives; the enforcers of today wear gray skin and carry instruments of light. The setting has changed, but the covenant has not. Humanity remains bound, our reproductive essence the price of another species' survival.

Surgical Precision as Signature

If there is one trait that unites the sacrificial remains of antiquity with the mutilations and abductions of today, it is precision. The covenant was never messy. It was never the wild tearing of predators or the chaotic bloodletting of mobs. It was procedural, deliberate, exact. The gods demanded blood, but they demanded it delivered with skill. Whether through obsidian blades on the steps of the Templo Mayor or laser-like incisions on the bodies of cattle, the mark of the covenant is the same: surgical efficiency.

Archaeological studies of Aztec sacrificial victims emphasize the speed and accuracy required for the rituals. Spanish chroniclers describe priests plunging obsidian blades into captives' chests, cutting free the heart in a matter of seconds, and raising it skyward while blood still pulsed from the aorta. To accomplish this with stone tools is astonishing. The cuts visible on skeletal remains confirm that the priests were trained, their motions exact, their knowledge of anatomy intimate. They were not butchers—they were surgeons. The covenant had taught them procedure.

In Egypt, mummification rituals reveal the same procedural focus. Embalmers routinely removed the brain and internal organs with remarkable dexterity, often through small openings in the skull or abdomen. Texts describe the use of hooked instruments and resins to preserve tissue. What appears to us as funerary ritual may also have been the echo of sacrificial procedure. The body was not desecrated randomly—it was opened with precision, its contents removed, its blood drained, its tissues preserved or offered. Even in death, surgical skill defined the interaction with the divine.

At Cahokia, the mass burials of Mound 72 also show evidence of method. The arrangement of bodies—some strangled, some executed by blows to the head, some buried alive—was not chaotic but categorized, as though each method served a distinct covenantal function. Archaeologists note the careful positioning of bones and artifacts, suggesting that executioners knew exactly what they were doing. Like their Mesoamerican counterparts, they were enacting a program, not improvising.

Fast forward to the modern era, and the same surgical logic reappears. Pathologists examining mutilated cattle consistently remark on incisions cleaner than any available scalpel. Tissue is excised without surrounding trauma, as though cut by a beam of heat or energy. Blood is removed without hemorrhage, vessels collapsed as if suctioned in a vacuum. The edges of wounds are cauterized, preventing insects from colonizing the remains. Predators do not cauterize; hoaxers with knives cannot replicate the effect. The surgical signature is unmistakable.

Linda Moulton Howe documented numerous cases in *A Strange Harvest* (1980), including veterinary testimony that the incisions appeared as if "machined." Ranchers described carcasses so bloodless that even the heart contained no clots. In one case, a sheriff noted that the excision of a cow's reproductive tract had been done "with the skill of a surgeon"—yet no blood was spilled on the ground. This is the same paradox we see in ancient remains: massive bloodletting but little evidence of chaos. The blood is always contained, always managed, always directed.

Abduction testimonies reinforce the surgical theme. Victims describe instruments applied to their skin that leave triangular marks, circular scoop scars, or straight-line incisions that heal overnight without infection. Some report waking with scars that fade within days, as if cellular repair had been accelerated. Others recall seeing rods, discs, or probes applied to their bodies, devices that operate without blades yet extract tissue or fluid with efficiency. The impression is not one of clumsy experimentation but of practiced procedure, repeated countless times.

My own experience confirms this signature of surgical detachment. In July 2022, I was taken by the Greys and subjected to an operation in which my left arm was removed and reattached. When I regained awareness, I found my elbow joint swollen, locked, and painful, leaving me debilitated for weeks. Yet what shocked me most was not the aftermath but the procedure itself: it was bloodless. Not a drop of blood spilled on the table beside me, nor on the side cart where my detached limb was placed. There was no pooling, no staining, no mess. Even at the point of separation, there was only sterile absence, as though the circulation had been sealed in an instant. The marrow deep within the bone may have been the true target, given the lingering swelling, but the surface was immaculate. It was one of the most haunting encounters I later described in my memoir, *Angst in the Shadows*—a moment that captured not only the fear of violation but the chilling precision that defines the covenant itself.

This is the same paradox veterinarians describe in cattle mutilations: carcasses drained of blood with no spillage on the ground, vessels collapsed without hemorrhage, wounds cauterized as if sealed by heat. It is also the same paradox archaeologists puzzle over at sacrificial sites: massive bloodletting described in chronicles, yet altars and floors that bear little trace of saturation. Again and again, the covenant reveals its signature. The gods harvest blood and tissue, but they do so with a precision that erases the act itself. My arm was not butchered. It was clinically removed and returned with the same sterile efficiency that has marked the covenant for millennia.

David Jacobs, in his decades of interviews, noted that abductees consistently described the beings as "coldly efficient." They rarely speak, rarely deviate from task, rarely display emotion. They move with the detachment of surgical teams, each performing a role. The abductee is not treated as an individual but as a subject. The procedures themselves are repeated across accounts: blood drawn from veins, semen extracted by devices or stimulation, ova removed with needles inserted through the abdomen. These are not random violations. They are standardized rituals, perfected over generations.

The signature of precision links past and present. Ancient victims bore marks of anatomical knowledge beyond expectation for their societies. Modern victims bear marks of technology beyond expectation for ours. The constancy of that precision suggests a continuity of instruction. The Greys may have been the original surgeons of the covenant, teaching human priests the motions of sacrifice, then continuing the work themselves in the present day with advanced instruments. The altar and the craft are two expressions of the same surgical theater.

This precision also explains why the covenant endured. Chaos invites resistance; order enforces awe. Victims who witnessed the skill of priests or the cold efficiency of Greys were more likely to interpret the act as divine. The clean cut, the swift removal, the absence of mess—these are psychological weapons as much as technical feats. They convey control, inevitability, authority. Sacrifice staged as surgery teaches the victim, and the culture, that resistance is useless. The gods know exactly what they are doing.

Skeptics often dismiss cattle mutilations as hoaxes or abduction accounts as hallucinations. But the very precision of the evidence undermines those explanations. Hoaxers do not cauterize wounds with invisible tools. Predators do not remove organs without tearing surrounding tissue. Sleep paralysis does not leave scoop marks, triangular burns, or missing pregnancies. The surgical signature is the through-line that defies dismissal. It is the fingerprint of the covenant.

We should not underestimate the significance of this signature. In antiquity, it shaped entire cultures: priests became surgeons of blood, kings became managers of sacrifice, temples became theaters of surgical ritual. In the modern world, it shapes our anomalies: ranchers bury cattle drained with impossible cleanliness, abductees carry scars that heal without infection, doctors record pregnancies that vanish without miscarriage. Precision is the link that binds archaeology to pathology, temples to laboratories, priests to Greys.

The covenant is not remembered only in myth. It is carved into bone, inscribed on tissue, recorded in scars. Its precision is its permanence. And wherever we find surgical efficiency without explanation —whether in mass graves at Cahokia, hearts excised in Tenochtitlan, cattle drained in Colorado, or abductees scarred in New York—we find the mark of the covenant still active. The gods' appetite is constant, but so is their discipline. Theirs is not a chaos of hunger but a procedure of survival. The covenant remains, written not only in blood but in the clinical cuts of its enforcers.

The Hybrid Program — Covenant's New Aim

If cattle mutilations and human abductions reveal the methods of the covenant, the hybrids reveal its aim. The Greys are not collecting blood and tissue out of curiosity. They are not conducting random experiments. They are building something. The procedures—clinical, repetitive, and relentless—converge on a single purpose: the creation of a new species. The covenant's ultimate goal is not simply extraction. It is transformation.

For decades, abductees have described encounters with beings that were neither fully human nor fully Grey. They are shown infants with disproportionately large eyes, thin limbs, and frail bodies, yet with recognizably human faces. Others describe adolescents who stare with unsettling intensity, who move awkwardly but display curiosity and emotion. Again and again, abductees report being told

—sometimes telepathically, sometimes aloud—that these are their children. The emotional manipulation is deliberate. It forges a bond between human abductees and hybrids, ensuring that the program is not viewed only as sterile procedure but as family entanglement.

One of the most painful examples comes from my own life. In Angst in the Shadows, I described how my former girlfriend, Samantha, experienced a pregnancy that ended without explanation. She passed tissue as though miscarrying, yet the fluid-filled sac that should have contained the fetus was missing. There was no fetus. While She was saddened and confused by what happened, I was left with the chilling suspicion that what had been taken was not lost but removed—transferred into the hands of the same beings who later showed me images of hybrid offspring.

That suspicion hardened into certainty when I was eventually introduced to the baby itself. During a later encounter in June of 2023, the Greys presented me with a living infant they identified as mine. I was conscious for only half a minute, long enough to see the child and to be told, bluntly, that he carried a genetic problem and that I was present to supply tissues needed to correct it. The moment was overwhelming, a collision of grief, awe, and helplessness. What Samantha had lost, the covenant had claimed for its own.

Her loss was not the end of a pregnancy but the beginning of a program. The child was proof that what disappears from the womb in these cases does not vanish into mystery—it continues elsewhere, in hidden chambers and sterile nurseries, nurtured for purposes beyond our choosing. Samantha's loss was not hers alone. It was conscription into the covenant.

Her case echoes countless others. Budd Hopkins documented women who reported pregnancies confirmed by doctors, only to find them vanish without miscarriage. David Jacobs recorded testimonies of women shown hybrid infants afterward, told that these were the very children they had once carried. Dr. John Mack at Harvard found the same pattern: missing pregnancies coupled with later presentations of hybrid children, often accompanied by overwhelming emotions of love, guilt, or despair. What modern researchers discovered in case after case, I saw play out firsthand in the life of someone I loved.

Men are not spared from this program. Many abductees report forced semen collection, sometimes through mechanical devices, sometimes through induced stimulation. The testimonies are chilling in their uniformity: a complete absence of intimacy, the act reduced to raw extraction. In ancient times, men were castrated or sacrificed in rituals that symbolized the gods' dominion over human fertility. In the covenant's modern form, the principle is the same: reproductive essence is taken, not offered.

The emotional dimension of the hybrid program distinguishes it from the blood harvest. Blood is taken clinically, impersonally. Hybrids are presented intimately. Abductees are urged to touch, to hold, to comfort. They are told that these fragile beings depend on them. The effect is profound. Where cattle mutilations provoke fear and outrage, hybrid encounters provoke confusion and grief. The gods understand that emotion binds more tightly than terror. By entangling humans emotionally with the hybrids, they ensure complicity in the covenant's next phase.

The continuity with ancient myth is striking. In Mesopotamian texts, the Apkallu were described as part human, part divine—beings sent to instruct and to rule. In Greece, gods descended to mate with mortals, producing demi-gods like Hercules. In the Hebrew Bible, the "sons of God" are said to have taken human women, producing the Nephilim, a race of hybrids so troubling that a flood was sent to cleanse them. These stories may be mythologized memories of the same program. Just as abductees today describe being used for reproductive purposes, ancient cultures remembered their gods demanding the same. The hybrid program is not new. It is a renewal.

From the covenant's perspective, the logic is clear. As Chapter 12 showed, the Greys are a species in decline. Their physiology is efficient but degenerate, stripped of digestion and reproduction, dependent on others for survival. To restore what they lost, they must graft their neurology onto human physiology. Hybrids are the bridge. By combining their intelligence with our reproductive resilience, they are engineering a species capable of thriving on Earth without dependence on constant harvest.

Abductees who describe hybrids often remark on their fragility. They appear weak, tentative, struggling to adapt. Some smile awkwardly, others try to imitate human gestures of comfort. They are not presented as perfected beings but as works in progress, prototypes of what is to come. Each generation appears slightly more human, more social, more viable. The message is clear: the program is advancing.

The hybrid program reframes the covenant in terrifying terms. It suggests that humanity's role is not only to supply blood and tissue but to supply the genetic foundation for its replacement. Where once our ancestors fed the gods with offerings, now we feed them with our very biology. The covenant has shifted from the management of sacrifice to the management of species.

Some abductees report being told directly that hybrids will one day live among us. They describe visions of cities where humans and hybrids coexist, of futures where the line between species is blurred. To skeptics, such visions sound hallucinatory. To those who know the covenant's history, they sound like prophecy. The gods are preparing not only to survive but to inherit.

Samantha's missing pregnancy stands as one of the most personal reminders of this truth. What she lost was not an accident but an offering, taken without consent, redirected to serve a program that neither of us understood at the time. Only later, when I was shown images of hybrid children, did the pieces align. Her absence of child was the presence of theirs. This is how the covenant operates: quietly, relentlessly, with surgical precision and emotional entanglement, transforming private grief into fuel for its agenda.

The hybrids themselves are the covenant's proof of continuity. They are not rumors but the living embodiment of millennia of sacrifice. Where once the gods consumed blood to sustain themselves, now they consume genes to renew themselves. Blood was the first covenant. Hybrids are the second. And just as the first reshaped civilization, the second will reshape humanity itself.

The chilling implication is that the covenant's aim has always been replacement. Humans were never meant to remain the endpoint. We were meant to be the means. Just as cattle serve as proxies for human blood, humans may serve as proxies for a new species—Homo sapiens reduced to scaffolding for Homo hybridus. The covenant began with blood, but it ends with inheritance.

Synthesis: The Covenant Alive

The evidence of the covenant surrounds us, hidden in plain sight. It is carved into the bones of sacrificial victims at Teotihuacan and Cahokia, preserved in the papyri of Egypt, whispered in the hymns of the Rig Veda. And it is recorded again today in veterinary reports of cattle drained of blood, in abductee testimonies of clinical procedures, in the scars that appear overnight, in the children born and then taken. The covenant was never abandoned. It simply adapted.

The cattle left behind in fields are not isolated anomalies. They are the open-air proxies of what once occurred on temple altars. Their husks are the modern equivalent of captives bled on pyramid steps, organs lifted to the sky in offering. The Greys no longer need priests to wield obsidian knives. They have technologies that cauterize as they cut, that drain without spilling, that harvest with sterility. The field is the altar; the carcass is the offering. The signature is the same: targeted extraction, surgical efficiency, ritual repetition.

The abductees carried into craft chambers are not simply experiencers of strange dreams. They are the modern victims of the covenant, taken into the new sanctuaries—the closed temples of metal and light. Their testimonies, consistent across continents and decades, describe the same ritual choreography: paralysis, elevation, placement on a central table, surrounding figures with tools, the removal of blood, semen, ova, or fetuses. These are not chaotic assaults but procedures, repeated with liturgical regularity. The priesthood is gone, but the ritual remains.

The precision of the acts links past to present with terrifying continuity. Archaeologists note the clean anatomical cuts in ancient sacrificial remains; pathologists note the clean cauterized incisions in cattle; abductees note scars that heal without infection. My own arm surgery bore the same mark: limb removed, marrow likely extracted, blood absent, surface immaculate. It was not butchery but procedure. The bloodless cut is the signature. It proclaims the presence of technicians, not predators, enforcers operating under a covenant as alive in 2022 as it was in 2000 BCE.

And what ties cattle, abductees, and surgical signatures together is the hybrids—the covenant's new aim. The blood and tissue taken from humans, the organs and plasma taken from cattle, are not collected at random. They are raw stock. They are the bricks and mortar of a genetic program whose goal is not curiosity but continuity. The Greys, stripped of digestion and reproduction, seek restoration through fusion. They seek to graft their intelligence onto human resilience. The hybrids shown to abductees, the missing pregnancies like Samantha's, the infants presented with the chilling insistence "this is your child"—all of it testifies to a project of replacement. The covenant has always been about survival. Now it is about succession.

The ancients sensed this trajectory. Their myths speak of gods who mated with mortals, of demi-gods who ruled cities, of Watchers who took women and produced offspring that disrupted the world. Their stories of floods, purges, and divine retribution may reflect attempts to reset the balance when hybrids proliferated beyond control. We dismiss these tales as myth, yet abductee testimonies repeat the same theme in clinical detail. Where the ancients told it in poetry, the moderns tell it in trauma. The covenant is the bridge between both.

To see these phenomena separately—cattle mutilations, abductions, hybrids—is to miss the continuity. To interpret them as folklore or anomaly is to ignore the precision of their repetition. Taken together, they form a tapestry as coherent as any scripture. The covenant has simply changed its garments. Where once it was clothed in feathers, stone, and incense, now it is dressed in steel, fluorescence, and silicon. But the bones beneath the garment are the same. The covenant harvests blood, extracts tissue, produces hybrids, and enforces its terms with clinical detachment.

The chilling truth is that humanity is still under contract. We never negotiated it. We never consented to it. But our civilizations were shaped by it, and our bodies continue to be harvested by it. The covenant is not metaphor. It is metabolic. It is reproductive. It is species-level. It is the engine of a program that has bound humanity to the Greys for millennia.

The ancients responded with awe and obedience. They built pyramids and temples, offered captives, codified rituals, and interpreted their dependence as divinity. Modern humanity responds with disbelief, ridicule, or silence. Yet the covenant persists, indifferent to belief. It continues in the bloodless carcasses, in the abductees who awaken with missing time, in the women who lose pregnancies without fetuses, in the men drained of their reproductive essence, in the hybrids who stare at us with half-familiar eyes.

The covenant is alive. It is not a relic of stone or scripture but a program operating now, here, in our own age. It surrounds us in the skies, in the fields, in the shadows of our bedrooms. It harvests not only our blood but our future. The question is no longer whether it existed, but how long we will endure it—and what will replace us when it reaches completion.

14

THE SAME RECIPIENTS?

The Question of Recipients

If ancient sacrifice and modern mutilation resemble one another so closely, then we must ask the inevitable question: who was receiving it all? Were the gods who demanded human hearts atop the pyramids of Teotihuacan the same intelligences who now harvest blood and marrow from abductees and cattle? Were the beings who accepted offerings in Egypt, Mesopotamia, and Cahokia the same who appear in bedrooms and pastures today?

Historians and anthropologists often pause at this threshold. They acknowledge that civilizations worldwide shared an obsession with blood. They catalog the scale of Aztec sacrifices, the precision of Egyptian embalming, the ritual slaughter detailed in Leviticus. They even note parallels to modern UFO lore, where abductees describe blood samples, reproductive harvests, and clinical detachment. Yet they stop short of asking the next question: were these offerings directed to the same recipients across millennia? Were the "gods" of antiquity and the "visitors" of today masks worn by the same enduring presence?

The continuity of form, function, and precision suggests that the answer is yes.

The ancients recorded their debts in stone and paint. Murals from Bonampak depict captives bleeding under the gaze of feathered attendants (Miller & Taube, *An Illustrated Dictionary of the Gods and Symbols of Ancient Mexico and the Maya*, 1993). Aztec codices show priests raising hearts to the heavens while jaguar- and eagle-costumed figures stand by as intermediaries. Mesopotamian stelae present Apkallu with buckets and cones applying substances to kings and sacred trees, acts that scholars describe as purification but which look more like procedure (Black & Green, *Gods, Demons and Symbols of Ancient Mesopotamia*, 1992). Egypt carved priests offering bowls of blood and organs to falcon- and jackal-headed gods, their altars drenched daily with animal life. The pattern was not symbolic alone. It was transactional. Life was taken, blood was gathered, tissue was extracted, and humanity was diminished in the process.

Modern experiencers describe the same choreography in different dress. Craft descend from the skies instead of winged disks; paralysis replaces binding ropes; clinical instruments replace obsidian knives. But the roles remain identical. Humans are immobilized, tissues are taken, blood is drawn, reproductive material is extracted. The recipients remain veiled, silent, and remote. They do not explain. They only collect.

Across millennia, the recipients have never revealed themselves in full. Instead, they have always worked through emissaries and technicians. The Apkallu with his cone, the Aztec priest with his obsidian knife, the Grey with his needle—all serve the same function: to collect, to deliver, to sustain. The intermediaries change, the costumes adapt, the settings shift from stone to steel. But the structure of the exchange remains intact.

If the roles are consistent, then so too must be the beneficiaries. The gods of antiquity and the visitors of today are not separate phenomena. They are expressions of the same enduring presence, hidden behind masks appropriate to each age. This continuity reframes history. It means that the covenant was never broken, never ended with the fall of Aztec temples or the closing of Egyptian sanctuaries. It was carried forward, adapted to new contexts, disguised under new names.

The chilling implication is that the covenant was never with priests or kings at all—it was with the species as a whole. Priests were only managers of delivery, kings only stage directors of ritual. Our ancestors delivered the covenant through ritual, believing themselves in service to gods. We deliver it now unwillingly, through abductions and mutilations we refuse to acknowledge. Either way, the flow of life-force continues uninterrupted. The debt is transgenerational, and the recipients appear unchanged.

This interpretation also makes sense of otherwise puzzling details. Why are the recipients never fully revealed? Because the intermediaries are sufficient. The Aztec commoner never saw the god directly; he saw only the priest, the mask, the blade, and the offering. The abductee never speaks with ultimate authority; he sees only the Greys, the instruments, and the procedure. The true beneficiaries remain concealed, their faces obscured by ritual or technology, their appetite shielded by distance. That continuity of concealment is itself evidence of continuity of identity.

Skeptics will object that we are conflating myth and anomaly, archaeology and abduction lore. Yet what is more implausible—that civilizations worldwide independently imagined identical obsessions with blood, or that a single enduring presence shaped them? The repetition of sacrifice in antiquity is already astonishing. Its reappearance in modern reports makes coincidence untenable. Continuity is the simplest explanation.

This is the question that must anchor the rest of this chapter. If the recipients are the same, then the sacrifices of the past and the violations of the present form a single, unbroken line. The Hebrew covenant carved in stone, the Aztec captives bled on altars, the cattle drained in Colorado fields, the abductee who wakes with tissue missing—these are not disconnected episodes. They are installments in the same relationship. To call the recipients gods, demons, or Greys is secondary. What matters is the continuity of appetite.

And no continuity is clearer than the one preserved in the Ark of the Covenant—stone in antiquity, paper in modernity, both sealed in arks of their age, both hidden from the people bound by them.

The Ark of the Covenant, Then and Now

Among all the civilizations that remembered their bond with the gods, none emphasized the language of "covenant" more than the Hebrews. Their scriptures record not only laws but contracts—agreements between a people and the being who claimed them. The covenant was not abstract. It was written, carved into stone tablets said to have been delivered directly by God, then preserved inside the Ark. The Ark itself was less important than its contents. It was a container, a chest that bore the physical evidence of the bargain. Only priests could approach it, and even then under strict ritual. For the ordinary Israelite, the Ark was never to be seen or touched. The covenant existed, but access was restricted. Its authority came from its concealment.

This principle fits the broader pattern of the covenant across civilizations. The people sacrificed, but only priests or rulers handled the mechanics of the agreement. The ultimate recipients remained hidden. Instead, intermediaries—prophets, priests, and guardians of sacred objects—administered the relationship. In Egypt it was the priests of Ra. In Mesoamerica, the priesthood of Huitzilopochtli. In Mesopotamia, the temple scribes. And in Israel, the Levites who carried and protected the Ark. The continuity is unmistakable: the covenant was always delivered to elites, mediated through ritual or text, and shielded from the common people.

The Ark was remembered as the most sacred possession of Israel, yet it was also the least accessible. It was placed within the Holy of Holies, a chamber entered only once a year by the high priest. It was carried into battle but covered with cloths so none could see it. It was the repository of the covenant, yet deliberately hidden from those whose lives were bound by it. This paradox—covenant declared, covenant concealed—matches the pattern of every age. The covenant is always real, but its terms are always withheld.

It is significant that the covenant was not given while the Hebrews remained in Egypt. In *Angst in the Shadows*, I suggested that the Hebrews may have been regarded as preferred breeding stock, singled out for a unique arrangement. Egypt, however, was a vast melting pot, teeming with peoples and bloodlines from across Africa and the Near East. If the covenant required a distinct, disciplined stock, then such a mixture would not suffice. Only in isolation could the contract be imposed. The Exodus, therefore, was not merely a liberation but a sequestration. By removing the Hebrews from the diversity of Egypt, their "God" established them as a separated people, suitable for covenant. The tablets could only be delivered once the people had been delivered—removed, purified, and redefined in the desert.

If we understand the Ark as the physical vessel of an agreement, then we must ask: what is the modern Ark? The Hebrews remembered theirs as a gilded chest with stone inside. But in the twentieth century, rumors describe another covenant, struck not with tribes in a desert but with generals and presidents. In 1954, President Eisenhower is said to have signed an agreement with the Greys—permission to abduct and harvest in exchange for technological concessions. The authenticity of this treaty remains debated, but its symbolism is undeniable. Like the tablets of Moses, it was a covenant not with humanity as a whole but with a chosen few empowered to speak on humanity's behalf.

And just as the Ark preserved the tablets, so too would this modern covenant have its vessel. Not gold-covered acacia wood, but paper pressed from pulp. Not engraved by divine fire, but typed by secretaries and signed in ink. Not placed in a tabernacle, but filed in a wooden or metallic bureau, deep within Pentagon vaults. If the Ark of the Hebrews was a sacred chest guarded by priests, the Ark of modernity is a filing cabinet guarded by clearances and classification. In both cases, the covenant was physically real, tangibly present, yet inaccessible to the people bound by it.

This continuity reframes the Hebrew story. The sacrifices prescribed in Leviticus—burnt offerings, blood sprinkled on the altar—were less about feeding the gods in bulk and more about demonstrating loyalty and obedience. The Hebrews may have been selected not for their quantity of blood but for their quality as breeding stock, their discipline, their willingness to follow. The covenant demanded proof of obedience, and the Ark served as the chest that testified to the contract. Just as modern abductions harvest specific individuals repeatedly, ancient Israel's covenant may have been more about maintaining a bloodline than feeding an altar.

When the Israelites left Egypt, the Bible frames it as liberation. But seen through the covenantal lens, it may have been a mandated relocation, a reassignment by their "God." The being who demanded sacrifice and obedience may have been no freer with Israel than with Egypt—merely repositioning its chosen stock. The covenant was not dissolved with departure; it was transferred. And the Ark, carried through the desert and into Canaan, was the chest that symbolized the continuity of that relationship.

In both cases—ancient and modern—the covenant was inscribed, contained, and concealed. The people lived under its demands, but the object that testified to it was always hidden from their eyes. The Israelites saw the Ark only as a veiled chest carried by Levites. Modern citizens see nothing at all, their "Ark" locked in vaults far below the Pentagon, their contract classified. But the pattern is the same: the covenant is always real, always physical, always preserved in writing, and always withheld from the masses it binds.

The chilling implication is that the covenant is not only biological but bureaucratic. It is not only written in blood but in documents. It exists both in the marrow taken from abductees and in the files sealed from public view. The Hebrews preserved their covenant in stone. Eisenhower preserved his in paper. Both were kept in containers—one gilded, one metallic—each hidden away, each guarded by an elite priesthood of its own age. And in both cases, humanity lived under agreements it neither saw nor approved, yet paid for with its lifeblood.

The ancients recorded their debt in stone. Murals, stelae, and codices depict beings who descend from the sky, accept offerings, and dictate ritual practice. Today, experiencers describe beings who descend in craft, immobilize their captives, and collect the same biological resources with clinical detachment. The forms differ in costume—winged serpent, bird-man, or Grey—but the transactions are identical. Life is taken, blood is gathered, tissue is extracted, and humanity is left diminished in the process.

Across millennia, the recipients have never revealed themselves in full. Instead, they have worked through emissaries, priests, and technicians. The Apkallu with his cone, the Aztec priest with his obsidian knife, the Grey with his needle—all serve the same function: to collect, to deliver, to sustain. If these roles are consistent, then so too must be the beneficiaries. The gods of antiquity and the visitors of today are not separate phenomena. They are expressions of the same enduring presence.

This interpretation reframes history. It means that the covenant was never broken, never ended with the fall of Aztec temples or the closing of Egyptian sanctuaries. It was carried forward, adapted to new contexts, disguised under new names. The recipients of blood and life were not myths fading with time, but enduring powers who continued to harvest in ways adapted to each age. Humanity, for all its supposed progress, has never escaped the debt.

The chilling implication is that the covenant was never with priests or kings at all—it was with the species as a whole. Our ancestors delivered it through ritual, believing themselves in service to gods. We deliver it now unwillingly, through abductions and unacknowledged mutilations. But the flow of life-force continues uninterrupted. The debt is transgenerational, and the recipients appear unchanged.

The parallels between then and now cannot be dismissed as coincidence. They form a timeline of continuity, one that binds the sacrifices of the past to the violations of the present. To name them differently is irrelevant. Whether called gods, demons, or Greys, the recipients appear to be the same. The covenant endures, and humanity remains bound by it.

The Ancient Recipients Recorded in Stone

If we ask who received the sacrifices of the ancient world, the most direct answer is given not in speculation but in art. Civilizations across continents carved, painted, and inscribed their transactions with the gods in ways that leave little ambiguity. The recipients of blood and life were not abstract forces. They were depicted in stone, fresco, and codex.

In Mesopotamia, the Apkallu are remembered on reliefs that adorned palaces at Nineveh, Nimrud, and Khorsabad. These hybrid beings—half-man, half-bird or fish—stand beside kings and sacred trees, cone in one hand, bucket in the other. Scholars describe them as "purifiers" or "guardians" (Black & Green, *Gods, Demons and Symbols of Ancient Mesopotamia*, 1992), but the consistency of their imagery is striking. They are always shown in action: applying the cone to a tree or king, extending a hand toward life-giving symbols, transferring something from bucket to target. They are never idle, never decorative. The message carved in stone is simple: the gods received offerings through procedure. The Apkallu were the technicians, the collectors, the hands of an unseen presence.

Egypt left the same testimony in temples and tombs. Walls show priests offering bowls of blood, organs, and animals to gods with falcon, jackal, or crocodile heads. In the Pyramid Texts, the king himself is described as feeding the gods through sacrifice (Faulkner, *The Ancient Egyptian Pyramid Texts*, 1969). Horus, Anubis, and Sobek loom larger than the humans who approach them, their scale proclaiming their superiority. The recipients are shown explicitly: gods with animal features standing over altars, watching as priests slit throats and pour blood. These images are not metaphors for "natural cycles." They are transactional scenes, depictions of debt being paid to higher powers.

A Blood Covenant 345

Mesoamerica recorded its recipients in even more visceral form. The murals of Bonampak, painted in the eighth century CE, depict captives bound and bleeding under the gaze of nobles wearing avian regalia. Aztec codices like the Codex Magliabechiano show priests cutting open chests, raising hearts skyward, and presenting them to feathered serpents and sun deities (Miller & Taube, *An Illustrated Dictionary of the Gods and Symbols of Ancient Mexico and the Maya*, 1993). At Teotihuacan, the Temple of the Feathered Serpent is lined with carved serpent heads, each with gaping jaws and protruding fangs, alternating with armored war-serpents. Beneath this temple, archaeologists found more than 200 sacrificed captives buried alive (Sugiyama, *Human Sacrifice, Militarism, and Rulership at the City of Teotihuacan*, 2005). The recipients were not left to the imagination. They were carved into the temple itself, stone mouths forever open to receive.

At Cahokia in North America, the Birdman Tablet tells the same story in a different idiom. On one side is a raptor-like figure with human form and outstretched wings. On the other is a crosshatched snakeskin pattern. Archaeologists interpret this as a symbol of power and fertility, but the covenantal lens sees more: a depiction of sky over serpent, enforcer over victim, recipient over offering. The Birdman stands as the hybrid being who demanded sacrifice, just as the Apkallu did in Mesopotamia and the feathered serpents did in Mesoamerica. His image was buried in Mound 72 alongside more than 250 sacrificial victims (Pauketat, *Cahokia: Ancient America's Great City on the Mississippi*, 2009). The pairing of icon and grave tells the truth: the Birdman was the recipient, the one for whom the sacrifices were made.

Across cultures, the recipients were recorded with startling consistency. They are always larger than humans, always hybrid in form, always depicted in the posture of receiving. They loom over kings, priests, and captives. They extend hands, jaws, cones, or beaks toward offerings. They are not abstract suns, rivers, or winds, but embodied beings demanding payment. Even when portrayed symbolically, their posture is transactional. The cone touches the tree. The god towers over the offering. The priest raises the heart toward the sky. In every scene, the same logic holds: humanity delivers, the recipients accept.

The consistency of these depictions undermines symbolic interpretations. Scholars may claim that the Apkallu represent "fertility," that the Aztec sacrifices "ensured agricultural cycles," or that Egyptian animal-headed gods were metaphors for natural forces (Hornung, *Conceptions of God in Ancient Egypt*, 1982). But why, then, the uniform emphasis on extraction and offering? Why the repeated depiction of blood, organs, and tissue being transferred to larger beings? Why the insistence on hybrid forms—part human, part predator—standing over the ritual? The art shows not abstraction but transaction. It memorializes who received the debt.

It is also telling that the recipients are never shown in full divine form. They are always masked, hybridized, partial. The Apkallu have human bodies but bird heads or fish skins. Egyptian gods have animal heads on human torsos. The Birdman of Cahokia is human in shape but raptor in features. Even Quetzalcoatl, the plumed serpent, combines bird and reptile. None appear as ultimate creators. All appear as intermediaries, emissaries, hybrids. The recipients are obscured, masked by animal forms, their true nature hidden. This concealment is itself continuity with the present. Just as abductees today report Greys who perform the procedures but rarely speak of higher authority, the ancients depicted intermediaries who received offerings on behalf of hidden powers.

The most striking continuity is in what was taken. In Egypt, bowls of blood. In Mesoamerica, human hearts. In Mesopotamia, cones applying substances to kings and sacred trees. In Cahokia, mass burials of young women. In every case, the focus is biological. Blood, organs, tissue, marrow, life. The recipients may change their masks, but their appetite does not. This is the signature that ties antiquity to modernity. Abductees today describe needles extracting blood, instruments collecting semen and ova, fetuses removed and presented later as hybrids. The procedure is the same. The offering is the same. The recipients, too, must be the same.

Taken together, the art of the ancients is testimony. It is courtroom evidence carved in stone and painted on walls. It records not only the rituals but the recipients. To walk through the ruins of Egypt, Mesopotamia, Teotihuacan, or Cahokia is to walk through archives of the covenant. Every mural and stele repeats the same truth: humanity gave, larger beings received. The intermediaries were priests and hybrids, but the beneficiaries were higher still. The ancients recorded them as best they could, through masks and animal forms, but the pattern is too consistent to ignore.

What the ancients recorded in stone, the moderns record in testimony. Abductees describe beings who immobilize, extract, and depart without explanation. Ranchers find cattle drained and organs removed without predators. My own experience of arm removal was bloodless, precise, and clinical—procedural, not chaotic. The recipients remain hidden, just as they were in antiquity. But the continuity between mural and testimony is unmistakable. Stone and memory testify to the same debt, the same transaction, the same recipients.

The Modern Recipients Hidden in Procedure

Across millennia, one truth stands out: humanity rarely, if ever, confronts the ultimate recipients directly. What we see instead are their emissaries—masks, hybrids, intermediaries who administer the covenant on their behalf. The pattern is unmistakable. In Mesopotamia it was Apkallu, half-man and half-bird, applying cones and buckets with ritual precision. In Egypt it was priests in jackal masks, or gods carved as human-animal composites, standing between worshiper and deity. In Mesoamerica it was bird-men and jaguar-warriors, hybrids whose very bodies declared predation. In our own time it is the smaller Greys, clinical technicians who perform procedures but rarely explain them. Always the middle layer. Always the hands of another.

It is tempting to see these emissaries as mere symbolism, or as the imaginative costumes of priesthoods. But the consistency across cultures argues for something deeper. These were not random archetypes. They were engineered. The Tall Greys—true recipients of blood, marrow, and reproductive essence—shaped emissaries to act as their visible face. They designed intermediaries to terrify, to enforce, to conceal. Just as they now engineer hybrids for their survival, so too did they once engineer hybrid overseers to administer the covenant in antiquity.

Their creation may have been driven not only by the need for enforcers but also by the Tall Greys' own limitations. As I suggested in chapter 12, their biology—optimized for absorption rather than protection—would render them fragile in Earth's biosphere and acutely vulnerable under ultraviolet sunlight. Prolonged exposure could damage their tissues, compromise their function, or prove fatal. By engineering emissaries—hybrids more robust in our environment, more terrifying in form—they could maintain control without exposing themselves to the dangers of direct contact. The emissaries became both mask and shield, carrying out enforcement where the Tall Greys themselves could not safely tread.

The evidence of engineering is embedded in the art itself. In Sumerian carvings, we find creatures with human heads mounted on animal bodies, so anatomically detailed that "stitching" appears at the neck, as though parts had been joined. These are not masks. They are constructs. They reveal a knowledge of anatomy—and a willingness to manipulate it—that suggests literal chimeras walked among the Sumerians. If such beings were present in Mesopotamia, then there is no reason to doubt their presence in Egypt as well. Figures like Anubis may not have been metaphor at all. His jackal head and human body may have been observed, not imagined—a real engineered overseer, designed to terrify and to administer ritual. Later, when such beings were gone or withdrawn, human priests preserved their image through masks and ceremonies, imitating the originals. The mask became memory of a construct.

This blended logic explains the consistency of the imagery. Why do Apkallu always appear with wings, buckets, and cones? Why does Anubis never appear as anything but jackal-headed? Why do bird-men in Colombia, Cahokia, and Mesoamerica stand in the same posture—avian head, human torso, serpent subdued beneath their claws? Such standardization is not the hallmark of human imagination, but of templates that were encountered and remembered. Standardized emissaries imply engineered emissaries. And engineered emissaries point to the Tall Greys as their creators.

This interpretation clarifies the continuity between past and present. The smaller Greys who paralyze abductees today are no different from the Apkallu who flanked Assyrian gates or the birdmen who loomed over Mesoamerican rituals. They are not the masters but the technicians. They are designed for procedure. Their scale, their repetition, their detachment—all suggest instruments rather than originators. Abductees describe them as robotic, emotionless, programmed. Ancient art portrays their equivalents as hybrids, part-human but more-than-human, always active, never contemplative. Both function as the enforcers of another's appetite.

Even priesthoods may have been shaped to the same purpose. The Aztec priest raising a heart skyward, the Egyptian priest draining blood into basins, the Levite slaughtering animals on the altar—all acted as technicians of the covenant. Their authority was not self-generated but borrowed. Their actions mirrored the gestures of hybrid beings carved in stone. They were trained to replicate procedure, to play the role of intermediary, to serve as hands of the hidden recipients. Whether through costume, mask, or genetic engineering, they too became emissaries of the covenant.

Seen this way, the diversity of emissaries across cultures is not evidence of different gods but of different masks. The Tall Greys adapted their emissaries to local contexts. In Egypt, predator-animal forms carried weight, so the overseers bore falcon and jackal heads. In Mesopotamia, sages and guardians fit the culture's imagination, so the overseers appeared as Apkallu. In Mesoamerica, avian and feline predators carried authority, so the overseers bore those forms. The underlying presence was the same. The masks were adjusted, the emissaries engineered to match local language and fear.

The smaller Greys of today are simply the latest mask, the most efficient form for our age. They no longer need feathers, masks, or animal heads. Their engineered features—large eyes, thin frames, uniform skin—suffice to terrify and to enforce. They appear standardized across abductee reports, just as Apkallu and falcon-headed gods appear standardized in ancient art. Their uniformity is their signature. They are emissaries, not originals. They are the visible administrators of the covenant, carrying out procedures for recipients who remain hidden but unchanged.

The chilling implication is that humanity has never once dealt directly with its gods. We have always dealt with their emissaries. The Tall Greys—recipients of blood and life-force—have never revealed themselves in full, preferring to hide behind engineered intermediaries. This concealment protects them from rebellion and ensures continuity. If the emissary is destroyed or disbelieved, another can be raised. The true recipients remain untouchable, preserved behind layers of masks.

The ancients may have sensed this truth. Their myths describe gods who disguise themselves, who appear in animal form, who cloak themselves in wings and feathers. They remembered that what they saw was not the ultimate presence but its mask. Abductees today echo the same: the smaller Greys are robotic, scripted, subservient, acting under higher command. The emissary is the continuity. The recipient is the constant. The Tall Greys, hidden but unchanged, are the same now as they were then.

The Covenant Never Broken

When we stand back from the fragments—murals in Mesoamerica, pyramid texts in Egypt, tablets in Mesopotamia, codices in Israel, testimonies in our own age—the picture that emerges is stark. The covenant was never broken. It has simply changed form, adapting to new contexts and disguises, but never ending its flow of blood, tissue, and life-force.

In antiquity, the covenant was staged openly. Captives were marched up pyramid steps, their hearts cut out and lifted to the sky. Priests in jackal masks drained blood into basins before gods who towered on temple walls. Scribes etched Apkallu administering rituals beside kings. These acts were communal theater, terrifying spectacles meant to awe whole populations. The covenant was visible, and the recipients—though masked in hybrid form—were carved in stone for all to see.

With the Hebrews, the covenant shifted to text. Stone tablets inscribed with commandments were preserved in a chest that could never be opened by common eyes. Sacrifice continued—burnt offerings, animal slaughter, ritual obedience—but the terms of the covenant were now hidden inside the Ark. The people lived under its weight, but its contents were kept veiled, guarded by a priestly elite. It was the same covenant of obedience and blood, but its vessel had changed.

In the modern era, the covenant has shifted again. It no longer plays out on the steps of pyramids or in temple courts, but in sterile craft and silent fields. Cattle are drained with surgical precision and left behind as husks. Humans are abducted, immobilized, and sampled, their reproductive tissues taken without consent. Missing pregnancies vanish without miscarriage. Hybrids are presented as offspring. Blood, marrow, and genetic essence are harvested as efficiently as ever. The covenant persists, but now it is hidden in procedure rather than spectacle. And if rumors of Eisenhower's treaty are to be believed, its terms are typed on paper and locked away in Pentagon vaults—the modern Ark of the covenant, sealed in filing cabinets rather than gilded wood.

Across all these phases, one thread is unbroken: humanity pays. Whether through the public death of captives in plazas, the slaughter of animals in temple courts, or the silent harvest of abductees in the night, the flow of life-force has never ceased. The recipients may hide behind emissaries, and the forms of the covenant may shift, but the debt remains constant. Blood, tissue, and obedience are always demanded, always delivered, always concealed from the masses who live under its shadow.

This is why the covenant has endured for millennia: because it is not symbolic. It is metabolic. It is not a pact of poetry or myth but a transaction of biology. The Tall Greys require sustenance, and they have ensured its supply through spectacle in antiquity, through obedience in scripture, and through secrecy in modernity. The covenant was never broken because the need never ended.

The chilling truth is that humanity has never outgrown this arrangement. Civilization may advance, empires may rise and fall, religions may shift, but the covenant adapts and continues. It is the same program written in different alphabets—stone, blood, parchment, paper, DNA. Each generation inherits the debt. Each age is bound anew. The covenant remains alive because its recipients remain the same.

Conclusion: The Same Debt

The question that began this chapter—are the same recipients behind both ancient sacrifice and modern abduction—now has its answer. The continuity of appetite, procedure, concealment, and intermediaries leaves little room for coincidence. The covenant has never shifted its beneficiaries. Whether through Apkallu with cones and buckets, Egyptian priests draining blood into basins, Aztec warriors raising hearts to the sun, or small Greys applying instruments in sterile chambers, the transaction has remained the same. Humanity gives, they receive. The debt is ancient, unbroken, and ongoing.

It is tempting to compartmentalize history. To imagine that the gods of Mesopotamia were separate from those of Egypt, that the Birdman of Cahokia was unrelated to Quetzalcoatl, that the Greys of modern abduction lore are an entirely new phenomenon. But the patterns tell otherwise. The uniformity of procedure—the demand for blood, the taking of tissue, the engineering of emissaries—points to one enduring presence. The Tall Greys, hidden behind masks and intermediaries, are the constant. Their appetite has bound humanity from the first ziggurats to the present night sky.

The debt they impose is not symbolic. It is biological. Blood is drained, marrow extracted, reproductive essence taken. What began as offerings on altars has become samples in laboratories of craft. What was once stone tablets hidden in a gilded Ark has become paper treaties hidden in Pentagon vaults. The continuity of form—stone to paper, altar to craft, priest to technician—only emphasizes the continuity of function. The covenant was never ceremonial. It was transactional, metabolic, genetic.

And across all its permutations, the cost is borne by us. The young women buried in Mound 72 at Cahokia, the captives sacrificed in Tenochtitlan, the livestock mutilated on American ranches, the abductees sampled in bedrooms—they are chapters in the same book. They are installments of the same debt, paid generation after generation. Each civilization believed itself unique, yet all fed the same recipients.

The chilling implication is that humanity has never stood outside this arrangement. We inherit it as we inherit language or myth, bound not by choice but by biology. The covenant was never negotiated with kings alone, though kings and priests played their parts. It was never merely Israel's covenant or Mexico's covenant or Egypt's covenant. It was humanity's covenant, imposed species-wide, maintained through spectacle, ritual, secrecy, and now clinical procedure.

If this is true, then history itself must be reread. The gods of the pyramids were not deities who died with their temples. They are the same intelligences who harvest in our age. The emissaries who enforced their will—whether jackal-headed or gray-skinned—were masks, not masters. The true recipients have always remained hidden, yet unchanged. And their covenant with us, written in blood and preserved in stone, paper, and DNA, has never been broken.

The debt continues. We are still paying it. And until we understand the continuity, we cannot begin to question its terms.

15

BLOOD COVENANT

Opening Frame

The evidence now lies before us like stones fitted into a pyramid. From the earliest rites of Mesopotamia to the equinox alignments of Chichén Itzá, from the blood bowls of the Aztecs to the bloodless corpses of cattle in our own fields, one thread binds them together: humanity has lived under covenant. Not a covenant of faith, as our ancestors believed, but one of necessity—written in blood, enforced by emissaries, and administered by unseen recipients who have never departed.

Civilizations that believed themselves unique were in fact installments of the same pattern. The Sumerians recorded Apkallu administering procedures that scholars call "purification," yet the imagery suggests dosage and delivery—hybrid overseers acting as technicians (Black & Green, *Gods, Demons and Symbols of Ancient Mesopotamia*, 1992). The Egyptians offered bowls of blood and organs before gods who stood taller than kings, their falcon and jackal heads hiding the hands that collected the tithe (Hornung, *Conceptions of God in Ancient Egypt*, 1982). The Aztecs marched captives up temple steps, their chests opened and hearts raised skyward in a theater of obedience

(Miller & Taube, *Gods and Symbols of Ancient Mexico and the Maya*, 1993). In North America, the Birdman of Cahokia loomed over mass graves, his likeness buried with victims who had been arranged with deliberate precision (Pauketat, *Cahokia: Ancient America's Great City on the Mississippi*, 2009). Everywhere we look, the covenant is present: life taken, blood spilled, tissue harvested, offered to powers greater than kings.

The Hebrews, delivered out of Egypt's melting pot and sequestered in desert, carried a covenant of their own. Their sacrifices were smaller, more symbolic, yet the principle was the same: obedience was measured in blood. The tablets inside the Ark, unseen by the people, testified not to liberation but to selection (Halpern, *The First Historians: The Hebrew Bible and History*, 1988). A breeding stock had been chosen, bound to ritual, instructed to remain separate. The covenant was not a myth of faith but a contract of control.

In our age the same thread continues, only its costume has changed. Cattle are discovered in pastures, drained with surgical precision, reproductive organs missing, tissues excised with an efficiency no predator could replicate (Howe, *A Strange Harvest*, 1980). Abductees describe procedures carried out by smaller Greys, their movements practiced, their demeanor cold (Strieber, *Communion*, 1987; Jacobs, *The Threat*, 1998). Samples are taken, fetuses removed, semen and ova collected. Some victims are presented with hybrids—children who look both alien and familiar—told that they are theirs, that they are part of a program whose purpose is never explained (Hopkins, *Intruders*, 1987; Mack, *Abduction*, 1994). This is the covenant of our era: clinical, concealed, yet unmistakably continuous.

What began as ritual debt evolved into systemic management. The gods demanded sacrifice, then lineage, then fertility itself. Populations were shaped, bloodlines tracked, genetic material harvested. In time the covenant moved underground, out of temples and into laboratories, out of myths and into the unmarked skies. The offerings never ceased. They only changed form.

The continuity is too consistent to dismiss as coincidence. The uniformity of procedure—the draining of blood, the excision of organs, the presentation of hybrids—argues for a single enduring recipient. Cultures as diverse as Mesopotamia, Egypt, Mesoamerica, and Cahokia all enacted the same gestures of offering. Modern abductees, unaware of those traditions, describe the same clinical harvests. Even the concealment is continuous: once in temples accessible only to priests, now in Pentagon vaults and hidden craft, the covenant is always withheld from the people it binds. The emissaries—whether Apkallu, jackal-headed gods, or smaller Greys—are visible masks. The true recipients remain veiled, their appetite unchanged.

This recognition forces us to confront what the covenant truly represents. It is not superstition, nor primitive ignorance. It is contract. Humanity was domesticated, its lifeblood collected like a tithe. The Tall Greys, or those who stand behind them, are not visitors newly arrived. They are creditors returning for payment, collecting what has been theirs since civilization's dawn.

The evidence of this contract is inscribed across our history. In ziggurats and temples aligned to the stars. In murals of captives drained of blood. In mass graves arranged with ritual care. In animal sacrifices repeated with monotonous precision. In the Ark of the Covenant, its contents hidden from the very people it bound. In mutilated cattle, drained without spillage. In abductees whose bodies bear scoop marks, scars, and memories of procedures they never consented to. These are the ledgers of the covenant, the receipts of an arrangement that has never lapsed.

And now we must ask: is the covenant nearing its fulfillment? Hybridization suggests it is. If the Greys' dependency on blood and marrow is only a stopgap, then the creation of hybrids signals a closing chapter. A new species—one that can survive on Earth's terms, yet carry the consciousness and continuity of the Greys—may be the intended outcome. The covenant, once sustained by sacrifice, would culminate in replacement. Humanity would not merely serve the gods; it would be rewritten as their descendants.

The old religions called this redemption, rebirth, ascension. But seen through the lens of evidence, it is absorption. Humanity's story may not end with apocalypse but with assimilation, its bloodlines merged into something no longer entirely human.

To recognize this is sobering. Yet to ignore it would be worse. The covenant's history warns us that ignorance never freed the victim. Only awareness can. Whether we resist, adapt, or accept, the first step is to understand the pattern: it was always about the blood.

Covenant as Domestication

To understand the covenant in its true light, we must strip away the illusions of faith and ritual and see it for what it has always been: domestication. Humanity has not been a partner in covenant but its livestock. Our blood was the tithe, our bodies the currency, our obedience the proof of ownership.

Domestication is the process by which wildness is broken, populations are shaped, and traits are selectively reinforced. Farmers practice it with animals, shaping docile herds from wild ancestors. The Tall Greys of Zeta 2 Reticuli - those who stood behind the gods of antiquity, practiced it with us. Temples were their barns, priests their herdsmen, sacrifices their harvest. Civilization itself may have been the pasture they created to manage us more efficiently.

The parallels are unsettling. Just as a farmer culls animals for breeding, so too were human bloodlines tracked and managed. The Hebrews were sequestered from Egypt, isolated to preserve their genetic profile. Royal lineages across Mesopotamia and Egypt claimed divine mandate, their marriages tightly controlled, their heirs guarded. Even in Mesoamerica, nobility claimed descent from gods, their blood shed on altars as proof of continuity. Everywhere we look, bloodlines were not only sacred—they were managed.

Sacrifice served as the most public display of domestication. Animals offered daily in temples, humans offered on feast days, captives paraded and slain before crowds. These were not random acts of superstition but systemic reinforcements of ownership. A domesticated herd does not merely graze—it is reminded constantly that it belongs to its keeper. Ritual sacrifice was humanity's branding iron, searing into memory the truth of dependence.

The archaeological record bears this out. In Egypt, animals were slaughtered in staggering numbers, their remains stacked in temple precincts (Wilkinson, *The Complete Gods and Goddesses of Ancient Egypt*, 2003). At Teotihuacan, mass sacrifices of captives were buried beneath the Temple of the Feathered Serpent, their bodies arranged with military precision (Sugiyama, *Human Sacrifice, Militarism, and Rulership*, 2005). At Cahokia, entire cohorts of young women were executed and interred as offerings to the Birdman, their arrangement as deliberate as cattle in pens (Pauketat, 2009). The scale and repetition suggest not random piety but systemic management.

Even the instructions preserved in sacred texts reinforce this interpretation. Leviticus is not a book of inspiration but a manual of slaughter, detailing which animals to kill, how to drain their blood, how to sprinkle it on the altar. It reads like herd management disguised as holiness. The logic is covenantal: obedience measured in blood, domestication maintained through ritual.

The same principle continues in the modern age. Cattle mutilations are perhaps the most literal echo. Animals discovered bloodless, organs removed with precision, reproductive tissues excised. They are livestock within livestock, offerings taken from herds already domesticated by humans. If ancient sacrifice was public theater, modern mutilations are hidden procedure. Yet the function is the same: extraction from managed populations, payment from stock that belongs to another.

Human abductions follow the same pattern. Just as farmers tag cattle, the Greys mark bloodlines, abducting the same families across generations. Reports abound of children taken because their parents and grandparents were also abductees (Jacobs, *The Threat*, 1998). This is not random. It is selective breeding, genetic tracking, husbandry. The Greys are not visitors—they are breeders. Humanity is their herd.

Even secrecy is part of domestication. Farmers do not explain to cattle why they are fed or bred. They only act. In the same way, the covenant has always been hidden from the masses. The Ark was kept in the Holy of Holies, unseen by the Israelites who lived under its terms. Aztec codices were the property of priests, not commoners. In our age, if Eisenhower's alleged treaty exists, it is locked in Pentagon vaults, its terms concealed from the very public it binds. Concealment is management. Ignorance is control.

Domestication explains why civilizations built with such obsessive alignment. Temples pointed to the stars not for abstract cosmology but because they were part of a system—structures designed to keep populations synchronized with cycles of offering. Chichén Itzá's equinox shadow, casting the serpent down the steps, was not astronomical curiosity but covenantal theater, ensuring offerings arrived on schedule. These were feeding stations disguised as holy sites, barns disguised as monuments.

Domestication also clarifies why emissaries were so consistent. Farmers use dogs to herd sheep, creating hybrids of wolf and man's purpose. The Tall Greys used engineered beings—Apkallu, jackal-headed gods, bird-men—as their herders, enforcing compliance where the masters themselves could not safely appear. Emissaries were not random monsters of the imagination. They were guard dogs of the covenant.

The emotional manipulation recorded in abduction testimonies also echoes domestication. Farmers soothe animals even as they lead them to slaughter, reducing resistance. Abductees report being calmed telepathically, urged to accept what was happening, shown visions that justify compliance. These are not acts of cruelty for cruelty's sake. They are acts of control. The herd must not stampede. The stock must remain manageable.

The chilling implication is that humanity has never been free. From the first temples to the latest abductions, we have been managed, culled, bred, and harvested. Civilization itself may have been a covenantal system designed not for our benefit but for theirs. Our monuments may not be testaments to our genius but to our captivity.

To call this domestication is not metaphor but recognition. We have been shaped as surely as cattle or wheat. Our rituals, our myths, our very bloodlines bear the mark of management. And the covenant that sustains this system is not one of faith but of necessity. The recipients need us. We have been domesticated to provide.

Hybridization as Fulfillment

If domestication explains the covenant's past, hybridization explains its future. For millennia the covenant has demanded blood, marrow, reproductive essence—offerings taken generation after generation. But these were not ends in themselves. They were steps toward something larger, a program with an ultimate aim. That aim is now becoming clear: replacement. The covenant is not endless harvest, but fulfillment through hybridization.

Hybrids represent the closing act of a process that began with ritual sacrifice. Where once hearts were cut from captives in Teotihuacan, where once lambs bled on the altars of Israel, where once blood was poured into bowls at Karnak, today the offerings are refined into ova, semen, and fetal tissue. What was once theatrical has become surgical. The same covenant that demanded public rivers of blood now works in hidden laboratories, drawing out not just life-force but the very blueprint of life.

Abductee testimonies converge on this truth with chilling consistency. Women speak of missing pregnancies—fetuses confirmed by doctors and then inexplicably absent weeks later. Men describe forced semen extraction, their reproductive material taken under paralysis. Both are later shown hybrid children: infants with enlarged eyes, thin limbs, but recognizably human features. They are pressed to accept a shocking claim—that these beings are not strangers, but kin. The message is as old as covenant itself: what you offer, we claim. But now the offering is not consumed—it is continued. Hybrids are the covenant made flesh, the tithe embodied in a new lineage.

I have seen this continuity firsthand. Years ago, I was confronted with a hybrid child connected to a former girlfriend, presented by the Greys themselves. The child was said to carry a genetic defect, and my role was to provide tissues to help correct it. In that remembered moment, the meaning of sacrifice shifts. It is no longer bowls of blood or piles of bodies—it is targeted extraction, deliberate and calculated, sustaining children who embodied both human and Grey. The covenant had evolved from altar to nursery, from sacrifice to succession.

The logic of hybridization aligns perfectly with what we know of Grey physiology. Their bodies, efficient yet degenerate, lack digestion and reproduction. Dependent on blood and marrow, they survive through what is essentially transfusion. But such dependency is unsustainable. A species cannot endure indefinitely by harvesting another. The only long-term solution is integration: to graft their neurology, their memory, their continuity onto a host body robust enough to thrive on Earth. That is what hybrids represent. They are the covenant fulfilled—living vessels into which the Greys may pour themselves, generation by generation.

Ancient myths preserve this trajectory in distorted form. The Mesopotamian tales of gods who "mingled" with mortals, the Greek stories of Zeus fathering demi-gods, the Hebrew memory of the "sons of God" taking daughters of men and producing the Nephilim—all echo the same truth: hybridization was always part of the program. What was once described in mythic poetry is today described in clinical testimony. Abductees speak the same language in different terms: the gods come, they take, they leave behind offspring not entirely human. The continuity of narrative is too exact to dismiss.

Hybridization also reframes the symbolism of ancient sacrifice. The Aztecs spoke of "feeding the sun" with human hearts, but what if those offerings were not consumed by gods but used to shape something new? Blood poured into bowls may have been the precursor to blood drawn into tubes. Marrow taken from sacrificial victims may have seeded experiments in genetic continuity. What was once crude and theatrical has become clinical and precise. The covenant was never about endless appetite—it was about reaching this moment, where bloodlines could be rewritten.

Nor is this trajectory confined to myth or ritual. The same theme recurs in modern testimonies: abductees shown nurseries of hybrid infants, rows of children who stare with a mixture of human familiarity and alien detachment. Some describe being urged to touch them, to hold them, to comfort them. Others recall a piercing sense of guilt, as though failing to recognize them as kin would doom them to neglect. The procedure is not only genetic—it is psychological. Just as priests once staged public sacrifices to bind whole populations in obedience, the Greys now stage emotional encounters to bind individuals to the program of hybrid succession.

The implications are profound. If hybrids are the fulfillment of the covenant, then humanity is not merely stock to be harvested but scaffolding to be dismantled once the structure is complete. A new species—capable of surviving in Earth's biosphere, yet carrying Grey consciousness and continuity—would make the old arrangement obsolete. No more altars, no more abductions, no more mutilations. The covenant would be paid in full, its terms executed, its debt closed. Humanity would persist only as memory within hybrid descendants.

The old religions promised redemption, ascension, rebirth. They told their followers that sacrifice led to renewal, that blood opened the path to eternity. Perhaps they were not wrong, only misled. For the renewal was never for us, but for them. The ascension was Grey, not human. The rebirth was hybrid. Our role was to pay into a covenant whose reward was always destined for the recipients.

This possibility is sobering. It suggests that what we call progress —writing, temples, technology, even our myths of salvation—may have been stages of a management system culminating not in our flourishing, but in our replacement. If hybridization is the covenant fulfilled, then we stand at the edge of humanity's final role. We were never meant to be the end. We were the bridge.

The Sobering Recognition

The evidence of the covenant, once scattered across civilizations, now lies assembled before us. Its stones are fitted, its shape unmistakable.

Yet recognition brings no comfort. To see the covenant clearly is to realize how deeply it is woven into the human story. From temple steps to operating tables, from bowls of blood to vials of DNA, humanity has been bound by a contract it never signed. And the recipients have never once relented.

The sobering truth is that ignorance has never freed the victim. The Aztec captive who marched up the pyramid steps may not have known the cosmology that justified his death. The Hebrew shepherd who brought a lamb to the priest may not have understood the supposed mysteries of covenant. The abductee who wakes in terror on a metallic table may not comprehend why her tissues are taken. But whether ancient or modern, the victim's ignorance does not spare the offering. The debt is collected regardless.

Civilizations that thought themselves enlightened still carried the covenant forward. Egypt, with its geometry and grandeur, was no freer than the tribal rites of Sumer. Mesoamerica, with its astronomical precision, was no less captive than the desert tents of Israel. Our own age, armed with satellites and silicon, is no less vulnerable. Domestication can coexist with brilliance; captivity can be masked as culture. The covenant requires only continuity, and continuity it has received.

The recognition of this truth is heavy, but it is also the only leverage humanity has left. To see the pattern is to stand outside of it, even briefly. For millennia the covenant has relied on concealment—on priests, on myths, on secrecy, on disbelief. To name it is to break one link in its chain. Awareness may not dissolve the debt, but it denies the recipients the advantage of invisibility. It forces the program into the light, where questions can at last be asked.

What humanity chooses to do with this awareness remains uncertain. Resistance may be futile against a species that has managed us since the dawn of cities. Accommodation may mean accepting assimilation, allowing ourselves to be rewritten as hybrids. Denial only ensures repetition, generation after generation. None of these choices are comfortable. But for the first time, choice itself becomes possible only when the covenant is recognized.

The old myths promised that blood bought redemption, that obedience secured favor. But history shows otherwise. The more we gave, the more was demanded. The covenant was never about humanity's ascent—it was about the recipients' survival. To see this is unsettling. Yet to look away is worse. For the program continues whether or not we acknowledge it. The only question is whether we will meet it blindly, as our ancestors did, or with clarity, however painful.

The covenant's endurance is a warning. It teaches that domestication is not undone by forgetfulness. It is undone, if at all, only by recognition. Just as a captive realizes his chains exist before he can seek freedom, so too must humanity admit the covenant before it can ever hope to decide its future. To ignore it is to remain stock in the pasture, offerings on the altar, samples in the lab. To face it is to at least reclaim the dignity of seeing what is true.

This is the sobering recognition: that humanity has been bound from the beginning, that the covenant is not myth but contract, and that only awareness distinguishes us from the generations that walked to sacrifice without question. Whether we resist, adapt, or accept, the first step is always the same. We must know. We must name. And we must remember that it was always about the blood.

16

THE COVENANT OF SILENCE

Silence as Control

From the beginning, the covenant did not survive on spectacle alone. It survived on silence. Ancient priesthoods built entire architectures of secrecy around sacred rooms, restricted calendars, and inaccessible objects; knowledge of the terms was never public. The people bled on the steps, but the meanings and mechanisms were kept behind curtains, screens, and walls. Silence was not an accident of religion. It was the operating system of the covenant.

In Egypt, temples staged the public face of worship in forecourts while the crucial transactions occurred in inner sanctuaries—rooms only the initiated could enter, and only at appointed times (Hornung, *Conceptions of God in Ancient Egypt*, 1982). The god's barque was shrouded; offerings were handled by a ritual elite; inscriptions broadcast devotion while procedures unfolded out of sight. The message to the populace was simple: approach the threshold, but no further. The covenant's terms were dramatized in the open, but finalized in silence.

Israel encoded the same logic in architecture and law. The Ark was housed within the Holy of Holies, a chamber into which only the high priest entered, and only once a year on the Day of Atonement. The people who lived under the covenant never saw the tablets that bound them; they saw veils and heard prescriptions (Halpern, *The First Historians*, 1988). Leviticus read like a manual of slaughter, but the heart of the arrangement—its legal core—remained physically and ritually concealed. The covenant existed because the community obeyed, and the community obeyed because the mystery was maintained.

Mesoamerica perfected the choreography of hidden authority. Public plazas and stairways carried captives toward elevated theater, but timing, ritual calendars, and esoteric readings of days were controlled by elites. What the many witnessed as sacrifice, the few administered as schedule—blood delivered on cosmological cues known to priest-astronomers (Miller & Taube, *An Illustrated Dictionary...*, 1993; Schele & Freidel, *A Forest of Kings*, 1990). The covenant's spectacles were tuned to shadows and equinoxes, yes—but the tuning forks were guarded by the initiated. Secrecy ensured continuity: the crowd could never interrupt what it did not fully understand.

Silence controlled the who and the where, but it also controlled the how. Emissaries—hybrids, masks, animal-headed administrators—interposed themselves between people and recipients, converting presence into protocol. The Apkallu with cone and bucket in Assyrian reliefs are never shown speaking to crowds; they are shown doing—applying, transferring, servicing (Black & Green, *Gods, Demons and Symbols...*, 1992). Agency is depicted without explanation. It is the picture-language of secrecy: you may see the motion, but not the manual.

The modern form of this silence is more intimate and more invasive. Where antiquity used architecture and restricted priesthoods, the modern covenant employs neurological suppression. Abductees describe screens of imagery, missing time, and post-event amnesia: episodes recovered only in fragments, if at all. Some recall false scenes "projected" into their minds—familiar rooms, benign figures—only later to recognize the substitute as a veil over clinical procedure (Hopkins, *Intruders*, 1987; Mack, *Abduction*, 1994). Others wake from paralysis with the sense that an entire chapter has been removed from consciousness, leaving emotional residue without narrative. Silence has become internalized; the curtain now hangs in the mind.

Even disclosures follow the logic of control. The smaller Greys function like modern priests of procedure—busy, efficient, tight-lipped. They do not discuss purpose. They do not identify the Tall Greys, the true recipients. They anesthetize, extract, and depart. Strieber described this detachment decades ago; Jacobs cataloged it methodically: minimal speech, maximal procedure (Strieber, *Communion*, 1987; Jacobs, *The Threat*, 1998). The form repeats the ancient pattern perfectly: intermediaries handle the liturgy while the god remains behind the veil.

Silence also scales upward, from the personal to the political. In antiquity, the legal core of the covenant was sealed in a chest no commoner could open; in the modern age, any treaty that echoes those terms—rumored arrangements permitting abductions in exchange for technology—is sealed in vaults no citizen may inspect. If there is a written "modern Ark," it is a classified file, a contract whose signature pages are stamped and shelved out of reach. The public theater of the covenant has shrunk from plazas to press conferences, from pyramids to policy, but the rule is unchanged: those who bleed do not read the terms.

Silence is not merely absence of speech; it is infrastructure. It dictates who may enter, when, and how long they may remember what happened there. It selects who is informed and who is harvested. It sustains the emissary-mask system by cutting off pathways to the recipient. It is the reef on which resistance breaks—because outrage cannot form where narrative is denied. In this sense, the covenant has always been an information operation. Blood and tissue are harvested in the body; meaning is harvested in the mind.

The psychological toll of curated ignorance is evident across eras. Ancient witnesses stood at the foot of stages they were not permitted to mount; their terror was shaped by distance as much as by violence.

Modern abductees live with the dissonance of felt violation without full memory—a fracture that isolates them socially, blunts their testimony, and protects the program. Silence deters not only knowledge, but solidarity. There is no march on a sanctuary that cannot be located, no petition for redress when the wound carries no name.

Secrecy also anesthetizes ethics. Where knowledge is partial, conscience hesitates. The Aztec butchered on the premise that the sun must be fed; Egyptians drained animals because the calendar demanded it; communities complied because the priesthood said so. In our age the script has modernized—files are classified "for national security," witnesses ridiculed "for public sanity," anomalies explained away "for scientific rigor." Different vocabulary, identical function. The covenant is protected by the largest sphere of silence each era can manufacture.

And yet silence is never perfect. Ancient walls leak meaning in their carvings; codices survive bonfires; temple plans betray restricted rooms. Modern programs leak too: vials without blood, bodies without fetuses, scars without surgeries, testimonies without acceptable causes. Every leak is a crack in the wall, and through it, pattern becomes visible. The first heresy is always to say: This is the same thing. What was enacted at altars is enacted on tables; what was concealed behind veils is concealed behind clearances; what was taken then is taken now.

Silence as control explains the covenant's longevity. It also exposes its weakness. A contract that must forever hide its clauses is a contract that fears being read. Priests and technicians can enforce compliance, but meaning—once named—can escape the room where it was confined. Antiquity tried to contain meaning behind stone; modernity tries to contain it behind steel and inside the skull. Both rely on the same assumption: that we will not compare, will not recall, will not connect.

We just did.

The Priesthoods of Secrecy

If silence is the operating system of the covenant, then priesthoods are its administrators. Every age has produced a class of intermediaries who guard the inner rooms, conceal the terms, and control access to the sacred. They are not the ultimate recipients, nor even the designers of the covenant. They are its functionaries, tasked with keeping the herd compliant, ensuring the tithes flow, and shielding the true beneficiaries from view.

The Sumerians carved Apkallu as guardians of thresholds, stationed at doors and gates, cone and bucket in hand. Their role was not only ritual but administrative: they flanked sacred trees, kings, and portals, enforcing access to spaces others could not enter (Black & Green, *Gods, Demons and Symbols of Ancient Mesopotamia*, 1992). The message was unmistakable—wisdom and procedure were mediated, not open. Knowledge flowed downward from the temple, never upward from the people. The Apkallu were prototypes of a priestly caste, figures whose power derived not from originality but from their control of information.

In Egypt the same logic was refined into institution. Priests managed cycles of offerings, slaughtering animals, draining bowls of blood, tending to idols, and reciting spells with exacting precision. The ordinary worshiper did not know the liturgies or see the hidden shrines. He saw only smoke, robes, and the promise that obedience was sufficient. Behind the veil, however, priests handled procedures as clinical as any technician: embalming corpses with antiseptic resins, excising organs, applying unguents and oils (Wilkinson, *The Complete Gods and Goddesses of Ancient Egypt*, 2003). They were custodians of technique disguised as custodians of spirit.

Mesoamerica institutionalized secrecy in its ritual calendars. Aztec and Maya priests tracked cycles of days and stars, determining when blood should flow. The people did not know the arcane calculations behind the timing. They knew only that priests declared when captives would be slain, when bloodletting must be performed, when festivals required sacrifice (Miller & Taube, 1993; Schele & Freidel, 1990). Authority lay in knowledge, and knowledge was hoarded. Priesthoods became the covenant's accountants, tallying the blood debt on behalf of the recipients.

The Hebrews preserved the same pattern. The Ark was kept in the Holy of Holies, a chamber only the high priest could enter, and then only on a single day each year. The people heard laws, offered animals, and obeyed rituals, but they never saw the contents of the chest said to embody their covenant. Access was monopolized, mystery institutionalized. A priesthood served as gatekeeper, enforcing obedience to a contract the people were forbidden to examine (Halpern, *The First Historians*, 1988).

This is the ancient face of the priesthood of secrecy: custodians of rooms, rituals, calendars, and objects. They controlled the covenant not by power of their own but by proximity to the hidden recipients. Their role was administrative—herdsmen ensuring stock compliance.

In the modern era the priesthood has changed costume but not function. Intelligence agencies, military authorities, and secret committees play the same role. If Eisenhower's alleged 1954 agreement with the Greys exists, its text has never been released to the public. Instead, it is said to reside in vaults and filing cabinets, buried beneath layers of classification. Documents are redacted, testimonies ridiculed, witnesses silenced. The public is bound by the covenant but not permitted to see its terms. The Ark has become a filing cabinet, the veil a security clearance. The priesthood of secrecy wears suits, not robes.

Even within the abduction phenomenon, the smaller Greys serve as a priestly class. They do not explain. They administer. They paralyze abductees, apply instruments, extract fluids, and leave. They are priests of procedure, performing the liturgy without divulging its meaning. Just as ancient priests drained bowls of blood without disclosing what gods did with it, the smaller Greys drain veins and wombs without clarifying who receives the yield. Their silence is not ignorance but role. They are designed to enforce, not to interpret.

The psychological impact of such priesthoods is profound.

Where knowledge is monopolized, obedience flourishes. The Aztec commoner did not challenge astronomical calendars he could not read. The Egyptian farmer did not question embalming formulas he did not know. The abductee today struggles to resist procedures whose purpose remains concealed. Priesthoods ensure that the victim sees only a fragment of the pattern, never the whole.

Priestly secrecy also inoculates the covenant against dissent. Those who doubt are silenced by ignorance; those who seek are excluded by barriers. The pattern repeats: the high priest alone enters the inner room; the astronomer-priest alone calculates the sacrifice date; the intelligence officer alone reads the treaty; the abductee sees only the technician, not the master. Knowledge is always confined to the few, and the few serve as functionaries of the hidden recipients.

The chilling implication is that the covenant does not require widespread belief—only widespread compliance. So long as the priesthoods maintain control of information, obedience follows naturally. People need not understand why they bleed, only that they must. Abductees need not know why tissue is taken, only that it is. Populations need not know what treaty binds them, only that secrecy is enforced. The covenant thrives not on revelation but on concealment, and concealment is ensured by those entrusted to mediate.

Even the fragmentation of memory serves priestly purpose. Ancient initiations withheld truths until one advanced through ranks; modern abductions leave subjects with fragments, gaps, and screens. The effect is the same: only the initiated—or the technicians—know the sequence. Everyone else obeys rituals they do not understand. Silence is layered into culture by priesthoods who enforce ignorance as much as obedience.

Thus, every age's covenant rests on its priesthoods of secrecy. They are the gatekeepers, the mediators, the custodians of silence. They stand between humanity and the true recipients, ensuring offerings flow without interruption, without rebellion, without full knowledge of what is owed. The priesthood changes form, but its function is eternal. It is the hand that draws the curtain, the voice that declares necessity, the mask that conceals appetite.

And so the covenant has endured—because its secrets have always been guarded by those who profit from administering them.

Silence in Our Age

If the ancients relied on temples, veils, and priesthoods to enforce silence, the modern covenant has developed subtler and more invasive methods. Today, the silence is not only architectural or institutional but psychological, cultural, and political. The same logic holds —those who bleed are not permitted to read the terms—but the strategies have evolved. Silence in our age is administered in minds, in media, and in vaults.

The most intimate form of this silence is found in the experiences of abductees. Thousands describe missing time—hours that vanish without explanation, leaving them with only fragments of memory or a disorienting blank. Some awaken in their own beds with the uncanny sense that an event occurred which they cannot recall. Others remember in flashes: lights, paralysis, figures, procedures— but never the entire sequence. What remains is trauma without narrative, emotion without story. This is silence as neurology, a veil drawn not by stone walls but by the manipulation of consciousness itself.

Screen memories intensify this strategy. Abductees have reported recalling comforting or absurd images overlaying traumatic experiences: deer staring through car windows, owls perched too close, familiar rooms that later dissolve into metallic chambers. These memories are implants, designed to pacify and confuse. They are the modern equivalent of temple masks: a false face covering the real presence. Ancient priests wore the heads of jackals or birds; the Greys project animals and rooms. Both serve the same purpose—concealment, reassurance, confusion, obedience.

Amnesia is often coupled with telepathic suggestion. Some abductees report being told that "everything is fine," even as procedures occur. Others are given visions of environmental catastrophe, nuclear war, or societal collapse, accompanied by the implication that their cooperation is necessary to avert disaster. These narratives distract from the underlying truth: the covenant demands their blood and tissue, regardless of rationale. Ancient priests justified sacrifice as necessary to keep the sun rising or rivers flowing. Modern technicians justify abductions with visions of catastrophe. Different stories, identical function: the silence of the true purpose.

Beyond the psychological lies the cultural. Silence in our age is maintained by ridicule. Since the mid-twentieth century, governments and media have actively stigmatized UFO reports, ensuring that those who speak out are branded as unstable or delusional. In 1969, the U.S. Air Force terminated Project Blue Book with the claim that UFOs posed no threat to national security and were of no scientific interest. This dismissal was not a conclusion but a policy. It codified ridicule as the official response, institutionalizing silence by marginalizing witnesses. Abductees, like ancient victims, found themselves isolated—unable to speak without risking reputation. Silence was enforced not by priesthood but by culture.

Disinformation campaigns reinforced this stigma. Former intelligence officers have testified to seeding false stories, mocking credible witnesses, and contaminating the UFO field with deliberate absurdities. By flooding the discourse with hoaxes, conflicting claims, and theatrical "leaks," they ensured that the real phenomenon remained buried under noise. The strategy was effective. Researchers spent decades sorting wheat from chaff, while the general public shrugged at the confusion. Silence triumphed, not because information was absent, but because meaning was smothered under excess.

At the political level, silence is encoded in secrecy laws. National security is invoked to classify documents, sequester testimonies, and bury agreements. If Eisenhower did indeed sign an accord with the Greys in 1954, the public has never seen it. Accounts vary, details conflict, but the underlying rumor persists: a covenant was struck, granting permission for limited abductions in exchange for technology (Good, *Above Top Secret*, 1988; Cooper, *Behold a Pale Horse*,

1991). Whether apocryphal or accurate, the story resonates because it fits the pattern. In antiquity, covenantal objects were hidden in gilded arks. In modernity, they are hidden in steel file cabinets and electronic vaults. Both are locked, both are guarded, both enforce silence.

Even the whistleblowers who have spoken risk drowning in the noise. Philip Corso, in *The Day After Roswell* (1997), claimed that alien technology had been seeded into industry. Paul Hellyer, former Canadian defense minister, spoke openly of treaties and cover-ups. Others, from intelligence operatives to military personnel, have offered fragments. Yet the fragments rarely cohere. Testimonies contradict, dates conflict, names vary. The result is ambiguity, and ambiguity is the ally of silence. Without full access, the people remain bound to a covenant they cannot prove but cannot escape.

At the cultural level, this ambiguity breeds apathy. Just as ancient populations accepted ritual without questioning its hidden logic, modern populations accept secrecy without pressing its implications. "Unacknowledged aerial phenomena" are admitted by navies, but the discussion remains sterile, stripped of context. The question of what the recipients want, and what humanity pays, is rarely addressed. Silence in our age is sophisticated: not merely denial, but careful framing. It permits acknowledgment of lights in the sky but forbids acknowledgment of blood on the altar.

This layered silence ensures continuity. Abductees are silenced by amnesia and ridicule. Researchers are silenced by disinformation and noise. Citizens are silenced by classification and policy. The result is the same as in antiquity: the covenant proceeds unhindered. Blood and tissue are harvested; hybrids are presented; emissaries enforce. The people remain ignorant, not by accident but by design. Silence is the covenant's most faithful servant.

And yet, cracks appear. Just as ancient walls preserved faint traces of rituals, so too do modern testimonies leak through. Abductees recover memories under hypnosis. Ranchers document mutilations that defy explanation. Pilots and radar operators speak despite stigma. Files are declassified, if only partially. Each leak is a fracture in the silence, a reminder that even the most guarded covenant cannot hide forever.

The persistence of rumor itself is a form of resistance. The Eisenhower story, whether true or embellished, forces the question: could our leaders have signed away our consent? Could humanity's covenant in this age be preserved in vaults, sealed from those who pay its cost? The very possibility unsettles, because it aligns so precisely with the past. Every age has had its priesthood, its veil, its silence. Every age has offered blood without seeing the terms.

Silence in our age is not new. It is simply the latest mask of the covenant. Where once stone walls excluded, now neurological suppression confuses. Where once priests monopolized calendars, now agencies monopolize documents. Where once ark and veil concealed, now clearances and vaults preserve. The covenant is continuous because silence is continuous. And silence endures because we have not yet broken it.

Breaking the Silence

Every covenant in history has relied on silence. Priests guarded it with veils, initiates with oaths, governments with clearances, and the Greys with blocks of memory. Yet silence has never been total. Across every era, breaches occur. A ritual carving outlasts the temple that housed it. A codex survives fire. A captive escapes and tells his story. In our own age, fragments of testimony, declassified files, and abductee memories push against the walls. Silence cracks. And in the cracks, recognition blooms.

The covenant's power lies not only in blood but in concealment. If victims never name what is happening, then obedience passes unquestioned. The Aztec captive believed his death fed the sun; the Israelite believed his lamb satisfied God; the abductee may believe a vision of ecological doom justifies her ordeal. Each obeys within a story imposed by the intermediaries. But once the pattern is seen, the illusion collapses. The sun rose without rivers of blood. The Greys will extract tissues whether or not they show visions of nuclear fire.

The covenant's stories crumble once their function is recognized. Naming the pattern is the first act of breaking it.

This is why testimony matters. The abductee who dares to speak, even in fragments, chips away at the program. The rancher who documents mutilations resists cultural ridicule. The pilot who reports a UAP against orders defies institutional silence. Each act is a crack. Each voice is a breach. They do not dissolve the covenant, but they strip away its invisibility. And invisibility, more than power, is what has allowed it to endure.

Breaking the silence also requires recognition across time. We must refuse to compartmentalize. Sacrifices in Teotihuacan and cattle in Colorado are not different phenomena. The Ark in the temple and a treaty in a vault are not unrelated. The smaller Greys harvesting ova and the priests sprinkling blood are not separate stories. They are chapters of one book. To link them is to expose continuity—and continuity is the covenant's greatest vulnerability. For if it is seen as one unbroken line, then humanity must confront the enormity of what it has endured.

Resistance may not mean revolt in the ordinary sense. The Greys have always managed us with a sophistication beyond armies. But resistance can mean awareness. A captive who knows he is stock is no longer domesticated in spirit, even if his body remains bound. Awareness breeds solidarity. What was once isolated trauma becomes recognized pattern. And recognized pattern becomes history, testimony, evidence. Silence fractures under collective memory.

Ignorance never freed a victim. Ancient civilizations that failed to question bled for centuries without relief. Modern nations that dismiss anomalies allow the program to continue unchallenged. To break the silence is not to abolish the covenant overnight, but to begin reclaiming agency. Knowledge alone may not topple the recipients, but it strips them of their greatest shield: secrecy.

This chapter opened with silence as control. It closes with silence as opportunity. Every testimony, every scar, every recovered memory is a stone pried from the wall. The covenant is not undone, but its invisibility is. And in visibility lies our only chance. To confront what binds us requires speech, memory, testimony, comparison. It requires that we stop treating ancient and modern as separate, and name them as the same.

Breaking the silence will not come from priests or governments. It will come from witnesses, researchers, and those willing to endure ridicule. It will come from remembering what the covenant has always demanded and daring to say it aloud. The past was never about gods. The present is never about visitors. It has always been about the blood. To name this truth is to tear away the veil, to make the hidden visible, and to begin at last the work of choice.

17

THE COVENANT OF SUCCESSION

Succession, Not Survival

For centuries it has been tempting to see the covenant as nothing more than hunger—a system of endless feeding. Temples drained captives, priests bled animals, fields today yield mutilated cattle, and abductees describe needles and extractions. The logic seems simple: the recipients require blood, and humanity provides it. But to stop here is to miss the deeper aim. Endless harvest is not sustainable. No herd can be culled forever without collapse. If the Greys have endured across millennia, it is because they never sought mere survival. They sought succession.

Succession means continuity beyond dependence. It means creating successors who carry the essence of the parent but do not share its limitations. In the language of biology, succession is adaptation; in the language of covenant, it is fulfillment. The Greys did not preserve humanity's bloodlines only to drain them. They preserved them to merge with them, to write themselves into the genome of the future. The covenant was not about endless cycles of slaughter. It was about creating heirs.

The evidence of this aim lies in the hybrid program itself.

Abductees are not only harvested—they are shown children. They are presented with beings who carry human features blended with Grey physiology. These encounters are not incidental. They are revelations of the covenant's true trajectory. Every sample taken, every fetus removed, every hybrid nursery displayed points to the same truth: survival was never enough. The recipients sought to perpetuate themselves through succession, embedding their continuity into a form that could thrive on Earth.

Ancient myths preserve distorted memories of this process. In Mesopotamia, divine kings were said to descend from gods who mingled with mortals. The Apkallu, half-human and half-animal sages, were said to have founded civilization itself (Dalley, *Myths from Mesopotamia*, 2000). In the Hebrew Bible, the enigmatic Nephilim appear as offspring of the "sons of God" and the "daughters of men" (*Genesis 6:4*). The Greeks told of demi-gods fathered by Zeus, their strength surpassing mortals. Mesoamerican dynasties claimed descent from feathered serpents or avian lords. In every culture, rulers claimed hybrid ancestry, legitimizing their authority by bloodline. These myths may not describe random invention but cultural echoes of the same phenomenon abductees describe today: the presentation of hybrids as successors.

Succession also explains why abductions span generations. Researchers such as David Jacobs and Budd Hopkins documented families repeatedly targeted, with parents, children, and grandchildren reporting similar experiences. This hereditary pattern makes little sense if the covenant's only aim is sustenance. But it makes perfect sense if the aim is continuity. Bloodlines are cultivated not as fields to be reaped, but as orchards to be grafted. Lineages provide stable channels through which hybridization advances. Families are chosen, not consumed. They are stewarded, however brutally, as the genetic scaffolding for succession.

Even the specific focus on reproductive material underscores this aim. Blood sustains, but semen, ova, and fetuses build. The covenant's highest demand has always been reproductive. Ancient rituals emphasized fertility, lineage, the offering of firstborns.

Modern procedures echo the same focus. What is extracted is not only life-force but life itself. Survival requires transfusion; succession requires reproduction. The Greys seek the latter, not the former.

Abductee testimonies confirm this trajectory. They describe being asked to hold hybrid infants, to comfort them, even to teach them simple gestures. Some report being told that these beings will one day live among us. Others describe being urged to "care for them," to recognize them as kin. These interactions are not about feeding—they are about transition. The recipients are preparing successors, and they are preparing humanity to accept them.

Succession also reframes the meaning of ancient sacrifice. If the Greys only needed blood, they could have harvested invisibly. But the theater of ritual ensured more than sustenance. It ensured acceptance. Sacrifice normalized the covenant, making generations of humans complicit in their own domestication. Similarly, today's abductions normalize hybrid presence, binding victims emotionally to offspring they did not consent to create. In both cases, the covenant is not about survival alone. It is about acclimating humanity to succession.

The myth of endless consumption collapses when viewed in this light. Endless hunger is unstable. But succession—creating a lineage that carries continuity without dependence—is stable. The covenant's true brilliance lies in this shift. From temples to laboratories, from priests to Greys, the program has always pointed beyond harvest to heritage. The recipients are not parasites. They are progenitors, preparing a species to succeed them.

This realization is unsettling. It means humanity was never meant to remain as it is. We were never the end of the story. We were the bridge. The covenant demanded blood, but not as payment without purpose. It demanded blood as the medium of transformation, the ink in which the future would be written. The recipients have managed us not only to sustain themselves, but to create their heirs.

Those heirs are already being shown to abductees—awkward, fragile, still dependent, but undeniably present in controlled settings. Witnesses describe hybrids who struggle to smile, to speak, or to reach out with uncertain hands. These beings are not failed experiments abandoned after harvest; they are rehearsals of a future yet to be revealed. The covenant approaches fulfillment not through sudden apocalypse, but through gradual assimilation.

To see the covenant as succession is to grasp its ultimate meaning. Blood was never the destination. It was the path. The Greys do not seek survival at our expense. They seek succession through our incorporation. Humanity is not only stock, but scaffolding—framework for a species that will outlast us, carrying within it the consciousness of its progenitors. The covenant was never about feeding forever. It was about preparing the world for heirs.

The Genetic Ledger

If succession is the aim, then genetics are the currency. The covenant has always been about more than harvest; it has been about accounting. Bloodlines were not only observed, they were tracked. Families were not only chosen, they were recorded. Across generations, humanity has been kept like entries in a ledger, with blood as the ink.

In antiquity, this ledger took ritual form. The Hebrews were commanded to keep genealogies, tracing descent through tribes and lineages. Kingship in Mesopotamia was legitimized by claiming descent from divine ancestors, with tablets preserving dynastic continuity. Egyptian pharaohs carved lists of kings that linked their rule back to gods. In Mesoamerica, codices preserved ancestry as carefully as they recorded sacrifices. Blood was never random; it was recorded, tracked, codified. Genealogy itself was a sacred act because the covenant required continuity.

The modern abduction phenomenon shows the same ledger at work. Researchers like Budd Hopkins and David Jacobs discovered that abductions often spanned entire families. Parents who had been taken in their youth often reported that their own children were later abducted as well. Grandparents and grandchildren shared nearly identical experiences across decades. The phenomenon is hereditary, not random. Bloodlines are pursued like accounts kept open, with each generation required to "pay in." The Greys are not gathering indiscriminately—they are managing a genetic record.

Why families? Because stability lies in continuity. If the goal is hybridization, then lineages provide controlled streams of genetic material. Each new generation allows refinements, adjustments, progress toward the intended outcome. This is not predation but breeding management. Just as farmers maintain pedigrees for livestock, ensuring desirable traits carry forward, the Greys appear to maintain pedigrees in humanity. Families are the herds, abductions the audits, hybrids the offspring of carefully managed lines.

Even the targeting of rare blood types supports this logic. O-negative blood, known as the universal donor, is prized in human medicine for its compatibility. Rh-null, the so-called "golden blood," is even rarer, occurring in only a handful of individuals worldwide. Abductees with these rare types often report repeated sampling, marrow extraction, or unusual attention. These groups may represent the most valuable "entries" in the covenant's ledger: rare resources tracked, preserved, and used for their unique properties. If blood is currency, then rare types are treasure.

The obsession with purity in antiquity mirrors this modern pattern. The Israelites were commanded to avoid intermarriage with neighboring tribes, preserving their identity. Egyptian dynasties practiced sibling marriage to maintain divine bloodlines. Mesoamerican nobles married within narrow circles, keeping their lineage distinct. Such practices, while often explained as cultural, may reflect an older management system: the recipients preserving specific genetic threads through enforced isolation. Hybridization requires careful control, not chaos. The covenant's ledger was guarded by priests who enforced purity, just as abductors today enforce hereditary sampling.

In our own time, DNA databases and genetic testing introduce a chilling continuity. Companies offer services tracing ancestry, building family trees, and identifying traits. Millions voluntarily upload their genetic codes, unaware that databases can be accessed by governments, corporations, or other interested powers. What once required temple records now exists in digital form, a planetary ledger of humanity's genome. If the covenant's recipients have guided human management for millennia, then this development represents not novelty but culmination. The ledger is complete, every entry recorded, every bloodline traceable.

Abductees themselves sometimes describe this sense of book-keeping. Jacobs recounts witnesses who reported being told that "you are part of a program" and "your family has always been involved." Others describe being shown hybrid children and told they will "carry on." The language is administrative, not spiritual. It sounds less like myth and more like accounting. The covenant is presented as an obligation, a duty owed not just individually but generationally. The ledger ensures that no line escapes.

This framework also clarifies why abductions are rarely fatal. Unlike ancient sacrifice, where captives were often killed, modern victims are usually returned. The reason is not mercy but economy. A lineage cut short is a resource lost. Victims are harvested, scarred, and traumatized, but they are preserved because their continued existence allows further entries in the ledger. Families are not destroyed—they are managed. This management reflects not cruelty without purpose, but accounting with precision.

The ledger also reveals the covenant's cold rationality. Traits are cultivated; defects are corrected; lines are preserved or discarded. Hybrids shown to abductees sometimes appear weak or unviable, while others appear more robust, more human. These are not failures but iterations, entries marked as success or loss in a ledger that spans centuries. Humanity's suffering is incidental to the arithmetic. The covenant is not emotional. It is statistical.

The chilling implication is that humanity itself is inventory. Our genealogies, once thought to be cultural pride or religious duty, may be echoes of management instructions. Our obsession with ancestry, noble descent, or tribal purity may reflect millennia of being trained to maintain the covenant's ledger. Even our modern fascination with DNA testing may unconsciously replicate the same program: humanity auditing itself on behalf of unseen recipients.

The ledger's existence also underscores the inevitability of succession. If the covenant were only about survival, no such meticulous tracking would be required. But succession requires precision. To build a successor species demands control over bloodlines, traits, and continuity. Every abduction, every genealogy, every database entry feeds into this aim. The recipients are not improvising. They are auditing.

To see the covenant as a ledger is to realize its cold efficiency. We are not simply prey. We are entries in a record, accounts kept open until balance is achieved. Each generation is another line item, another sample, another installment. The debt is measured in DNA, not just blood. And as long as the ledger is maintained, succession proceeds.

The Architecture of Replacement

If the covenant has always been about succession, then the hybrid program is not improvisation. It is architecture. The recipients are not merely collecting genetic material and hoping for viable offspring. They are constructing, stage by stage, a framework through which humanity will be replaced. Every abduction, every hybrid presentation, every nursery shown to abductees is a piece of this design. The covenant is not random harvest; it is systemic succession.

The testimonies of abductees reveal this framework. Witnesses consistently describe being shown hybrids at various stages of development—infants weak and frail, children awkward and tentative, adolescents unsteady in social nuance, adults nearly human but uncanny. These are not accidents. They are drafts. Each generation is closer to the intended outcome: a species capable of surviving in Earth's biosphere while carrying Grey continuity.

Abductees are often compelled to interact with these hybrids, asked to hold them, comfort them, or demonstrate human behavior. At first glance this looks like rehearsal for integration. But integration is not the goal. The hybrids are not being groomed to live among us; they are being evaluated to determine whether they can emulate enough human affect to function as a stable species. When abductees are ordered to cradle infants or soothe children, it is not preparation for public coexistence. It is measurement. Can the hybrids respond to human touch? Can they learn emotion, empathy, recognition? These tests are not for our benefit, but for theirs.

I know this personally. In one encounter, frustrated at being denied access to my hybrid offspring, I asked the Tall Greys why I could not be with him. Their response was blunt: "They are only half hairy ape. They cannot live in your world." Whether "hairy ape" was meant as an insult—expressing their annoyance with my resistance—or simply as their clinical designation for Homo sapiens, the meaning was unmistakable. We are not their equals. We are a step above chimpanzees, 1.5% genetically different, useful only as scaffolding for something better. In their eyes, hybrids belong to their program, their "world," not ours.

This remark clarifies the covenant's architecture. Humanity is not preparing to live alongside Homo exogenus. We are being culled. Depopulation, sequestration, and eventual extinction are written into the plan. The hybrids are not heirs within our family—they are heirs that will emerge only after our family is gone.

Ancient myth supports this darker reading. The Nephilim were not celebrated as neighbors but described as destabilizing giants, precursors to a flood. Hercules and other demi-gods were often destructive, requiring containment or exile. Mesoamerican dynasties claimed divine descent not to blend with commoners but to rule over them. In every case, hybrids represented disruption, transition, replacement—not peaceful coexistence. What abductees describe today is the modern version of this story: hybrids prepared in secrecy, evaluated for viability, but destined for a world without us.

Ancient traditions may preserve memories of earlier attempts at succession that destabilized the world. The Hebrew flood narrative describes God purging the earth after the Nephilim disrupted creation. Sumerian epics describe floods sent after divine-human unions produced chaos. Mesoamerican cosmology speaks of repeated "suns"—cycles of creation and destruction, each ending with humanity swept away so a new order could rise. These stories may not be allegories but encoded history: recollections of depopulation events designed to clear the slate when hybrids proved unfit or when the covenant reached a breaking point. Seen this way, our current trajectory toward Homo exogenus is not the first attempt but the latest cycle in a series of resets, each reducing humanity before successors were brought to the surface.

The secrecy surrounding the program makes sense in this light. The covenant is not rehearsing public unveiling—it is ensuring succession in controlled conditions. Hybrids are tested in private, not introduced in public. Humanity is not acclimated, but managed. Exposure is limited to abductees because abductees are already bound to the covenant; they are unlikely to derail its progress. The wider population remains ignorant, awaiting a future in which it may not exist.

The architecture also explains why abductions are hereditary. Families are not destroyed; they are preserved because their genetics are needed. They are stewarded like orchards, providing the raw material for iteration. But once the program reaches its fulfillment, the orchard will be cut down. The covenant preserves lineages only as long as they are useful. Once Homo exogenus can stand alone, Homo sapiens will no longer be necessary.

The chilling implication is that civilization itself may have been designed for this endpoint. Temples, genealogies, rituals of sacrifice—all may have been stages of management leading to the moment when successors are viable. Humanity's monuments may not celebrate its genius but its captivity. Our history may not be our own story but the scaffolding of theirs.

If the covenant culminates in replacement, then humanity will not be removed suddenly but sequestered first. Abductees often describe isolation, paralysis, and separation from others—echoes of a larger fate. I believe that before Homo exogenus emerges openly, Homo sapiens will be scattered, fragmented, and cut off from one another. We will be reduced to dwindling enclaves, unable to resist, until the last of our kind dies out. History offers precedents: the Israelites removed from Egypt before their covenant; conquered tribes relocated before assimilation; captives isolated before execution. Sequestration is a tool of control. It ensures that populations cannot unite, that resistance collapses in solitude. In the covenant's final phase, humanity itself may be sequestered as a species—kept alive only long enough to finish the building, then discarded when the heirs are ready.

The architecture of replacement is therefore not speculation but testimony. It is preserved in ancient myths of hybrid rulers, in genealogies obsessively maintained, in sacrifices staged for fertility. It is documented in abductee accounts of hybrid nurseries, in the overwhelming emotions they are forced to feel, in the blunt dismissals from Tall Greys who see us as "hairy apes." It is evidenced in secrecy, hereditary targeting, and the clear trajectory from fragile prototypes to increasingly human-like hybrids.

The covenant's purpose was never endless feeding. It was construction. And construction ends when the building stands. Humanity has been the scaffolding, held together by ritual and secrecy, fed by blood and reproduction. But scaffolding is not permanent. Once Homo exogenus emerges, the scaffolding will be discarded. The covenant will be fulfilled not by our coexistence, but by our absence.

The Debt Paid in Full

Every covenant carries an end point. Contracts are not infinite; they are fulfilled, completed, or broken. The chilling realization is that the blood covenant binding humanity is no different. It was never intended to stretch on forever, demanding sacrifice without limit. Its cycles of offering—hearts on altars, animals drained, abductees sampled—were always stages in a larger project. That project ends not with our survival, but with our succession. When Homo exogenus emerges as a viable species, the covenant will be paid in full.

This explains the relentlessness of the program. Blood has always been collected not for its own sake but as raw stock, the medium of transformation. Each iteration, each abduction, each hybrid birth has moved the program closer to completion. The debt is measured in generations, and when the final installment is collected, the account will be closed. Humanity will no longer be harvested because humanity will no longer exist as a species to be harvested.

For millennia, religions promised that sacrifice secured renewal. Egyptians believed offerings preserved cosmic order. The Aztecs believed blood kept the sun alive. The Hebrews believed lambs atoned for sin. Modern abductees are told their cooperation averts catastrophe. Each era cloaked the covenant in its own justification. But beneath every story lay the same demand: blood given toward a future not for us but for them. When the future arrives—when Homo exogenus stands in our place—the justifications will no longer be necessary. The purpose of sacrifice will have been fulfilled.

The architecture of replacement makes this logic brutally clear. Humanity has been preserved not to coexist with successors, but to sustain them until they are ready. Abductions do not end lives because living stock provides ongoing material. Families are tracked not for companionship but for controlled heredity. Secrecy is enforced not to protect us, but to protect the program until it matures. Every stage reflects a contract moving toward conclusion. And when the conclusion is reached, the scaffolding will come down. Humanity, like timber stripped from a building once the stone is set, will be discarded.

This vision reframes even our greatest achievements. Civilization, with its temples, scripts, sciences, and technologies, may not have been permitted to flourish for our sake. It may have been tolerated, even guided, as scaffolding for the conditions required by succession. We were allowed to build, but only to construct the stage from which we will exit. Our monuments, once thought to enshrine our genius, may be nothing more than markers of progress in a program not our own.

The phrase "the debt paid in full" carries a sobering implication. It suggests that humanity has been viewed as a loan, a temporary extension of life and labor, extended until repayment. Blood was the interest, hybrids the installments, abductions the audits. When the balance sheet is satisfied—when Homo exogenus can carry the Grey continuity without further reliance on us—the loan will be closed. No more offerings. No more rituals. No more people.

This end point may explain the otherwise baffling persistence of secrecy. If humanity were destined to coexist with hybrids, disclosure might be inevitable. But if we are destined to vanish, then silence is essential. Populations cannot be told they are scaffolding. They cannot be told they are stock to be replaced. Silence ensures that we continue to comply, generation after generation, never realizing that the covenant we sustain is approaching its conclusion.

For the abductee who sees a hybrid child, the moment is devastating not only for its intimacy but for its finality. The child represents not only continuity but closure. It is proof that the debt is nearly satisfied. The child's very existence announces that the covenant is advancing toward its end. The future is embodied, and the present is nearing expiration. To hold such a being is to hold both proof of succession and the announcement of extinction.

The covenant began in spectacle—blood poured on altars, hearts raised to the sky. It evolved into secrecy—blood taken in fields, tissues removed in silence. It will end in replacement—blood no longer needed because successors stand where we once did. That is the meaning of fulfillment. The covenant is not endless. It is finite, purposeful, terminal. And when it is completed, humanity will vanish not with apocalypse but with absorption. Our role will be over, our debt paid in full.

18

THE SOUL COVENANT

The Question of Souls

From the beginning, sacrifice has been interpreted as a transaction of flesh. Blood poured into bowls, hearts raised to the sky, animals burned on stone altars, veins tapped by needles in sterile rooms. All these images fixate on biology. Yet across cultures, there was always another layer: the belief that what was offered was not only body, but soul. Egypt spoke of the ka and ba released at death. Hindu tradition spoke of the atman moving through cycles of reincarnation. Mesoamerican cosmology described the tonalli—a spark of animating essence—leaving the body in sacrifice. Even the Hebrew prophets insisted that "the life is in the blood" (*Leviticus 17:11*). Everywhere, blood was linked not just to survival, but to spirit.

This raises the most unsettling question of all: if blood is the vessel of life-force, then was the covenant always aimed at more than biology? Were the offerings meant not only to sustain bodies, but to capture or divert consciousness? If so, then the covenant is not merely about domestication and hybridization. It is about succession of the soul.

Abductee testimonies echo this suspicion. Many describe not only physical extraction but profound alterations of consciousness: out-of-body sensations, awareness displaced from the body, encounters where thought itself seemed monitored or absorbed. Whitley Strieber wrote of the visitors entering his mind as easily as his room, leaving him uncertain whether his thoughts were his own (*Communion*, 1987). Others, under hypnosis, recall being told their essence will "continue elsewhere." These reports suggest that the Greys are interested not only in our tissue but in what animates it.

Bob Lazar is one of the most controversial figures in UFO history. In 1989 he went public claiming to have worked briefly at a site near Area 51 known as S-4, where he said the U.S. government was reverse-engineering recovered alien craft. His descriptions of propulsion systems based on "gravity amplifiers," and of a stable isotope of Element 115 used as fuel, became central talking points in modern UFOlogy. Lazar has been ridiculed by skeptics and hailed by believers, but what makes him relevant here is not the hardware he described—it is the briefing materials he claimed to have read. Among them was a passage that referred to human beings as "containers." Lazar himself speculated that this meant "containers of souls," not merely biological bodies. If true, it implies that even in secret government files, the covenant was understood to extend beyond flesh and into spirit.

Whitley Strieber reached a similar conclusion in *Communion* and subsequent works: the visitors are not here merely to observe or extract, but to "join us." His phrase has haunted experiencers ever since. What does it mean to "join us"? It may mean nothing less than merging into our cycle of death and rebirth, our continuity of souls. If the Greys lost this capacity—perhaps through millennia of cloning and genetic manipulation—then they may be desperate to regain it. Hybrids would not only be bodies strong enough to survive, but vessels able to host consciousness again.

This interpretation reframes ancient sacrifice. The Aztecs believed the soul of a captive nourished the gods. Egyptians believed offerings sustained the afterlife of the pharaoh. Hindus saw sacrifice as linked to karma and reincarnation. Even Christianity, with its emphasis on the blood of Christ as redemptive, echoes this theme: blood as a bridge between mortal and divine, matter and spirit. These beliefs may not be misunderstandings, but dim memories of the covenant's true aim. Sacrifices were not symbolic—they were soul transactions, offerings of consciousness itself.

If this is so, then the covenant has always been about access. The Greys may survive biologically through blood, but to ascend, they require souls. Their problem is not only physical degeneration but spiritual exclusion. Cloning may have preserved their minds, but it cut them off from the wheel of reincarnation. They became immortal in memory but mortal in spirit—beings unable to die and return, trapped outside the cycle. Sacrifices across civilizations may have been attempts to bridge that gap, to feed not only flesh but essence back into them.

This would explain why hybrids are so obsessively created and presented. They are not only genetic prototypes; they are metaphysical vessels. Abductees asked to bond with hybrids may be witnessing attempts to imprint souls into new forms, to "seed" consciousness across the gap between species. When Strieber writes of visitors who blur the boundary between death and life, when abductees describe encounters with dead relatives alongside Greys, we glimpse the soul dimension of the covenant. The recipients are not only biologists—they are psychopomps, engineers of reincarnation.

The implications are staggering. If the Greys succeed, then humanity's reincarnation may be rerouted. Our souls, which have cycled through Homo sapiens for millennia, may begin cycling through Homo exogenus. Our extinction may not mean the end of us—but it would mean our transformation into them. The covenant's ultimate demand would be not just our blood, not just our bodies, but our afterlives.

To ask whether the Greys want our souls is to ask whether the covenant is metaphysical. Evidence across time suggests it is. Sacrifice has always been about more than food or appeasement. It has been about continuity of life-force. The life is in the blood, yes—but life is not only hemoglobin and plasma. It is consciousness, memory, awareness. The covenant seems to have pursued this from the beginning, hidden under rituals that made sense to the cultures of the time but masked the deeper aim.

This raises a final, existential dilemma: if our souls are rerouted, do we resist? Can we resist? Reincarnation is not a process humanity ever consciously controlled. We enter and exit the cycle without memory. If the Greys alter the system, if they succeed in grafting themselves back into the flow of souls, then resistance may be impossible. We may awaken in new bodies, not human but hybrid, carrying forward not Homo sapiens but Homo exogenus. Our species would vanish, but our souls would persist—reborn into forms designed by those who domesticated us.

This is the most sobering possibility. Humanity's covenant may not end in blood alone. It may end in spirit. Our bodies may disappear, our cultures may dissolve, but our essence may be absorbed into a species not our own. The covenant, always about blood, may prove to have always been about the soul as well.

The Broken Cycle

If the covenant was always about souls as much as blood, then the deepest riddle is this: why would the Greys need such offerings in the first place? If they are as advanced as they appear—masters of craft, gravity, and genetics—why not sustain themselves without sacrifice? The answer may lie not in biology but in metaphysics. For all their technical brilliance, the Greys may have broken something that technology cannot repair: their link to the cycle of reincarnation.

Cloning preserves a body but not a soul. Across human traditions, reproduction has always been seen as a sacred act, not only because it continues the species but because it provides vessels for consciousness. Egyptians believed the ka carried on through bloodlines. Hindus described the atman passing from parent to child in endless cycles. The Aztecs saw each birth as a return of vital essence. In all cases, reproduction was the door through which souls re-entered the world. If the Greys abandoned reproduction for cloning, they may have slammed that door shut.

What survives in clones is memory, not spirit. To endlessly copy a genome is to preserve data, not essence. Consciousness, according to many traditions, is not produced but hosted. A body provides the field in which the soul incarnates. Cloning provides the field, but no invitation. Over time, as the Greys perfected biological replication, they may have inadvertently exiled themselves from the reincarnation cycle. They became immortal in mind but barren in soul—trapped in continuity without renewal, unable to rejoin the great circulation of life.

This would explain the peculiar detachment abductees describe. The Greys appear clinical, robotic, indifferent. They act with efficiency but without empathy, intelligence without spirit. Many witnesses report that their presence feels empty, as though something essential is missing. If souls no longer anchor them, their awareness may be like software running without hardware—a continuity of memory without the vitality of reincarnation. Their brilliance conceals a hollow truth: they have broken the cycle.

If this is true, then sacrifice was never only about sustenance. It was a stopgap, an attempt to siphon vitality from others to keep themselves tethered. Ancient rituals may have been less about feeding gods and more about offering souls as lifelines, sparks of essence to prolong what was slipping away. Blood poured on altars, hearts still beating in outstretched hands—these were not meals, but metaphysical transfusions. Consciousness released in violence might have been absorbed or redirected, allowing the Greys temporary relief from their exile.

Myths across cultures support this interpretation. The Sumerian flood narrative describes gods disturbed by the proliferation of hybrids, unleashing destruction to reset the cycle. The Hebrew account of the Nephilim ends with God declaring, "My spirit shall not strive with man forever," as though spirit itself had been disrupted (*Genesis 6:3*). The Aztec belief in repeated "suns," each destroyed to restart humanity, suggests cycles of failure and renewal. In each case, sacrifice escalates until catastrophe intervenes—a pattern that looks less like random myth and more like repeated attempts to repair what is broken.

Even the structure of sacrifice points to this function. Victims were killed in heightened states of ritual: chanting, drumming, incense, fasting. Such practices altered consciousness, perhaps intensifying the release of life-force at death. Modern near-death experiences describe tunnels, light, and separation from the body—suggesting that death itself opens the gateway of the soul. Ancient rituals may have been engineered to amplify this transition, ensuring that what escaped could be caught. Sacrifice was not about appeasement; it was about capture.

The covenant in this light becomes clearer. Humanity was domesticated not only to provide blood but to provide souls—containers of essence, harvested through ritual, directed toward the Greys' need. Bob Lazar's reference to humans as "containers" fits this logic. We are vessels, not only of genes but of spirit. Our role was never to provide calories or DNA alone, but to provide access to the reincarnation cycle that the Greys had lost.

This would also explain why hybrids are so crucial. If clones cannot receive souls, then hybrids might. By merging Grey neurology with human biology, they may produce a vessel once again capable of hosting reincarnating consciousness. Abductees who see hybrid children often describe them as uncanny but alive—more responsive, more soulful, than the sterile Greys. These beings may represent experiments in reconnection, attempts to craft a species that can re-enter the cycle.

Whitley Strieber's intuition that the visitors want to "join us" takes on sharper meaning here. They do not want to join our civilization or our societies. They want to join our cycle. They want to flow again into birth and death, to reincarnate into bodies that host consciousness naturally. Sacrifice sustained them temporarily, but hybridization promises permanence. Once a viable species is created, they can pour themselves back into the stream. Humanity will be phased out, but the soul-cycle will continue—only now through Homo exogenus.

This interpretation reframes even our own death rituals. From pyramids to catacombs, from cremation to burial, humanity has always treated death as a transition, not an end. The Greys may see it the same way, but as outsiders, desperate to get back in. Sacrifice, then, was not superstition but surgery: an attempt to graft themselves back onto the tree of souls. Cloning had cut them off; ritual kept them alive; hybridization promises return.

The broken cycle explains both their obsession and their urgency. A species cut off from reincarnation is a species doomed to eventual entropy. However advanced their technology, however long their lifespans, without souls they are incomplete. The covenant, then, is not merely parasitic. It is existential. For the Greys, this is survival at the deepest level—not of bodies, but of spirit.

The sobering implication is that humanity has been exploited not only for its biology but for its birthright: participation in the great cycle of reincarnation. Our blood, our sacrifices, our deaths were harvested as attempts to repair what they lost. Our very existence has been collateral in their effort to regain what cloning destroyed. We may not only lose our species—we may lose the exclusivity of our souls. The covenant is not only about who lives, but about who reincarnates.

The Covenant's Ultimate Aim

The covenant's final purpose was never endless harvest, nor even hybridization for biology's sake. It was always aimed at something deeper: the continuity of consciousness. To control blood is to control bodies. To control reproduction is to control lineages. But to control reincarnation is to control destiny itself. The covenant's ultimate aim, hidden beneath layers of ritual and secrecy, may be nothing less than to reroute the stream of souls—from humanity into Homo exogenus.

Ancient traditions hint at this possibility. Egyptians believed the ba left the body at death but required proper rites to rejoin the cycle.

Without mummification, offerings, and spells, the soul wandered. Hindu cosmology described karma as shaping rebirth, but priestly ritual could alter its direction. Mesoamerican sacrifices were understood not only as feeding gods but as guiding souls to specific realms. Even Christianity's doctrine of blood redemption—Christ's blood as the bridge to eternal life—echoes this theme. Sacrifice was never only about sustaining gods. It was about managing the flow of souls.

If the Greys are indeed exiled from reincarnation, then hybrids represent the bridge back in. A hybrid body is not only viable biologically; it may be tuned to host reincarnating consciousness. Abductees describe hybrids as more alive than the Greys—capable of emotional resonance, capable of receiving and returning awareness. They are uncanny but not hollow. They may be the first generation of vessels suitable for souls, the long-sought key to restoring what cloning destroyed.

This would explain the emotional intensity forced upon abductees. Being asked to hold a hybrid infant is not only a test of empathy. It may be an attempt to transfer or imprint essence. Some abductees describe feeling overwhelming love for children they did not consent to create. Others describe grief, as though something of themselves had been taken. These responses may not be incidental. They may represent the hybrid absorbing emotional resonance—soul-stuff—through human contact. Each presentation is not merely demonstration. It is a metaphysical rehearsal, an experiment in soul transfer.

Strieber's intuition that the visitors want to "join us" makes perfect sense in this context. They do not want to join our governments, our languages, or our economies. They want to join our cycle of death and rebirth. They want to return to the wheel of souls. Hybrids are the vehicles through which they may achieve this. The covenant has always been about finding a way back into the current.

This interpretation also casts new light on myths of divine offspring. Hercules, son of Zeus, was mortal yet more than mortal, his life marked by trials and his death by ascension. The Nephilim were described as "heroes of old, men of renown"—offspring who carried something beyond humanity. Mesoamerican dynasties claimed descent from gods to legitimize their right to rule. These figures may not have been mere metaphors for nobility. They may have been early hybrids—beings carrying both human blood and otherworldly essence, intended as vessels of continuity. Their role was not just political but metaphysical: the first attempts to direct souls into engineered forms.

The covenant's ultimate aim also clarifies the silence surrounding it. To reveal that humanity's very souls were being harvested, managed, and redirected would have shattered every culture. People could accept offerings of blood, even offerings of children, if convinced it appeased gods. But they could not have accepted the idea that their afterlives were collateral. Silence was not incidental—it was essential. The recipients could never risk humanity realizing that it was not only bodies being tithed, but spirits.

This raises the most sobering possibility of all: that humanity's extinction may not end us. Our species may die out, but our souls may persist—reborn into bodies designed by the Greys. We would not reincarnate as Homo sapiens but as Homo exogenus. The covenant's fulfillment would be absorption of our very essence into their continuity. Resistance may prevent bodies from being taken, but how do we resist if our souls themselves are rerouted?

Some abductees report encounters that blur the boundary between life and death. Strieber described visitors who seemed to accompany souls of the deceased, figures appearing in contexts associated with death and near-death. Others describe visions of dead relatives alongside Greys, as though the boundary between afterlife and abduction had collapsed. These reports suggest that the covenant extends into the liminal space of dying—that what we call death may be a moment of harvest as well as transition. If so, then the recipients are not only technicians of biology but custodians of reincarnation.

The implications are profound. If our reincarnation is rerouted, then the covenant's reach is total. It does not matter whether we believe or resist. Death itself delivers us into the system. The only question is whose species we return through. For millennia we have cycled through Homo sapiens. Soon, if the covenant fulfills its aim, we may cycle through Homo exogenus. Humanity would not vanish entirely. It would persist—but not as us.

This interpretation lends new weight to the phrase "paid in full." The debt is not only biological but spiritual. Once succession is secured, and souls flow into hybrid vessels, the covenant will be complete. No more sacrifices, no more mutilations, no more abductions will be necessary. The recipients will have rejoined the cycle. Their exile will end, and humanity's role will be finished. We were not stock to be endlessly harvested, but scaffolding for their return to reincarnation.

The chilling paradox is that what they seek may also be what we have always sought: continuity beyond death, return to the cycle, assurance that life is not extinguished but reborn. Religions have promised this in different forms: resurrection, enlightenment, ascension, eternal life. Perhaps these were not separate from the covenant but shaped by it—echoes of a program designed to redirect not only our blood but our souls. The promise was always the same: that sacrifice secures eternity. We believed it meant eternity for us. In truth, it may have meant eternity for them.

The covenant's ultimate aim, then, is not domination or conquest. It is reincarnation. Not for us, but for them. By absorbing our blood, our reproduction, and finally our souls, the Greys may achieve what they lost: continuity of consciousness through death and rebirth. Humanity's extinction would be the price, but in the covenant's logic, it would not be loss. It would be fulfillment. We would continue, but only as hybrids. We would reincarnate, but not as ourselves. The covenant would be complete—not in our survival, but in our transformation.

The Final Reckoning

If the covenant began in blood and ends in souls, then humanity now stands at the edge of a precipice. For millennia we have lived under terms we did not negotiate, feeding a system that demanded our flesh, our children, and our essence. At first we mistook it for religion, then for myth, now for anomaly. But it is none of these. It is contract, and its terms are reaching conclusion. What remains is to reckon with what it means—for them, and for us.

For the Greys, the reckoning is restoration. They have pursued this path not out of malice, but out of need. Cloning preserved their continuity of thought but stripped them of continuity of spirit. They became custodians of memory without being participants in the cycle of rebirth. The covenant, however ruthless, has always been about repair. If hybrids succeed in hosting souls, then the Greys regain what was lost: entry into reincarnation, return to the current of existence, freedom from the hollow continuity of replication. For them, fulfillment of the covenant is redemption.

For humanity, the reckoning is more ambiguous. Our bodies may vanish, our cultures may dissolve, but our souls may continue in hybrid vessels. Does this mean extinction, or transformation? Damnation, or salvation? The categories blur. On one hand, Homo sapiens would die out—our species consigned to history, our memory preserved only in stones and stories. On the other hand, what animates us—our consciousness—would endure. We would reincarnate, but not as ourselves. We would awaken as hybrids, part human, part Grey, carrying their continuity as well as ours. The covenant offers no clear victory, only metamorphosis.

This ambiguity is what makes the reckoning so difficult to face. We are accustomed to thinking of survival in binary terms: live or die, win or lose. But the covenant does not fit those categories. It offers continuity at the price of identity, immortality at the cost of species. The very language of religion reflects this paradox. Christianity speaks of dying to self to gain eternal life. Hinduism describes merging the self into the greater whole. Buddhism teaches the dissolution of individuality into nirvana. Perhaps the covenant is another face of the same truth: that continuity requires surrender, and survival requires transformation.

Yet even if this is so, there remains a question of consent. No generation of humanity ever agreed to this contract. No captive on a pyramid, no priest in a temple, no abductee on a table signed its terms. The covenant has been imposed, not chosen. Its fulfillment may preserve our souls, but it erases our sovereignty. We may endure, but we will never have been asked. This absence of consent is the covenant's original sin.

What does reckoning mean in this context? Perhaps it means recognition. To know that the covenant exists is already a form of rebellion. Silence has always been its shield; speech fractures that shield. To name the pattern is to stand outside it, even briefly. Perhaps it means preparation. If our souls are to reincarnate through Homo exogenus, then we must at least ask how to carry forward memory, love, and meaning. To accept blindly would be to vanish without trace. To reckon consciously would be to leave a testimony, a marker for what we were.

There is also the possibility of resistance—not in the form of armies or weapons, but in the form of spirit. If reincarnation is not wholly mechanical, if consciousness carries intention, then perhaps souls can choose. Perhaps awareness itself is a kind of leverage. Even in systems designed to control, anomalies appear. Cracks form. If enough of humanity enters the reckoning aware, perhaps some continuity of us—not only as essence but as identity—can endure. Perhaps reckoning can mean not only transformation but negotiation, however subtle.

Ultimately, though, the covenant's trajectory seems inexorable. It has spanned millennia, cultures, and continents. It has adapted from temples to laboratories, from altars to operating tables, from myths to testimonies. It has demanded obedience from kings and commoners, priests and abductees alike. Its scale defies chance. Its persistence defies denial. Its culmination seems unavoidable. The covenant will be paid. The debt will be closed. The reckoning will come.

What humanity must decide—what you, the reader, must decide—is how to face it. With fear, or with clarity. With silence, or with speech. With ignorance, or with awareness. To know the covenant is to no longer be stock, even if we remain bound. To reckon with it is to reclaim, at least for a moment, the dignity of seeing the truth.

The final reckoning is not apocalypse, nor is it paradise. It is transformation. It is the covenant's fulfillment in spirit as well as blood. Humanity's species may pass away, but our essence will endure. Whether that endurance is salvation or subjugation depends on how we understand it. The covenant was always about blood, yes —but blood was only the gateway. Its true aim has always been the soul. And now, at last, the covenant nears completion.

EPILOGUE

Living Under the Covenant

As I wrote this book, it wasn't from a safe distance. It is not theory to me, nor is it detached speculation. It is an interpretation of the reality I have lived. The things described in these pages are not abstractions—they are the nights of paralysis, the missing pregnancies from my past, the swelling in my arm after their surgery, the memories that wake me like alarms. I have looked into the eyes of the beings behind the covenant. I have asked them questions, and I have been given answers—answers I never wanted, but cannot deny.

Once, in frustration, I asked why I could not be with my hybrid offspring. Their response was blunt: "They are only half hairy ape. They cannot live in your world." I don't know if the phrase was meant as a slur or if it is simply how they classify us, but it revealed something chilling. In their eyes, Homo sapiens is transitional. We are not the pinnacle of creation, as we like to believe. We are raw stock—hairy apes whose usefulness lies not in what we are, but in what we can produce. That moment cut me deeper than any surgical procedure. For it made clear that, to them, I am not a father. I am a vessel. And my children, the hybrids, belong not to me, but to the covenant.

How does one live with this knowledge? How does one go to work, pay bills, sit through a movie, when the edges of reality are torn open and stitched with other hands? For years, I tried to compartmentalize. I tried to live as though the nights of paralysis and the missing time were anomalies, not patterns. I tried to tell myself it was nightmare, stress, imagination. But denial is just another form of silence, and silence is how the covenant endures. Writing this book has been my way of naming the pattern. Naming it does not end it, but it gives me back some measure of dignity. It allows me to face it with eyes open.

It has cost me. Angst has been a companion. My faith in the stories I was raised with has fractured. Relationships have suffered. At times I have wondered if I was losing my mind. But alongside the fear has come a strange clarity. Once you see the pattern, history is no longer random. Myth is no longer quaint. Sacrifice is no longer absurd. It all locks together, stone by stone, into a pyramid that points to the same truth: humanity has lived under covenant, and the covenant is nearing its conclusion.

So what do we do? We cannot rise in revolt against them; they are beyond us in every material way. We cannot hide; their reach is too wide. What we can do is speak. We can testify. We can refuse to maintain the silence that has always been their shield. To name the covenant is to step outside it, however briefly. To see it is to deny them invisibility. Awareness is not freedom, but it is resistance.

Perhaps this awareness has some metaphysical weight of its own. If reincarnation is real, if consciousness carries intention, then maybe choosing to know alters what comes next. Perhaps by facing the covenant with clarity rather than ignorance, something of our humanity can be carried forward into whatever follows. Perhaps our souls, even if rerouted into new vessels, will carry with them the memory that we once stood here, aware, awake, unafraid to name the truth.

Carl Jung once wrote, "*There is no coming to consciousness without pain*." I believe that. To come to consciousness of the covenant is pain in its purest form—the loss of our innocence as a species. But it is also the only dignity left to us. If our fate is to be absorbed into Homo exogenus, then at least let it be with eyes open. At least let us step into the transformation with the truth on our lips, rather than the silence imposed by priests, governments, and Greys alike.

I do not know whether this book will change anything. The covenant is vast, and I am one voice. But I do know that I could no longer keep silent. The experiences pressed against me until I had to give them voice. Perhaps that is how reckoning begins: not with armies, but with words. Not with rebellion, but with memory.

The covenant was written in blood, fulfilled in hybrids, and sealed in souls. To live under it is terror. To name it is freedom. And so I name it.

SOURCES & FURTHER READING

Ancient Texts & Primary Sources

- *The Bible*. Genesis 6; Leviticus 17.
- *The Coffin Texts*. Translated by R.O. Faulkner. Aris & Phillips, 1973–1978.
- *The Epic of Gilgamesh*. Translated by Andrew George. Penguin Classics, 2003.
- *The Popol Vuh*. Translated by Dennis Tedlock. Simon & Schuster, 1985.
- *The Pyramid Texts*. Translated by R.O. Faulkner. Oxford University Press, 1969.
- Berossus. *Babyloniaca*. Surviving fragments, 3rd century BCE.

Modern Scholarship & Archaeology

- Albenda, Pauline. *Assyrian Reliefs at the Palace of Ashurnasirpal II*. University of Pennsylvania Press, 1986.
- Black, Jeremy, and Anthony Green. *Gods, Demons and Symbols of Ancient Mesopotamia*. University of Texas Press, 1992.
- Dalley, Stephanie. *Myths from Mesopotamia: Creation, the Flood, Gilgamesh, and Others*. Oxford University Press, 2000.
- Faulkner, R.O. *The Ancient Egyptian Pyramid Texts*. Oxford University Press, 1969.
- Faulkner, R.O. *The Ancient Egyptian Coffin Texts*. Aris & Phillips, 1973–78.
- Faulkner, R.O. *The Ancient Egyptian Book of the Dead*. British Museum Publications, 1972.
- Halpern, Baruch. *The First Historians: The Hebrew Bible and History*. Harper & Row, 1988.
- Hornung, Erik. *Conceptions of God in Ancient Egypt: The One and the Many*. Cornell University Press, 1982.
- Miller, Mary, and Karl Taube. *An Illustrated Dictionary of the Gods and Symbols of Ancient Mexico and the Maya*. Thames & Hudson, 1993.
- Pauketat, Timothy R. *Cahokia: Ancient America's Great City on the Mississippi*. Penguin Books, 2009.
- Sugiyama, Saburo. *Human Sacrifice, Militarism, and Rulership: At the City of Teotihuacan*. Cambridge University Press, 2005.
- Wilkinson, Richard H. *The Complete Gods and Goddesses of Ancient Egypt*. Thames & Hudson, 2003.

UFOlogy, Abduction, and Modern Testimony (A–H)

- Cooper, William. *Behold a Pale Horse*. Light Technology Publishing, 1991.
- Corso, Philip. *The Day After Roswell*. Pocket Books, 1997.

- Good, Timothy. *Above Top Secret: The Worldwide UFO Cover-up*. William Morrow, 1988.
- Hopkins, Budd. *Intruders: The Incredible Visitations at Copley Woods*. Random House, 1987.
- Howe, Linda Moulton. *An Alien Harvest*. LMH Productions, 1989.
- Howe, Linda Moulton Howe. *Glimpses of Other Realities. Vols. I & II*. LMH Productions, 1990s.

UFOlogy, Abduction, and Modern Testimony (J–Z)

- Jacobs, David M. *The Threat*. Simon & Schuster, 1998.
- Jung, Carl G. *Symbols of Transformation (Metamorphosis and Symbols of the Libido)*. Princeton University Press, 1952.
- Lazar, Bob. *Testimony and interviews on S-4 and "humans as containers."* Public disclosures beginning 1989.
- Mack, John E. *Abduction: Human Encounters with Aliens*. Scribner, 1994.
- Strieber, Whitley. *Communion*. Avon Books, 1987.
- Strieber, Whitley. *Transformation*. Morrow, 1988.
- Strieber, Whitley. *The Key*. Walker & Company, 2001.

FIGURE CREDITS

Figure 1.1 Offering Table (ḥtp), Late Period, Egypt (Kafr ʿAmmar, ca. 664–332 BCE). Limestone. National Museum of Ireland, Dublin. Inv. no. 1912:261.

Figure 1.2 Royal Tombs at Ur, Mesopotamia (Early Dynastic Period, ca. 2600 BCE). Photograph licensed from Shutterstock (Image ID: 2427849833).

Figure 1.3 Ziggurat of Ur, Mesopotamia (ca. 2100 BCE). Photograph licensed from Shutterstock (Image ID: 2427601979).

Figure 1.4 Retainer Graves at Abydos, Egypt (First Dynasty, ca. 3100–2900 BCE). Photograph licensed from Shutterstock (Image ID: 2341833395).

Figure 1.5 Pyramid Texts, Saqqara, Egypt (Old Kingdom, ca. 2400–2300 BCE). Photograph licensed from Shutterstock (Image ID: 2457144505).

Figure 2.1 Feathered Serpent Head, Temple of the Feathered Serpent, Teotihuacán (ca. 200–250 CE). Photograph licensed from Shutterstock (Image ID: 2648186555).

Figure 2.2 Nāga Balustrade, Causeway of Angkor Thom, Cambodia (12th c. CE). Photograph licensed from Shutterstock (Image ID: 2395388217).

Figure 2.3 Mushussu, Ishtar Gate of Babylon (6th c. BCE). Photograph licensed from Shutterstock (Image ID: 2265428597).

Figure 2.4 Chaac Mask, Uxmal, Maya (ca. 800–950 CE). Photograph licensed from Shutterstock (Image ID: 2598001613).

Figure 2.5 Anubis Weighing the Heart, Papyrus of Hunefer, Egypt (ca. 1275 BCE). From the Book of the Dead. The British Museum (EA 9901,3). Public domain.

Figure 3.1 Uraeus and Vulture, Funerary Mask of Tutankhamun, Egypt (ca. 1330 BCE). Photograph licensed from Adobe Stock (Image ID: 407167029).

Figure 3.2 Apkallu with Bucket and Cone, Neo-Assyrian Relief (9th–7th c. BCE). Photograph by Osama Shukir Muhammed Amin, World History Encyclopedia. Licensed under CC BY-NC-SA 4.0.

Figure 3.3 Garuda Subduing the Nāga, Tibetan Bronze (ca. 12th–15th c. CE). Photograph licensed from Shutterstock (Image ID: 2652710037).

Figure 3.4 "Handbag" Motif and Bird-Man Figure, Göbekli Tepe (c. 10,000 BCE). Photograph licensed from Shutterstock (Image ID: 2320059091).

Figure 3.5 Bird-Man Statue, San Agustín, Colombia (ca. 1–400 CE).

Photograph by MegavasCol, Wikimedia Commons. Licensed under CC BY-SA 3.0.

Figure 3.6 Birdman Tablet, Cahokia, Illinois (ca. 1200 CE). Courtesy of the Illinois State Museum. https://story.illinoisstatemuseum.org/content/cahokia-mounds-bird-man-tablet

Figure 3.7 Vishnu with Consorts, India (ca. 5th–6th c. CE). Sri Pratap Singh (SPS) Museum, Srinagar. Source: Wikimedia Commons. Public domain.

Figure 3.8 Kinich Ajaw with Attendants, Maya (ca. 8th–9th c. CE). Museo Nacional de Arqueología y Etnología, Guatemala. Source: Vladimir Krym, LiveJournal.

Figure 4.1 Great Pyramids of Giza, Egypt (ca. 2550–2490 BCE). Aerial view. Photograph licensed from Shutterstock (Image ID: 2064892322).

Figure 4.2 Belt Stars of Orion's Constellation. Photograph by Martin Mutti, Astronomy Picture of the Day (NASA), 10 February 2009. Public domain.

Figure 4.3 Avenue of the Dead & Pyramid of the Sun, Teotihuacan, Mexico (ca. 1–500 CE). Photograph licensed from Shutterstock (Image ID: 1128967919).

Figure 4.4 Angkor Wat, Cambodia (12th c. CE). Photograph licensed from Shutterstock (Image ID: 127204730).

Figure 4.5 Borobudur Temple, Java, Indonesia (8th–9th c. CE). Photograph licensed from Adobe Stock (Image ID: 654157559).

Figure 4.6 Temple of the Feathered Serpent, Teotihuacan, Mexico (ca. 200 CE). Photograph licensed from Adobe Stock (Image ID: 555549565).

Figure 4.7 Temple of the Great Jaguar, Tikal, Guatemala (ca. 8th c. CE). Photograph licensed from Shutterstock (Image ID: 1473174113).

Figure 4.8 Bakong Temple, Cambodia (ca. 9th c. CE). Photograph licensed from Shutterstock (Image ID: 73465384).

Figure 4.9 Keyhole Kofun Tomb, Japan (3rd–6th c. CE). Photograph licensed from Adobe Stock (Image ID: 37801345).

Figure 5.1 Abu Simbel Solar Alignment, Egypt (13th c. BCE). Photograph licensed from Adobe Stock (Image ID: 324244760).

Figure 5.2 Dresden Codex — Venus Table, Maya (11th–12th c. CE). Public domain. Saxon State and University Library, Dresden (SLUB).

Figure 5.3 Codex Borgia — Venus as Spear-Thrower, Aztec (ca. 15th–16th c. CE). Public domain. Biblioteca Apostolica Vaticana, Rome.

Figure 5.4 El Castillo, Chichén Itzá, Mexico (ca. 10th–12th c. CE). Photograph licensed from Adobe Stock (Image ID: 359103307).

Figure 5.5 Equinox Sunrise, Angkor Wat, Cambodia (12th c. CE). Photograph licensed from Adobe Stock (Image ID: 104338673).

Figure 5.6 Oracle Bone, Shang Dynasty, Anyang, China (ca. 1600–1046 BCE). Photograph licensed from Adobe Stock (Image ID: 78079528).

Figure 6.1 Ocelotl Cuauhxicalli, Aztec (Posclásico Tardío, ca. 1250–1500 CE). Andesite. Museo Nacional de Antropología, Mexico City. © INAH, Proyecto de Digitalización de las Colecciones Arqueológicas.

Figure 6.2 Sacred Cenote, Chichén Itzá, Mexico (ca. 9th–16th c. CE). Photograph by Enrico Pescantini, Adobe Stock. Courtesy of Ancient-Origins.net.

Figure 6.3 Bronze Ding Vessel, Shang or Zhou Dynasty, China (ca. 1200–771 BCE). The Metropolitan Museum of Art, New York. Public domain.

Figure 6.4 Libation Basin of Lady Ruiu with Hathor Head, Egypt (New Kingdom). Photograph © Glencairn Museum.

ACKNOWLEDGMENTS

I am deeply grateful to Linda Moulton Howe, whose decades of fearless investigative work not only laid the foundation for understanding the cattle mutilation phenomenon, but whose encouragement and insight continue to inspire me. Her generosity in contributing the foreword to this book is an honor beyond measure.

To Whitley Strieber, whose writings and willingness to listen opened a door when I needed it most. While he illuminated a room I never wanted to enter, his light offered comfort and guidance, easing the angst that once ruled my shadows.

To Timothy Aines of MUFON, who investigated my case with professionalism, compassion, and rigor, and who presented my experiences at the 2025 International Symposium. Your support and integrity have meant more than I can express.

To my family—especially my parents, Betty and Norman Nanstiel, Sr.—for raising me not only with love, but with the love of inspiration. You were perfect. And to those closest to me now, who have walked with me through the shadows, listened without judgment, and helped me find the courage to speak: thank you.

I would also like to thank the pioneers of the Ancient Astronaut and Ancient Alien field — from Erich von Däniken, Zecharia Sitchin, and Charles Hapgood, to more recent investigators like Giorgio Tsoukalos, Graham Hancock, David Hatcher Childress, and so many others.

Their early efforts opened the door to this vast and interconnected world of history rediscovered. Whatever refinements, connections, and continuities I've attempted to trace in these pages stand on their shoulders. They introduced me — and millions of others — to the possibility that humanity's story is far stranger and more profound than we were taught

And finally, to the many experiencers who have reached out with their own testimonies. Your stories are part of a larger human story. I hope this book honors your courage, and that together our voices break the silence that has endured too long.

ABOUT THE AUTHOR

Erik Nanstiel is a designer, nonprofit founder, and lifelong experiencer whose abduction case has been investigated by MUFON and featured at their 2025 International Symposium. He is the author of *Angst in the Shadows: A True Story of Alien Abductions,* a memoir that brought his case to national attention.

His story has been featured on Ancient Aliens and Whitley Strieber's *Dreamland* podcast, and he continues to appear on programs exploring the UFO phenomenon and human–alien contact. He lives in Illinois, where he pursues research into the deeper patterns behind abduction, hybridization, and the alien agenda shaping human history.

www.ingramcontent.com/pod-product-compliance
Lightning Source LLC
Chambersburg PA
CBHW050524100526
44581CB00006B/125/J